D1608395

STUDIES IN THE HISTORY OF MUSIC 5

Lewis Lockwood and Christoph Wolff, General Editors

ELAINE R. SISMAN

Haydn and the Classical Variation

Harvard University Press
Cambridge, Massachusetts, and London, England   1993

Library of Congress Cataloging-in-Publication Data

Sisman, Elaine Rochelle.
 Haydn and the classical variation / Elaine R. Sisman.
  p.   cm.
 Includes bibliographical references and index.
 ISBN 0-674-38315-X (acid-free paper)
  1. Haydn, Joseph, 1732–1809. Variations.
2. Mozart, Wolfgang Amadeus, 1756–1791.
Variations.   3. Beethoven, Ludwig van, 1770–1827.
Variations.   4. Variation (Music)—Analysis, apprecia-
tion.   I. Title.
MT90.S58   1993
781.8'25'09033—dc20   92-28292
CIP
MN

To Martin Fridson

Contents

Preface   ix

1   Introduction: Repetition and Decoration   1

2   The Rhetoric of Variation   19

Rhetoric and Classical Composers   22   Rhetoric and Variation   25
Figures of Rhetoric and Music   30   Figures for Variation Form   35
Rhetorical Analysis   40

3   Variation as Form and Technique in Eighteenth-Century Musical
Writings   48

Improvised and Composed Variation Technique   51   Improvised and
Composed Variation Form   63

4   The Variation in the Universe of Classical Musical Forms   79

Expansion Techniques   80   Principal Periods   87   Haydn's
Expansions   92   Variation and Expanded Forms   101

5   Convention and Innovation in Haydn's Variations to 1780   109

Early Variations   109   The Watershed of 1772   135   Haydn's "Creative
Periods"   146   Hybrid Variations: Principles and Development   150

6   Synthesis: Haydn's Variations in the 1780s and 1790s   164

Symphonies   168   Quartets   172   Keyboard Works   185

7   Mozart's Variations   196

Inventio: Choice and Adaptation of Themes   198   *Dispositio:* Ordering of
Variations   210   *Elaboratio:* Figures and Figurations   223

8   Conclusion: Beethoven and the Transformation of the Classical
Variation   235

Decorum 236   Piano Variations and the "New Way" 249
Eroica: Transformation of the Alternating Variation 254

*Appendix A   Variations of Haydn, Mozart, and Beethoven
(Tables A.1–A.3)* 265

Appendix B   Extended Original-Language Quotations 276

Selected Bibliography   281

Index   303

Preface

"It is not sufficiently considered," said Dr. Johnson, "that men more frequently require to be reminded than informed." In the musical form we know as theme and variations, we are typically "informed" only once, during the theme, and then "reminded" subtly or overtly ever after. Perhaps the long history and popularity of this form, which for its first few hundred years was associated exclusively with dances and with well-known melodies, rest upon its tireless assertions of the familiar. Sometimes found as movements in suites or, later, sonatas, most variations were free-standing or "independent" works usually for keyboard. It is the thesis of this book that Haydn and a few of his contemporaries developed and popularized the variation movement and its aesthetic, but that Haydn's own innovations—placing it in every position of a multi-movement cycle, broadening its array of theme types, and transforming its larger shape—created, in effect, the Classical variation. Mozart and Beethoven in individual and innovatory ways drew on Haydn's achievements and were thus both generally and specifically indebted to him as participants in the Classical variation aesthetic. Independent sets of variations, nearly always for keyboard or keyboard and strings, share in that aesthetic in matters of technique rather than overall shape, and with a few exceptions are less central to it; in a sense they are documents primarily of social history. The arguments adduced in support of this thesis are reasonably wide-ranging, drawing not only on the music itself but on discussions of variation in eighteenth- and early nineteenth-century writings and on related ideas in contemporaneous aesthetics and rhetoric.

In the first four chapters I explore several sets of apparent oppositions: between variation as a ubiquitous musical technique and variation as a circumscribed musical form; between rhetoric as a speaking art and rhetoric as a critical tool; between the mechanical and the meaningful in musical figures; between the sonata aesthetic and the variation aesthetic; and between repetition and return. To eighteenth-century writers on music, variation had three different, though related, connotations. First, it was a method of composition, by which a simple melody or bass line could be elaborated in shorter note values to create a fully worked-out piece.[1] In this sense, all music could be seen as composing out a simple framework. Indeed, the source of melodic invention itself was sometimes thought of as variations or permutations of a basic underlying harmony.[2] Second, it was a technique designed to add interest to a composition by modifying simpler material previously heard, usually in unmediated repetition; this could be accomplished by either the composer or the performer or both. Finally, variation could be elevated to the dominating structural principle of a musical work, resulting in the well-known form of theme and variations. Here, both pattern and elaboration are experienced in a temporal series. The pleasure of the pattern, arising from its "ordering of elements by identity and difference,"[3] is the chief *raison d'être* of the Classical variation. As a form and as a technique, variation may also be elucidated by the rhetorical modes of thought still broadly informing musical thinking in the later eighteenth century. Indeed, ideas derived from a study of rhetoric in both musical and non-musical sources, together with eighteenth-century discussions of variation, can illuminate a new approach to Classical variations.

In the second half of the book I examine and evaluate the variations of Haydn, Mozart, and Beethoven (to the middle period), as well as, although to a lesser extent, those of mid-century Vienna. Composers working in Vienna, of the generation before Haydn, generally did not cultivate the variation. Most of the works I have found by contemporaries of "the great triumvirate," in Charles Rosen's words, are of indifferent quality.[4] My survey of over 1,300 multi-movement works in all instrumental genres, by fifty-five composers working in and around Vienna, has yielded 110 variation movements written between about 1760 and 1800, most from the later part of that period.[5] Many sources remain to be investigated; since variation movements are often not headed as such (with "Andante con variazioni," for example, or even with individual headings such as "Var. 1"), the difficulties of locating variations in the first place are not trivial. Perhaps this book will inspire other scholars to undertake a comprehensive survey of the eighteenth-century variation. Although the variation *oeuvres* of Haydn and Mozart themselves also contain the run-of-the-

1. Friedrich Erhard Niedt, *Handleitung zur Variation des Generalbasses* (Hamburg, 1706; rev. ed. [Mattheson] 1721); Friedrich Wilhelm Marpurg, *Anleitung zum Clavierspielen* (Berlin, 1755; 2nd ed. 1765); Johann Friedrich Daube, *Der musikalische Dilettant* (Vienna, 1773) and *Anleitung zur Erfindung der Melodie* (Vienna, 1797). See also David Schulenberg, "Composition as Variation: Inquiries into the Bach Circle of Composers," *CM* 23 (1982), 57–87.

2. Johann Mattheson, *Der vollkommene Kapellmeister* (Hamburg, 1739), Part II, par. 24ff.; Daube, *Der musikalische Dilettant,* chap. 7; Joseph Riepel, *Grundregeln zur Tonordnung insgemein* (Regensburg, 1755), passim.

3. E. H. Gombrich, *The Sense of Order: A Study in the Psychology of Decorative Art* (Ithaca, N.Y., 1979), p. 72.

4. Charles Rosen, *The Classical Style: Haydn, Mozart, Beethoven* (New York, 1971), p. 19. Although there are some good variations by *Kleinmeister,* their contributions to the form seem to me not to merit a prominent place in this book. I mean no disparagement to the achievements of these composers in other areas.

5. Most of these works have no modern edition, and exist in autograph, manuscript copies, or in early editions. Library sigla throughout the book are taken from *RISM.*

mill, their many artfully crafted movements include variations of greatness, even sublimity, concepts not usually invoked to describe these pieces. My aim is not to provide a complete descriptive survey but rather to refocus attention, through the means suggested in the first half of the book, on achievements that are imperfectly understood and hence undervalued. Locating the transformation of the Classical variation aesthetic in the defamiliarizing ethos of Beethoven's works of the decade beginning in 1799, rather earlier than is usually supposed, forms the subject of the final chapter.

The title of this book, and some of its working hypotheses as outlined here, use the term "Classical" to describe the era of Haydn and Mozart.[6] In Chapters 5 and 6, I make a case for turning points in Haydn's style in 1772 and "after 1780," thus stepping into the middle of the debate over the issue of periodization, cogently formulated by James Webster.[7] I do not imply, however, that Haydn's variations before 1772 are "not Classical," nor that those after 1780 are "fully Classical." While it is hard to avoid tautologically transferring the term "Classical" from the realm of historical chronology to the realm of musical style—because Haydn and Mozart are Classical composers (that is, composers of the Classical era), they wrote Classical variations—nonetheless the aesthetics, rhetoric, and decorum of Haydn's and Mozart's mature variations may be termed Classical by more than simple analogy. The flowering of variation movements in the larger multi-movement genres (for example, symphony and string quartet) appears to be based on Haydn's efforts, as his contemporaries recognized; and the abandonment of suite variations, contrapuntally organized variations, and passacaglias by mid-century composers, including Haydn, marks a distinct era in terms of genre and technique. In addition, both of the turning points just mentioned concern generic issues, the new weighting of variations in a slow movement in 1772, for example, and the powerful ways in which a "variation principle" suffuses several movements in an instrumental cycle in Haydn's music after 1780. The rhetorical force of Mozart's variations is viewed in these contexts. Beethoven's participation in "the Classical variation," on the other hand, ultimately entails an irrevocable altering of its decorum as well as a reconceived rhetorical model of repetition in variation movements.

My interest in variations goes back many years, to the senior recital I prepared with Malcolm Bilson at Cornell University which fortuitously included Sweelinck's variations on "Mein junges Leben hat ein End," Beethoven's E-major Sonata, Op. 109, and the Brahms Handel-Variations, Op. 24. I would like to thank James Webster for early encouragement of that interest, and Kenneth Levy and Harold Powers for their advice on an earlier version of some of the material in Chapters 3, 4, and 5. Research for the present study has been generously supported by a fellowship from the National Endowment for the Hu-

6. I use the term "classical" to refer to classical antiquity and its writers on rhetoric.

7. See the "Historiographical Conclusion" to his *Haydn's Farewell Symphony and the Idea of Classical Style: Through-Composition and Cyclic Integration in the Instrumental Music* (Cambridge, 1991), pp. 335–373. See also Daniel Heartz, "Classical," in *The New Grove*, vol. 4, pp. 449–454.

manities, and by grants from the Columbia University Research Council in the Humanities and the Horace Rackham Faculty Research Program of the University of Michigan. The directors and staffs of music collections in libraries and archives in Austria and Germany have also been extremely helpful; I would like to note especially the unstinting access afforded by the archive of the Gesellschaft der Musikfreunde in Vienna and the help of its director, Dr. Otto Biba; the Wiener Stadtbibliothek, and its director, Dr. Ernest Hilmar; the archive of Melk Monastery, and its director, Dr. Bruno Brandstetter; as well as the assistance of the Nationalbibliothek in Vienna, the Archivio "Benedetto Marcello" in Venice, and the Bayerische Stadtbibliothek in Munich.

It is a pleasure to acknowledge the colleagues who have asked me just the right questions, put just the right volume in my hands, sounded just the right note of encouragement, or prodded me in a fresh direction: Eva Badura-Skoda, Ian Bent, Mark Evan Bonds, Richard Crawford, Mark De Bellis, Michelle Fillion, Walter Frisch, Sonja Gerlach, Janet Sisman Levy, Katherine T. Rohrer, László Somfai, Richard Taruskin, Maynard Solomon, Neal Zaslaw. Michael Long was generous with his time and his considerable knowledge of rhetoric in discussing with me some of the issues in this book. I am deeply grateful to James Webster and Eugene Wolf for reading the entire manuscript and providing exceptionally helpful detailed comments and materials. I have also benefited from conversations with A. Peter Brown, Georg Feder, George Gopen, Carla Pollock, David Rosen, Hollace Schafer, Alan Tyson, and Alexander Weinmann, all of whom generously shared unpublished materials with me. None of those mentioned here is implicated in the errors and omissions that remain.

I would like to thank Margaretta Fulton and Mary Ellen Geer of Harvard University Press, the former for her continuous encouragement of this project from its early stages and the latter for her excellent copyediting of the manuscript. Johanna Baldwin cheerfully provided beautifully engraved musical examples under trying time-pressured circumstances.

Thanking my family for their love and support seems too small a token for the size of the gift. My parents, Dr. Irving and Margot Sisman, have been a source of strength throughout. My children, Arielle and Daniel Fridson, have come up through the nursery-school ranks clamoring to take my place at the word-processor, and often succeeding; it was through their efforts ("Again!") that I understood viscerally the joys of repetition discussed in the text. To my husband, Marty Fridson, an extraordinarily gifted writer and scholar of high-yield debt, I owe more than any traditional avowals of love and gratitude could express. This book is dedicated to him.

Haydn and the Classical Variation

Abbreviations

AfMw	*Archiv für Musikwissenschaft*
AM	*Acta Musicologica*
AMZ	*Allgemeine musikalische Zeitung*
CM	*Current Musicology*
HSt	*Haydn-Studien*
HYb	*Haydn Yearbook*
JAMS	*Journal of the American Musicological Society*
JbÖK	*Jahrbuch für Österreichische Kulturgeschichte*
JHW	*Joseph Haydn: Werke,* ed. Joseph-Haydn Institut, Cologne (Munich: Henle)
JM	*The Journal of Musicology*
JMT	*The Journal of Music Theory*
JRMA	*Journal of the Royal Musical Association*
Mf	*Die Musikforschung*
MF	*The Music Forum*
MJb	*Mozart-Jahrbuch*
ML	*Music and Letters*
MQ	*The Musical Quarterly*
MR	*The Music Review*
MMR	*Monthly Musical Record*
MusA	*Music Analysis*
New Grove	*The New Grove Dictionary of Music and Musicians,* ed. Stanley Sadie (London: Macmillan, 1980)
19CM	*19th-Century Music*
ÖMz	*Österreichische Musikzeitschrift*
PRMA	*Proceedings of the Royal Musical Association*
SM	*Studia Musicologica*
ZfMw	*Zeitschrift für Musikwissenschaft*

CHAPTER ONE

Introduction:
Repetition and Decoration

Variation is the victim of a curious paradox: while variation technique is extolled as one of the most basic, natural, and essential principles underlying all music, indeed as a powerful stimulus to human creativity, variation form is routinely denigrated from nearly every perspective, whether historical, social, aesthetic, structural, or technical.[1] Although a number of masterworks in variation form by Bach, Beethoven, and Brahms have been admitted to the canon, the later eighteenth century is usually viewed as a valley between the peaks of the Goldberg Variations and the *Eroica*.

Why has variation form in general and the Classical variation in particular received such treatment? Simply put, its common practices do not accord with several cherished assumptions about musical value. First, the form is associated with borrowing a theme and keeping it in more or less full view, thus violating the principle of original thematic invention. Indeed, the eighteenth century presided over the shift in the meaning of invention from finding to making.[2] Second, as a repetitive series of short, discrete segments with the same structure, variations seem artificial and arbitrary, incapable of a sustained organic structure, and thus violate one of the central tenets of German Romanticism.[3] Third, the ornamental and decorative techniques assumed to prevail in the variations of Haydn and Mozart are considered "surface" features, failing to penetrate and transform the thematic model like "deeper" contrapuntal, character-

---

1. Perhaps the most acerbic of these is Jan LaRue's assessment: not only does he find it the most restrictive of any form, but its external shape turns it into "a kind of musical link sausage." See his *Guidelines for Style Analysis* (New York, 1970), p. 174.

2. Lawrence Manley, *Convention: 1500–1750* (Cambridge, Mass., 1980), p. 330. See also Carl Dahlhaus, *Between Romanticism and Modernism,* trans. Mary Whittall (Berkeley and Los Angeles, 1980), pp. 42–43. George Gopen has pointed out to me that the source of the Greek word for poem is *poiein,* to make, and that the medieval Scottish term for poet was *makar.*

3. On the acceptance of organicism as a locus of value, see Ruth Solie, "The Living Work: Organicism and Musical Analysis," *19CM* 4 (1980), 147–156, and Janet Levy, "Covert and Casual Values in Recent Writings about Music," *JM* 5 (1987), 3–27.

istic, developmental, or transformational techniques.[4] Finally, the enormous numbers of variation sets produced by virtuosos between about 1790 and 1840 provoked a reaction against their empty display, or what Momigny called "much speech but little sense."[5]

Two values associated with the peaks of Bach and Beethoven were not shared by pieces of the intervening generations. In the Goldberg Variations, the harmony rather than the melody of the theme forms the basis of the variations, which are themselves both brilliantly contrapuntal and characteristic. And the *Eroica* finale is seamless, its variations on two themes yoked together by transitions, fugatos, alterations in period structure, as well as many departures from and one dramatic return to the tonic. That these techniques can operate within a single set condemns variations of the Classical era, a period in which no single set continuously mitigated or abandoned the melodic and structural model of the theme.

The traditional view of variations written by Haydn, Mozart, and their contemporaries goes something like this: in the early part of the eighteenth century, composers explored several different options for constructing a variation set, including decorating the melody of a well-known piece or creating contrapuntal complexities over a harmonic progression or an ostinato bass. Sometime after mid-century, the melodic type came to the fore, mandating decoration as the exclusive technique. Thus, the required figurative elaboration of the theme restricted Haydn's and Mozart's freedom and resulted in only a few stereotyped designs. Indeed, their variations were most successful when taking on aspects of other forms, that is, exhibiting contrast and return or recurrence, or development. Finally, after a weak start decorating popular tunes, Beethoven began to write variations in an "entirely new manner," liberating the variation from its trivial Classical phase.

The remarkable element of this view is its tenacity. Even in the groundbreaking studies of the last two decades on the Classical period by Charles Rosen and Leonard Ratner and on the variation itself by Kurt von Fischer, assessments of the variation have not substantially changed.[6] Because discussions

4. For example, Arrey von Dommer's *Musikalisches Lexikon* (Heidelberg, 1865), a thoroughgoing revision of Heinrich Christoph Koch's dictionary of the same title (Frankfurt am Main, 1802; facs. ed. Hildesheim, 1964), divided variations into two classes, the higher one of which provided "deeper and freer transformations" of the theme.

5. Jérome-Joseph de Momigny, *Encyclopédie méthodique: musique*, II (Paris, 1818; rpt. New York, 1971), s.v. "Variations." Negative reaction to virtuosity in general was of course a widespread critical attitude of the late eighteenth as well as the nineteenth century; cf. Theodor Adorno, *Aesthetic Theory*, trans. C. Lenhardt, ed. Gretel Adorno and Rolf Tiedemann (London, 1984), pp. 155–156.

6. Charles Rosen, *The Classical Style: Haydn, Mozart, Beethoven* (New York, 1971); Leonard Ratner, *Classic Music: Expression, Form, and Style* (New York, 1980); Kurt von Fischer, "Arietta Variata," in *Studies in Eighteenth-Century Music*, ed. H. C. Robbins Landon with Roger Chapman (New York, 1970), pp. 224–235; idem, "Variations," *The New Grove*, ed. Stanley Sadie (London, 1980), vol. 19, pp. 536–556 (a translation of "Variation," in *Die Musik im Geschichte und Gegenwart* [Kassel, 1962], vol. 13, pp. 1284–1309); idem, *The Variation* (= *Anthology of Music*) (Cologne, 1962); Robert U. Nelson, *The Technique of Variation* (Berkeley and Los Angeles, 1948).

of eighteenth-century instrumental music invariably focus on the rise of the sonata aesthetic, sectional or additive forms are evaluated by how closely they adhere to this aesthetic and by how "organic" they become. Recent Schenkerian studies of variations also seek and not surprisingly find such organic unity.[7] Rosen even defines as truly Classical only Beethoven's variations with sonata-like elements; Mozart and Haydn retained the "Baroque" reliance on ornamentation.[8] In the five pages he devotes to variations, Ratner spends three of them discussing Beethoven. Although the comments he draws from contemporaneous theorists are valuable on other topics, he finds nothing on variation deeper than "fresh" and "tuneful."[9] And while Fischer comes closest to showing how diverse the variations of the period actually were—differentiation of character in C. P. E. Bach, hybrid structures in Haydn, improvisatory styles in Mozart—he seeks to show that the variation finale of the *Eroica* is a sonata movement.[10]

Up to a point, the critics of the Classical variation are correct: variations of that period may be seen as a series of frozen moments, of decorative tableaux, each maintaining a certain decorum, a certain melodic and harmonic resemblance, and a nearly inevitable pattern of cadences. Yet the resemblances are not immutable: a variation may be transparent, offering a window onto the theme, or it may be opaque, relegating the theme to the position of "absent signifier," in Genette's term.[11] The variation may refer literally to the theme via a feature common to both, or it may refer metaphorically to the theme via a feature the theme does not share.[12] Concepts of decoration, ornamentation, or figuration apply in both their technical (note-based) and rhetorical senses. And each final cadence calls attention to its own temporary status as it gives way either to a repeat or to the next variation.[13]

Variation form is founded on repetition: a discrete thematic entity—a complex of melody, harmony, phrase structure, rhythm, and the character resulting from these—is repeated several (or many) times, with various modifications. While the principle of repetition may seem among the sturdiest possible, it is

7. For example, Esther Cavett-Dunsby, *Mozart's Variations Reconsidered: Four Case Studies (K. 613, K. 501, K. 421/417b, K. 491)* (New York, 1989); Nicholas Marston, "Analysing Variations: The Finale of Beethoven's String Quartet Op. 74," *MusA* 8 (1989), 303–324.

8. Rosen, *Classical Style*, pp. 435–439.

9. Ratner, *Classic Music*, pp. 255–259.

10. Kurt von Fischer, "Eroica-Variationen op. 35 und Eroica-Finale," *Schweizerische Musikzeitung* 90 (1949), 282–285.

11. Gérard Genette, *Figures of Literary Discourse* (New York, 1982), pp. 49–50.

12. See Nelson Goodman and Catherine Z. Elgin, *Reconceptions in Philosophy and Other Arts and Sciences* (Indianapolis and Cambridge, 1988), chap. 4, "Variations on Variation—or Picasso back to Bach" (the latter is never mentioned), pp. 66–82. Goodman calls these ways of referring "literal exemplification" and "contrastive exemplification." I am grateful to Mark DeBellis for turning my attention to this book.

13. On the issue of repeats, see Michael Broyles, "Organic Form and the Binary Repeat," *MQ* 66 (1980), 339–360; Jonathan Dunsby, "The Formal Repeat," *JRMA* 112 (1986/87), 196–207. The former is largely concerned with first movements, the latter with the analytical significance of repeats.

actually surprisingly fragile, because at any moment a greater-than-usual contrast can upset the perception of a repetitive form and seemingly reorganize the whole.[14] To critics of the variation, this is greatly to be desired, and thus they read a *minore* variation as a central contrast creating an ABA form, recurrences of the theme's melody lending elements of rondo form, and an Adagio-Allegro set of concluding variations as evidence for a "slow movement and finale."[15] A similar phenomenon obtains with the ostensible reliance of Classical variations on melodic decoration: any complication of texture is read as the composer's attempt to go below the surface and increase musical value.

The Achilles' heel of the Classical variation would seem to be its dual reliance on repetition and decoration. But these two elements, for all that their musical meaning appears self-evident, may be rendered less vulnerable to reflexive critical attack when we broaden the interpretive scope beyond the musical. Although the difficulties of applying models from literature, rhetoric, and art to the kind of repetition found in variation form soon become clear, these models offer ways of evaluating variation form that seem never to have been applied to it. Among the problems of comparing repetition in literature and poetry with repetition in music is, of course, that verbal meanings and musical structures may simply be incommensurable. To this may be added the inevitable problem of explaining the aesthetic effect of repetition: as the author of the [*Rhetorica*] *Ad Herennium* stated, "The frequent recourse to the same word is not dictated by verbal poverty; rather there inheres in the repetition an elegance which the ear can distinguish more easily than words can explain."[16] Finally, literary critics and theorists do not consistently distinguish between repetition and recurrence, nor between these terms and return.[17] Such distinctions are important for musical analysts, for whom the repetitions of variation form, the recurrences of rondo form, the symmetrical return of *da capo* form, and the resolving return of sonata form yield quite different structural, not to mention aesthetic, results.[18] In fact, for variation the distinction between repetition and recurrence or return could not be more crucial, affecting as it does the very

14. Leonard B. Meyer suggests that in some cases repetition actually leads to less stability. See *Explaining Music: Essays and Explorations* (Chicago and London, 1973), p. 51.

15. On the tendency of all Classical forms to take on characteristics of ABA form, see Rudolf von Tobel, *Die Formenwelt der klassischen Instrumentalmusik* (Bern, 1935); on melodic reprises and rondo as well as the "final pair," see Kurt von Fischer, "Variations," pp. 546–547. I disagree with Adorno's identification of sonata form with closed form and rondo form with open form (*Aesthetic Theory*, p. 314). Adorno thinks the latter is open because it is open-ended, but the actual musical techniques employed in both reveal the open (or openable, or expanded or expandable) techniques in the former, and the closed (small) techniques in the latter. See Elaine R. Sisman, "Small and Expanded Forms: Koch's Model and Haydn's Music," *MQ* 62 (1982), 444–478.

16. [Pseudo-Cicero], [*Rhetorica*] *Ad Herennium*, trans. and ed. Harry Caplan (Cambridge, Mass., 1954), p. 281. More on this treatise will appear in the next chapter.

17. Julie Ellison is more consistent in this regard than other writers; cf. her *Emerson's Romantic Style* (Princeton, 1984), pp. 160–174, to be discussed below.

18. A valuable discussion of the differences between repetition and return, as well as different effects of repetition, can be found in Meyer, *Explaining Music*, pp. 44–54.

existence of an autonomous variation form as opposed to variation technique embedded in another type of form entirely. In the rest of this introduction I consider repetition and decoration, the issues underlying variation form that are essential to understanding both its nature and its current valuation.

I

Repetition is a topic of daunting size. Even the list purporting to reflect the "modern history of ideas about repetition," given by J. Hillis Miller, seems to be grandly proportioned while identifying itself as ominously selective: Vico, Hegel, and the German Romantics, Kierkegaard *(Repetition)*, Marx *(The Eighteenth Brumaire)*, Nietzsche (the eternal return), Freud (repetition-compulsion), Joyce *(Finnegan's Wake)*, Jacques Lacan, Gilles Deleuze, Mircea Eliade, and Jacques Derrida.[19] Drawing on Deleuze's opposition of Platonic and Nietzschean repetition, Miller claims that modes of repetition within a literary work embody some form of the "contradictory intertwining" of these two types. The Platonic type is based on a "solid archetypal model which is untouched by the effects of repetition," while the Nietzschean type argues that everything in the world is "intrinsically different from every other thing."[20] That the distinction rests on the presence or absence of a "ground in some paradigm or archetype" suggests a parallel, not explored by Miller, with musical variations: the archetype is the theme, and the nature of the variations rests not only on the relationship between variations and theme, but on the extent to which the theme itself is perceived as being transformed during the course of the piece. The piece may indeed provoke a response in the contradiction between the "truth of correspondence" and the background of difference.

Occasionally, the musical analogue of the idea of repetition is invoked explicitly by a literary critic; two such writers are Edward Said and Barbara Herrnstein Smith.[21] In his essay "On Repetition," Said compares Vico's ideas about large-scale cycles in human history with variation form:

> Formally speaking, Vico's understanding and use of repetition bears a resemblance to musical techniques of repetition, in particular those of the *cantus firmus* or of the chaconne or, to cite the most developed classical instance, Bach's *Goldberg Variations*. By these devices a ground motif anchors the ornamental variations taking place above it. Despite the proliferation of changing rhythms, patterns, and harmonies, the ground motif recurs throughout, as if to demonstrate its staying power and its capacity for endless elaboration. As Vico saw in the phenomenon of human

---

19. J. Hillis Miller, *Fiction and Repetition: Seven English Novels* (Cambridge, Mass., 1982), p. 5. Of course, many of the larger historical or autobiographical aspects of repetition are largely irrelevant to the present study, such as Kierkegaard's notion that recollection is living backward while repetition is living forward *(Repetition*, ed. and trans. Howard V. Hong and Edna H. Hong [Princeton, 1983]).

20. Miller, *Fiction and Repetition*, pp. 5–6, citing Gilles Deleuze, *Logique du sens* (Paris, 1969), p. 302.

21. The latter will be discussed in section II.

history, there is in these musical forms a tension between the contrariety or eccentricity of the variation and the constance [sic] and asserted rationality of the *cantus firmus*. Nothing Vico could have said about the mind's triumph over irrationality can equal the quiet triumph that occurs at the end of the *Goldberg Variations,* as the theme returns in its exact first form to close off the aberrant variations it has generated.[22]

Said's reading of a purely instrumental composition in a conceptual framework is provocative, principally because the notion of the "asserted rationality" of the theme's return after the "variations it has generated" implies that the theme acts as agent rather than as first in a series. Yet his terms point up some of the problems with language about the elements of variation. For example, *cantus firmus* and "ground motif" usually mean a literally recurring bass-line (or less often, melodic) pattern; what the Goldberg Variations have instead is a constant harmonic progression. Similarly, "ornamental" usually describes a quality of melody, not texture generally. Here the variations have new melodies, figurations, and textures that are elaborate projections of the harmonic plan. Moreover, describing the variations, which are by turns brilliantly contrapuntal, dance-like, *cantabile,* and richly topical in other ways, as contrary, eccentric, bizarre, and aberrant seems misconceived, more dependent on an analogy with Vico than on Bach's music.

Jerome Robbins's brilliant choreography and staging of the Goldberg Variations for the New York City Ballet includes a detail that gives visual substance to the idea of theme as agent: the theme is danced—replete with elaborate hand-gestures—by a couple in full eighteenth-century courtly dress, while the invention-like first variation strips to leotards an energetic corps of dancers. Contrapuntal exegesis has nothing in common with decoration. About halfway through the piece bits of courtly apparel begin to appear on the dancers in successive layers of accretion until the final, thirtieth variation, which is fully decked out again. Then, with dramatic simplicity, the return of the theme features the original couple in leotards. What had originally seemed frippery, a superficial rococo ornateness, can in retrospect be interpreted as the underlying substance of the unadorned body, indeed, *pace* Said, the source of rationality in every variation.

II

Repetition in prose fiction and repetition as a philosophical and historical idea inevitably require a broadening of pure repetition to include such recurrences and returns. Some forms of nonfiction also lend themselves to types of repetition. In Julie Ellison's sensitive analysis of Emerson's *Essays,* for example, repetition is a preeminent structural principle, including "classification . . . ; word association that generates a chain of synonyms; metaphoric variations; self-

---

22. Edward W. Said, *The World, the Text, and the Critic* (Cambridge, Mass., 1983), pp. 113–114 (from the essay "On Repetition," pp. 111–125).

paraphrase that both repeats and elaborates an initial statement; quotation and allusion."[23] Particularly useful is Ellison's differentiation between "the repeated elements as substitutes for one another implicitly connected by 'or,'" and "repetitions . . . related by addition, by an implied 'and.'" In the former type, "[r]epetition forces us to take out one interchangeable part and substitute another . . ., intensifying the figural or fictive quality of language." With repetition by addition, on the other hand, "the original statement is persuasively extended, enriched, and complicated. We rise above the local difficulties of the catalogue and feel its terms cumulatively gather into hyperbole."[24] Variations exist in a series that has a necessary and identifiable beginning but no predetermined end; the organization of that series may be substitutive ("or") or cumulative ("and"), or may deploy figurative elements to both ends.

Two art forms embody unmediated structural repetition: poetry and decorative art, the latter constituting a separate aesthetic problem to be considered in the following section. Poetry offers a primary model for variations in stanza forms with metrical and rhyme schemes; these are literal counterparts to the strophic structure of variations with fixed phrase-lengths and cadential patterns.[25] Barbara Herrnstein Smith describes repetition as the "fundamental structure of poetic form" in her study *Poetic Closure*.[26] She identifies the principal varieties of repetition by means of three sets of oppositions: systematic versus occasional repetition; unmediated versus mediated repetition, with the latter referring more precisely to recurrence, as of refrain lines, rather than repetition; and formal versus thematic repetition, in which the former term posits a kind of rhythm and the latter a definable meaning for elements in the work.[27] Largely unproblematic, these distinctions run into trouble when too rigidly maintained or when, as in the first, the elements are overlapping. For example, systematic repetition is defined as structural or metric, while occasional is described as "rhetorical," as in "Come forth, come forth, the gentle Spring"; yet structural repetition, as Chapter 2 will make clear, is just as rhetorical, even if based on a different understanding of figures.

Herrnstein Smith also differentiates between paratactic and sequential structures of poetry, two formal types of great importance to the present study.[28] Perhaps because her subject is poetry, she does not make the more common distinction between parataxis and hypotaxis, terms from classical grammar commonly applied to oratory and prose composition. Parataxis in both contexts sheds light on musical variations, but its older usage will be taken up first.

23. Ellison, *Emerson's Romantic Style*, pp. 172–173.

24. Ibid., p. 173.

25. An older study that considers this issue is J. P. Dabney, *The Musical Basis of Verse* (New York, 1901).

26. Barbara Herrnstein Smith, *Poetic Closure: A Study of How Poems End* (Chicago, 1968).

27. Ibid., p. 39.

28. Ibid., pp. 98–138. I will not address her third type of structure, "associative or dialectical," which she relates primarily to poems reflecting an "interior monologue" or other train-of-thought speech.

The rounded, hypotactic, or Ciceronian periodic style of antiquity *(oratio periodica)* featured sentences with many relative clauses and a central climax; it differed substantially from the more fragmented, "chopped-up," Senecan, or paratactic sentence structure *(oratio perpetua)* with shorter clauses and sentences, parallelisms, and the aspect of a linear series.[29] Hugh Blair's *Lectures on Rhetoric and Belles Lettres* differentiated between them as the *style périodique* and the *style coupé,* identifying the former as the "most pompous, musical, and oratorical manner of composing . . . [which] gives an air of gravity and dignity to composition." The latter, on the other hand, "suits gay and easy subjects . . . [and] is more lively and striking." His examples bear this out. For the periodic style, here is William Temple in a letter to Lady Essex:

> If you look about you, and consider the lives of others as well as your own; if you think how few are born with honour, and how many die without name or children; how little beauty we see, and how few friends we hear of; how many diseases, and how much poverty there is in the world; you will fall down upon your knees, and, instead of repining at one affliction, will admire so many blessings you have received from the hand of God.[30]

For the *style coupé,* Blair's example from Alexander Pope suffices:

> I confess it was want of consideration that made me an author. I writ, because it amused me. I corrected, because it was as pleasant to me to correct as to write. I published, because I was told, I might please such as it was a credit to please.[31]

The ideal in composition was to intermix both styles.[32] Seventeen-year-old Mozart sent to his sister an apparent parody of a high-flown periodic sentence:

> I hope, my queen, that you are enjoying the highest degree of health and that now and then or rather, sometimes, or, better still, occasionally, or, even better still, qualche volta, as the Italians say, you will sacrifice for my benefit some of your important and intimate thoughts, |: which ever proceed from that very fine and clear reasoning power, which in addition to your beauty, and although from a woman, and particularly from one of such tender years, almost nothing of the kind is ever expected, you possess, O queen, so abundantly as to put men and even grey-beards to shame :|. There now, you have a well-turned sentence [|hier hast du was gescheides|].[33]

29. See Aldo Scaglione, *The Classical Theory of Composition from Its Origins to the Present: A Historical Survey* (Chapel Hill, 1972), pp. 26–37.

30. Hugh Blair, *Lectures on Rhetoric and Belles Lettres* (rpt. New York, 1826), p. 118.

31. Cited from the Preface to Pope's works by Blair, *Lectures,* p. 118.

32. As Scaglione put it in *The Classical Theory of Composition* (p. 36), "the *perpetua* and the *periodica* . . . are sufficient to produce the perfect mix by balancing the complication of sustained hypotaxis with the relative simplicity of smooth-flowing parataxis."

33. Letter of 14 August 1773. Emily Anderson, ed. *The Letters of Mozart and His Family,* 3rd ed. (New York, 1985), no. 179a, p. 238; the Anderson edition does not include Mozart's unusual markings that call attention to the clause. See Mozart, *Briefe und Aufzeichnungen,* ed. Wilhelm Bauer and Otto Erich Deutsch [Bauer-Deutsch], 8 vols. (Salzburg, 1962–1975), I, no. 290, p. 488. Mozart might be making a pun on the idea of something clever *(gescheit)* that is separated off *(geschieden)* by vertical lines; it is also the most flowery part of the sentence.

In their sustained forms, parataxis had traditionally been associated with the low style, hypotaxis with the elevated, although this began to change with medieval epic.[34] Eric Blackall shows that in Herder, the antirational writer aligned with the *Sturm und Drang* movement and with the rediscovery of folk ballads, there is a "steady progress away from the periodic sentence. Parataxis rather than hypotaxis renders thoughts which often come in successive gusts, each amplifying and perhaps clarifying the last."[35] And Ronald Paulson describes the difference between "coherent" formal gardens and "more intimate" natural gardens as the distinction between the periodic sentence and a paratactic structure, respectively; in the natural garden, "one scene follows another apparently unsubordinated, but in fact related by clever juxtapositions."[36]

The periodic form seemed to represent the traditional ideal, but was often surpassed by the paratactic. Despite the inroads of the latter, the former retained the moral high ground in such terms as "coherent." In the eighteenth-century musical realm, choppy or episodic forms like variation and rondo were considered hierarchically lower than rounded or recapitulatory forms like sonata form.

Herrnstein Smith's paratactic and sequential structures do not refer to such concepts as "rounded" or "choppy." Focusing instead on repetitive structures, she bases these opposing categories on the internal connections among segments in the series:

> When repetition is the fundamental principle of thematic generation, the resulting structure will tend to be *paratactic;* that is, the coherence of the poem will not be dependent on the sequential arrangement of its major thematic units. In a nonparatactic structure (where, for example, the principle of generation is logical or temporal), the dislocation or omission of any element will tend to make the sequence as a whole incomprehensible or will radically change its effect. In paratactic structure, however (where the principle of generation does not cause any one element to "follow" from another), thematic units can be omitted, added, or exchanged without destroying the coherence or effect of the poem's thematic structure . . . "Variations on a theme" is one of the two most obvious forms that paratactic structure may take. The other one is the "list" . . . [A] generating principle that produces a paratactic structure cannot in itself determine a concluding point . . . The coherence of development in a paratactic structure does not depend upon the sequential order of its thematic elements. In most sophisticated poems, however, it does; for the lines or verses usually "follow" from one another, either logically, temporally, or in accord with some principle of serial generation.[37]

34. See Erich Auerbach, *Mimesis: The Representation of Reality in Western Literature,* trans. Willard R. Trask (Princeton, 1953), pp. 109–110.

35. Eric Blackall, *The Emergence of German as a Literary Language, 1700–1775,* 2nd ed. (Ithaca, 1978), pp. 459–460. Blackall also discusses the controversies over the rounded, Ciceronian style and the looser, Senecan style in eighteenth-century German writings in chap. 5.

36. Ronald Paulson, *Emblem and Expression: Meaning in English Art of the Eighteenth Century* (Cambridge, Mass., 1975), pp. 21–22.

37. Herrnstein Smith, *Poetic Closure,* pp. 98–100, 109.

In discussing poetic structure and its relation to closure, then, Smith has isolated the problems central to composers as well as critics of variations: how coherence may be achieved in a form based on repetition, how paratactic structure may sometimes take on aspects of sequential structure, and how a piece may have closure and not merely end.[38] A similar idea on the relationship between structure and meaning is brought out by Paul Fussell:

> In a short multistanza poem, . . . the number of stanzas into which the poem is divided should itself express something; the number should not give the impression of being accidental . . . Another way of saying the same thing is to suggest that the white space between stanzas means something. If nothing is conceived to be taking place within it, if no kind of silent pressure or advance or reconsideration or illumination or perception seems to be going on in that white space, the reader has a legitimate question to ask: Why is that white space there, and what am I supposed to do with it?[39]

This passage raises important questions for the critic of variation form: What impels one variation to succeed another? Is there any motivation for the number and order of variations? Leonard Meyer has already suggested a negative answer to the latter question by defining strophic variation form as a "formal" and not "processive" structure, because closure is established at the end of each variation, because no one segment implies any other, and because there is no "functional differentiation" between parts.[40] Not until Beethoven did composers routinely fill up the "white space" between variations; Meyer even claims that "the history of the theme and variations in the eighteenth and nineteenth centuries might be understood as the search for a way of transforming a 'naturally' flat, additive hierarchy (as in most Baroque and early classical variations) into an arched, processive one—one with functionally differentiated parts."[41] Another way of putting this is that before the nineteenth century, variations were purely paratactic, and that composers sought ways to overcome this. Rosen argues that every Classical form takes on sonata-like features, including, by the time of Beethoven's *Appassionata* sonata, Op. 57, variation form.[42] In effect, paratactic form represents the abstract model of variation form, its objective external shape, while sequential form might be thought of as the ideal inner shape to which it aspires.

Yet to consider paratactic or stanzaic structure as a negative value in music—that is, to assume that composers would want to "overcome" it and to consider them successful only when they did so—is to miss that the aesthetic experience of variation (and thus one measure of a composer's success) depends as much

---

38. The issue of closure, also drawing on Smith's categories, is explored by V. Kofi Agawu in "Concepts of Closure and Chopin's Opus 28," *Music Theory Spectrum* 9 (1987), 1–17.

39. Paul Fussell, *Poetic Meter and Poetic Form,* rev. ed. (New York, 1979), p. 155.

40. Meyer, *Explaining Music,* pp. 94–97.

41. Ibid., p. 96.

42. Rosen, *Classical Style,* p. 438. He also suggests that Mozart's handling of variation form is influenced by sonata style (p. 226).

upon the independence of individual segments as upon their ordering. Paratactic structure in variation form is one of its strengths precisely because at any moment a variation may be considered as a totality, as a species of relationship with the theme, and as a building block in the larger edifice. Repetition enables a multiplicity of interpretations along such temporal and spatial lines. Correlations exist not just in the experience of walking through a "paratactic garden," but in the field of visual perception, the eye following a decorative pattern created by what Gombrich calls the "graded complication" of a hierarchical design rooted in movement.[43] A network of "progressive intricacy" in design arises from a three-step creative process: framing, filling, and linking. There are even sets of visual variations, such as the didactic set of one hundred designs, by a Victorian architect, based on three circles inscribed within a circle.[44] Yet Gombrich also asserts that repetition devalues the motif while isolation enhances its potential meaning.

III

At this juncture, repetition begins to overlap with decoration, and poses a different sort of aesthetic problem. Decoration, also variously called embellishment, figuration, and ornamentation, has had a checkered history since antiquity, with its emphasis on the superficial and suggestion of the excessive. Most critics of any period applauded the idea of unity and variety within a work of art *(variatio delectat)*, but ornament itself was seen as hiding true worth, obscuring the merits of simplicity, or giving an unfair advantage in oratory.[45] In the rhetorical treatise of Bernard Lamy, *L'Art Rhétorique ou l'art de parler* (1676), categories of verbal ornamentation included the extremes of "natural ornament," which "produces a pleasing picture of what one wishes to make known," and "false ornament," the primary goal of which is to please without care for truth; in an intermediate category of "artificial ornaments," embellishments add grace and charm but could be removed without harming the speech's essential persuasive force. In fact, only when these figures detract from the message by calling attention to themselves do they become false.[46]

43. E. H. Gombrich, *The Sense of Order: A Study in the Psychology of Decorative Art* (Ithaca, 1979), p. 75.
44. Robert William Billings, *The Power of Form Applied to Geometric Tracery* (London, 1851), cited in Gombrich, *The Sense of Order*, p. 82. Gombrich explicitly links these to the "game" of playing variations on a simple theme.
45. For an excellent account of the various debates, see Gombrich, *The Sense of Order*, pp. 17–62. On recurring arguments about the plain and natural versus high-flown sophistry, see Brian Vickers, *In Defence of Rhetoric* (Oxford, 1988), and Richard Lanham, *The Motives of Eloquence: Literary Rhetoric in the Renaissance* (New Haven, 1976).
46. Thomas M. Carr, Jr., *Descartes and the Resilience of Rhetoric: Varieties of Cartesian Rhetorical Theory* (Carbondale and Edwardsville, 1990), pp. 155–156, citing Lamy's *L'Art Rhétorique* (Paris, 1676), pp. 236, 261, and 157–158, respectively. The vexed question of rhetorical figures and their relationship to musical figures will be explored in Chapter 2, while eighteenth-century critical judgments of musical embellishments will be taken up in Chapter 3.

The centrality of ornament to eighteenth-century thinking about art and architecture led to a variety of evaluations of decorative styles of the past. A mid-century Italian treatise on architecture upheld a style both simple and varied, decrying the Gothic style because of its profusion of small ornaments but lauding the regular divisions of the Greek arch, which enable the mind to take it all in.[47] Winckelmann similarly admired the symbolic motifs of Greek design while attacking the lack of meaning in decoration of the mid-eighteenth century.[48] Thus, decoration was held to be central to beauty, while at the same time—both paradoxically and inevitably—beauty itself was found less and less satisfying as an aesthetic ideal. The gendered quality of much aesthetic criticism of the period arose from increasingly explicit associations of both beauty and ornament with women and with feminine taste.[49]

General aesthetic theories of the eighteenth and early nineteenth centuries may be applied to musical decoration by analogy or extension. These larger issues—the imitation of nature, the expression of the passions, theories of the beautiful and sublime, and organic metaphors in art—called forth endless written considerations. The mimetic theories of art that enjoyed wide currency from Aristotle up to the end of the eighteenth century find only two echoes in musical writings on variation, both meant in a fairly wide sense: Mattheson's derivative dictum "Variation is the joy of Nature" and Daube's peroration "It is certain that everything that has been and will be composed is subject to the art of variations."[50] A natural sanction for variety went without saying; the questions concerning most writers were the limits on that variety. But since varying and figuring a melody were generally agreed to give the music greater character and expressiveness, according to the authors of *Melodielehren,* we might also claim for decoration an important role in expressing the affect or passion of a piece. By extension, then, variation technique at least could participate in the central aesthetic purpose of a piece of music, moving the emotions.

Repetition too could be described in terms of producing a response. As a technique of the "verbal arts"—hence rhetoric—repetition was defined narrowly by Johann Georg Sulzer in his *Allgemeine Theorie der schönen Künste* as a "figure of speech in which a word or thought is repeated, for the sake of greater emphasis."[51] Recommending that the repetition be performed in a stronger or

47. Francesco Milizia, *Saggio sopra l'Architettura* (1768), cited in Gombrich, *The Sense of Order,* p. 28.

48. Johann Joachim Winckelmann, *Thoughts concerning the Imitation of Greek Works* (1755), cited in Gombrich, *The Sense of Order,* p. 26.

49. Gombrich noted that an overly ornamented style was criticized as reflecting feminine taste; *Sense of Order,* p. 23. See the discussion of beautiful and sublime below. On the relationship between ornamental details and the feminine in this period, see Naomi Schor, *Reading in Detail: Aesthetics and the Feminine* (New York and London, 1987), pp. 11–22. My thanks to Michael Long for recommending this book.

50. Johann Mattheson, *Große Generalbaß-Schule* (Hamburg, 1731), pp. 161–162: "Variation ist der Lust der Nature"; Johann F. Daube, *Der musikalische Dilettant* (Vienna, 1773), p. 148; "Das ist einmal gewiß, daß alles, was bisher in der Welt in die Musik ist gebracht worden, und was noch ins künftige komponieret werden wird: was ist miteinander der Variationskunst unterworfen."

51. Johann Georg Sulzer, *Allgemeine Theorie der schönen Künste,* 4 vols. in 2 (Leipzig, 1771–1774; 2nd ed., 1794; rpt. Hildesheim, 1969), IV, p. 730, s.v. "Wiederholung."

more affecting voice, he suggested that the figure be used sparingly. Other types of repetition, with other effects, seemed to Sulzer not important enough to be recounted; in a footnote, he merely referred the reader to the ninth book of Quintilian's *Institutio Oratoria* (chap. 3.28ff.). Although these sections of the treatise are among the most important for an understanding of specific rhetorical figures of repetition, many of them have the same effect as that described by Sulzer. His interest is less in enumerating techniques of repetition than in the general affective quality they produce.

Theories of the beautiful and sublime, on the other hand, seemed more likely to belittle variation as the century progressed, because language used to describe the sublime inevitably downgraded beauty. Hogarth's well-known criterion for beauty, the "sinuous line," given in *The Analysis of Beauty* (London, 1753), might by analogy champion figured melody: if the eye delights in curvature, then the ear might well enjoy similarly "curling" melodic patterns. But other writers described beauty as bounded by orderliness, even limitation, in comparison with the vast, free, awe-inspiring sublime. Edmund Burke is notorious in this regard: beautiful objects are small, smooth, delicate, show gradual variation without angular contour, and have clear and bright (but not glaring) color.[52] The sublime, on the other hand, has a more compelling source: "Whatever is fitted in any sort to excite the ideas of pain, and danger, that is to say, whatever is in any sort terrible, . . . is a source of the *sublime;* that is, it is productive of the strongest emotion which the mind is capable of feeling."[53] The dark and powerfully disordered elements of the Burkean sublime which cause astonishment, horror, and admiration cannot be reconciled with the more pleasing elements of beauty. An even more explicit association of the beautiful with the superficial and the sublime with the powerful and deep appeared in Kant's pre-Critical treatise, *Observations on the Feeling of the Beautiful and Sublime* (1763); indeed, such binary oppositions abound.[54] Although Kant clearly stated that beautiful and sublime were complementary and needed each other, there is no question of their relative valuation; simply contrast a man's nobility and depth of understanding with a woman's "strong inborn feeling for all that is beautiful, elegant, and decorated."[55]

Kant's *Critique of Judgment* (1790) established a new and complex differentiation between the beautiful and sublime, as well as modifying his earlier categories into two different sublimes: "Beauty in nature concerns the form of the object; and this consists in limitation. The sublime, on the other hand, may be discerned even in a formless object in so far as it has or evokes the idea of limitlessness even though the object's totality may be adduced as well."[56] Even

52. Edmund Burke, *A Philosophical Enquiry into the Origin of our Ideas of the Sublime and Beautiful,* 2nd ed. (1759), ed. James T. Boulton (Notre Dame, 1968), pp. 113–117.

53. Ibid., p. 39.

54. Immanuel Kant, *Observations on the Feeling of the Beautiful and Sublime,* trans. John T. Goldthwait (Berkeley, Los Angeles, Oxford, 1960; 1991).

55. Ibid., pp. 76–77.

56. Translated in Peter LeHuray and James Day, eds., *Music and Aesthetics in the Eighteenth and Early-Nineteenth Centuries* (Cambridge, 1981), p. 223.

within beautiful form, however, decorations deemed extrinsic to it are hierarchically denigrated:

> That which is only incidental to and not an inner component of the complete representation, is called a *decoration (parerga)*. It increases the pleasure of taste, though only by its form; such are picture-frames, draperies for statues, or colonnades round palaces. If however the decoration is not integral to the beautiful form itself, if as with the golden frame it is there as an attraction simply to arouse admiration for the painting, it is then termed an *embellishment (Schmuck)* and it has nothing to do with beauty.[57]

Thus, even at their best, formal decorations contribute only peripherally to beauty; and beauty, deriving from the form of an object and creating harmony in our faculties of sensibility and understanding, cannot compete with the sublime experience, based as it is upon formlessness. Kant's sublime, in the words of Paul Guyer, "makes demands upon the imagination which imagination cannot fulfill, it presents objects which seem to exceed the organizing capacities of mind."[58] The sublime does this in two ways—by magnitude or extent (the "mathematical sublime") and by power or force, the "might of nature" (the "dynamical sublime"). Ascribing such sublime qualities to the world, the mind actually locates them in our rational being, since we are superior to nature: as Kant put it, *"the sublime is that, the mere ability to think which, shows a faculty of the mind surpassing every standard of Sense."*[59]

A similar, though more inexorably Romantic train of thought compares the restrictions of form unfavorably to sublime freedom in two passages from Schiller's *On the Sublime* (1801):

> Who does not prefer to tarry among the spiritual disorder of a natural landscape rather than in the spiritless regularity of a French garden? Who would not marvel at the wonderful battle between fecundity and destruction in Sicily's plains, or feast his eyes on Scotland's wild cataracts and mist-shrouded mountains, Ossian's vast nature, rather than admire in straight-diked Holland the prim victory of patience over the most defiant of the elements? . . .

> To noble minds freedom, for all its moral contradictions and physical evils, is an infinitely more interesting spectacle than prosperity and order without freedom, when the sheep patiently follow the shepherd and the autonomous will reduces itself to an obedient cog in a machine.[60]

Perhaps we should resist the temptation to see in "straight-diked Holland" the rigid succession of double bars in variation form, but Schiller's approval of "spiritual disorder" at the expense of "spiritless regularity" enables us to iden-

57. Ibid., p. 220.

58. Paul Guyer, *Kant and the Claims of Taste* (Cambridge, Mass., 1979), p. 500.

59. Kant, *Critique of Judgment,* trans. J. H. Bernard (London, 1914), 2nd ed., I, par. 25. See Ernst Cassirer, *Kant's Life and Thought* (New Haven: Yale University Press, 1981; first pub. 1918), pp. 327–329.

60. Both translated in *Two Essays by Friedrich Schiller. Naive and Sentimental Poetry and On the Sublime,* trans. Julius A. Elias (New York, 1966), pp. 204–206.

tify the same aesthetic response to variation form. Here the concepts of repetition and decoration are conjoined for a devastating critique.[61]

The final blow to aesthetic acceptance of the variation form in this period came with the full emergence of the organic metaphor in the arts, in the works of Schlegel, Coleridge, and many others.[62] Growing, becoming, and flowering were not terms that readily described variation forms.[63] Variations throughout history to that point had obeyed an externally imposed law, that of enforced structural resemblance to a theme; different "solutions" were always found to that "problem." Yet as separable entities, individual variations could not lay claim to a continuous process of growth, even though they all derived from the germinating seed, the theme, unless one fancifully allows for the plant with regular striations, possibly culminating in the "flower" of a fugue or coda. The processes of sonata form, on the other hand, fulfilled this new locus of value.

The new age in variations presaged by this aesthetic was heralded by Schumann. In 1836, crusading against the empty figuration of the salon variation, he wrote that "variations should create a whole, whose center is the theme . . . The time is past when one can create astonishment with a sugary figure, a yearning suspension, an Eb-major run over the keyboard. Now one strives for *thoughts,* for inner *connections,* for poetic *totality,* with the whole bathed in fresh fantasy"; he claimed that the age of variation was ending to make room for the capriccio.[64] The "wholeness" of a set of variations and the centrality of its theme argued for a deep relationship—"inner connections"—between theme and variations.

IV

The scope of eighteenth-century thinking about *musical* repetition can be suggested by Neefe's unusual slant on the topic in an article of 1776 and by Koch's more matter-of-fact summary in the entry on repetition [*Wiederholung*] in his *Musikalisches Lexikon* (1802). I begin with the later of these, because it sensibly covers the points raised by most earlier writers on compositional techniques:

> *Wiederholung.* In the general sense of the word . . . every mediated or unmediated return of a previous segment [*Satzes*] in a composition; the returning segment may appear in the same or in a different key.
>
> In a still narrower sense, we use this word when in the theory of composition we

61. Schiller's many specific discussions about music, some of them contradictory, would be relevant here only with the most procrustean efforts. See Rey M. Longyear, *Schiller and Music* (Chapel Hill, 1966), pp. 94–129.

62. M. H. Abrams's *The Mirror and the Lamp* (London, 1953) remains the classic study of this phenomenon in historical context. See also Solie, "The Living Work," and Brian Primmer, "Unity and Ensemble," *19CM* 6 (1982), 97–140.

63. See Janet M. Levy's mention of this phenomenon, with its concomitant "absolute derogation of the mechanical," in "Covert and Casual Values," 27.

64. Schumann, *Gesammelte Schriften über Musik und Musiker,* 2 vols. (Leipzig, 1854; 3rd ed., Leipzig, 1875), I, no. 34, pp. 221, 223, 218.

distinguish between immediate repetitions of a melodic section [*Theils*] in a sequence [*Versetzung*] from those in a transposition [*Transposition*] . . . and imitation [*Nachahmung*] . . . These different types of repetition have not only the most excellent qualities that help to convey the unity of a piece, but they also belong to those means through which a piece is realized [*Ausführung*]. *Repetition in the broader sense of the word, however, contributes to the peculiar form of various pieces, as in, for example, the rondo.* [Emphasis added.] A piece can gain so many advantages through suitable repetitions, especially through those in which the repeated segment always appears in new harmonic garb; just as disadvantageous is a piece in which too many of those repetitions are used that are purely mechanical without harmonic variety, in order to give the piece its customary dimensions.[65]

The broader sense of form-generating repetition, for which Koch here gives the example of rondo, also gives rise to variation, which Koch in a different place defined as "multiple immediate repetitions of a short piece."[66] Differentiating between small-scale procedures and broader repetitions nicely encapsulates the term's meanings, but Koch only alludes to the role of repetition in the more historically significant features of "unity" and "realization."

An entirely different approach to *Wiederholung* was outlined in 1776 by Christian Gottlob Neefe, later Beethoven's teacher. Neefe's essay "Ueber die musikalische Wiederholung" suggested that the issue was on many people's minds; it is worth quoting at length:

It is customary today for critics of musical compositions in newspapers, journals, societies, and audiences that they reproach composers [for their] repetition, and they least of all know what they properly mean by it. It is true that repetition, in music as in the other arts and sciences, can cause error when it is used without basis, and it can cause annoyance in the listener when it appears too often. A musical idea, however, can be often and perhaps immediately upon itself repeated, and this repetition can be a true merit of the composer. I will set out here a few fleeting thoughts on repetition . . .

Musical repetition is divided into two categories: repetition with respect to invention [*in Ansehung der Erfindung*] and for the purpose of realization [*in Absicht auf die Ausführung*].

According to the first, a composer can repeat either his own thoughts or those of another. The repetition of his own ideas springs from different sources. Either he is actually poor in invention, in which case he lacks the most essential characteristic of a composer and his repetition is certainly open to censure . . . or [he is] . . . deficient in memory, so that the composer can imagine his ideas to be current when they had already been introduced previously. Or it arises from the necessity of working hard and fast; then it is an error that deserves [our] indulgence . . . Even Hasse and Graun . . . have not been free from these mistakes . . .

65. Heinrich Christoph Koch, *Musikalisches Lexikon* (Frankfurt am Main, 1802; rpt. Hildesheim, 1964), s.v. "Wiederholung."

66. Ibid., s.v. "Variazionen, Variazioni" (quoted in Chapter 3). Koch did not refer to the numerous techniques of repetition that he had outlined in the *Versuch einer Anleitung zur Composition* (Rudolstadt and Leipzig, 1782–1793), trans. by Nancy K. Baker as *Introductory Essay on Composition* (New Haven and London, 1983). See Chapter 3.

The repetition whereby the composer brings to light the ideas of another composer may arise from just the same causes as the previous type:

a) a deficiency in power of invention. Young composers are generally inclined to this error . . . Pergolesis, young geniuses, . . . are rare. Philidor . . . knows how to use the Italians and others . . . He transposed an aria of Hasse's.

b) from excessive haste;

c) from a weak memory . . .

There is still another category of repetition, namely with respect to realization . . . This [type] you want not only to criticize but to abolish? What kind of monstrosity would a musical piece become if we piled up idea upon idea without connection, if we wanted to employ only an unrestrained fantasy, not heart and understanding. No listener would be able any longer to understand and feel a [piece of] music. All the rules, the periodicity of melody [*Periodologie des Gesanges*], by which we have worked for such a long time, even the true expression of affect, the situation of the character of a singing person, would disappear. Genius ought not to be oppressed by rules . . .

I said above that if you want to wipe out this second type of repetition, expression would often be completely lost. I will illustrate this with an example. There are cases where the composer has to express a certain affect in the first lines of his text. He invents a musical idea for it. In the following lines the interest of the same affect intensifies. Should he invent a new idea to each of the following lines? Or should he more strongly repeat the first thought? I think the latter . . .

Repetition is also necessary for another reason. Our soul longs to seize hold of all that is interesting to it. I leave it to the composer: he must repeat an interesting, flattering thought with which the soul can be satisfied. In poetry and painting this repetition is not necessary, because I can reread an excellent place in a poem to myself two or three times, view a charming painting to and fro, fro and to. A listener cannot do this, the music goes by quickly; he can lose much that he would not like to lose, if the composer does not recoup it for him by repetition.

These are my fleeting thoughts on this subject. Perhaps at least someone will see that he criticizes the repetition of a composer without knowing whether he is rendering an overhasty judgment or whether he is inadvertently paying the composer a compliment. I have applied my thoughts to vocal compositions; they can with a bit more limitation also be applied to instrumental compositions.[67]

Neefe's outline has significance beyond providing a means of evaluating the creative capacities of a composer and evaluating current responses to repetition. First, his argument was revived in 1803 by Michaelis, who took the opportunity to summarize and elaborate on Neefe's remarks on repetition with his own on variation; we will examine Michaelis's article in Chapter 8.[68] Second, in setting out *Erfindung* and *Ausführung* as his principal areas of discussion, Neefe staked a major claim in intellectual history: not only did he reflect contemporaneous ideas of the compositional process, as set out by Mattheson and

67. Neefe, "Ueber die musikalische Wiederholung," *Deutsches Museum* 1 (August, 1776), 745–751; see Appendix B for German.

68. C. F. Michaelis, "Ueber die musikalische Wiederholung und Veränderung," *AMZ* 6 (1803), cols. 197–200.

Sulzer, but his discussion also clearly alluded to the first three of the five parts of classical rhetoric: (1) invention *(inventio)*, (2) arrangement *(dispositio)*, (3) style *(elocutio)*, (4) memory *(memoria)*, and (5) delivery *(pronuntiatio)*.[69] Repetition, according to Neefe, is central to the invention of the ideas in a piece, to the connection of those ideas, as well as to their affective expression, which arises from the third element of rhetoric—how language was to be beautified and made expressive through the judicious application of figures, called embellishments or ornaments of style. Many of these figures are in fact figures of repetition, as Sulzer made clear. Neefe's article, then, is suffused by rhetorical thinking. The twin topics of repetition and decoration in rhetoric, and their relevance to variation form, will constitute our next point of departure.

69. On eighteenth-century discussions of the compositional process, see Ian Bent, "The Compositional Process in Music, 1713–1850," *MusA* 3 (1984), 29–55. For a provocative recent formulation of the relationship among the parts of rhetoric, see Tzvetan Todorov, *Theories of the Symbol,* trans. Catherine Porter (Ithaca, 1982), chaps. 2–3.

CHAPTER TWO

The Rhetoric of Variation

The idea that models for variation form might be found in rhetoric arises not only from the explanatory vividness and sheer historical staying power of the latter, but also from features common to both—their shared modes of display and their understanding of the persuasive power inherent in repetition and ornament. At once a speaking art, a compositional guide, and a critical tool, rhetoric had been a more vital force in public life and letters earlier in its long and venerable history, but its influence was still ubiquitous in the eighteenth century. Not only did *gymnasium* and church-school instruction in Germany and Austria include the study of rhetoric, but evidence is growing for its influence even on such major and forward-looking works as Schiller's *On the Aesthetic Education of Man* and Hegel's *Phenomenology of Spirit*.[1] And though the course of study called "rhetoric" did not appear in the curriculum until the sixth year, rhetorical concepts had been included in studies of grammar and literature undertaken in previous years.[2]

Writers on music had since the sixteenth century routinely invoked rhetorical ideas and made comparisons with rhetorical figures: rhetoric as a model of composition, extemporizing, and evaluation was an ingrained habit of thought.[3] Indeed, analogies were made as a matter of course. For example,

1. See Herman Meyer, "Schillers philosophische Rhetorik," in *Zarte Empirie* (Stuttgart, 1963), pp. 337–389; John H. Smith, *The Spirit and Its Letter: Traces of Rhetoric in Hegel's Philosophy of Bildung* (Ithaca and London, 1988). Leopold Mozart's education in Augsburg included considerable instruction in rhetoric; see Adolf Layer, *Eine Jugend in Augsburg—Leopold Mozart 1719–1737* (Augsburg, [1975]). And C. F. D. Schubart read Quintilian, as reported in *Schubart's Leben und Gesinnungen von ihm selbst, im Kerker aufgesetzt* (Stuttgart, 1791–1793; rpt. Leipzig, 1980), vol. 1, p. 92. Important recent histories of rhetoric include George A. Kennedy, *Classical Rhetoric and Its Christian and Secular Tradition from Ancient to Modern Times* (Chapel Hill, 1980) and Brian Vickers, *In Defence of Rhetoric* (Oxford, 1988). See also Ursula Stötzer, *Deutsche Redekunst im 17. und 18. Jahrhundert* (Halle, 1962).

2. Fritz Keller, "Rhetorik in der Ordenschule," in *Die Österreichische Literatur: ihr Profil an der Wende vom 18. zum 19. Jahrhundert (1750–1830)*, ed. Herbert Zeman (*JbÖK* 7–9 [1977–79]), p. 57.

3. As George J. Buelow put it, "The humanistic basis of education aspiring to teach every student the art of rhetorical eloquence permeated musical thought for centuries"; see "The *Loci Topici* and Affect in Late Baroque Music: Heinichen's Practical Demonstration," *MR* 27 (1966), 161. Among

Leopold Mozart's violin treatise echoed Quintilian without citing him on the naturalness of rhetorical figures and their use even by the uneducated. In discussing extemporized embellishments, Mozart noted:

> The Appoggiature are little notes which stand between the ordinary notes but are not reckoned as part of the bar-time. They are demanded by Nature herself to bind the notes together, thereby making a melody more song-like. I say by Nature herself, for it is undeniable that even a peasant closes his peasant-song with grace notes . . . Nature herself forces him to do this. In the same way the simplest peasant often uses figures of speech and metaphors without knowing it.[4]

Quintilian had commented that metaphor is "so natural a turn of speech that it is often employed unconsciously or by uneducated persons," and that hyperbole "is employed even by peasants and uneducated persons, for the good reason that everybody has an innate passion for exaggeration."[5] If the naturalness of adding ornament is justified by rhetorical example, so too are cautions against an excess of ornamentation, which will sacrifice intelligibility. C. P. E. Bach's comments fall into the latter category:

> Regard [embellishments] as decorations which can overload the best building and as spices which can ruin the best dish. Notes of no great moment and those sufficiently brilliant by themselves should remain free of them, for embellishments serve only to increase the weight and import of notes and to differentiate them from others. Otherwise, I would commit the same error as orators who try to place an emphatic accent on every word; everything would be alike and consequently unclear.[6]

the principal modern surveys on rhetoric and music are Hans-Heinrich Unger, *Die Beziehungen zwischen Musik und Rhetorik im 16.–18. Jahrhundert* (Würzburg, 1941); Willibald Gurlitt, "Musik und Rhetorik," *Helicon* 5 (1943), 67–86; Rolf Dammann, *Der Musikbegriff im deutschen Barock* (Cologne, 1967), pp. 93–180; and especially Mark Evan Bonds, *Wordless Rhetoric: Musical Form and the Metaphor of the Oration* (Cambridge, Mass., 1991), which convincingly demonstrates the importance of rhetoric in eighteenth- and nineteenth-century aesthetics, theory, and criticism. See also Carl Dahlhaus, "Das rhetorische Formbegriff H. Chr. Koch und die Theorie der Sonatenform," *AfMw* 35 (1978), 155–177; Hartmut Krones, "Rhetorik und rhetorische Symbolik in der Musik um 1800. Vom Weiterleben eines Prinzip," *Musiktheorie* 3 (1988), 117–140. Buelow includes an extensive bibliography of more specialized studies in "Rhetoric and Music," *The New Grove,* vol. 15, pp. 793–803.

4. Leopold Mozart, *Versuch einer gründlichen Violinschule* (Augsburg, 1756); trans. as *A Treatise on the Fundamental Principles of Violin Playing* by Editha Knocker (Oxford, 1945; 1988), p. 166. Mozart used Gottsched's *Deutsche Sprachkunst* when preparing his treatise; his letters to this effect are cited by Mark Evan Bonds, "Haydn's False Recapitulations and the Perception of Sonata Form in the Eighteenth Century" (Ph.D. diss., Harvard University, 1988), p. 103.

5. Quintilian, *Institutio Oratoria,* trans. H. E. Butler, Loeb Classical Library, vol. 126 (Cambridge, Mass., 1921), VIII.vi.4 and VIII.vi.75, respectively. (Conventional citations of Quintilian and other rhetorical treatises are given as book/chapter/section.) Cited by Vickers, *In Defence of Rhetoric,* p. 299.

6. C. P. E. Bach, *Versuch über die wahre Art, das Clavier zu spielen* (Berlin, 1753–1762; facs. Leipzig, 1976), I, p. 54 (at chap. II, par. 9); trans. slightly modified from William J. Mitchell, *Essay on the True Art of Playing Keyboard Instruments* (New York, 1949), p. 81.

The rhetorical analogies that had taken hold were thus particularly appropriate to discussions of embellishments.

As an improvised technique and form comprising "ornaments" and "figurations," variation invites a comparison with the art of extemporizing a persuasive speech using verbal figures.[7] And as a form founded on repetition, variation implicitly reminds us that perhaps the majority of rhetorical figures are figures of repetition. With the exception of Koch, no musical writers discussed the importance of repetition to variation form, and practically no attempt was made to distinguish between repetition and recurrence. But repetition as a rhetorical figure sometimes put in an appearance in these writers' works.

As we have seen, Neefe's article on musical repetition (1776) described repetition in the same terms as the first three parts of classical rhetoric: invention *(inventio, Erfindung)* of the subject and its treatments; its disposition or articulation *(dispositio, Ausführung* or *Anordnung)* into a coherent speech; and its expression of the affect, which would have been part of *elocutio (Ausdruck, sometimes Ausschmückung),* by means of figures—also called schemes—and tropes. Some musical writers attempted to fit musical structures to the six-part structure of an oration: introduction *(exordium),* statement of facts *(narratio),* division *(partitio* or *propositio*—what is agreed upon and what is contested), arguments and their confirmation *(confirmatio* or *probatio),* destruction of enemies' arguments *(confutatio* or *reprehensio),* and conclusion *(peroratio* or *conclusio).*[8] Greater enthusiasm for the third part of rhetoric, style and expression, led to the wide-ranging application of figures and tropes to music by theorists of the late sixteenth and seventeenth centuries—notably Burmeister, Bernhard, and Herbst—a task taken up with equal enthusiasm by their musicological counterparts of the first half of the twentieth century—Schering, Brandes, Gurlitt, Unger, and Bukofzer.[9] With the renewed interest in rhetoric in all fields since the late 1960s, and since the publication in 1980 of George Buelow's article "Rhetoric and Music" in the *New Grove Dictionary* with its extensive tables of musico-rhetorical figures, a strong reaction against "figure-finding" has set

7. If nothing else, the use of the term "figure" bears further scrutiny in the context of instrumental music; its textual associations have already been applied to vocal music.

8. See Vickers, *In Defence of Rhetoric,* pp. 67–72, for a summary of these persuasive functions, as well as Richard Lanham, *A Handlist of Rhetorical Terms,* 2nd ed. (Berkeley and Los Angeles, 1991), pp. 171–174. Versions of this structure appear in Mattheson (see n. 16) and Forkel (see n. 19), among others; on Mattheson, see Bent, "Compositional Process," pp. 47–48.

9. Joachim Burmeister, *Musica poetica* (Rostock, 1606; facs. ed. Kassel, 1955); Christoph Bernhard, *Tractatus compositionis augmentatus,* ed. in Joseph Müller-Blattau, *Die Kompositionslehre Heinrich Schützens in der Fassung seines Schülers Christoph Bernhard* (Kassel, 1926), trans. Walter Hilse, "The Treatises of Christoph Bernhard," *Music Forum* 3 (1973), 1–196; Andreas Herbst, *Musica poetica* (Nürnberg, 1643); Arnold Schering, "Die Lehre von der musikalischen Figuren," *Kirchen-Musikalisches Jahrbuch* 21 (1908), 106–114; Heinz Brandes, *Studien zur musikalischen Figurenlehre im 16. Jahrhundert* (Berlin, 1935); Gurlitt, "Musik und Rhetorik"; Unger, *Beziehungen zwischen Musik und Rhetorik;* Manfred Bukofzer, "Allegory in Baroque Music," *Journal of the Warburg and Courtauld Institutes* 3 (1939–40), 1–21. See the bibliographies in Buelow, "Rhetoric and Music," and in his "Music, Rhetoric, and the Concept of the Affections: A Selective Bibliography," *Notes* 30 (1973–74), 250–259.

in. Peter Williams argues scathingly that unless one can document a composer's intentions, labeling figures accomplishes virtually nothing; his title, "The Snares and Delusions of Musical Rhetoric," accurately conveys his tone.[10] In a more judicious but still thoroughly skeptical article, Brian Vickers claims that little seems to remain of the original meaning of the figure when applied to non-semantic notes, and thus that any large-scale application of rhetorical figures to music beyond purely illustrative purposes is suspect.[11]

Here for once Vickers is himself guilty of not heeding his own admonition: "In the study of rhetoric, as with all other disciplines, a narrow conception leads to narrow thinking, facile rejections, and hasty abandonment of the subject. Give rhetoric a trivial function and you trivialize it; conceive of it as widely as it originally existed, and you may begin to do justice to it."[12] That early seventeenth-century theorists gave inappropriate musical analogues to rhetorical figures says more about the theorists than about the ultimate applicability of figures to music. Vickers's real difficulty is in imagining instrumental music as rhetorically conceived or as able to be elucidated by recourse to rhetorical concepts.[13] Nor has he considered models outside the structure of an oration or the expression of affections through figures and text-setting. He deplores the application of rhetoric to music because it seems more suited to "critics than to creators."[14] Yet precisely that critical potential makes rhetorical concepts seem most attractive.

Rhetoric and Classical Composers

Rhetoric can indeed be broadly applied to eighteenth-century music, and, as Leonard Ratner has reminded us, musical writers of the period discussed rhetorical concepts in a pervasive, all-encompassing way.[15] Mattheson, for example, discussed not only melodic invention but also musical structures—from phrase to piece—in terms of the parts of an oration.[16] Scheibe claimed that in vocal music the parallel to oratory went without saying, but that the

10. Williams, "The Snares and Delusions of Musical Rhetoric: Some Examples from Recent Writings on J. S. Bach," in *Alte Musik: Praxis und Reflexion*, ed. Peter Reidemeister and Veronika Gutmann (Winterthur, 1983), pp. 230–240. See also David Schulenberg, "Musical Expression and Musical Rhetoric in the Keyboard Works of J. S. Bach," paper delivered at the Annual Meeting of the American Musicological Society, Vancouver, 1985; Maria Rika Maniates, "Music and Rhetoric: Faces of Cultural History in the Renaissance and Baroque," *Israel Studies in Musicology* 3 (1983), 44–69.

11. Vickers, "Figures of Rhetoric/Figures of Music?" *Rhetorica* 2 (1984), 1–44.

12. Vickers, *In Defence of Rhetoric*, p. 105.

13. He resists Ursula Kirkendale's virtuoso performance identifying Quintilian as "the source" for Bach's *Musical Offering* ("The Source for Bach's *Musical Offering*: The *Institutio oratoria* of Quintilian," *JAMS* 33 [1980], 88–141). One wonders what he would make of Alan Street's even more detailed, historically based application, "The Rhetorico-Musical Structure of the 'Goldberg' Variations: Bach's *Clavier-Übung* IV and the *Institutio oratoria* of Quintilian," *MusA* 6 (1987), 89–131.

14. Vickers, "Figures of Rhetoric," p. 41.

15. Ratner, *Classic Music*, pp. 31–206. See also Bonds, *Wordless Rhetoric*.

16. Mattheson, *Der vollkommene Capellmeister*, Part II, chap. 14, pars. 1–25.

rhetorical element was necessary even in instrumental music, as long as one wished to draw in, please, and move the audience.[17] Marpurg claimed that rhetoric included every aspect of musical composition and performance.[18] Forkel specified six large areas controlled by rhetoric: (1) the construction of musical periods; (2) musical styles; (3) the different genres of music; (4) the ordering of musical thoughts, also called "aesthetic ordering," including the study of figures; (5) the performance of a piece; and finally (6) music criticism.[19] And Koch quoted extensively from Forkel in his own *Musikalisches Lexikon* of 1802.[20]

That Haydn knew Mattheson's work is certain.[21] He also owned the relevant works by Marpurg, as well as earlier ones by Herbst and Beer.[22] Haydn had an Italian edition of Aesop's fables, a paradigmatic work for instruction in rhetoric, for purposes of paraphrase and as a source for themes and moral characters.[23] His studies at St. Stephen's included, according to Griesinger, "the scant

17. Scheibe, *Compendium Musices Theoretico-practicum, das ist Kurzer Begriff derer nöthigsten Compositions-Regeln* (c. 1728–1736), ed. by Peter Benary as the appendix to *Die deutsche Kompositionslehre des 18. Jahrhundert* (Leipzig, 1960), p. 75.

18. Marpurg, in the introduction to his *Anfangsgründe der theoretischen Musik* (Leipzig, 1757; facs. ed., New York, 1966), divided music into five categories: philosophical, rhetorical, grammatical, historical, and mechanical. Rhetoric includes the practical aspect of music, namely its composition and performance; grammar merely clarifies its rules (pp. 1–3).

19. Johann Nikolaus Forkel, *Allgemeine Geschichte der Musik* (Leipzig, 1788–1801), I, p. 39: Periodologie, Schreibarten, Musikgattungen, Anordnung musikalischer Gedanken, Vortrag or Declamation, musikalische Kritik.

20. Koch, *Musikalisches Lexikon*, s.v. "Rhetorik."

21. Both Griesinger and Dies transmit comments from Haydn about *Der vollkommene Capellmeister*. Griesinger said "he came to know it" during his stay at the St. Stephen's Choir School, while Dies put his acquaintance with the work during the 1750s in Vienna: "He found the exercises in this book nothing new for him, to be sure, but good. The worked-out examples, however, were dry and tasteless. Haydn undertook for practice the task of working out all the examples in this book. He kept the whole skeleton, even the same number of notes, and invented new melodies to it." Georg August Griesinger, *Biographische Notizen über Joseph Haydn* (Leipzig, 1810), and Albert Christoph Dies, *Biographische Nachrichten von Joseph Haydn* (Vienna, 1810), both translated in Vernon Gotwals, *Haydn: Two Contemporary Portraits* (Madison, 1968), pp. 10 and 96, respectively. In fact, one of the comments Haydn made to his biographer Griesinger, that "vocal music is easier to compose than instrumental music," is similar to a remark given in boldface in Mattheson's text, in the section on melodic invention and the rhetorical commonplaces *(loci topici)*, p. 127.

22. Herbst, *Musica poetica;* Johannes Beer, *Musicalische Discurse* (Nuremberg, 1719). One of the books recommended in Mattheson's *Der vollkommene Capellmeister,* Beer's work was hardly current, and was purchased by Haydn perhaps from Monath, who had published the Beer and maintained a Nürnberg shop run by his son. See Hannelore Gericke, *Der Wiener Musikalienhandel von 1700 bis 1778* (Graz, 1960), p. 38. Haydn's claim to Griesinger that his ear knows better than the rules is prefigured in Beer's two chapters (11–12) entitled "Ob die Regel aus dem Gehör oder das Gehör aus dem Regel komme?" and "Ob in der Music mehr auf die Regeln oder auf das Gehör zu sehen?" Joseph Elßler's list of Haydn's book holdings is given in H. C. Robbins Landon, *Haydn: Chronicle and Works* (Bloomington, 1976–1980), V, pp. 314–316.

23. *Favole d'Isopo* (Venice, 1568), listed in Maria Hörwarthner, "Joseph Haydns Bibliothek—Versuch einer literarhistorischen Rekonstruktion," *Joseph Haydn und die Literatur seiner Zeit,* ed. Herbert Zeman (JbÖK 6 [1976]), p. 164.

instruction usual at the time in Latin, in religion, in arithmetic and writing."[24] Latin instruction of the period, such as that undergone more rigorously by Leopold Mozart in Augsburg or, later, by Hegel in Stuttgart, included grammar, rhetoric, and letter-writing. It is not unreasonable to suppose that similar instruction took place in Vienna. Indeed, it might have been difficult to learn any Latin without also learning some rhetoric.[25] Haydn was also no stranger to currents in literary and intellectual life.[26]

A new reading of Haydn's autobiographical sketch of 1776, supplied in letter form for publication in a book about notable Austrians, suggests that his education did include rhetoric, and that he had, consciously or unconsciously, assimilated the rhetorical modes of thought required for communication in public discourse.[27] The sketch is noteworthy for its shape: a charmingly self-deprecating opening, with clear cognizance of the honor inherent in the request for information; a narrative version of the events of his life to that time (with a few asides about God, and the care and feeding of genius), the narrative concluding that he still works for "Prince Esterházy, in whose service I wish to live and die"; then a listing of his best-received pieces, with a few details of their reception; a strikingly long refutation of his Berlin critics (sixty percent as long as the biographical narrative itself); and finally a conclusion touching on his honesty, belief in God, and respect for his Prince, as well as for the man who commissioned the biography.

In short, the sketch is a classic rhetorically organized composition, drawing particularly on the medieval *ars dictaminis,* the art of letter-writing: first an introduction *(exordium),* incorporating the so-called "securing of good-will" *(benevolentiae captatio,* in this case by self-deprecation); then the narration of facts *(narratio,* his biography); the supporting evidence *(corroboratio,* the list of pieces); the refutation of his enemies' arguments *(confutatio,* the Berlin critics); and the conclusion, revealing again his good qualities as well as those whom he admires and respects *(peroratio).*[28] Haydn's autobiographical letter reveals the persistence of rhetorical approaches to such documents.[29] It also suggests that

24. Gotwals, *Haydn,* p. 10. See also Gerda Mraz-Koller, "Bildungsanspruch und Bildungsmöglichkeiten im aufgeklärten Österreich," *Joseph Haydn und seine Zeit (JbÖK* 2 [1972]), pp. 105–120.

25. See Keller, "Rhetorik in der Ordensschule"; Georg Jäger, "Zur literarischen Gymnasialbildung in Österreich von der Aufklärung bis zum Vormärz," *Die Österreichische Literatur: ihr Profil an der Wende vom 18. zum 19. Jahrhundert (1750–1830),* ed. Herbert Zeman *(JbÖK* 7–9 [1977–79]), pp. 85–118. On Leopold Mozart's education, see Layer, *Eine Jugend in Augsburg;* on Hegel, see Smith, *Spirit and Letter,* p. 67.

26. See the interesting study by David C. Schroeder, *Haydn and the Enlightenment: The Late Symphonies and their Audience* (Oxford, 1990), part 1.

27. The text of the letter is given in *Joseph Haydn. Gesammelte Briefe und Aufzeichnungen* [hereafter *Briefe*], ed. Dénes Bartha (Kassel, 1965), pp. 76–78; trans. in Landon, *Haydn Chronicle,* II, pp. 397–399.

28. On the *ars dictaminis,* see James J. Murphy, *Rhetoric in the Middle Ages* (Berkeley and Los Angeles, 1974), pp. 194–268.

29. The autobiography of C. P. E. Bach also contains, toward the end, a discussion of the shortcomings of critics. See William S. Newman, "Emanuel Bach's Autobiography," *MQ* 51 (1965), 363–372.

the reason composers did not leave documentation about their own use of rhetoric is that it was completely assimilated and natural.

Mozart's more formal letters also show just such a reliance on this approach. In fact, the best-known letters to his Masonic brother Michael Puchberg written in 1788 and 1789 reveal not the frigidly stylized elements of *opera seria,* with which they were stigmatized by Wolfgang Hildesheimer, but rather the stylized effects of the *ars dictaminis.*[30] Indeed, this goes a long way toward explaining one of their more jarring effects, Mozart on his knees suddenly reverting to a practical tone. In the first lengthy plea, dated before June 1788, Mozart secures goodwill with "the conviction that you are *indeed my friend* and that you know me to be *a man of honour* encourages me to open my heart to you completely." His case, the request for a sizable amount of capital, proceeds by a list of the benefits of such a loan. Supporting evidence consists of his prospects for subscriptions and patrons, and the depth of responsibility of friendship and brotherhood. Protestations of his means of economizing serve as an indirect refutation of arguments by enemies that he might have spendthrift habits. Finally, the peroration stresses confidence and devotion. The long letter of 12 July 1789 is even more detailed in these respects, at once more heartrending ("poor sick wife and child") and factual ("Meanwhile I am composing six easy clavier sonatas for Princess Friederike"). That Puchberg was a Mason is significant: it seems more than likely that the rituals and formalized relationships of Freemasonry, with its orations, mix of social classes, and proliferation of commonplace books *(Stammbücher),* offered Mozart many opportunities for stylized discourse.[31]

Rhetoric and Variation

A correlation between rhetoric and variation can be grafted onto the common fund of rhetorical knowledge on which composers and theorists can be assumed to have drawn. These correlations are of three kinds: first is explicit connection, such as that made by Georg Joseph Vogler in 1793; second is the existence of rhetorical models for the structure of variation form; and third is the vast topic of figures and figuration. These will be taken up in turn.

All of the Abbé Vogler's musical writings betray a consistent interest in and

---

30. Wolfgang Hildesheimer, *Mozart,* trans. Marion Faber (New York, 1983), p. 21. See especially the letters of "before 17 June 1788" (Anderson no. 554) and 12 July 1789 (Anderson no. 567).

31. The mix of social classes within the lodges may have made rhetoric a kind of rank-free neutralizing force. For the percentages of the different groups in the Viennese lodges of this period, see Eva Huber, "Zur Sozialstruktur der Wiener Logen im Josephinischen Jahrzehnt," in *Aufklärung und Geheimgesellschaften: Zur politischen Function und Sozialstruktur der Freimaurerlogen im 18. Jahrhundert,* ed. Helmut Reinalter (Munich, 1989), pp. 173–187. Important recent studies of Haydn, Mozart, and Masonry include Joachim Hurwitz, "Joseph Haydn and Freemasonry," *HYb* 16 (1985), 5–98; H. C. Robbins Landon, *Mozart and the Masons: New Light on the Lodge "Crowned Hope"* (London, 1989); and Volkmar Braunbehrens, *Mozart in Vienna, 1781–1791,* trans. Timothy Bell (New York, 1989), chap. 6.

application of rhetorical ideas, and his description of variation form is among the most interesting and suggestive of the period:

> Variations are a type of musical rhetoric, where the given meaning appears in different guises, with the distinction that the boundary lines are much more rigorously determined in music than in oratory. Already in prose there is a certain rhythm *(numerus;* un certo, non so, che; un, je ne sais, quoi) that has the effect of a caesura, a rhythm that is more easily felt than described. However, neither this rhythm, nor a prescribed incise, nor even the rhyming syllables needed to make a verse can be compared with the narrow path the theme shows us and to which it is limited. . . .
>
> Notwithstanding this strict connection with the theme, which one must never lose sight of, there opens on the other side the prospect of the broadest scope for elaboration [*Einkleidung*]. In order to write variations, the composer need not be a great Melopoet, but should possess all the more Phraseology. His main task is to invent new styles of playing [*Spielarten*], to adapt new forms and new figures to the model; he must successfully retain in the variations the same analogy between harmony and harmony, between melody and melody that obtains in the theme; in short, each character which he assigns to the first measure must be continued throughout . . .[32]

These are important issues indeed. Meaning is invoked, then quickly recharacterized on a smaller scale, although still with a literary accent: the composer should be more of a phrasemaker than a tunesmith, and must maintain the "analogies" of the theme.[33] And the character to be maintained throughout results from the figuration introduced in the first measure. Vogler also gave Haydn high marks for writing his own themes for variations, the hallmark of a superior *inventio.*

Models for the actual form of theme and variations are also to be found in rhetoric. One of these was the medieval rhetoric of preaching, or *ars praedicandi,* which was alive and well in the eighteenth century.[34] To construct a sermon, one was advised to choose a theme, a quotation from scripture, and then illuminate and amplify it in a series of divisions, often in groups of three. Each division could be a word from the quotation. The continuing relevance of this practice is demonstrated in the second volume of Riepel's *Anfangsgründe zur musicalischen Setzkunst,* in which the student and teacher argue about how

32. Georg Joseph Vogler, *Verbesserungen der Forkel'schen Veränderungen über "God Save the King"* (Frankfurt, 1793), pp. 5–7; for German, see Appendix B.

33. A similar allusion to meaning appears in Hoyle's *Dictionarium Musicae* (London, 1770), s.v. "Variation": "In the first part or strain you have the plain notes of the composition, and the next part is variated, that is, the notes here and there are altered, and more notes made than in the first part, but yet it is to the same signification." Quoted in Paul Willem van Reijen, *Vergleichende Studien zur Klaviervariationstechnik von Mozart und seinen Zeitgenossen* (Buren, 1988), p. 12.

34. See Murphy, *Rhetoric in the Middle Ages,* pp. 269–355; John W. O'Malley, "Content and Rhetorical Forms in Sixteenth-Century Treatises on Preaching," in *Renaissance Eloquence: Studies in the Theory and Practice of Renaissance Rhetoric,* ed. James J. Murphy (Berkeley and Los Angeles, 1983), pp. 238–252.

much contrast to allow in a composition; the student claims that the composer, like the preacher quoting Scripture, must stick to his theme, while the teacher says that digressions strengthen the sermon if the theme remains in memory.[35] The term *division* was also the English synonym for variation, like the Italian *partita* and French *double*.[36]

A second source for the linkage of variation form and rhetoric is the widely circulated early sixteenth-century treatise by Erasmus on abundant language or copiousness *(De copia)*, based on the necessity for developing the ability to say the same thing in many different ways.[37] Copiousness had already been deemed essential by Quintilian; indeed, *De copia* has been called Erasmus's *Institutiones oratoriae*.[38] After providing the means of variety (namely, the different figures), Erasmus gave a practical demonstration: 150 variations of the sentence "Your letter pleased me mightily," and 200 variations on "I will remember you as long as I live." Variations of the first include:

> Your epistle exhilarated me intensely.
> Your brief note refreshed my spirit in no small measure.
> Your pages engendered in me an unfamiliar delight.
> Your communication poured vials of joy on my head.
> The perusal of your letter charmed my mind with singular delight.
> Your honoring me with a letter was the most agreeable of occurrences.
> Your letter promptly expelled all sorrow from my mind.
> Good God, what a mighty joy proceeded from your epistle.
> May I perish if I ever met with anything in my whole life more agreeable than
> your letter.[39]

Erasmus advised students to keep notebooks in which they would jot down phrases, maxims, proverbs, and novel bits of information under suitable headings, as an important source of *copia;* the new availability of books and paper

35. Joseph Riepel, *Anfangsgründe zur musicalischen Setzkunst*, II: *Grundregeln zur Tonordnung insgemein* (Leipzig, 1755) [hereafter *Tonordnung*], p. 76; the image of preacher and sermon appears again on pp. 99 and 104. Evan Bonds kindly shared this reference with me.

36. An interesting comparison between the "runs and embellishments of 'the music of division'" and the "similes, metaphors, puns, and fanciful allusions" of the "witty manner" is drawn by J. W. Smeed, *The Theophrastan 'Character'* (Oxford, 1985), p. 179.

37. Erasmus, *De duplici copia rerum ac verborum commentarii duo* (Paris, 1512; later enlarged editions until 1534); modern critical edition in *Collected Works of Erasmus, Literary and Educational Writings*, ed. Craig R. Thompson, vol. 24: *Copia: Foundations of the Abundant Style*, trans. and ed. Betty I. Knott (Toronto, 1978). There were many editions and translations of this work into the nineteenth century; the Union catalogue lists several Latin publications in German and Swiss cities in the late seventeenth and eighteenth centuries. Arthur Quinn goes so far as to call it "the most influential work written in early modern Europe on the figures of speech" *(Figures of Speech* [Salt Lake City, 1982], p. 61).

38. John D. Schaeffer, *Sensus Communis: Vico, Rhetoric, and the Limits of Relativism* (Durham and London, 1990), p. 29. Quintilian's materials on *copia* were a source for Erasmus; see Kennedy, *Classical Rhetoric*, p. 119. The relevant sections in Quintilian are VIII.iii.87 and X.i; the latter is primarily concerned with gaining a store of ideas and words by studying the principal classical authors.

39. Erasmus, *De copia*, pp. 349–354.

"made note-keeping an innovation."[40] In pointing out the dangers inherent in the pursuit of copiousness, Erasmus appeared to echo the concerns of the rhetoricians of antiquity, concerns which find many echoes in music treatises about variation technique in the eighteenth century:

> The speech of man is a magnificent and impressive thing when it surges along like a golden river, with thoughts and words pouring out in rich abundance. Yet the pursuit of speech like this involves considerable risk. . . . We find that a good many mortal men who make great efforts to achieve this godlike power of speech fall instead into mere glibness, which is both silly and offensive. They pile up a meaningless heap of words and expressions without any discrimination, and thus obscure the subject they are talking about, as well as belabouring the ears of the unfortunate audience. (p. 295)

On the other hand, the subject had natural advantages, as Erasmus made clear in a passage that also relates directly to the necessity of studying and applying its principles:

> First of all, exercise in expressing oneself in different ways will be of considerable importance in general for the acquisition of style. In particular however it will help in avoiding *tautologia,* that is, the repetition of a word or phrase, an ugly and offensive fault. It often happens that we have to say the same thing several times. If in these circumstances we find ourselves destitute of verbal riches and hesitate, or keep singing out the same old phrase like a cuckoo, and are unable to clothe our thought in other colours or other forms, we shall look ridiculous when we show ourselves to be so tongue-tied, and we shall also bore our wretched audience to death. Worse than *tautologia* is *homoiologia* [identical repetition], which, as Quintilian says, has no variety to relieve the tedium and is all of one monotonous colour. . . . Nature above all delights in variety. (p. 302)

These ideas recall Neefe's discussion of repetition, and the last sentence finds eighteenth-century adherents in Mattheson and Daube, among others.[41] Because of Erasmus's considerable influence on vernacular literature as well as on Latin rhetoric, his ideas seem to have diffused into a kind of conventional wisdom; *copia* became a "source of creative energy."[42]

Thus, rhetorical variations were seen as a means of acquiring and polishing style. A display of copiousness, or varied repetition, might be called into action in many oratorical situations.[43] Student exercises along these lines were a necessity. For example, Hegel gave a valedictory address as an eighteen-year-old student in 1787, on the educational values of his *gymnasium* in Stuttgart; his

---

40. Betty I. Knott, Introduction to *De copia,* p. xxxviii. By the eighteenth century, this habit had become a commonplace, as evidenced by the notebooks and sketchbooks kept by composers.

41. See Introduction, n. 50.

42. Knott, Introduction to *De copia,* p. xli.

43. Brian Vickers comments that Raymond Queneau, in *Exercices de Style* (Paris, 1956), "takes a banal incident on a Paris bus and retells it in ninety-nine different ways (a procedure that a Renaissance writer would have instantly recognized as a form of 'varying,' practised to increase facility in expression, as in Erasmus' *De copia)*." *In Defence of Rhetoric,* p. 379.

peroration was an "eightfold variation of gratitude formulas."[44] Certainly epideictic or demonstrative rhetoric needed such resources as part of its mode of display. Cicero, whose doctrine of *decorum* set out the conditions under which display was acceptable and even necessary, wrote that epideictic orations are

> produced as show-pieces, as it were, for the pleasure they will give, a class comprising eulogies, descriptions, and histories, and exhortations like the *Panegyric* of Isocrates, and similar orations by many of the Sophists . . . and all other speeches unconnected with the battles of public life. Not that their style is negligible; for it may be called the nurse of that orator about whom we design to speak more particularly. This style increases one's vocabulary and allows the use of a somewhat greater freedom in rhythm and sentence structure [*Ab hac et verborum copia alitur et eorum constructio et numerus liberiore quadam fruitur licentia*]. It likewise indulges in a neatness and symmetry of sentences, and is allowed to use well-defined and rounded periods; the ornamentation is done of set purpose, with no attempt at concealment, but openly and avowedly, so that words correspond to words as if measured off in equal phrases, frequently things inconsistent are placed side by side, and things contrasted are paired [Cicero's translation of *antithesis*], clauses are made to end in the same way and with similar sound.[45]

> The epideictic oration, then, has a sweet, fluent and copious style, with bright conceits and sounding phrases. It is the proper field for sophists, as we said, and is fitter for the parade than for the battle; set apart for the gymnasium and the palaestra, it is spurned and rejected in the forum.[46]

The love of display and the pleasure it takes (and gives) in "open and avowed ornamentation," as embodied in epideictic, characterize the creator of musical variations. Indeed, as a manifestation of *homo ludens,* the man who enjoys playing, we may see in the variation-composer the personification of Richard Lanham's "*homo rhetoricus*": self-conscious about language and creating pleasure.[47] And as a means of acquiring and polishing style, variations were sometimes considered an early step in compositional training; Brahms urged his only composition student, Gustav Jenner, to begin with variations.[48]

Aristotle identified two other important and relevant features of epideictic rhetoric: first, "amplification is most suitable for epideictic speakers, whose

44. Smith, *The Spirit and Its Letter,* p. 57. The entire speech is discussed on pp. 55–57. Smith comments that "the art of varying such formulas belongs under the rhetorical categories of *copia et amplificatio verborum.*"

45. Cicero, *Orator,* trans. H. M. Hubbell, Loeb Classical Library vol. 342 [Cicero vol. V] (Cambridge, Mass., and London, 1939), xi.37–xii.38, p. 333. The Panegyric was "in the form of an exhortation to the Greeks to unite against Persia, but largely devoted to praise of Athens." On decorum, see *Orator,* xxi.70–74, pp. 357–361, and Chapter 8.

46. Ibid., xiii.42, p. 337.

47. Richard A. Lanham, *The Motives of Eloquence: Literary Rhetoric in the Renaissance* (New Haven, 1976), pp. 3–7 and passim; this book is a brilliant treatment of, among other things, the noxious effects of the "serious" view of life and its usurpation of terms of value in philosophical and literary discourse. See also Jan Huizinga, *Homo Ludens: A Study of the Play-Element in Culture* (Boston, 1955); E. H. Gombrich, *The Sense of Order,* p. 166.

48. Gustav Jenner, *Johannes Brahms als Mensch, Lehrer, und Künstler* (Marburg, 1905), p. 45.

subject is actions that are not disputed, so that all that remains to be done is to attribute beauty and importance to them."⁴⁹ Quintilian, for his part, provided a lengthy discussion of amplification, which was intended to reveal in ever stronger terms the importance of the subject: augmentation *(incrementum,* increasing the power of words and images), comparison *(per comparationem),* reasoning *(per ratiocinationem,* especially by drawing inferences), and accumulation *(congeries).*⁵⁰ Aristotle's second point is that epideictic was the only type of oratory similar to written prose because it was meant to be read; the other two types are political or deliberative, which seeks to exhort or dissuade, and forensic or judicial, which accuses or defends.⁵¹ The latter point seems to mitigate George Kennedy's dichotomy between primary and secondary rhetoric: "Primary rhetoric is the conception of rhetoric as held by the Greeks when the art was, as they put it, 'invented' in the fifth century B.C. Rhetoric was 'primarily' an art of persuasion, it was primarily used in civic life; it was primarily oral. . . . 'Secondary' rhetoric, on the other hand, is the apparatus of rhetorical techniques clustering around discourse or art forms when those techniques are not being used for their primary oral purpose."⁵² Epideictic, in existing at the intersection of oral and written forms, conjoins primary and secondary rhetoric as a technically rich and "analyzable" mode of persuasive discourse. Variation also straddles improvised and written forms. And the equal phrases and equivalent phrase endings described by Cicero match the variations themselves. Of the three types of oratory, epideictic is the most suitable model for variation.

Figures of Rhetoric and Music

Recent attacks on the applicability of rhetorical figures to music or on the character of the *elocutio* (or *elaboratio)* have not taken into consideration the striking similarity between "figures" in both contexts: the nature, application, and control of figures is in fact a problem considered in almost identical terms both by writers on rhetoric and by writers on variation in particular. The first question these writers consider is whether such figures are natural, inevitable, necessary. One view had it that figures are deviations from the norm.⁵³ This was explicitly contradicted by some eighteenth-century writers, who claimed that there is nothing so natural and necessary as figures; it would be more unnatural to do without them.⁵⁴ Vickers points out that *ornatus,* the general topical name for

49. Aristotle, *"Art" of Rhetoric,* trans. and ed. J. H. Freese, Loeb Classical Library vol. 193 [Aristotle vol. XXII] (Cambridge, Mass., 1926), I.ix.38–40, pp. 103–105. He identified examples as most important for deliberative speakers and enthymemes as most suitable for forensic speakers.

50. Quintilian, *Institutio oratoria,* VIII.iv, pp. 263–281.

51. Aristotle, *"Art" of Rhetoric,* III.xii.6, p. 423, on epideictic, and I.iii.3, p. 33, on the three types of oratory.

52. Kennedy, *Classical Rhetoric,* pp. 4–5.

53. See Roland Barthes, *The Semiotic Challenge,* trans. Richard Howard (New York, 1988), pp. 88–89. See also Todorov, *Theories of the Symbol,* pp. 87–97.

54. See Vickers, *In Defence of Rhetoric,* p. 302, citing Du Marsais (1730) and Fontanier (1818) in this context.

the figures, is translated as "ornament" and thus seems to connote incidental and largely unnecessary decoration; actually, however, it connotes distinction and excellence, *ornamentum* itself signifying equipment or accoutrements, a soldier's gear or weapons. Musical treatises similarly discussed the nature of ornamentation, always concluding that it was essential for the true expression of a melody; an entire class of ornament was even termed "essential ornament."

The oratory treatises of antiquity first discussed the question of restraint in ornament, and its rejection has always been a sign of classical influence,[55] especially in the periodic resurfacings of the plain style. In the eighteenth century, many voices called for restraint. Thomas Gibbons, in a work of 1767 entirely devoted to tropes and figures, spent the larger parts of two chapters advocating restraint in the use of tropes and concealment, even effacement, in the use of figures, which should not inflame the passions until reason has convinced the intellect.[56] He quotes Addison on the overly ornate style of a contemporary (p. 4):

> Great COWLEY then, a mighty Genius, wrote,
> O'errun with wit, and lavish of his thought;
> His turns too closely on the reader press:
> He more had pleas'd us, had he pleas'd us less.

Musical ornamentation and figuration were similarly taken to be natural and necessary, but cautions and constraints were sounded at every turn. Unbridled figuration in improvising had to be curtailed, as did doubling (varying) of suite movements with "crooked leaps and many-tailed notes."[57] In 1721, Mattheson commented that the varying of a bass line was similar to figures in rhetoric, precisely in that the variations must not be overused: "This 'doubling' or 'varying' has, in a way, the same quality as figures have in rhetoric, or the so-called compliments in conversation. If they are used *cum grano salis* then they are beautiful; but if they appear affected, forced and *mal à-propos,* then one would prefer a more simple and gracious language."[58] Marpurg commented on the simple and direct rhetorical character of the Berlin style: "A special distinction of Ber-

---

55. Gombrich, *The Sense of Order,* p. 18.

56. Thomas Gibbons, *Rhetoric; or, a View of its Principal Tropes and Figures, in the Origin and Powers: with a variety of Rules to escape Errors and Blemishes, and attain Propriety and Elegance in Composition* (London, 1767), part I, chap. 1 ("The general Nature of the Tropes," pp. 1–20) and part II, chap. 2 ("The general Nature of Figures," pp. 119–127). Gregory G. Butler points out "the almost total preoccupation of late Renaissance English rhetoricians with . . . elocution, the decoration or ornamentation of speech by means of various rhetorical colors or figures"; "Music and Rhetoric in Early Seventeenth-Century English Sources," *MQ* 66 (1980), 54. While some scholars find this a degenerate form of rhetoric, Vickers ringingly defends it: "*elocutio* provided the passage from potentiality to realization, via the control of language and the force of feeling . . . [E]*locutio* was the hinge around which the whole of Renaissance moral and civic philosophy turned." See his "Rhetorical and Anti-Rhetorical Tropes: On Writing the History of *Elocutio,*" *Comparative Criticism* 3 (1981), 129.

57. Mattheson, *Der vollkommene Capellmeister,* p. 232.

58. Mattheson included this in a footnote to his edition of Friedrich Erhard Niedt's *Handleitung zur Variation* (Hamburg, 1721 [orig. ed. 1706]), p. 3n; trans. Pamela L. Poulin and Irmgard C. Taylor as *The Musical Guide* (Oxford, 1989), p. 74.

lin music is that it makes very sparing use of manners and embellishments; but those that are used are the more select and the more finely and clearly performed. The performances of the Grauns, Quantz, Benda, Bach, etc. are never characterized by masses of embellishments. Impressive, rhetorical, and moving qualities spring from entirely different things, which do not create as much stir, but touch the heart the more directly."[59] And at the beginning of the nineteenth century, as we have seen, Momigny complained that modern variations seemed to carry the slogan "much speech but little sense."[60] Prolixity of notes could easily be compared to prolixity of words. And the problem was compounded by necessarily vague notions of what the "sense" should be. After all, the tension between *res* and *verba*, or *Gedanke* and *Ausdruck*—how the thought is to be clothed in words—is considerably greater in music than in verbal arts. In purely instrumental music, what is the *res?* Even the theme has its own figural "clothing."

Just as in verbal rhetoric, then, figures were the means necessary to adorn and make expressive a simpler musical entity, as well as the culprits in freighting it down unnecessarily. The term "figure" and its synonyms also referred to the two means by which a theme may be varied: by breaking up the principal notes of the theme's melody into smaller note values or by adding ornaments to them. These two approaches essentially summarize the distinction between the *Setzmanieren* and *Spielmanieren*—"figures of composition" and "figures of performance"—drawn by Marpurg in 1755.[61] The figures of composition are grouped in classes according to their shape: (1) repeated notes *(Schwärmer)*, with or without octave leaps and including anticipations; (2) running figures *(lauffenden Figuren)* filling in the main notes; (3) turning figures *(rollende Figuren)*, including the "roller" *(Walze)* and "half-circle"; (4) arpeggiated figures *(gebrochne Figuren)*; and finally (5) mixed figures (called *Passagen, Gänge, Wendungen*). Riepel differentiated among them by interval-type *(Läuffer, Springer, Schwärmer, Singer)*, while Daube called for alternations of character *(rauschende, singende)*.[62] Whereas ornaments are additions only, figures of composition may be either additions, when the main notes appear at analogous parts of the measure, or substitutions for the main notes.

Marpurg also distinguished specifically between *Setzmanieren* and *Spielmanieren* on the one hand and rhetorical figures on the other: the figures of composition and performance are mechanical means of elaborating basic melodies, while the figures of rhetoric are meaningful, text-based expressions.[63] That

59. Marpurg, *Der Critischer Musicus an der Spree* (1750–1751), cited and translated by Mitchell in Bach, *Essay*, p. 81.

60. See Chapter 1, n. 5. We can see that rhetorical analogies continued to hold sway.

61. Marpurg, *Anleitung zum Clavierspielen* (Berlin, 1755; 2nd ed., Berlin, 1765; facs. Hildesheim, 1970), pp. 36–37.

62. Joseph Riepel, *Anfangsgründe zur musicalischen Setzkunst*, I: *De Rhythmopoeïa oder von der Tactordnung* (Augsburg, 1752; Regensburg, 1754) [hereafter *Tactordnung*], p. 39; Daube, *Der musikalische Dilettant*, chap. 7, "Von der Variation." See George J. Buelow, "The Concept of 'Melodielehre': A Key to Classic Style," *MJb 1968/70*, 182–195.

63. Marpurg, *Anleitung zum Clavierspielen*, p. 39: "In engerm Verstande aber versteht man durch *Figuren*, die Anwendung der Setzmanieren auf einen gewissen Affect oder Gegenstand, und werden

"figure" has two senses goes back to classical theories of rhetoric. Quintilian, for example, stated that "In the first [sense] it is applied to any form in which thought is expressed, just as it is to bodies which, whatever their composition, must have some shape. In the second and special sense, in which it is called a *schema,* it means a rational change in meaning or language from the ordinary and simple form, . . . that which is poetically or rhetorically altered from the simple and obvious method of expression."[64]

Rhetorical figures, termed "aids to expression" by Forkel,[65] were also variously identified and classified in the eighteenth century, especially by Mattheson, Scheibe, and Forkel himself, following the tradition inaugurated by Burmeister's *Musica poetica* in 1606. Mattheson had claimed that "One must add some ornamentation to one's melodies, and the abundant figures or tropes from rhetoric can really do good service here, if they are well arranged";[66] comparing words to tones, he went on to distinguish between musical word-figures (changing individual pitches) and figures of "sentence" or a complete thought *(Figurae sententiae),* referring to the variations, imitations, and repetitions of complete phrases *(Sätze).*[67] In 1739 Mattheson clearly expected his readers to recognize the rhetorical figures and merely listed them, while a half-century later Forkel felt he had to explain "the most striking examples of figures expressing feelings." These are *ellipsis* (a quickening of motion, only to break off abruptly and move to a new idea; or a deflected cadence going to an unexpected key); *Wiederholung* (repetition of both notes and phrases, and even words in the text), especially in conjunction with *paronomasia (Verstärkung),* repetition with stronger additions (more notes or more powerful performance); *suspension (Aufhalten),* or delaying, not to be confused with *Dubitation (Zweifel),* or uncertainty in feeling; *epistrophe (Wiederkehr),* in which the close of the first phrase of a melody returns at the ends of other phrases; *Gradation (Steigerung),* one of the most beautiful and effective figures, most usually occurring as crescendo, but also through continual expansion of ideas and modulations. Almost all the other figures are figures of repetition, wherein individual segments are either varied or unvaried, expanded or contracted, or repeated at beginning, middle, or end.[68] Rhetorical figures may be used in instrumental as well as vocal music; Forkel's lengthy discussion of musical rhetoric gives an

---

solche mit gewissen aus der Rhetorik entlehnten Nahmen beleget. Diese gehen uns in diesen Blättern nicht an, wo wir es mit der blossen Mechanik der Figuren zu thun haben."

64. Quintilian, *Institutio oratoria,* IX.i.10–11, 13.

65. Forkel, *Allgemeine Geschichte der Musik,* I, p. 53.

66. Mattheson, *Der vollkommene Kapellmeister,* part II, chap. 14, par. 40; Harriss, p. 480: "Etwas Zierath muß man seinen Melodien beilegen, und dazu können die häuffigen Figuren oder Verblümungen aus der Redekunst, wenn sie wol angeordnet werden, vornehmlich gute Dienste leisten."

67. This meaning of figures of diction and of sentence is to be found in Johann Christoph Gottsched's influential treatise, *Ausführliche Redekunst* (Leipzig, 1736; 5th ed., 1759; ed. Rosemary Scholl, *Johann Christoph Gottsched Ausgewählte Werke* 7 [Berlin and New York, 1975]). It differs from the meaning of *sententiae,* which are reflections inserted into the speech at the conclusions of individual paragraphs. See Quintilian, *Institutio oratoria,* VIII.v.

68. Forkel, *Allgemeine Geschichte der Musik,* I, pp. 56–59.

example of *ellipsis* in a C. P. E. Bach sonata.[69] In fact, Forkel offered not a single texted example. Marpurg, on the other hand, appeared to be severely limiting the analogy in purely instrumental music, despite his identification of rhetoric, in the *Anfangsgründe der theoretischen Musik,* as the branch of music dealing with both composition and performance (and grammar the branch of music giving its rules).

Forkel also differentiated between "figures for the understanding," which included contrapuntal devices and textures to evoke intellectual pleasure, and "figures for the imagination," comprising musical "painting" and "imitations" of externally visible and aural phenomena *(Gegenstände)* and, more profoundly, of internal feelings. Whereas to Mattheson, then, the figures of rhetoric were basic resources for ornamenting a simple melody, to Marpurg and Forkel rhetorical figures were primarily expressive devices, to be distinguished from figurations in the general sense. This offers the possibility of distinguishing between figures in the theme and in the variations, to reveal expressive crosscurrents within a piece, and to employ terminology from earlier theorists for such expressive figures as the *pathopoeia,* an affective chromatic half-step, and *saltus duriusculus,* a larger chromatic leap. Metrically based figures, according to a somewhat obscure remark by Marpurg, cause variations themselves to arise, when a piece constructed from alternations of metrical patterns, or the so-called "sound-feet" *(Klangfüsse),* is repeated with figurations.[70] The term *Klangfuss* had been introduced by Mattheson in one of his many musicoliterary parallels.[71]

A useful typology of figures from the Renaissance writer George Puttenham may help to unite some of these musical categories. In the third part ("Of Ornament") of his treatise *The Arte of English Poesie* (1589), Puttenham first describes "Poeticall" ornament in general:

> This ornament then is of two sortes, one to satisfie & delight th'eare onely by a goodly outward shew set upon the matter with wordes, and speaches smoothly and tunably running: another by certaine intendments or sence of such words & speaches inwardly working a stirre to the minde: that first qualitie the Greeks called *Enargia* . . . because it geueth a glorious lustre and Light. This latter they called *Energia* . . ., because it wrought with a strong and vertuous operation; and figure breedeth them both, some seruing to giue gloss onely to a language, some to geue it efficacie by sence.[72]

69. Ibid., pp. 57–58.

70. Marpurg, *Anleitung zum Clavierspielen,* p. 43: "Anmerkung. Mit diesen itzt erklärten Setzmanieren werden die sogenannten Cadenzen ingleichen die willkührlichen Veränderungen gemacht, mit welchen man aus dem Stegereif ein Stück auszuzieren pfleget. Wenn ein gewisser Klangfuß bey dergleichen Auszierungen angenommen, und bey jeder Wiederholung eines dazu gemachten Stückes derselbe mit einem andern abgewechselt wird: so entstehen daraus alsdenn die sogenannten *Variationen.*"

71. Mattheson, *Der vollkommene Capellmeister,* first mentioned in part II, chap. 5, par. 110, then elaborated in part II, chap. 6.

72. George Puttenham, *The Arte of English Poesie,* ed. Gladys Doidge Willcock and Alice Walker (Cambridge, 1936), pp. 142–143.

In a further typology, Puttenham names and expands upon this basic antithesis between "enargetic" figures that serve the ear and "energetic" figures that serve the "conceit" or intellect. The former he calls *auricular figures,* and assigns them to the poet, the latter *sensable [sic] figures,* assigned to both poet and orator. He adds another synthesizing category that serves the ear as well as the understanding: *sententious figures,* assigned to the orator, "not only . . . properly apperteine to full sentences, for bewtifying them with a currant and pleasing numerositie, but also giuing them efficacie, and enlarging the whole matter besides with *copious amplifications* [emphasis added]."[73] These categories suggest the ancestry of Forkel's figures for the understanding and imagination, because Puttenham was apparently the first to classify "according to receptive rather than formal criteria."[74] That is, the speaker/writer/composer would choose particular figures based on the faculties of the audience he or she wished to engage, rather than on properties inherent in the figures.

Puttenham's distinction between sonority and sense seems strikingly well-suited to instrumental music. And the sententious—also called rhetorical—figures contain, in addition to their copious amplification,

> a certaine sweet and melodious manner of speech, in which respect, they may, after a sort, be said *auricular:* because the eare is no lesse rauished with their currant tune, than the mind is with their sententiousnes. For the eare is properly but an instrument of conueyance for the minde, to apprehend the sence by the sound. And our speech is made melodious or harmonicall, not onely by strayned tunes, as those of *Musick,* but also by choice of smoothe words.[75]

His inclusion of seven figures of repetition among the sententious figures makes them seem even more appropriate to variations.

Figures for Variation Form

Abundant speech, with its figural recasting of a given theme, obviously has its musical analogue. That a correlation exists between rhetorical and music figures seems not open to question. That the correlation is especially rich with respect to variation form may be claimed on the basis of the model of copiousness. Part of the problem with previous attempts to label figures, especially in instrumental music, has been the equating of figure and motive. But figures need not be considered necessarily coextensive with motives. Indeed, each of Erasmus's variations embodies a figure. In the model of *copia,* variations emerge from the search for copiousness as the locus of "pure style," deriving from a delight in play and an assertion of technical mastery in varied repetitions. In the model of *ars praedicandi,* variations can be viewed as a series of exegeses, of interpretations of a theme, an elaboration of its "motives," as it

73. Ibid., pp. 159–160.
74. Heinrich F. Plett, "The Place and Function of Style in Renaissance Poetics," in *Renaissance Eloquence,* ed. Murphy, p. 371.
75. Puttenham, *Arte of English Poesie,* p. 197.

were.[76] Recent criticism has shown a propensity to consider variations as interpretations or criticisms of a theme.[77]

As a means of showing mastery of style while elaborating on a theme, varied repetition may itself be seen as a kind of rhetorical figure that could include other figures. Such an inclusive figure, *refining,* was set forth in the major treatise of antiquity formerly attributed to Cicero, the [*Rhetorica*] *Ad Herennium:*

> *Refining* [*expolitio*] consists in dwelling on the same topic and yet seeming to say something ever new. It is accomplished in two ways: by merely repeating the same idea, or by descanting upon it. We shall not repeat the same thing precisely—for that, to be sure, would weary the hearer and not refine the idea—but with changes. Our changes will be of three kinds: in the words, in the delivery, and in the treatment . . . Our changes will be verbal when, having expressed the idea once, we repeat it once again or oftener in other, equivalent terms, as follows: "No peril is so great that a wise man would think it ought to be avoided when the safety of the fatherland is at stake. When the lasting security of the state is in question, the man endowed with good principles will undoubtedly believe that in defence of the fortunes of the republic he ought to shun no crisis of life, and he will ever persist in the determination eagerly to enter, for the fatherland, any combat, however great the peril to life." Our changes will reside in the delivery if now in the tone of conversation, now in an energetic tone, and now in variation after variation of voice and gesture, repeating the same ideas in different words, we also change the delivery quite strikingly . . . The third kind of change, accomplished in the treatment, will take place if we transfer the thought into the form of Dialogue or into the form of Arousal. *Dialogue* [*Sermocinatio*] . . . consists in putting in the mouth of some person language in keeping with his character . . . Again, the idea is changed in the treatment by means of a transfer to the form of Arousal [*exsuscitatio*], when not only we ourselves seem to speak under emotion, but we also stir the hearer . . . But when we descant upon the same theme, we shall use a great many variations. Indeed, after having expressed the theme simply, we can subjoin the Reason [a figure of diction], and then express the theme in another form, with or without the Reasons; next we can present the Contrary [a figure of diction]; . . . then a Comparison and an Example . . .; and finally the Conclusion . . . A Refinement of this sort, which will consist of numerous figures of diction and of thought, can therefore be exceedingly ornate . . . [I]t is by far our most important means of training for skill in style.[78]

76. I am indebted to Michael Long for this comparison.

77. Edward Cone expressed this idea in "Schubert criticizes Schubert," a paper read at the International Schubert Festival-Conference in Detroit, November 1978. See also George Steiner, *Real Presences* (Chicago, 1989), p. 20: "[T]he criticism of music truly answerable to its object is to be found within the music itself. The construct of theme and variation, of quotation and *reprise,* is organic to music, particularly in the West. Criticism is, literally, instrumental in the ear of the composer. . . . Consider the critical authority . . . in Beethoven's ten variations, at once attentive and critically magisterial, on a duet from Salieri's *Falstaff.*"

78. [Pseudo-Cicero], [*Rhetorica*] *Ad Herrenium,* trans. and ed. Harry Caplan, Loeb Classical Library vol. 403 [Cicero vol. I] (Cambridge, Mass., and London, 1954), IV.xlii.54–xliii.56, pp. 365–375.

A long example of a speech based on this figure appears on pp. 371–375, and includes the Theme expressed simply, the Theme expressed in a new form, arguments from Comparison, Contrary, and Example, and a Conclusion which restates the theme. The topic of the speech, the necessity for defending the fatherland, is an ethical theme, or *chria,* perhaps the earliest extant example of one.[79] Writing such a moral essay, as well as writing aphorisms *(sententiae)* and character delineations *(ethologiae),* remained part of a Latin education.

Puttenham gives *expolitio* an entire chapter, renaming it "the Gorgious" because it has the same effect on speech and language as "rich and gorgious apparell" has on the "bare and naked body," making it "more comely and bewtifull than the naturall": "So doth this figure . . . polish our speech & as it were attire it with copious and pleasant amplifications and much variety of sentences all running upon one point & to one intent: so as I doubt whether I may term it a figure, or rather a masse of many figurative speaches, applied to the bewtifying of our tale or argument."[80]

Other figures similarly lend brilliance to style by varied repetition of one kind or another. Great effect may be produced by *Dwelling on the Point (commoratio),* that is "repeating the point several times in different words,"[81] or "remain[ing] rather long upon, and often return[ing] to, the strongest topic on which the whole cause rests. . . . No opportunity is given the hearer to remove his attention from the strongest topic."[82] Or *Digression* may be used to delight the audience, punctuated by neat and elegant returns to the main theme.[83] *Dinumeratio* appears to be the equivalent of *congeries* on the higher structural level of the sentence: because the speaker loves to amplify, he heaps up sentences *(dinumeratio)* as opposed to words *(congeries).*[84] *Comparison (similitudo, parabole)* "carries over an element of likeness from one thing to a different thing. This is used to embellish or prove, or clarify or vivify. Furthermore, corresponding to these four aims, it has four forms of presentation: Contrast, Negation, Detailed Parallel, Abridged Comparison."[85] The *Ad Herrenium* also includes *Synonymy* or *Interpretation (Interpretatio)* as a figure "which does not duplicate the same word by repeating it, but replaces the word that has been used by another of the same meaning, as follows: 'You have overturned the republic from its roots; you have demolished the state from its foundations.'"[86] Puttenham described *Sinonimia* as "When so euer we multiply our speech by many words or

79. Caplan notes this in *Ad Herrenium,* p. 370n. See also Chapter 4 for a connection between a *chria* and a short musical piece.

80. Puttenham, *Arte of English Poesie,* p. 247.

81. Quintilian, *Institutio oratoria,* IX.1.27.

82. *Ad Herrenium,* p. 375.

83. Quintilian, *Institutio oratoria,* IX.i.28.

84. Henry Peacham, *The Garden of Eloquence* (1577; 2nd. ed. 1593; facs. ed. of both, Gainesville, Fla., 1954), [p.] R i. See also Willard R. Espy, *The Garden of Eloquence: A Rhetorical Bestiary* (New York, 1983).

85. *Ad Herrenium,* p. 377.

86. Ibid., p. 325. Caplan notes that Quintilian (IX.iii.98) denies that this is a figure.

clauses of one sence," by using "plenty of one manner of thing" that we have stored up.[87] And Henry Peacham identified it as "when by a variation and change of words that be of like signification, we iterat one thing diuerse times."[88]

To my knowledge, the figures just mentioned are rarely if ever found in treatises of *musical* rhetoric, probably because these figures refer to the structuring of a fair portion of a speech, as opposed to individual turns of phrase.[89] Music theorists took over word-figures, which repeat words for emphasis or for parallelism of phrase structure, in order to describe imitative, expressive, and harmonic procedures, primarily at the level of the *motive*. Some figures work at the level of the motive and phrase—especially those with an expressive theme or locally expressive variation. Others have implications for an entire variation and even for the structuring of entire variation movements.

Two figures only occasionally cited by music theorists become central to such a view of variation, although they have not been so applied: *periphrasis (circumlocutio)*, the substitution of many words for one in order to amplify, and *pleonasm,* the addition of superfluous words for purposes of decoration and emphasis. In his treatise *On the Sublime,* Longinus even tells us that periphrasis can contribute to sublimity, if not overused, and relates it to ornament in music:

> No one, I think, would dispute that periphrasis contributes to the sublime. For as in music the sweetness of the dominant melody is enhanced by what are known as the decorative additions, so periphrasis often harmonizes with the direct expression of a thought and greatly embellishes it, especially if it is not bombastic or inelegant, but pleasantly tempered. . . . However, periphrasis is a dangerous business, *more so than any other figure,* unless it is used with a certain sense of proportion. For it quickly lapses into insipidity, akin to empty chatter and dullness of wit.[90]

In terms of musical figuration, pleonasm may be seen in the *Spielmanieren,* that is the addition of ornaments to a melody, while periphrasis seems more typical of the *Setzmanieren,* written-out figures of composition, although such figures may be pleonastic as well as periphrastic depending upon their relationship to the notes of the original melody. Puttenham's notion of periphrasis is instructive: the figure *dissembles,* "by reason of a secret intent not appearing by the words, as when we go about the bush, and will not in one or a few words expresse that thing which we desire to haue knowen, but do chose rather to do

87. Puttenham, *Arte of English Poesie*, p. 214.

88. Peacham, *Garden of Eloquence,* p. 149.

89. As Gregory Butler has shown, however (in "Rhetoric in Seventeenth-Century English Sources"), several seventeenth-century English rhetorical treatises apply a musical analogy to their verbal figures.

90. [Pseudo-] Longinus, *On the Sublime,* trans. T. S. Dorsch (Middlesex, 1965), pp. 137–138 (chaps. 28 and 29); emphasis added. This treatise was widely known in the eighteenth century in Boileau's translation of 1694. Leonard Ratner identifies periphrasis as a type of rhetorical figure applied to music by eighteenth-century theorists: "Many notes where one will do." See his *Classic Music,* p. 91.

it by many words."[91] Thus, periphrastic figuration may even conceal its relationship with the theme. Together with many other writers, Puttenham considers pleonasm a fault of style, although not a serious one.

The notion of substitutive and additive figures is further complicated by the dimension of simultaneity in musical texture, which music does not share with the verbal arts. A variation may contain both a pleonastic and a periphrastic line, for example a reprise of the theme melody and a simultaneous ornate countermelody. That is, the countermelody is periphrastic in substituting for the original *Hauptnoten* of the melody, but it is heard in addition to the melody itself. Yet the new line is not really "superfluous" and, hence, not pleonastic *per se*, as Haydn's "Surprise" Symphony (No. 94, second movement) clarifies: all the variations but the *minore* (var. 2) consist either of pleonastic figurations applied to the theme melody (var. 3 first reprise, var. 4 varied repeat) or literal melodic reprises with an added countermelody (var. 1, var. 3 varied repeat, var. 4 with varied accompaniment). Entirely new melodies can be evaluated as types of comparisons (for example, by detailed parallel), or as examples of synonymy. Thus, individual variations, segments of variations, as well as variation groups may embody different sorts of figures with respect to the theme and to each other.

The idea of applying an inclusive figure like *refining* to a set of variations brings up the larger issue of the structure of an oration itself. After Aristotle asserted that speeches needed only two parts, statement and proofs, he continued to describe the different effects required by different sections of the speech; later writers of antiquity expanded and clarified the presentation of ideas into a basic six-part oration: *exordium (proemium), narratio, partitio (divisio, propositio), confirmatio, confutatio (refutatio, reprehensio),* and *peroratio (conclusio).*[92] Forkel tried to apply these parts of the oration, as well as new ones of his own devising, to sonata form. My belief is that these elements—introduction, statement of facts, announcement of the relevant arguments, positive arguments, refutation of critics' or enemies' arguments, and conclusion—may with a certain amount of tinkering be applied to any piece of music of sufficient length to distinguish among the beginning, the middle, and the end. I do not find it a particularly compelling model for variation form except in the notion of a series of proofs compared to a series of variations, and in the more problematic area of the peroration. The means of achieving closure in a variation form, as suggested in Chapter 1, must be imposed from without: the variation, unlike recapitulatory forms, "need not" end at a particular point. An interesting question about a rhetorical model of closure, therefore, might be the location of that peroration: can it occur in a final variation or must it be outside the series entirely in a coda, to make the most convincing close? Can it impart a sense of "internal necessity" for the conclusion? Some solutions to the problem, whether conventional ones like the theme *da capo* or innovative cadenza-like or

91. Puttenham, *Arte of English Poesie*, p. 193.
92. See n. 8. The basic six parts were given in *Ad Herrenium* I.iii.4.

developmental codas, will be treated in Chapters 5 through 8. In variation movements, Haydn and Mozart were more likely to include codas than were their contemporaries; in independent sets for piano, on the other hand, cadenzas (sometimes called *fermas*) and short codas were more common.

Rhetorical Analysis

Applying some of the rhetorical ideas described above to two little-studied but widely criticized variation movements—a piano-concerto movement by Mozart and a keyboard sonata by Haydn—suggests a few directions that such rhetorical analysis might take.[93] Mozart's first set of concerto-variations, a piece known as the Rondo in D major, K. 382, was composed in March 1782 as a new finale for the earlier D-major Concerto, K. 175. A striking discrepancy exists between Mozart's description of this movement and the twentieth-century reception of it. In sending it to his father on 23 March 1782, Mozart noted that it was making a "big noise" in Vienna, and was always greeted with torrents of applause; he asked that Leopold "guard it like a *jewel*—and not give it to a soul to play . . . I composed it *specially* for myself—and no one else but my dear sister must play it."[94] Mozart continued to perform it for over a year,[95] and Artaria issued it in piano arrangement in 1787 as a "Rondeau varié." Modern commentators, on the other hand, almost universally criticize its (ostensible) triviality, superficiality, and mediocrity.[96] To concur in the latter view essentially requires a cynical assessment of Mozart's statements as consciously pandering to the public, or as using self-praise as a tactic to reinforce his success to his father. On the other hand, perhaps our traditional modes of understanding and valuation have not been fully adequate to deal with this piece, and have taken insufficient account of its design. Indeed, it is the design of the piece that is its most persuasive—hence rhetorical—element. In the musical discussions

93. For a different approach to rhetorical analysis, see the valuable recent study by Daniel Harrison, "Rhetoric and Fugue: An Analytical Application," *Music Theory Spectrum* 12 (1990), 1–42. See also the imaginative study by Zahava Karl McKeon, *Novels and Arguments: Inventing Rhetorical Criticism* (Chicago, 1982), for a new rhetorical reading of beginning-, middle-, and end-oriented novelistic structures.

94. Anderson no. 445, p. 798.

95. Mozart listed it in the program of his concert of 23 March 1783 that he sent to his father on 29 March 1783: "I played my concerto in D major, which is such a favourite here, and of which I sent you the variation rondo [*Variazion rondeau*]." (Trans. adapted from Anderson no. 484, p. 843. See Bauer-Deutsch, III, pp. 261–262.)

96. Cuthbert Girdlestone, *Mozart and His Piano Concertos* (New York, 1964), pp. 127–128, refers to the "distressing banality of these variations," which make a "woeful contrast with the sturdy personality of the other two movements"; he refers to the original finale as "splendid" and its substitution the result of "submissiveness to prevailing taste." David R. B. Kimbell, "Variation Form in the Piano Concertos of Mozart," *MR* 44 (1984), 95–103, remarks that K. 382, "the earliest (1782) and by far the least interesting, may be rapidly disposed of." For an interesting recent account of this movement, see Bernd Sponheuer, "Zum Problem des doppelten Finales in Mozarts 'erstem' Klavierkonzert KV 175: Zwei Versuche der Synthetisierung von 'Gelehrtem' und 'Galantem,'" *AfMw* 42 (1985), 102–120.

that follow, and in succeeding chapters, the principal theme will be designated A, and its variations A_1, A_2, and so on, whenever there is a rondo-like, alternating, or ternary organization (otherwise the conventional "var. 1" will be used). When relevant, a second theme in a set of alternating variations will be called B and its variations B_1 and B_2. Modifications will be introduced as necessary.[97]

Mozart referred to K. 382 as a "Variazion rondeau" or, simply, "rondeau," a term that in the late eighteenth century was sometimes synonymous with "finale."[98] The form of the movement is a theme and variations in which the first reprise of the sprightly contredanse-theme returns periodically like a ritornello or rondo refrain, the repeated notes of that first reprise serving as punctuation for the rest of the movement.[99] The format of K. 382 exploits its ritornello in a brilliant and hitherto unremarked sectional arrangement: the ritornello recurs first after a single variation (A_1), then after two variations (A_2, A_3), then after three variations (A_4, A_5, A_6), as follows:

$$\textcircled{A}\,A_1\,\textcircled{A}\,A_2\,A_3\,\textcircled{A}\,A_4\,A_5\,A_6\,\textcircled{A}\,A_7\,\text{Coda}$$

Further, the three segments thus demarcated each reveal a different set of issues (Example 2.1): A_1, as the solo foil to the tutti ritornello, functions as the generic signal of the piano concerto and stakes out a more personal mode of expression, softening the repeated notes of the tutti into chromatic appoggiaturas; A_2 and A_3 introduce progressive diminution by moving from the theme's eighth-note melody and sixteenth-note accompaniment to sixteenth triplets and then thirty-second notes. The third segment of the piece, A_4–A_6, offers expressive and characteristic reinterpretations of the theme: A_4 is the *minore*, A_5 a scherzando with trill accompaniment and (initially) no bass register, A_6 the florid Adagio. When the ritornello reappears in A_7, it is as a triple-meter Allegro flanking a real variation. The scoring confirms this reading of the movement: only the ritornellos include trumpets and timpani. And only in the coda are ritornello, solo, and "festive" scoring united.

Mozart's perceptions of this movement were, in my view, justified. I know of no other movement with topical groupings of variations asserting first genre, then technical strategy, then expressive values. Even Mozart's stereotyped meter and tempo change at the close is given new meaning. It is tempt-

97. Similarly, episodes in rondo-variations, as in typical rondos generally, will carry contrasting alphabet designations (ABA_1CA_2), as will ternary variations (ABA_1).

98. Albrechtsberger copied a Gassmann symphony and labeled the finale "rondo," although the movement is actually a set of variations (an example from this movement is given in Chapter 5, Ex. 5.2); modern edition by László Somfai, *Musica Rinata* 18 (Budapest, 1972).

99. Malcolm Cole, in "The Rondo Finale: Evidence for the Mozart-Haydn Exchange?" *MJb 1968/70*, 246, cites Brossard's *Dictionaire de Musique* of 1703 as evidence that pieces whose first period ends in the tonic were said to be "en rondeau." However, as Eugene K. Wolf has pointed out to me, the article in question ("Minuetto," not cited by Cole), merely states that the first period of a minuet may not end on the tonic unless it is to be "en Rondeau": "& jamais sur la *Finalle*, à moins qu'il ne soit en *Rondeau*."

Example 2.1. Mozart, Rondo in D major, K. 382 ("Variazion Rondeau").

Example 2.1   (continued)

ing to compare Mozart's method with the speech illustrating refining in *Ad Herrenium:* the theme expressed simply (ritornello), the theme stated in a new form (piano solo), arguments from Comparison *(Setzmanieren* becoming more brilliant as note values decrease), from Contrary (contrasting affective variations: minor, scherzando, Adagio), and Example (triple-meter variation), before restating the theme. The frequent returns of the ritornello help to delineate the arguments, while at the same time dwelling on the point. In addition, there is the *dialogue* between tutti and solo; the *arousal* of heightened sensibility in the minor variation; the change in *delivery* mandated by scherzando and brilliantly technical topics. In these ways, sentences are heaped up for purposes of comparison to the ubiquitous ritornello theme.

The simple finale of Haydn's A-major Sonata, Hob. XVI:30, will reveal other advantages of the rhetorical models for variations. One of six sonatas *"anno 776,"*[100] coincidentally the year of Haydn's autobiographical letter, its Tempo di Menuet finale with six easy variations might easily be dismissed as quotidian and unserious. Yet it concludes a sonata in which not a single previous movement came to a final cadence, the first and only such fully linked cycle in Haydn's *oeuvre;*[101] indeed, the theme provides the first structural final cadence in the sonata. That the theme is then followed by six such final cadences in the variations drives home the point emphatically: the finale acts as a kind of reiterated cadential pattern for the sonata as a whole.

Haydn's longest strophic set among the sonatas (six variations, his limit in a variation movement) is punctuated by melodic returns of the theme (Example 2.2). Here, pleonastic additions take the form of new contrapuntal lines added to the original theme melody. For example, var. 1 is pleonastic by additions to the melodic line itself (internal pleonasm), while var. 2 is pleonastic by addition of a countermelody (external pleonasm). In the periphrastic var. 3, the shape of the figuration has been altered. The contrapuntal aspect of var. 2 also exhibits refining, in particular descanting upon the theme in a dialogue, as set out by *Ad Herrenium,* here between middle voice (the theme reprise) and upper voice. But the contrasting nature of the first two pleonastic variations reorganizes the

100. Grouped this way in Haydn's *Entwurf-Katalog* (facs. ed. Jens Peter Larsen, *Three Haydn Catalogues* [New York, 1979], p. 22).

101. James Webster's important recent study, *Haydn's "Farewell" Symphony,* deals with the issues raised by linked cycles; he analyzes this sonata on pp. 288–294.

Example 2.2. Haydn, Sonata in A Major, Hob. XVI:30/iii.

set. The first variation is closely linked to the theme in bass line and melodic direction, while the contrapuntal var. 2 inaugurates a series of contrapuntal, invention-like variations: var. 3 in two parts, var. 4 in three parts, both a culmination and a partial disintegration in the arpeggiated flourishes of var. 5. The final variation, var. 6, is straightforwardly pleonastic in the enriched first statements of each reprise, then half and half (mm. 1–4 pleonastic, 5–8 periphrastic) in the varied repeats.

But each of the variations between the first and the last has a kind of dual identity (see Table 2.1). Var. 2 is a melodic reprise in the same lower register as var. 6 and so acts as a link between the theme and the end, while var. 4, despite its counterpoint, returns to the initial melodic pitches and contour of the theme in its original register. The set thus features *digression,* and evokes the joy of return. At the same time, variations 3 and 5 exhibit an increase in the speed of figuration, or progressive diminution; this increase may be compared to the rhetorical figure *gradatio,* although not in its purest form. Music theorists from Burmeister on applied this term to any garden-variety ascending sequence, whereas its rhetorical meaning is clearly that of intensification. Not every sequence has this effect, nor need *gradatio* refer only to sequence. The intensification of rhythmic *gradatio* is here interrupted as well as framed by frequent references to the theme, which at the same time play into the larger *dinumeratio,* or heaping up of sentences in counterpoint. If an entire variation can be considered a figure, then each structural element plays a part in building the eloquent variation set.

A final consideration in the rhetorical analysis of Haydn's Sonata 30 is that several segments of the finale recall elements of the first two movements, and thus help to explain the apparently incongruous placement of a paratactic form at the end of a through-composed cycle. In the opening Allegro, the eight-measure theme (a) ends in the tonic, only to be followed immediately by another melody in a lower register (b); the second of these melodies closes with a fanfare passage (c) that recurs at the end of the exposition (Example 2.3). It is

Table 2.1 Haydn, Sonata 30/iii: Organization

Theme	
Var. 1	pleonasm (internal: embellished melodic line)
	rhythm: some sixteenths
Var. 2	pleonasm (external: countermelody)
	melodic reprise in lower register
Var. 3	periphrasis ("invention à 2")
	rhythm: sixteenths
Var. 4	pleonasm ("invention à 3")
Var. 5	periphrasis (culmination of contrapuntal group [2–5] and rhythmic *gradatio* [1, 3, 5])
	rhythm: sixteenth-triplets
Var. 6	melodic reprise in lower register; varied repeats in higher register, with pleonasm (mm. 1-4) and periphrasis (mm. 5-8), and with left-hand arpeggiation recalling Adagio

Example 2.3. Haydn, Sonata 30/i. (a): higher-register theme; (b): lower-register theme; (c): fanfare.

this fanfare that is denied at the point of transition into the slow movement, denied with a shocking harmonic and textural *abruptio:* an arpeggiated flourish (on V_7) and dotted deceptive chords that set off a recitative-like interruption with sequential staccato arpeggios in the left hand (Example 2.4). In the finale, not only does var. 2 bring back the theme in a lower register, but the final variation, no. 6, unites a first reprise in a lower and its varied repeat in a higher register, at the same "heights" as the themes of the Allegro (see Ex. 2.2). Moreover, during the Adagio—which sustains two-part texture nearly throughout—the left hand has a series of arpeggiations of the same type that appear in the varied repeats of var. 6 (Example 2.5). Since the passages in question in var. 6 also recall the eighth-note counterpoints in vars. 2 and 4, the reemergence of the slow-movement version at the close motivates a retrospective reading of the contrapuntal variations as a reclothing of the "archaic" style of the Adagio.

Both of these aspects—registral and figural—suggest that the finale moves beyond necessary reiterative cadencing and into the rhetorical mode of a series

Example 2.4. Haydn, Sonata 30/ii.

Example 2.5. Haydn, Sonata 30/iii, var. 6: varied repeat (mm. 9–12).

of proofs (theme through var. 5) in defense of the theme and the structure of the sonata as a whole, followed by the peroration, var. 6, one purpose of which is to summarize the facts, thus reminding the audience of the strongest arguments. Thus, the finale synthesizes the galant aspect of the Allegro with the through-composed and *empfindsam* Adagio via a kind of galant counterpoint. Such a reading offers a first step in freely applying rhetorical concepts to a piece recently described, outside of its run-on construction, as "conservative" and "commonplace."[102] And it suggests one answer to the question of meaning posed by James Webster's analysis of the sonata.[103] The next step will be to put into a different sort of context the melodic and contrapuntal approaches to variation just described. Thus, we move from a global perspective—a broad rhetorical analogy—to the specific local discussions of variation technique and variation form in eighteenth-century writings.

102. A. Peter Brown, *Joseph Haydn's Keyboard Music: Structure and Style* (Bloomington, 1986), pp. 308, 312.

103. Webster, *Haydn's "Farewell" Symphony,* p. 293, comments that "its aesthetic and rhetorical import remains obscure."

CHAPTER THREE

Variation as Form and Technique in Eighteenth-Century Musical Writings

On one basic point, normally contentious eighteenth-century Europe could agree: variation meant the artful elaboration of given material. Beyond this, agreement ended, and what the given material was or how it was to be elaborated artfully depended on one's point of view as a performer, composer, or writer of a performance manual, composition manual, dictionary article, or critical essay; or as an Italian, Frenchman, or German; or from the vantage points of, say, 1740, 1770, or 1795. Variation could be a technique of improvisation, to be used by the soloist at center stage as well as by the accompanist. It could be a technique in composition by which melodies might be extended, "improved," or even invented in the first place. It was also a form—the technique elevated to a structural principle—and this form could itself be improvised by the virtuoso instrumentalist or set down on paper by the composer for a variety of social and musical contexts; composer and performer were often the same person. Music critics and theorists, serving an ever-growing musical public during this period, tried to clarify the situation by offering admonitions, prescriptions, and analyses based on their own reactions to the contemporary scene.

As this chapter will demonstrate, the changes in the concept and usage of variation as both a technique and a form reflected the principal developments in musical style. The treatises must be our first guide to a performance practice that is no longer extant; their examples and the few elaborated versions written down by composers are the only surviving links with eighteenth-century improvised variation technique. And we shall see that the aesthetic attitudes chronicled in the first chapter created hospitable environments for certain variation types, while consciously or inadvertently denigrating others.

Several types of eighteenth-century musical writings discussed variation: performance-practice manuals, composition treatises, dictionaries and encyclopedias, collections of critical essays, and prefaces to published keyboard works.[1] Each type reflected facets of the musical and intellectual life of the

1. For a chronologically ordered discussion of many of these writings, see Kurt von Fischer, "Zur Theorie der Variation im 18. und beginnenden 19. Jahrhundert," *Festschrift Joseph Schmidt-Görg zum 60. Geburtstag,* ed. Dagmar Weise (Bonn, 1957), pp. 117–130.

48

time. The century plots a rise and fall of both thoroughbass practice and improvised ornamentation, evidenced by the thoroughbass treatises and guides for singing or playing a particular instrument that together constitute performance-practice manuals. Because the basso continuo declined after 1770, few significant thoroughbass treatises were published after this time, while keyboard treatises toward the end of the century, still concerned with ornamentation, gave more space to execution and finger dexterity.

That performance practice correlated with compositional practice is attested by several types of evidence, of which Heinichen's thoroughbass treatise, *Der Generalbass in der Composition* (1728), was only the most visible example. Indeed, the connection of composition with thoroughbass may be regarded as central to the "Bach circle of composers."[2] Niedt declared in 1706 that "Varying justly begins with the thoroughbass, for the latter is the entire fundament of music."[3] The decline in added ornamentation as the outcome of a change in melodic composition was pungently expressed by Charles Burney in 1789: "It was formerly more easy to compose than to play an *Adagio,* which generally consisted of a few notes that were left to the taste and abilities of the performer; but as the composer seldom found his ideas fulfilled by the player, *adagios* are now made more *chantant* and interesting in themselves, and the performer is less put to the torture for embellishments."[4]

The approach and materials of composition manuals changed completely over the course of the period, sometimes overlapping with other kinds of writings. Seventeenth- and some early eighteenth-century composition treatises were concerned with musical and rhetorical figures and rules of counterpoint in different musical styles—church, theater, and chamber are only the best known of these—and described consonance and dissonance in a contrapuntal framework.[5] To writers such as Christoph Bernhard in the mid-seventeenth century, *variatio* meant varying an interval or artfully resolving a dissonance in small note values, and could also be seen as a rhetorical figure; to Riepel in the mid-eighteenth century, *variatio* was the decoration of a cadence.[6] Mid- and

2. See David Schulenberg, "Composition as Variation: Inquiries into the Compositional Procedures of the Bach Circle of Composers," *CM* 23 (1982), 57–87.

3. Niedt, *Handleitung zur Variation* (Hamburg, 1706), chap. 2, par. 1. Mattheson corrects him in his revised edition (1721) of Niedt: "nicht das *ganze,* sondern nur das *vollkommenste* Fundament der Music sey" (p. 162). See also Walter Gerstenberg, "Generalbasslehre und Kompositionslehre in Niedtens *Musicalische Handleitung,*" in *Bericht über den internationale Musikwissenschaftliche Kongress Bamberg 1953* (Kassel and Basel, 1954), pp. 152–155; Peter Benary, *Die deutsche Kompositionslehre,* pp. 61–67. Niedt's work was known to J. S. Bach, who used the first part for his own teaching of thoroughbass.

4. Charles Burney, *A General History of Music,* 4 vols. (1776–1789), 4 vols. in 2, ed. Frank Mercer (1935; rpt. New York, 1957), III, from the prefatory "Essay on Musical Criticism," p. 10.

5. See Benary, *Die deutsche Kompositionslehre,* pp. 39–40.

6. On Bernhard, see Josef Müller-Blattau, *Die Kompositionslehre Heinrich Schützens in der Fassung seines Schülers Christoph Bernhard* (Leipzig, 1926), pp. 73–75, 149–150; translation by Walter Hilse in *Music Forum* 3 (1973), 96–100. Scheibe defined *variatio* as the resolution of a dissonance "durch kleinere Noten variire" in his *Compendium Musices Theoretico-practicum,* p. 62. Joseph Riepel discussed improvising cadenzas, in which the decorated cadence is called *Variatio; Anfangsgründe zur musicalischen Setzkunst,* IV: *Erläuterung der betrüglichen Tonordnung* (Regensburg, 1765), pp. 89–90.

later eighteenth-century theorists approached composition in terms of melodic invention and phrase structure—as Riepel termed them, *Tonordnung* and *Tactordnung*—which gave rise to the main musical forms.[7] The forms themselves, however, tended to be discussed in the context of genres in which they appeared, like symphony, concerto, and sonata. The early nineteenth-century treatises examined for this study considered all constructive features of music, but gave the most detailed attention for the first time to the forms themselves, and this remained the focus of such manuals well into the twentieth century.[8]

The large-scale development encompassed by these composition manuals goes in two directions. On the level of context for the discussion of compositional techniques, we see a kind of continuing contraction of focus from style to genre to form. At the level of the individual techniques, however, we see the process reversed, increasing in size, so to speak, from the intervallic figures of the seventeenth century, to the phrase-oriented constructions of the eighteenth century, to the larger formal recipes of the nineteenth century. The intersection of these rhetorical concepts was most vivid in the later eighteenth century, and as we will see assumed special significance for variation.

An intellectual ιage for comprehensiveness led to unprecedented numbers of dictionaries and encyclopedias aiming to classify, compile, and transmit the entire store of human knowledge (to which they also sought to add).[9] In a number of musical articles in such works, controversial stylistic issues were presented in an ostensibly objective manner, but overt polemic also found its place. Critical essays by such writers as Mattheson, Marpurg, and Scheibe tried to be similarly comprehensive in asking searching questions about the nature of musical styles and genres and their attendant technical problems.[10] Their

7. Buelow, "'Melodielehre'"; on Riepal, see Chapter 2, nn. 35, 62. The problem of the primacy of melody or harmony, the subject of considerable polemic by Rousseau and Rameau and their adherents, occupied writers until Koch's elegant solution that both were projections of basic tonal material, the "Urstoff der Musik," described by Ian Bent as "a kind of tonal 'plasma.'" See Bent, "Compositional Process," p. 30, and Nancy K. Baker, "Heinrich Koch and the Theory of Melody," *JMT* 20 (1976), 1–48.

8. Treatises on fugue are not considered here because they do not discuss variation. It ought to be noted, however, that the article by Johann Abraham Peter Schulz on variation in Sulzer's *Allgemeine Theorie der schönen Künste*, IV, pp. 636–638, treats some fugues as embodying variation, such as a D-minor fugue by J. S. Bach "varied twenty times," and fugues by D'Anglebert (p. 637). Moreover, Albrechtsberger's influential treatise on counterpoint, *Gründliche Anweisung zur Composition* (Leipzig, 1790), p. 189, described certain fugal procedures (e.g., inversion, augmentation) as "ornaments" *(Zierlichkeiten)*.

9. An "encyclopedic" tendency is found in other kinds of works as well. Mattheson's *Der vollkommene Capellmeister* (Hamburg, 1739) is an encyclopedic reference work on the theory and practice of its time. Not organized like an encyclopedia or dictionary, it actually cuts across many other categories by combining *Melodielehre, Verzierungslehre, Formenlehre, Kompositionslehre,* and criticism. See Margarete Reimann, "Nachwort" to the facsimile edition (Kassel, 1954).

10. See Georgia Cowart, *The Origins of Modern Musical Criticism: French and Italian Music, 1600–1750* (Ann Arbor, 1981); Imogen Fellinger, "Mattheson als Begründer der ersten Musikzeitschrift *(Critica musica),"* in *New Mattheson Studies,* ed. George J. Buelow and Hans Joachim Marx (Cambridge, 1983), pp. 179–197.

collections of essays, periodicals, and pamphlets dealt with wide-ranging issues of musical practice, taste, and composition. Later critics, writing primarily in newspapers, rarely dealt with such big topics, partly because they were striving simply to keep up with the tremendous expansion of musical life in the number of performances and publications to review.

Improvised and Composed Variation Technique

Writers on performance practice, whether in dictionaries, essays, or manuals devoted entirely to the subject, considered variation chiefly to be an extemporaneous technique in which the main notes of the melody or bass were broken up into smaller note values called diminutions, or in which ornaments were added to the melody. A few composers published pieces with written-out diminutions and ornaments, with the express purpose of guiding performers in the correct method of varying them extemporaneously.[11] In some cases, these were supplied in early published editions, in the shaping of which the composer might or might not have played a role.[12] Together with occasional examples in treatises, such as those by Quantz and Türk, these written-out elaborations are the only surviving keys to eighteenth-century improvised variation technique.[13] The ornamental approach was sometimes associated with the French style, the freer diminutions with the Italian, and the German with a mixture of the two.[14] Ornamentation and diminution were treated separately by these writers, because the so-called "essential ornaments" like the mordent and trill, indicated with special signs, were quite different in practice and effect from the "arbitrary" or more freely prescribed figurations.[15] Different terms are given to these classes of "figures" by Marpurg, who called diminutions "figures

11. J. S. Bach, English Suites in A minor and G minor (with "Agréments du même Sarabande"); Telemann, *Sonates méthodiques* (1731, 1732); Corelli, *VI Sonate a Violino Solo e Violino o Cimbalo* (Op. 5 [1700], embell. ed. pub. 1710); Franz Benda, Sonatas for Violin and Bass (MS, c. 1733–1763); C. P. E. Bach, *Sechs Sonaten fürs Clavier mit veränderten Reprisen* (1760); Löhlein, Sonatas Op. 2 (1765). On Benda, see Douglas Lee, "Some Embellished Versions of Sonatas by Franz Benda," *MQ* 62 (1976), 58–71.

12. For example, the slow movement of the well-known Mozart sonata in F major, K. 332, was extensively embellished in the first edition, published in Vienna by Artaria (1784). The Roger edition of Corelli's Op. 5 (1710) supposedly used Corelli's own embellishments for the slow movements (Michael Talbot, "Corelli," in *New Grove*, vol. 4, p. 773).

13. Quantz varied an Adagio in his *Versuch* (Johann Joachim Quantz, *Versuch einer Anweisung die Flöte traversière zu spielen* [Berlin, 1752; 3rd ed. Breslau, 1789; facs. ed. Kassel, 1953], chap. 14); a generation later, Türk similarly gave simple and varied versions of a piece (Daniel Gottlob Türk, *Klavierschule* [Leipzig and Halle, 1789; facs. ed. Kassel, 1962; 1967], pp. 362–369). See Ernest T. Ferand, *Improvisation in Nine Centuries of Western Music* (Cologne, 1961); Hans-Peter Schmitz, *Die Kunst der Verzierung im 18. Jahrhundert: Instrumentale und Vokale Musizierpraxis in Beispielen* (Kassel, 1955).

14. Quantz, *Versuch,* chap. 14, par. 2, and chap. 18.

15. See Joan E. Smiles, "Improvised Ornamentation in Late Eighteenth-Century Music" (Ph.D. diss., Stanford University, 1976), pp. 5–9, and "Directions for Improvised Ornamentation in Italian Method Books of the Late Eighteenth Century," *JAMS* 31 (1978), 495–509.

of composition" *(Setzmanieren)* and ornaments "performance figures" *(Spiel-manieren).*[16]

James Grassineau, in his *Musical Dictionary* of 1740, elegantly differentiated between the two types of improvised variation: "Variation, is the different manner of playing or singing the same song, air, or tune, either by subdividing the notes into several others of less value, or by adding of graces in such a manner, however, as that one may still discern the ground of the tune thro' all the enrichments."[17] Grassineau here (and most other writers) noted the obvious point that in repetitions of the given material, something must stay the same while something is varied. What Grassineau referred to as the "ground" was variously identified by other writers as the bass line, series of harmonies, or the main notes of the original melody. Variation is thus a surface technique imposed upon a more basic structural design which retains its shape throughout. This structural design—the "ground"—may answer the question posed in Chapter 2: what is the *res* in such a piece? Music derived from the given material that completely alters its shape may be considered "transformation" or "development" in the Romantic or modern sense, but it was not part of the discussions of variation by writers of this period. To learn how to create such variations, however—and here improvised technique came very close to compositional technique—writers suggested practicing varying different intervals (Niedt, Quantz, Riepel, and Daube), or chords (Daube), sometimes applying the permutation techniques of *ars combinatoria.*[18]

Extemporaneous varying—that is, variation as performance practice—dominated all discussions of varying in the first half of the century, and found its aesthetic justification in the imitation of nature: "Nature delights in varying," proclaimed Mattheson.[19] The age of figured bass was obviously concerned with "certain niceties of accompaniment,"[20] and discussions of varied figurations in such realizations appear in treatises by Niedt, Gasparini, Hein-

16. See Chapter 2. On other distinctions among figures for composers and performers, see the valuable study by John Butt, "Improvised Vocal Ornamentation and German Baroque Compositional Theory—An Approach to 'Historical' Performance Practice," *JRMA* 116 (1991), 41–62.

17. James Grassineau, *A Musical Dictionary* (London, 1740; facs. ed. New York, 1966), s.v. "Variation." This part of the definition is taken from Sebastien de Brossard, *Dictionaire de Musique,* 2nd ed. (Paris, 1705; facs. ed. Hilversum, 1966): "Les différentes manières de jouer ou de chanter un Air, soit en subdivisant les Notes en plusieurs de moindre valeur, soit en y ajoûtant des agréments, etc. de manière cependant qu'on puisse toûjours reconnoître le fond de cet Air . . . au travers . . . de ces enrichissements." Grassineau's dictionary carried the explanatory subtitle: "the whole carefully abstracted from the best authors."

18. See Leonard Ratner, "*Ars combinatoria:* Chance and Choice in Eighteenth-Century Music," *Studies in Eighteenth-Century Music,* ed. Landon, pp. 343–363; Ian Bent, "Analytical Thinking in the First Half of the Nineteenth Century," in *Modern Musical Scholarship,* ed. Edward Olleson (Stocksfield, 1980), pp. 157–161.

19. Mattheson, *Grosse Generalbass-Schule,* p. 162.

20. C. P. E. Bach, *Versuch über die wahre Art das Clavier zu spielen,* II (1762), title of chap. 2 ("Von gewissen Zierlichkeiten des Accompagnements"), cited by F. T. Arnold, *The Art of Accompaniment from a Thoroughbass as practiced in the XVIIth and XVIIIth Centuries,* I (London, 1931; New York, 1965), p. 438.

ichen, Mattheson, Geminiani, and C. P. E. Bach. Geminiani even worked out a bass line a number of times and referred to the successive realizations as variations.[21]

Niedt's treatise is entirely devoted to variations of the bass line as well as the upper line via diminutions, consisting of scalar and arpeggiated figurations and filled-in intervals. In the early chapters, his examples vary the same bass line over and over, but it is clear that this is a pedagogical tool; he does not expect the performer to play consecutive variations on the bass. His tour-de-force conclusion is the generation of an entire series of suite movements from a single bass line, altering meter and rhythm in the manner appropriate to the character of each dance.[22] And following the Allemande and Courant are one or more *Doubles,* which Niedt defined in his glossary as "an arpeggiated *(gebrochene)* variation"; the *Double* marks the only occasion for an actual varied repetition of a short piece, or a variation in the modern sense.

In 1721, Mattheson brought out an edition of Niedt's treatise, enlarged and copiously annotated by himself. He barely concealed his irritation with Niedt's rhapsodizing and sometimes confusing prose, and took it upon himself to define variation in the sense used in the treatise: "Certain slow bass notes, keeping their direction [*Ganges*] and progression, come to be varied in different ways in smaller notes, so that basically the composition retains its essence, but by being diminished, divided, and dismembered, it gets more life, strength, grace, and embellishment. What the French call a *double* (doubled or a doubling), we call, although not appropriately, a variation."[23] This improvised variation of a dance joins thoroughbass practice with the practice of decorating melodies in performance, and also intersects with composed variation forms in written-out *Doubles.* Walther defined *Double* in his *Musicalisches Lexicon* of 1732: "The *Double* of an Air, or second couplet in diminution, means: the second verse of an Aria varied, that is, broken into smaller notes. A doubling, or a variation, usually of Allemandes and Courantes."[24]

21. Francesco Geminiani, *The Art of Accompaniment* (London, 1755), part I, example 9.

22. Kurt von Fischer points out that this procedure connects thoroughbass practice with the variation suite of the seventeenth century, citing a Florentine manuscript (Bib. naz. centr. XIX 110) in which a series of dances is notated only by the bass line and a few figures. ("Zur Theorie der Variation," p. 118). Niedt never refers to his dance movements as a variation suite, but the concept is clearly applicable.

23. Mattheson, *Niedtens Musicalische Handleitung,* p. 3n; for German see Appendix B. Poulin and Taylor translate *Gang* as interval, in *The Music Guide,* p. 74n.; Harriss, in *Mattheson's Der vollkommene Capellmeister,* part III, chap. 5, translates it as "passage." Mattheson also discussed variations as projections of the bass line in his *Grosse Generalbass-Schule.*

24. Johann Gottfried Walther, *Musicalisches Lexicon* (Leipzig, 1732; facs. ed. Kassel, 1967), s.v. "Double": "*Double . . . Le Double d'un Air, ou second Couplet en diminution,* bedeutet: den zweyten Vers einer Arie variirt, d. i. in kleinern Noten vorgestellt und angebracht. Eine Verdoppelung, oder eine Variation, gemeiniglich bey Allemanden und Couranten." Hans Heinrich Eggebrecht suggested that Walther used Niedt's *Handleitung* in making his own dictionary ("Walthers Musikalisches Lexicon in seinen terminologischen Partien," *AM* 29 [1957], 10–27, cited in Poulin's introduction to *The Musical Guide,* p. xi). See also Margarete Reimann, "Zur Entwicklungsgeschichte des *Double,*" *Mf* 5 (1952), 317–332; 6 (1953), 97–111.

Niedt's work resembles Christopher Simpson's much earlier treatise *The Division-Violist,* which itself stands near the end of a long line of manuals teaching the art of diminution.[25] Although Niedt and Simpson differ in two crucial respects—Simpson wrote about a solo line which happened to be in the bass register, not a figured bass, and he did intend the performer to play a series of variations (divisions)—the specific variation techniques he described coincided to a remarkable extent with those of Niedt. In fact Simpson's first type of division, "breaking the ground" (p. 33), consisted of precisely the same kind of bass-line elaboration presented by Niedt nearly fifty years later (chap. 3, pp. 27–28). The gamba plays these divisions over the notes of the ground held by the harpsichord or organ. And Simpson's "descant to the ground" (p. 43), a series of quasi-melodic figurations over the ground, resembles Niedt's right-hand elaborations over the bass (chap. 6, p. 54). The "descant to the ground" makes a "different-concording-part unto the Ground" (p. 35), and does not always "meet every succeeding note of the Ground in the Unison or Octave," but rather in any consonant interval (Example 3.1). Niedt assigns a similar meaning to descant in his definition of "ciacona," in which the bass is repeated and "in the upper voice or discant variations are made, which, as it were, so thoroughly dissert [*durchtractiren*] upon the theme that it is quite smashed and shattered."[26] Niedt's ciacona is a form generated by a simple thoroughbass; Simpson's divisions result *de facto* in a ciacona as well, as a result of improvised descant division by a solo instrument.

In addition to figured-bass realization, keyboard players and other instrumentalists needed to know how to add ornaments and diminutions to the melodies they played. Here the terrain was fraught with peril; indeed, the dust has not yet settled on several of the more enduring controversies of performance practice. The following discussion is limited to a few of the writers most significant for the present study. Friedrich Wilhelm Riedt affords a good starting point because he contrasted current indiscriminate practices with the cautious and judgmental critic's voice. His essay, "Observations on the optional variations of a musical thought in the elaboration of a melody," published by Marpurg in 1755,[27] attempted to answer the question: "How can a good variation-

---

25. Christopher Simpson, *The Division-Viol, or the Art of Playing Ex Tempore to a Ground,* 2nd ed. (London, 1667; facs. ed. London, 1955). The similarity in "scope and intention" between Niedt's and Simpson's treatises was noted by Arnold, *The Art of Accompaniment,* I, p. 213 n.1. The earliest known diminution manual is the *Fontegara* of Sylvestro di Ganassi (Venice, 1535); the *Tratado di Glosas* of Diego Ortiz (Rome, 1553) describes the different ways a violone may play with a cembalo. In 1584, Girolamo della Casa's *Il vero modo di diminuir* included a list of diminutions for all intervals of the scale within the time values of a semibreve and a minim. See Howard Mayer Brown, *Embellishing Sixteenth-Century Music* (London, 1976); Imogene Horsley, "Improvised Embellishment in the Performance of Renaissance Polyphonic Music," *JAMS* 4 (1951), 3–19; Ernest R. Ferand, "Didactic Embellishment Literature in the Late Renaissance: A Survey of Sources," in *Aspects of Medieval and Renaissance Music,* ed. Jan LaRue (New York, 1966), pp. 154–172; Robert Lach, *Studien zur Entwicklungsgeschichte der ornamentalen Melopöie* (Leipzig, 1913), pp. 411–525.

26. Niedt, *Handleitung zur Variation,* chap. 10, s.v. "Ciacona."

27. Riedt, "Betrachtungen über die willkührlichen Veränderungen der musicalischen Gedanken bey Ausführung einer Melodie," in *Historisch-Kritische Beyträge zur Aufnahme der Musik,* II, ed. Marpurg (Berlin, 1755; facs. ed. Hildesheim, 1970), pp. 95–118.

(a)

(b)

Example 3.1. (a): Christopher Simpson, descant to the ground; (b): Friedrich Erhard Niedt, right-hand elaborations to bass line.

maker be distinguished from a bad one?" Riedt systematically presented not only his own point of view, but currently opposing attitudes as well, in a bewildering array of "basic principles," "basic rules," "working rules," and the like. The basic rules *(Grundregeln)* represented his own beliefs: namely, that the main idea of a piece should never be varied, only those ideas that are "incompletely formed" or "in the shade." Like other writers of mid-century, Riedt stressed the importance of fidelity to the composer's intentions, by which he meant not contravening the character of the melody and of the composition.[28] Four "working rules" *(Ausübungsregeln)*, by contrast, showed the more extreme, laissez-faire view of his contemporaries:

28. Riedt, "Betrachtungen," pp. 101–102.

1. The more diversity the performer brings to the melody, the more beautiful is the performance;
2. The theme of a piece must be performed unvaried only in its first and last appearances; otherwise it must be varied as often as it appears again, and each time by a different method;
3. Since music is a free art, thus each performer has the freedom to make his variations as he pleases; and
4. If one performs his own composition, he can vary it as he wants, and he is not bound to observe the rules so exactly as he must do in the performance of the composition of another.[29]

Having presented both sides of the issue, Riedt left the final determination to the judgment of the performer, but stood by his basic rules and two additional "main rules" *(Hauptregeln)*: that a variation must never clash with the underlying harmony, and that the motion *(Bewegung)* of the variation must resemble the motion of the idea.[30]

Quantz, in his influential treatise on playing the flute, also tried to curb the zeal of the inept variation-maker: "So many incorrect and awkward ideas appear that it would be better in many cases to play the melody as the composer set it, rather than to spoil it repeatedly with such wretched variations."[31] His frequently cited example of an entire Adagio movement—the most proper location for variation technique—showed two melodies, simple and florid, the latter incorporating both ornaments and diminutions.[32] Quantz wanted the variations to be added only after the simple melody has already been heard, "otherwise the listener cannot know if variations are actually present."[33] And the variations must maintain the character of the original melody: "Gay and bold variations must never be interspersed in a melancholy and modest melody, unless you seek to render them agreeable through your execution."[34] An example of a specially written-out embellishment of a piece thus far unknown to the literature on this subject is the "Andante variatio" of a "Concerto" for keyboard preserved in the practice-book of Maria Theresia's daughter, Archduchess Maria Elisabeth, in the Vienna National Library (Example 3.2).[35]

29. Ibid., pp. 102–107; for German, see Appendix B. Fischer claims that the second *Ausübungsregel* refers to the theme and da capo of a variation set, because these would be the "first and last appearances" of the theme, but because Riedt never alluded to variation form, I believe that he was simply describing a contemporary performance practice which allowed one to vary everything but the first and last appearance of a musical idea. The first *Ausübungsregel* is mistakenly represented as Riedt's own opinion by Hans Joachim Marx, "Some Unknown Embellishments of Corelli's Violin Sonatas," *MQ* 61 (1975), 74.

30. Riedt, "Betrachtungen," p. 108; for the *Hauptregeln* in German, see Appendix B.

31. Quantz, *Versuch,* chap. 13, par. 2, p. 118; idem, *On Playing the Flute,* trans. and ed. Edward R. Reilly (New York, 1966; New York, 1975), p. 136.

32. The adagio is reprinted in Ferand, *Improvisation,* p. 132.

33. Quantz, *On Playing the Flute,* p. 139.

34. Ibid., p. 138. That variations should not alter the original character of a melody is found as early as 1555 in Vicentino's *L'antica musica ridotta alla moderna prattica.* See Horsley, "Improvised Embellishment," p. 17.

35. S.m.11085, p. 92. This source is described in Brown, *Haydn's Keyboard Music,* pp. 173–176.

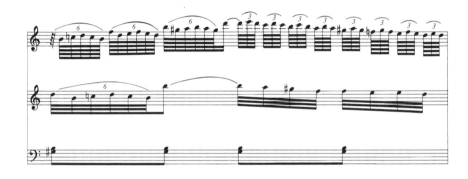

Example 3.2. Leopold Hofmann, Concerto. (a): Adagio; (b): Andante [*sic*] variatio.

Here, in contrast to Quantz's example, the original Adagio is already quite ornate, a highly expressive *minore* aria by Leopold Hofmann.

Leopold Mozart's treatise on playing the violin had similarly strong words for would-be embellishers:

> It is clear as daylight that a violinist must know well how to decide whether the composer has intended any ornamentation, and if so, what kind . . . Those unmusicianly musicians who wish to befrill each note, can see here the reason why a sensible composer is indignant when the notes set down by him are not played as they are written . . . [L]et us make no embellishments, or only such as spoil neither the harmony nor the melody . . . All these decorations are used, however, only when playing a solo, and then very sparingly, at the right time, and only for variety in often-repeated and similar passages. And look well at the directions of the composer; for in the application of such ornaments is one's ignorance soonest betrayed.[36]

In commenting that decorations are permissible only in a solo, Mozart added his voice to the many contemporaneous injunctions against varying the melody in ensemble playing, a fault often laid at the door of violinists in particular.[37] Determining the composer's intentions, however, was a task for which many performers were unsuited, and which C. P. E. Bach sought to simplify.

Bach described the "present practice of varying extemporaneously the two reprises of an allegro" at the end of the first part of his *Versuch über die wahre Art, das Clavier zu spielen*.[38] He continued:

> The concept is excellent but much abused. My feelings are these: Not everything should be varied, for if it is the reprise will become a new piece. Many things, particularly affettuoso or declamatory passages, cannot be readily varied . . . All variations must relate to the piece's affect, and they must always be, if not better than, at least as good as the original . . . [T]here must be a vision of the whole piece so that the variation will contain the same mixture of the brilliant and the simple, the fiery and the languid, the sad and the joyful, the singable and the instrumentally idiomatic. In keyboard pieces the bass too may be modified as long as the harmony remains unchanged. Despite the present popularity of elaborate variations, it is of first importance always to make certain that the lineaments of a piece, by which its affect is recognized, remain unobscured.[39]

A few years later, Bach published a set of *Sechs Sonaten fürs Clavier mit veränderten Reprisen,* dedicated to Princess Anna Amalie of Prussia (1760). Here he took audiences as much as performers to task for current abuses. To suggest

36. Leopold Mozart, *Versuch einer gründlichen Violinschule* (Augsburg, 1756), trans. by Edith Knocker as *Treatise on the Fundamentals of Violin Playing* (Oxford, 1948; 1988), pp. 179–180, 214. Similar admonitions are found in chap. XII, "Of reading music correctly, and in particular, of good execution," pp. 215–216.

37. See John Spitzer and Neal Zaslaw, "Improvised Ornamentation in Eighteenth-Century Orchestras," *JAMS* 39 (1986), 524–577, not only for other such citations but also for extensive documentary evidence of the practice.

38. See Bach, *Essay,* pp. 165–166.

39. Translation modified from Mitchell in *Essay.*

the immediacy of his argument, I have taken the translation from the first English edition published by Walsh between 1760 and 1763 (the German appears in Appendix B);[40] where Walsh departs significantly from Bach, the original appears in curved brackets; where Walsh abridged the preface, the missing portions appear in square brackets:

Alterations in the several Repetitions in a Piece of Musick are in our Days become almost necessary {indispensable}; as being expected from every Performer. Some {one of my friends} give themselves all pains imaginable to play every single Note as it stands, with due Accuracy and Distinction, according to the true Intent of the Composer {rules of good performance}. Which indeed is very commendable. {Can applause be rightfully denied him?} Others again, urged often by necessity, throw in so many Flourishes (though misapplied) to make up for that Deficiency, in not being skil'd sufficiently, to play the Plain Notes as they stand with Propriety and Justness. [Nevertheless, the public holds him above the former. Performers want to vary every idea at the repeat without stopping to ask whether such variation is permitted by the organization of the piece and the ability of the performer. Often it is simply this varying, especially when it accompanies a long and much too peculiarly decorated cadenza, that draws bravos from most listeners . . . No longer is there patience enough to play the first part of the piece as written; the long delay of the Bravos would be intolerable.] Such embellishments often prove to be quite contrary to the Subject and Passion, and to the Just Proportion which ought to subsist in a well regulated disposition of Thoughts; {Often these untimely variations are contrary to the theme, the affect, and the relationship of ideas}; A thing very disagreeable to many a composer. But supposing a Performer to be possess'd of all necessary requisites for introducing proper Variations, he cannot at all times be alike dispos'd for it; not to mention the many Difficulties he must have to encounter within a variety of new and uncommon turns and Passages. Should it not be a principal View with every Performer to do credit not only to the Composer {piece} but also to himself? Must not of Consequence his own Invention by varying the repetitions at least be equally as good as that of the Composer? [However, despite these difficulties and abuses, good variations always retain their value. I refer moreover to what I asserted at the end of the first part of my *Versuch*.] In consideration of these Difficulties, the following SONATAS have chiefly been appropriated for such Beginners and lovers of Musick, as for various Reasons have neither Time nor Patience enough to adhere to a constant Practice, and besides being Compos'd in an easy and familiar Stile, I at the same time aimed at procuring to them that particular Satisfaction and Convenience as to enable them to introduce proper Variations without puzzling their Heads about Inventions of their own, or to have them prescribed by others, and learning them afterwards by Heart. Lastly, every thing concerning the manner of playing these SONATAS with Propriety, Delicacy, and Expression has been particularly mark'd, so that one might perform them properly even by an indifferent Disposition. [I am delighted to be the first, so far as I know, to have worked in this fashion for the profit and enjoyment of pa-

40. *Sei Sonate/per/Cembalo/Composte Dal/Sigr. Carl Philipp Emanuel Bach.* London. Printed for I. Walsh in Catherine Street in the Strand. Copy in USBE with inscription "H. L. Serces, 1763." See also the modern Schirmer edition by Eiji Hashimoto (New York, 1988), with facsimile and translation of the dedication and preface.

trons and friends. How happy I would be if the special liveliness of my diligence in service should be recognized hereby.]

The language of this translation suggests that the ornaments should coordinate with the rhetorical nature of musical compositions; one might even see in "Subject" and "disposition of Thought" the first stages in composing an oration *(inventio, dispositio)*, after which embellishments make up the *elaboratio*.

In deploring contemporary performing practices while offering new compositional alternatives, these pieces in effect herald the decline of ex tempore varying. They offered not a guide but a substitute. But the techniques used to vary the repeats reflected ex tempore variation pure and simple: melody undergoes the greatest change, via ornamentation, diminution, and changes of register and contour. Modifications of the bass are minimal, and although inner voices are added, the harmonies remain the same.[41] Significantly, when Haydn and Mozart adopted the varied-reprise idea in their sonata forms, they did so only in slow movements, which had remained the locus for expressive melodic figuration. In fast outer movements, varied returns in rondos may be more or less systematically carried through a piece (for example, Mozart's Eb-major Piano Concerto K. 449/iii, Haydn's Bb-major String Quartet Op. 33/4/iv); Kollmann claimed to imitate Bach's varied-reprise sonatas in his composition treatise of 1799, when he included a rondo "with variations of the subject."[42] Mozart also referred to varied refrains in a rondo as variations: the autograph of Mozart's Fantasy and Sonata in C minor (K. 457/475), rediscovered in 1990, reveals that the first version of the slow movement did not contain varied refrains (the refrains were noted as "da capo 7 täckt"), but subsequent pages added first a hitherto-unknown embellished version "bey der ersten Reprise" and "bey der 2ten Reprise," and then the embellishments of the final version, headed "Variationen."[43] On the other hand, the occasional decorated return of a theme in the recapitulation (for example, Mozart's G-major String Quartet K. 387/i) does not constitute a thoroughgoing application of the varied reprise. When in 1789 Türk claimed that "the rage for variations was never bigger than it is today,"[44] he recommended Bach's varied-reprise sonatas and suggested that the Allegro was a good place for varying. Indeed, many of his admonitions and prescriptions still echo those of the mid-century treatises by Bach, Mozart, and Quantz.

41. See Donald Francis Tovey, "Haydn's Chamber Music," in *The Main Stream of Music and Other Essays* (Cleveland and New York, 1959; first pub. 1949), pp. 28–30; Erich H. Beuermann, "Die Reprisensonaten C. P. E. Bachs," *AfMw* 13 (1952), 168–179; A. Peter Brown, "Haydn and C. P. E. Bach: The Question of Influence," in *Haydn Studies,* ed. Jens Peter Larsen, Howard Serwer, and James Webster (New York, 1981), pp. 158–164; idem, *Haydn's Keyboard Music,* pp. 219–221.

42. Augustus Frederick Christopher Kollmann, *An Essay on Musical Composition* (London, 1799; facs. ed. New York, 1973), p. 11 and Appendix. See below, in the following section, for Koch's description of a type of variation finale with episodes, "after the fashion of the rondo."

43. Eugene K. Wolf, "The Rediscovered Autograph of Mozart's Fantasy and Sonata in C Minor, K. 475/457," *JM* 10 (1992), 23, 39–46. I am indebted to Eugene Wolf for sharing this information before publication.

44. Türk, *Klavierschule,* p. 322.

Variation technique as a compositional tool appears in two guises in compositional manuals of the eighteenth century. First is *ars combinatoria (Verwechselungskunst)*, by which all the permutations and combinations of melodic intervals could be used to create an ornate and attractive composition.[45] For example, in an unpublished composition treatise from 1739, Christian Gottlieb Ziegler discussed such permutations in extraordinary detail. In an early chapter on melody, Ziegler described the invention of new melodies as the setting down of a series of musical intervals from which arise musical thoughts called *inventiones* or *Einfälle*. Then, in a chapter entitled "De Artificio Variandi, oder von der Wissenschaft zur Variiren,"[46] he identified the two types of variation as those that make many notes from a few and vice versa. Ziegler also distinguished between pure variations of an interval, those which vary just the pitches of the interval, and impure ones, which add passing and neighbor notes. He finally showed an entire "*Grund Melodie*" and "*algemeiner Bass*" [sic] together with six *Veränderungen* of the melody (Example 3.3).

Ars combinatoria served as a source of melodic invention in treatises through the end of the century, especially those by Riepel and Daube.[47] But to Riepel and Koch, whose treatises were the first to systematize the essential periodicity of musical style from about mid-century on, variation also became a way to expand and balance melodies, by inserting a varied bar or two into the middle or end of a phrase, or by varying the entire phrase at its immediate or subsequent repetition. The techniques identified by Koch, most of which he took over from Riepel, call for the varied presentations and insertions of small melodic cells, as well as repetitions of entire phrases. Koch helpfully listed the ways in which varied repetition might be handled aesthetically:

1. through increasing or decreasing the strength of the tone in the execution of the repeated section,
2. through varying of figures with which the principal notes are decorated,
3. through new configuration [*Wendungen*] in the accompanying voices,
4. through increasing or decreasing the accompanying instruments, and
5. through the combination of several of these individual means.[48]

Koch pointed to the Andante of Haydn's Symphony No. 42 (1771) as a piece for which variation is the sole means of melodic extension, expansion, and

45. See Ratner, "*Ars combinatoria,*" for a detailed discussion.

46. Christian Gottlieb Ziegler, *Anleitung zur musikalischen Composition* (Quedlinburg, ms. dated 1739), chap. 2, pp. 12–13, and chap. 3, pp. 68ff, respectively. This treatise, heavily indebted to Mattheson, was first described by Ratner in "Eighteenth-Century Theories of Musical Period Structure," *MQ* 42 (1956), 439–454. The apparently unique copy in NYPL (Drexel 3290) is missing most of Part II, on harmony.

47. Riepel, *Tonordnung*, pp. 112–121; see Ratner, "*Ars combinatoria,*" pp. 346–348, 351, 353–354. Daube, *Der musikalische Dilettant* and *Anleitung zur Erfindung der Melodie;* see Buelow, "'Melodielehre'"; Susan Snook, "Daube's 'Der Musikalische Dilettant': Translation and Commentary" (Ph.D. diss., Stanford University, 1978); Michael Karbaum, "Das theoretische Werk Johann Friedrich Daubes: ein Beitrag zur Kompositionslehre des 18. Jahrhunderts" (Ph.D. diss., Vienna, 1968).

48. Koch, *Versuch*, III, pp. 155–156; Baker, *Introductory Essay*, p. 130 (trans. differs slightly). Riepel's examples of varied repetition appeared in his *Tactordnung*, p. 26, and *Tonordnung*, p. 56; his discussion of permutations appeared in the former, pp. 12–13, and the latter, pp. 25–32.

Grund Melodie

Example 3.3.   Christian Gottlieb Ziegler [from top to bottom]: "Grund-Melodie, erste Veränd., 2ᵗᵉ, 3ᵗᵉ in lauter triolen, 4ᵗᵉ in lauter geschwinden Noten, 5ᵗᵉ in lauter punctirten Noten, 6ᵗᵉ noch andert punctirt, algemeiner Bass."

balance. Melody, accompaniment figuration, and dynamics are all varied. The effect of varied repetition in Haydn's symphonic movement, however, clearly changes as the size and formal function of the varied segment change. An embellished version of the first eight-measure period of a movement focuses attention on sheer sonic beauty, on surface melodic events, on the relationship of melodic to accompanying voices. Variation of shorter segments during modulatory passages creates a delaying action, as the goals are deferred during the repetition. Finally, varied repetition of cadence patterns, actually another category of repetition in Koch's view, strengthens the closural force of such passages.[49]

49. This piece is discussed further, with an example (4.2), in Chapter 4.

Example 3.3   (continued)

Improvised and Composed Variation Form

The writers surveyed thus far never offered explicit guides to improvising variation forms, even though systematic applications of the techniques they described would result in variation form.[50] Simpson, in discussing the "ordering of division," had in effect indicated that a variation series with contrasting types of figuration would be the result.[51] Mattheson had discussed improvising chorale variations for the organ; he quoted extensively from an earlier writer, Christoph Raupach, whose approach was to set *Doubles* to the cantus firmus in counterpoint.[52] And Marpurg's remark about the way variations arise from *Klangfüsse* and *Setzmanieren* perhaps implied an improvised form.[53]

50. Schmitz, *Die Kunst der Verzierung*, p. 25, believes that all pieces labeled "Variation," "Alternatio," "Passacaglia," "Chaconne," "Double," "Division," and "Partita" are written versions of performance practice.

51. *Division-Viol*, p. 56. He advocated playing the ground first, then breaking it into crotchets and quavers or playing a slow descant to it; then a quicker division; then a slower descant; then a "skipping division," always showing variety.

52. *Der vollkommene Capellmeister*, part III, chap. 25, par. 37–46; Harriss, pp. 853–855.

53. See Chapter 2, n. 70.

The distinction, then, between improvised and composed variation form was too obvious to be made explicit by prescriptive writers. Kollmann, who included variations as a type of "Fancy" or improvised piece, merely remarked that "Extemporary variations are the same as written ones," requiring "perfect knowledge of harmony and a lively imagination."[54] He advised the reader to learn from his previous chapter on how to compose variations, where the student would be happy to find only three basic types of figurations: arpeggios, "transitions" (scale-step figures), and syncopations. Even Czerny, who forty years later devoted a chapter to variations in his *L'Art d'improviser,* never made useful distinctions between improvised and composed variation sets.[55] But he indicated that it was necessary to learn how to improvise variations because there are many opportunities that present themselves for varying a theme, whether the returns of a theme in another genre or in a set of variations *per se.* Czerny's list of the techniques to employ in individual variations might be regarded as good advice for the composer of variations:

> The number of forms at the disposal of the artist is infinite. For example:
> 1. triplets, sextuplets, etc., for right hand, left hand or both, with the sole condition that the melody be retained or at least the harmonic progression of the theme in its first part;
> 2. trills and ornaments of all sorts;
> 3. a new cantabile theme on the bass and harmony of the theme;
> 4. strict style [*style lié*], in which the theme could be placed in a higher or lower voice;
> 5. using the theme in the form of canons or fugues;
> 6. changing the tempo, meter, and key, as in an Adagio, Polonaise, Rondo, and in a finale with free development.[56]

Czerny advised the student to study works by Hummel, Moscheles, Kalkbrenner, and Ries, but particularly recommended Mozart's variations on "Je suis Lindor" (the same piece used as a model by Momigny),[57] Clementi's variations on the same theme in the Finale of a Bb-major sonata, Hummel's variations on the march from Rossini's *Cendrillon* Op. 40, and Beethoven's F-major set Op. 34, Eb-major set Op. 35, and C-minor set WoO 80.

Most of our information about variation forms actually improvised in public comes from reports of concerts and contests, as in Mozart's letters, and from such famous rivalries as Mozart-Clementi and Beethoven-Steibelt.[58] And the

---

54. A. F. C. Kollmann, *An Essay on Musical Harmony* (London, 1796; Utica, N.Y., 1817), p. 274. Interestingly, Kollmann grouped variations with the "grammatical" chapters of his first treatises, saving rondos and sonata forms for his second treatise on "practical composition." His explanation of the distinction between these two aspects of the musical "language" forms the introduction to the *Essay on Musical Harmony.*

55. Carl Czerny, *L'Art d'improviser* (Paris [1836]).

56. Ibid., p. 92.

57. Jérôme-Joseph de Momigny, *Cours complet d'harmonie et de composition* (Paris, 1803), pp. 608–612.

58. See Katalin Komlós, "Mozart and Clementi: A Piano Competition and Its Interpretation," *Historical Performance* 3 (1989), 3–9; idem, "'Ich praeludirte und spielte Variazionen': Mozart the

reports themselves focus only on the fact of variations being improvised, not on their content and technique. A typical comment is in Mozart's letter to his father about a concert in Vienna in June 1781: "When the concert was over I went on playing variations (for which the Archbishop gave me the theme) for a whole hour and with such general applause that if the Archbishop had any vestige of humanity, he must have felt delighted."[59] At a concert in Prague in January 1787, Mozart improvised a dozen "most interesting and most artful variations" on Figaro's aria "Non più andrai" and received a "roaring ovation."[60] Mozart never wrote down these variations. We know that some of his published independent keyboard sets also originated in performance, but there is no evidence of their pre-publication states. Evidence of improvisation may be in their free passages and cadenzas, especially when these serve to link the variations of a strict series into more fantasia-like combinations.[61] The variations on a theme of Gluck that Mozart improvised in March 1783 at the Burgtheater in the presence of Gluck and the Emperor Joseph II were not published until the summer of 1784 (K. 455). One wonders if the significant stylistic differences between this set and the variations on a theme of Paisiello (K. 398) originally improvised at the same concert reflect the differences in the themes or their sources, the fact of *hommage à* Gluck, or the nearly eighteen-month span of "composition" for the Gluck set.[62]

Discussions of variation form generally addressed three issues, some more directly and lengthily than others:

1. The nature of the resemblance between theme and variations, clearly the central issue concerning the relationship between the constant and changing elements of the theme. This relationship changed considerably during the period.
2. The character of the theme and the variations. This issue is connected by many writers with the next item:
3. The type of melodic figuration, and, occasionally, the texture, in individual variations.

Because the term "variation" connoted both the technique, often improvised, and the form, many eighteenth-century writings include commentary on both. Variation form itself, even when its structural component was not clearly isolated, was to a considerable degree defined by a relationship between

Fortepianist," in *Perspectives on Mozart Performance,* ed. R. Larry Todd and Peter Williams (Cambridge, 1991), pp. 27–54.

59. Letter of 13 June 1781, Anderson no. 410, p. 742.

60. Recollection of Jan Nepomuk Stepánek, quoted in Georg Nikolaus von Nissen, *Biographie W. A. Mozarts* (Leipzig, 1828), p. 517, cited and trans. in Komlós, "Mozart and Clementi," p. 4.

61. Komlós, "Mozart the Fortepianist," pp. 35–38.

62. This issue will be taken up again in Chapter 7.

constant and changing elements. To illustrate the change in that relationship over the period that spanned the careers of Haydn and Beethoven, several writers will be adduced here, although not in chronological order.

The principal types of variation, and the issues surrounding them, were set out by J. A. P. Schulz in 1774, in his article entitled "Veränderung; Variationen" for Sulzer's *Allgemeine Theorie der schönen Künste:*

> To a series of harmonies or chords, one can set several melodies, all of which are correct according to the rules of harmonic setting. Therefore, when a melody is repeated by singers or instrumentalists, they can sing or play many things completely differently the second time from the first time, without violating the rules of composition. Experienced composers, however, sometimes construct on one kind of harmony several melodies that retain the character of the first to a greater or lesser degree. For both cases, one uses the word *Variation,* which we [prefer to] express as *Veränderungen* [variations, alterations].[63]

He then employed his preferred synonym, *Veränderungen,* throughout the rest of the article.

Schulz's two cases oppose improvised variation and composed variation. In the first case, the given melody may be greatly modified in many of its details. In composing variations, on the other hand, composers write more than one melody, and these melodies may resemble the first or be quite different from it. Here, within Schulz's second case, we have in a nutshell the distinction between the two types of melodic treatment most favored by eighteenth-century composers: the first retains both the harmony and melodic outline of the theme, while in the second only the theme's harmony remains constant. Since no pithy eighteenth-century terms are available, we may term the first type *melodic-outline* variation and the second *constant-harmony* variation. Both terms are catchalls, to some extent, and both may include highly figured as well as unfigured variations, countermelodies, and so on.

In his use of the term "character" to mean "essential melodic characteristics" (as in "retain the character of the first"), Schulz revealed a typical eighteenth-century approach. Writers of this period, propounding the familiar ideal of creating variety while maintaining unity, identified the character changes resulting from melodic manipulations as a central element in the composition of variations, and showed that the style of figuration is an important determinant of character. Rousseau, for example, asserted that each variation should have a different character to keep up the interest of the listener, while Daube maintained that brilliant figuration should be broken up with gentler material.[64]

63. Johann Abraham Peter Schulz, "Veränderungen; Variationen," in Johann Georg Sulzer, *Allgemeine Theorie der schönen Künste,* cited from the 2nd improved ed., 1778–1779), II, p. 361. The definition remained the same in the "new, expanded 2nd ed." of 1792–1799 (facs. ed. Hildesheim, 1970), IV, pp. 636–638; for German, see Appendix B.

64. Jean-Jacques Rousseau, *Dictionnaire de Musique* (Paris, 1768), s.v. "Variation": "Il faut que le caractère de chaque *variation* soit marqué par des différences qui soutiennent l'attention et préviennent l'ennui"; Daube, *Der musikalische Dilettant,* p. 144: "Das Rauschende soll jederzeit mit etwas zartlichen, Singenden unterbrochen seyn."

Further evidence is provided by Riepel's distinctions among types of figurations appropriate in different contexts: his main figures, although not mentioned in connection with variation form, are the *Singer* (singing longer notes), *Springer* (leaping intervals), *Läuffer* (running figuration), *Schwärmer* (repeated notes), and *Rauscher* (any "noisy" or active figurations).[65] Daube later simplified this to three melodic types, *Singbar, Rauschend* or *Brillant,* and *Vermischt.*[66] And Koch advised composers to "alternate the variations with regard to their individual character, that is, brilliant or enthusiastic variations must not follow one another immediately, but rather between two or more brilliant ones . . . insert one of gentler character."[67]

In the nineteenth century, A. B. Marx introduced the term "character variation" to refer to a variation that changes the form of the theme, sometimes into a character piece (that is, a march or dance) but also into a rondo, sonata form, or fugue. He distinguished this type from "formal variations," which vary melody, modulation, accompaniment, mode, rhythm, and form.[68] Later writers apparently misunderstood his distinction, and downplayed or denied the notion that melodic-outline variations—principally those written between Bach and Beethoven—could fully change the character of the theme.[69] Pertinent here is Schoenberg's comment: "A distinction is often made between formal variations and character variations. But there is no reason to suppose that a variation can be so formal as not to possess character."[70] Thus, to the eighteenth-century mind, changing character did not simply mean incorporating "characteristic" variations like the "alla marcia," "siciliana," or "Ouverture" variations, although these types are also found in works by composers between Bach and Beethoven. The variations by Forkel on "God Save the King" (Leipzig, 1791), so roundly criticized by Vogler a few years later, contain all of these, as well as an "Alla Polacca"; Vogler's own variations on "Willem van Nassau" (c. 1789) include a "Minuetto grazioso," "Gigue," "Fanfare," and "Marche."[71] Beethoven as the originator of the "character variation" is a notion that must be laid to rest; the term "characteristic variation," on the other hand, is appropriate to many pieces of the era.[72]

65. Riepel, *Tactordnung* and *Tonordnung,* passim. He also showed how pieces could be expanded through the judicious use of *Rauscher (Tonordnung,* pp. 97–100, and passim).

66. Daube, *Anleitung zur Erfindung der Melodie,* p. 10.

67. Koch, *Musikalisches Lexikon,* s.v. "Variazionen, Variazioni."

68. Adolf Bernhard Marx, *Die Lehre von der musikalischen Composition,* 4 vols. [Leipzig, 1837–1847], III, 2nd. ed. [1848], pp. 59–93. The character variation thus represents an *Umwandlung,* or transformation, of the theme.

69. An influential modern account with this view is Robert U. Nelson, *The Technique of Variation* (Berkeley and Los Angeles, 1948), pp. 103–104.

70. Arnold Schoenberg, *Fundamentals of Musical Composition,* ed. Gerald Strang (New York, 1967), p. 172.

71. The latter example is given in Reijen, *Vergleichende Studien,* p. 45. Reijen also discusses issues of character on pp. 19–22.

72. Steps toward abandoning this terminology have already been taken. See the valuable study by András Batta and Sandor Kovács, "Typbildung und Grossform in Beethovens frühen Klaviervariationen," *SM* 20 (1978), 125–156.

Schulz also offered a rank-ordered list of variation types, in which he placed the constant-harmony type above the melodic-outline, especially in a particular subtype of the former, the *contrapuntal* variation.[73] Lowest are the *Doubles* of suite movements (Couperin and Bach are cited), then come the sonatas with varied reprises (C. P. E. Bach), and finally, as "incontestably the highest type," are contrapuntal variations with imitation and canons, as in Bach's Goldberg and "Vom Himmel hoch" variations. Included here also are sets of fugues by Bach *(Art of Fugue)* and d'Anglebert. Contrapuntal variations appeared as individual numbers in sets by Haydn and Mozart, became more prominent in Haydn's works in the 1790s, then emerged more forcefully with Beethoven's Opus 35. It is possible that Schulz's critical assessment of variation types influenced Beethoven, who is now known to have studied at least one article from Sulzer's encyclopedia during the period in which both Opus 35 and the *Eroica* were composed.[74] Schulz did not use the term *Double,* perhaps reflecting the decline of the suite, but his low assessment of such variations has precedents in Mattheson (1739):

> The Sarabande: In playing on the clavier and on the lute, one lowers oneself in this category of melody and takes more liberties, indeed even makes doublings or arpeggios on it, which are generally known as variations, but by the French, *Doubles* . . . Aria, with and without doublings, which are called *Partitas* in Italian, *Doubles* in French . . . is generally a short, singable, simple melody in two parts, that for the most part should be so simply drawn that one may decorate, adorn, and vary it in countless ways, so that, along with the retention of its basic motion, one's own virtuosity can be seen . . . In Froberger's time, perhaps 70 to 80 years ago, this partita-spirit was so abused, that not only at least a half-dozen variations had to be performed on special little arias or ariettas, e.g. on a so-called little *Lantürlü* song; but also the allemandes, courantes, etc. were so infected with it and did not escape without fractures, crooked leaps, and many-tailed notes.[75]

Another subtype of constant-harmony variation, described earlier in the century, may be termed *constant-bass* variation. In his *Critischer Musicus* of 1740, Scheibe discussed variations in the minuet finale of a solo sonata, whose "bass notes remain unvaried through all the variations of the melody. Thus, the variations affect only the upper voice, and must always show the power of the instrument and new and ingenious ideas."[76] Over the unchanging bass, then a

73. Schulz, "Veränderungen; Variationen," p. 637.
74. Richard A. Kramer has shown that Beethoven read Schulz's article on recitative for his studies with Salieri; see "Beethoven and Carl Heinrich Graun," in *Beethoven Studies* [I], ed. Alan Tyson (New York, 1973), pp. 18–44.
75. Mattheson, *Der vollkommene Capellmeister,* pp. 230–232; Harriss, pp. 461–464.
76. Johann Adolph Scheibe, *Critischer Musicus,* new enl. ed. (Leipzig, 1745; facs. Hildesheim, 1970), p. 682: "Wenn es ein Menuet mit Veränderungen sey: so müssen die Baßnoten bey allen Veränderungen der Melodie durchaus unverändert bleiben. Die veränderungen betreffen also nur der Oberstimme, und müssen allemal die Stärke des Instrumentes und neu und sinnreiche Gedanken beweisen." Kurt von Fischer refers to this type as *Generalbassvariation* in "Zur Theorie der Variation," passim.

series of possibly unrelated melodies is played. In mid-century Vienna, chamber compositions even without explicit basso continuo featured minuet finales with constant-bass variations, as in works by Dittersdorf, Hofmann, Vanhal, and Haydn.[77] The designation also describes nearly all the rest of Haydn's early variation movements and many other movements by his contemporaries. Closer to Scheibe's circle were the constant-bass variation movements by C. P. E. Bach, most written for flute and continuo. This subtype seems to have flourished only until about 1770.

As constant-bass and contrapuntal variations fell by the wayside, the melodic-outline variation became the preferred type of constant-harmony variation. This change is attested by composition treatises from the 1770s and 1780s, particularly those by Daube and Christmann.[78] Although these writers stressed the harmonic underpinnings of the form—Daube's teaching used thoroughbass, while Christmann incorporated part of Schulz's definition—their examples confirmed that, in addition to the harmony, the notes of the theme's melody were present during the elaborations. Christmann even explicitly called the simple melody the theme, a term which in the context of variations was previously used only in definitions of chaconne.

Christmann identified "theme" with the "melody" of the first "piece," yet Schulz's definition—"several melodies set to a series of harmonies without violating the rules of composition or varying the bass"—apparently suggested to him no contradiction. His example of a "Menuetto con Variazioni" showed that melodic-outline techniques carried the day. He even varied the bass, confirming that "bass" in his definition referred to the harmonic progression, not to the literal bass line. Daube's *Dilettant,* the only important composition treatise published in Vienna in this period, showed how to vary the basic chords in any key (I, II$_5^6$, V) using *ars combinatoria.* When one has mastered the figuration of basic chords and melodic intervals, different figures may then be combined in variations on a short piece like a Menuet or Aria, resulting in "now singing, now brilliant, running, leaping variations." An Andante with seven variations illustrates this with a different figure predominating in each one; the upper lines conform closely to the Andante, while the bass is varied only in the final variation (Example 3.4).

In his *Verbesserung der Forkel'schen Veränderungen über "God Save the King,"* a small, polemical treatise published in 1793, Abbé Vogler devoted himself to upbraiding Forkel for the inadequacies of his variations on "God Save the King." Several rather valuable observations about the nature of variation and about Haydn and Mozart appear in this unpromising venue; indeed, what Vogler has to say surpasses many other period writings in astuteness and sensitiv-

---

77. Manuscript copies of these works write out the bass part only once, and then indicate how many times it is to be repeated. See Example 5.5.

78. Daube, *Der musikalische Dilettant;* Johann Friedrich Christmann, *Elementarbuch der Tonkunst* (Speyer, 1782), p. 151, and *Praktische Beyträge zum Elementarbuch der Tonkunst* (1782), no. 51 (Minuet with variations).

Example 3.4. Johann Friedrich Daube, Andante and Var. 7.

ity. He began with the sweeping statement cited in Chapter 2 that variations are a type of musical rhetoric, and that the variation composer might devise new figures *(Spielarten, Wendungen, Figuren)*, but each had to be continued throughout an entire variation.[79]

Vogler's comments about Haydn and Mozart captured the principal features of their variations that set them apart from their contemporaries:

> The first man who taught us variations in general, who distributed them to all instruments, who, added to the merit of being great in phraseology, can invent songs and themes himself, is the inimitable Haydn. He, a true Phoebus, whose labor needed no external warmth, whose works already shine forth enough without being illuminated by the borrowed glimmer of a popular theme, showed us in symphonies how we should vary. Hindered by no preference, restricted by no shortsightedness, he was equally beneficent to all instruments. Since he knew very well the merit and effect of all, thus he assigned each its vantage point from which to shine, without eclipsing anyone.
>
> His student Pleyel imitated this great spirit on a small scale, that is, successfully in quartets; even his elegant keyboard variations were applauded . . .
>
> [Mozart:] This powerhouse [*Kraftmann*], inexhaustible in expression, universal in character, full of pathos in the Adagio, powerfully stirring in the Allegro, who (I almost dare say) extravagantly endowed so many themes with variations, showed in all these spiritual creations how one could combine the unity of the subject-matter to be arranged and carried through with the diversity of phrases. [He] showed how each variation must alternate in character [and be] individual in figure, instead of [the practice of] H. F. [Herr Forkel, who] never strongly sustains the first measure, introduces not a single unusual figure, and in some variations anxiously has recourse to three or more figures.[80]

79. In some respects, these figures resemble Schoenberg's "motive of the variation" *(Fundamentals of Musical Composition*, pp. 169–172).

80. Vogler, *Verbesserung*, pp. 8–10; for German, see Appendix B.

These comments prepare Vogler's attack on Forkel for failing to understand idiomatic writing—his keyboard variations would sometimes sound better on guitar or mandolin—and for inappropriately changing figuration within a variation; both of these were areas in which Haydn and Mozart were considered exemplary. Not surprisingly, Vogler thought most successful the three variations by Forkel that maintained a particular rhythmic pattern throughout: the sixteenth (syncopated motive), seventeenth (a "Marcia" with dotted rhythm), and nineteenth (a "Siciliana" with swaying rhythm). Many of Vogler's quibbles are minor, but some are perfectly justified, especially concerning the inadequate "Fugetta" (no. 14), to which Vogler took exception from the spelling of its title to the clumsy counterpoint.

Forkel's twenty-four variations are indeed undistinguished, but Vogler's criticisms sometimes seem obtuse. Citing the measures which departed from the melody notes of the theme, he claimed that Forkel must have "forgotten his theme" or "forgotten that he was writing variations." He made the bizarre suggestion that one should be able to sing the theme along with any variation. And his objection to Forkel's imaginative recasting of "God Save the King" in minor—precisely the same relative-minor reharmonization which Beethoven usually receives credit for inventing in his Opus 35, var. 6—is narrow-minded. Although Vogler's little work has its problems, it offered nonetheless some revealing comments about the form from a leading theorist of the period. The assertion that variations are a type of rhetoric has already been shown to be especially fruitful.

By 1790, variation theory implied that every constructive thematic element— the principal notes of the melody, the harmonic scheme, and, by association, the period structure—is fixed. Moreover, the type of variation form described was invariably *strophic,* based on repetitions of a given structure; although this term was not used by eighteenth-century writers, Walther's definition of *Double* makes it appropriate: "the second verse of an air, varied."[81] But new directions opened when Vogler invoked a rhetorical analogy and when Koch, in the same year, described new formal designs with which the variation was associated. In the third volume of his monumental *Versuch einer Anleitung zur Composition* (1793),[82] Koch offered different options for variations depending on their context. His first definition is of the type of short piece used in "das sogenannte Thema zu Variationen," a short piece of no particular character (that is, not a dance piece): "The so-called theme for variations . . . requires a somewhat simple but flowing melody, capable of many variations, which is at the same time so constituted that it allows sufficient, unforced changes of harmony. In the variations themselves, the main melody should always be recog-

81. See n. 24.
82. See Chapter 1, n. 66. On the significance of Koch's *Versuch,* see the Introduction to Nancy K. Baker's translation, *Introductory Essay,* pp. xi–xxii.

nizable, though an exception is often made in these pieces, especially when they are intended to show skill on the instrument for which they are composed."[83]

The rest of Koch's comments in the *Versuch* on variation form describe movements in larger works. The longest explanation concerns the symphony, the genre which is in any case central to Koch's descriptions of form. Variations may occur in the slow movement of a symphony, on a "short Andante or Adagio, which usually comprises two parts, . . . and which often has a coda [*Anhang*] which recurs between each variation like a ritornello. The variations of the main melody are played either by the first violin alone, or by the other voices in alternation."[84] More interesting is Koch's assertion that Haydn was the first to write variations in the slow movements of symphonies.[85] For the last Allegro of a symphony, Koch wrote, "variations on a characteristic dance melody or on a short Allegro . . . are usually mixed with short interpolated episodes in closely related keys, after the fashion of the rondo."[86] This combination of variation and rondo has been called "variation rondo," perhaps inappropriately.[87] Modern writers often consider this type of piece to be rondo form, to which variation technique is incidentally applied.[88] Koch's order of presentation suggests the opposite view: the amalgamated form is introduced as a type of variation finale, not of rondo finale.[89] In this book I will maintain a distinction between "rondo-variation," as here described by Koch to be a variation movement with *Zwischenperioden,* and "variation-rondo," as a rondo with incidental varying—primarily that involving changes in the accompaniment and the occasional melodic embellishment—in the refrains. Haydn wrote "true" rondo-variations much more often than did Mozart or Beethoven.

Koch's final formulation, in his *Musikalisches Lexikon* (1802), sums up most of his earlier comments:

Variazionen, Variazioni . . . multiple immediate repetitions of a short piece [*Tonstück*], in which the melody each time is varied through different methods of sub-

83. Koch, *Versuch,* III, p. 52; *Introductory Essay,* p. 83.

84. Ibid., pp. 313–314; *Introductory Essay,* p. 202.

85. Ibid., p. 314: "Beyspiele dieser Form findet man in sehr vielen Sinfonien von Haydn, der sich nicht allein im Andantesatz dieser Form zuerst bedienet, sondern auch vorzügliche Meisterstücke in derselben geliefert hat."

86. Ibid., p. 314: "zuweilen enthält es auch Veränderungen über einen characteristische Tanzmelodie, oder über einen kurzen Allegrosatz; diese Veränderungen aber werden gewöhnlich mit kurzen Zwischenperioden in nahe verwandten Tonarten, nach Art des Rondo vermischt."

87. See Witold Chrzanowski, *Das instrumentale Rondeau und die Rondoform im 18. Jahrhundert* (Leipzig, 1911), p. 60; H. C. Robbins Landon, *The Symphonies of Joseph Haydn* (London, 1955), p. 323; Sonja Gerlach, "Die chronologische Ordnung von Haydns Sinfonien zwischen 1774 und 1782," *HSt* 2 (1969–70), 60–62.

88. See Malcolm Cole, "The Vogue of the Instrumental Rondo in the Late Eighteenth Century," *JAMS* 22 (1969), 444; idem, "The Rondo-Finale," 252.

89. On the other hand, Kollmann's description of "rondos with variations of the subject," comparing them to C. P. E. Bach's sonatas with varied reprises, suggests a different viewpoint; see n. 42.

dividing its main notes, and the passing and neighbor notes connected therewith, yet without completely mitigating the similarity with the main melody. One can use such variations as independent pieces for private enjoyment, or in connection with other movements in larger works, as for example in sonatas, concertos, and symphonies. So that such variations may have a good effect, one must (1) choose a cantabile melody . . . which is already interesting in and of itself and which . . . easily impresses itself upon the memory, (2) alternate the variations with regard to their individual character . . . , and (3) retain the similarity with the main melody in each variation, so that the attention of the listener is thereby fixed; for as soon as the similarity ends, so does the interest of the variations, and they give the impression of a group of arbitrarily related pieces [*Sätze*] which have nothing in common with each other, and for whose existence and ordering [*Daseyn und Folge*] one can imagine no basis.[90]

Invoking social and generic context, structural principle, thematic essence, and character, Koch's definition goes beyond any previous published assessment of variation form. And his last sentence opens a new area in the evaluation of how the listener imaginatively participates in the relationship among variations and their ordering.

Anton Reicha occupies a unique place among the theorists examined for this study because he was a friend of both Haydn and Beethoven. While he particularly revered the former, his relationship with the latter was apparently somewhat ambivalent.[91] In both his *Traité de Melodie* (Paris, 1814) and his *Traité de haute composition musicale* (Paris, 1824–1826), he suggested that Haydn's Andantes be used as a model for variation writing. The earlier treatise is more conservative, claiming right at the outset that the discussion will not be concerned with "the modern manner of varying, where the harmony is more than the melody and where one can almost never recognize the object that one varies" (p. 87), and stating that highly figured variations using several different techniques for varying the melody should be used only in pieces with large numbers of variations because they "disfigure" the theme so much (p. 88).

In Reicha's later treatise, on the other hand, melody, chords, and accompaniment patterns were all considered variable elements. Reicha's list of the possible permutations of these elements reveals that, at times, all of them may be changed within a single variation:

1. Embroidering or decorating a motif without tampering with its harmony;
2. Changing the accompaniment figuration without tampering with the chords or melody;

90. Koch, *Musikalisches Lexikon,* s.v. "Variazionen, Variazioni"; for German, see Appendix B.
91. Stefan Kunze describes Reicha's uneasy relationship to the classical masters of whom he was both a contemporary and a reverent follower; see "Anton Reichas 'Entwurf einer phrasirten Fuge.' Zum Kompositionsbegriff im frühen 19. Jahrhundert," *AfMw* 25 (1968), 289–307. John A. Rice suggests that Reicha's and Beethoven's falling-out in Vienna stemmed from a rivalry caused by too many similarities, rather than too many differences; "Anton Reicha, Beethoven, and the *Sinfonia Eroica*," paper delivered at the Annual Meeting of the American Musicological Society in Philadelphia, October 1984.

3. Changing only the chords;
4. Changing simultaneously chords and accompaniment figuration without tampering with the melody;
5. Varying the motif and the accompaniment figuration without changing the chords;
6. Varying at the same time the melody, accompaniment figuration, and chords.[92]

That Reicha's conception of the theme was primarily melodic is revealed by his equation of melody and motif in the fifth item. The following chart puts his list of changeable elements in tabular form:

1.	Melody	—	—
2.	—	Accompaniment	—
3.	—	—	Harmony
4.	—	Accompaniment	Harmony
5.	Melody	Accompaniment	—
6.	Melody	Accompaniment	Harmony

Reicha omitted only the possibility of varying melody and harmony while retaining the accompaniment, an infrequently used device. Key or mode was also allowed to change. This table bears some resemblance to the permutations applied to melodic notes in various eighteenth-century discussions of *ars combinatoria,* but entire musical elements themselves (such as melody, harmony, rhythm) were not subject to permutation, at least not before Kollmann in *An Essay on Musical Harmony* (1796). Kollmann's three variation types—those which vary the harmony and melody of the theme, those in which different harmonies are put to the same melody, and those in which different melodies are put to the same harmony—depend upon an important concept of melodic difference: "Two or more melodies, which depend on the same essential notes, and proceed in the same motion, are one and the same melody, though they be different in simplicity and figuration, and accompanied by different harmonies. But two or more melodies, which do not depend on the same essential notes, or not proceed in the same motion, though they be founded on the same harmony, and even much resemble each other, are different melodies."[93] All three types, "commonly intermixed" within a single set, may be found in works of Bach, Handel, Corelli, Haydn, Mozart, Forkel, and Fasch (p. 270). This eclectic list oddly places the strikingly different stylistic results of individual composers' "intermixtures" of variation techniques on the same level.

Reicha's accompanying example of a set of variations for string quartet was rather unadventurous, as befitted his pedagogic purpose, less interesting than the Andante variations by Haydn on which his discussion was ostensibly based, and far less innovative than the set of fifty-seven variations for piano he had published earlier as *L'Art de Varier,* Op. 57 (Leipzig, c. 1803–4).[94] Perhaps

92. Reicha, *Traité de haute composition musicale,* II, p. 304.
93. Kollmann, *Essay on Musical Harmony,* p. 268.
94. Reicha's Op. 57 received a scathing review in the *AMZ* 10 (1807–1808), cols. 141–142.

as one of the elder statesmen of the Paris Conservatoire, he felt it incumbent upon him to present a noncontroversial recipe rather than the daring flights of fancy of his youth (Example 3.5). Nonetheless, his expanded list of variable elements shows a redefinition of the limits of variation form. And when his list is examined in conjunction with his string quartet example, with his Opus 57, and with the example of, say, Beethoven's Diabelli Variations, it becomes evident that each permutation must have both a narrower and a broader application. A variation which changes melody, accompaniment, and harmony, for instance, may stray no farther from the theme than a melodic-outline *minore* variation, but on the other hand may replace the original thematic elements with a more remotely related or even a new melody, accompaniment, and harmony.

Reicha's other comments expanded structural as well as technical possibilities. In giving an overall plan for a set of variations on a 16-bar "motif" with two reprises, he included a central episode of 24 to 30 bars "to rest the motif . . . change the key . . . modulate . . . [and] introduce new ideas," and, "in place of a sixth variation, a type of coda, in which one turns the theme to account, by partly developing it a little and by passing through a few keys that have not yet been heard" (p. 304). The central episode thus has a quite different function from the rondo-like episodes mentioned by Koch. Since central episodes are not readily apparent in variations by Haydn and Mozart, unless one includes the middle section of Haydn's ternary (ABA) variation movements, Reicha may have been referring to *minore* variations with a much-changed melody, or simply to something he found desirable that his contemporaries did not yet put into practice. Reicha was also the only writer of this period to discuss the alternating variations on two themes that were practically Haydn's trademark. He illustrated the latter form, however, with a plan never used by Haydn: four variations on each theme, followed by partial development and coda, to an ending invariably in major.

Theoretical and critical discussions of variation form thus show two trends: first, toward greater limitations, in fixing harmony and melody, and then toward increased possibilities, in freeing harmony, melody, and large-scale structural organization. The latter development embodied internal, technical modifications, in fewer constant and more variable elements, as well as external, structural changes, in the combination of variations and episodes, or variations on two themes. By the end of the eighteenth century, theorists routinely modeled their discussions of variation on well-known composers, instead of simply listing composers whose works they admired. And, beginning with Schumann and Marx, the spiritual and poetic component of variations began to hold sway in published descriptions and criticisms.[95] To the period after Reicha, then, belonged the canonization of Beethoven by Marx and the concomitant denigration of "mechanical" Classical models. In the realm of variation, the prolifera-

95. See my article "Brahms and the Variation Canon," *19CM* 14 (1990), 132–153.

Example 3.5.   Anton Reicha, string-quartet variations.

tion of superficial salon variations, already under way in the 1790s with Steibelt and Gelinek, expanded further with Herz, Hunten, and Kalkbrenner.

Examination of publishers' catalogues, extant prints and manuscript copies, and sundry work-lists confirms the veritable explosion of independent sets of variations in the 1790s after the already significant increase in the 1780s. Of the twenty-one variation sets published by Artaria in the 1780s—its first decade of publication—fully nine, or more than 40 percent, were by Mozart; next were Haydn and Vanhal, tied at three each. In the sixty-six published during the 1790s, the number of otherwise distinguished composers decreased relative to the total; thus, even though another nine sets by Mozart were published, this accounted for only 15 percent, and the Abbé Gelinek surpassed him with ten sets. André, who had published hardly any variations during the 1770s, increased the number during the 1780s and especially after 1787. And the vast majority of these works were based on vocal models, mostly operatic tunes but also folk songs (a variety from the Tyrol spawned many particularly dull works), reflecting the expansion of theatrical life in both city and suburban venues, as well as the increase in the number of concerts.[96] While other musical centers had had vogues for certain kinds of variations in previous decades—the variations on "national airs" in the British Isles during the 1760s and 1770s, for example, or the extravagant number of virtuosic violin variations in Paris from the 1740s to the 1760s[97]—it was the simultaneous expansion of performance, publishing, and the home music market that debased the currency. Even criticism of published variations rarely exceeded platitudes; especially common was invoking the term "fantasy" to imply that the piece showed imaginative figurations. An article of the 1820s surveyed the depressing situation, and longed for the days of the sonata:

> "Sonate, que me veux-tu" exclaimed Fontenelle, and we are tempted to bestow a similar apostrophe upon the fantasias and variations by which the reign of the sonata has been succeeded. Augmenting in number every day, not a theme is suffered to escape which offers the slightest appearance of a melody; it is seized upon with eagerness by composers of every description, and not an air from "*God Save the King*" down to the newest French quadrille can now aspire to be unvaried . . . From what has this *furor mutandi* arisen? Or may it not be fairly traced to those musicians of the third and fourth classes in which London abounds? people who find it much easier to produce variations than compose a sonata, and whose efforts are highly acceptable to such amateurs as desire to be *showy*, without much expense of either time or trouble.[98]

96. See the concert calendar in Mary Sue Morrow, *Concert Life in Haydn's Vienna, 1760–1810* (New York, 1988).

97. La Borde claimed that Jean-Pierre Guigon (1702–1774) began the variation vogue single-handedly; Jean-Benjamin de La Borde, *Essai sur la musique ancienne et moderne*, 4 vols. (Paris, 1780), III, p. 353, cited in Lionel de La Laurencie, *L'École Française de Violon de Lully à Viotti*, 3 vols. (Paris, 1922–1924), II, p. 74. See also Rousseau, *Dictionnaire*, s.v. "Variations."

98. *The Monthly Magazine of Music*, 1 January 1823, quoted in Arthur Loesser, *Men, Women, and Pianos: A Social History* (New York, 1954), p. 290.

Three principal topics, treated broadly if not deeply in a number of writings on variation in the eighteenth century, emerge from this chapter: the nature of the theme and its resonance in the variations, characteristics of melodic figuration, and the ordering of a repetitive structure. Taken together with the rhetorical models suggested in the previous chapter, they begin to define a classical variation aesthetic. Before examining the works themselves, it will be useful to probe further into eighteenth-century theory to evaluate the descriptions of formal processes typical of variations with respect to those typical of other classical forms, particularly sonata form, which has long been assigned a supreme value. The placement of variations in the hierarchy of size and value granted to individual members of multi-movement works has been compromised by an implication in modern writings that might be stated as a paraphrase of Pater: all forms aspire to the condition of sonata form. The sonata aesthetic and the variation aesthetic ought to be compared in light of their eighteenth-century conceptions. It is to this topic that I now turn.

CHAPTER FOUR

The Variation in the Universe of Classical Musical Forms

Variation form, often counted as part of the basic equipment of a composer, occupied a particular place in the spectrum of classical musical structures. Composition manuals of the later eighteenth century enable us to locate it rather precisely in a hierarchy ranging from simple dances to complicated sonata forms, by stressing the fundamental similarities among musical forms rather than their more obvious external differences. These manuals focused first on details of the melodic and harmonic construction of phrases and then on their combination and expansion. That small musical segments could be expanded into larger segments linked the formal designs of small pieces, such as minuets, to large pieces, such as symphony Allegros. Indeed, Riepel and Koch both considered the minuet to be the model for larger compositions.[1] As Riepel explained at the outset of his first chapter, "a Minuet, according to its realization [*Ausführung*], is no different from a concerto, an aria, or a symphony . . . thus, we wish to begin therewith, [with the] very small and trifling, simply in order to obtain out of it something bigger and more praiseworthy."[2] And Koch, after enumerating and analyzing three types of small pieces, concludes that "these forms are, together, models in miniature of the larger compositions."[3] This method of composition was an important part of pedagogical

1. The theorists' predilection for minuets and other dance pieces has often been noted. See Heinrich Besseler, "Singstil und Instrumentalstil in der europäischen Musik," in *Kongressbericht Bamberg 1953* (Kassel and Basel, 1954), pp. 223–240; Leonard Ratner, "Eighteenth-Century Theories of Musical Period Structure," *MQ* 42 (1956), 443–444, 446–447; Wolfram Steinbeck, *Das Menuett in der Instrumentalmusik Joseph Haydns* (Munich, 1973), pp. 7–10; Nancy K. Baker, "From Teil to Tonstück: The Significance of the *Versuch einer Anleitung zur Composition* of Heinrich Christoph Koch" (Ph.D. diss., Yale University, 1975), pp. 222–223; Wolfgang Budday, *Grundlagen musikalischer Formen der Wiener Klassik: An Hand der zeitgenössischen Theorie von Joseph Riepel und Heinrich Christoph Koch dargestellt an Menuetten und Sonatensätzen (1750–1790)* (Kassel, 1983).

2. Riepel, *Tactordnung*, p. 1.

3. Koch, *Versuch*, III, p. 129. Koch greatly admired Riepel's earlier treatise, and wrote: "Riepel was the first (and is also the only theorist yet known to me) who has treated these matters [lengths of melodic sections, their cadences] in detail . . . [and] shed the first rays of light over these matters which, at that time were, theoretically speaking, still entirely hidden in darkness." *Versuch*, II (1787), p. 11, cited and translated in Baker, "Heinrich Koch and the Theory of Melody," *JMT* 20 (1976), 4.

techniques employed by composers as well; instruction that moved from smaller to larger structures, also beginning with the minuet, characterized Thomas Attwood's studies with Mozart.[4]

The relationship between phrase and form, alluded to by Riepel and systematically worked out by Koch, has several consequences. In the first place, both its terminology and its hierarchical nature provide further evidence for the influence of rhetorical modes of thought on eighteenth-century composition; indeed, Koch's topics and procedures appear to derive not just from the many handbooks of rhetoric published between the 1720s and the 1760s but even more specifically from the *Anfangs-Gründe der Teutschen Oratorie* of Daniel Peucer, published in Dresden, which went through four editions between 1736 and 1765.[5] Second, Koch's model for analyzing the expansions of small pieces is directly applicable to Haydn's own expansions of the themes of two variation movements, one from the earlier and one from the later stages of his career: the theme of a divertimento finale (Hob. II:11) became a symphony Andante (No. 14/ii, written before 1764), and one of the two themes of a piano trio (Hob. XV:19/i, 1794) was expanded as the final Presto variation in the movement. Moreover, Koch's model, in disclosing the construction of smaller forms, especially variation, and larger ones, especially sonata form, will be useful in determining the precise relationship between them.[6] Finally, it will also enable us to evaluate claims that variations later acquired elements of sonata form. That Haydn's sonata forms also reveal elements of variation will suggest that the variation principle, however differently realized in a small and an expanded form, was central to Haydn and is essential to an understanding of Haydn's instrumental music.

Expansion Techniques

Koch's scheme of musical organization consists, in effect, of three levels of structure (see Table 4.1). Applying one or more compositional techniques at each level results in the next higher level.[7] He began with the phrase *(Absatz* or *Satz)*, outlining its possible constructions, including its subdivision, the incise *(Einschnitt)*.[8] Two or more phrases combine to form a period *(Periode)*, the intermediate level.[9] And combining this period with other periods creates the

4. See Daniel Heartz, "Thomas Attwood's Lessons in Composition with Mozart," *PRMA* 100 (1974), 175–183.

5. See Nicole Schwindt-Gross, *Drama und Diskurs: Zur Beziehung zwischen Satztechnik und motivischem Prozess in die Streichquartetten Haydns und Mozarts* (Laaber, 1989), pp. 73–106.

6. Parts of this argument appeared in my article "Small and Expanded Forms."

7. I am indebted to Harold S. Powers for this tri-level view of Koch's scheme.

8. Koch, *Versuch*, II, pp. 362–464; Baker, *Introductory Essay*, pp. 1–59. Riepel used similar terminology in his discussion of phrases; for a clear-eyed recent assessment of Riepel's "muddled achievement" in this area, see Justin London, "Riepel and *Absatz*: Poetic and Prosaic Aspects of Phrase Structure in 18th-Century Theory," *JM* 8 (1990), 505–519.

9. Koch, *Versuch*, III, pp. 3–12; Baker, *Introductory Essay*, pp. 63–66. Koch's entire third volume is the final section on the mechanical rules of melody, "On the connection of melodic segments, or on the construction of periods."

Table 4.1 Koch's Levels of Musical Structure

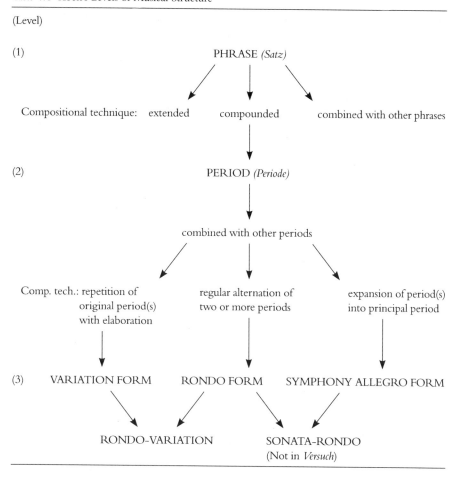

(Level)

(1)   PHRASE *(Satz)*

Compositional technique: extended   compounded   combined with other phrases

(2)   PERIOD *(Periode)*

                                    combined with other periods

Comp. tech.: repetition of   regular alternation of   expansion of period(s)
    original period(s)   two or more periods   into principal period
    with elaboration

(3)   VARIATION FORM   RONDO FORM   SYMPHONY ALLEGRO FORM

            RONDO-VARIATION   SONATA-RONDO
                                           (Not in *Versuch*)

third level, which is a type of form.[10] For example, if the period is combined
with one or two other periods, and the whole arranged into two repeated sec-

10. Koch discussed the nature of musical form earlier in the *Versuch,* in a section on the process
of composition (II, pp. 15–135, not translated by Baker), stating there that the form of a composition results from the number, size, and arrangement of periods, as well as their modulations and
repetitions. Although Riepel had classified phrases according to their endings, and combined them,
he had not named larger levels of structure; the other major theorist of the second half of the
eighteenth century to treat the structure and combination of melodic segments is Johann Philipp
Kirnberger, in *Die Kunst des reinen Satzes in der Musik,* 2 vols. (Berlin and Königsberg, 1771–1779),
II, pp. 137–153; trans. by David Beach and Jürgen Thym, *The Art of Strict Musical Composition*
(New Haven and London, 1982), pp. 403–417. His structural hierarchy is quite similar to Koch's:
phrase *(Einschnitt* or *Rhythmus),* period *(Abschnitt* or *Periode),* and piece *(Tonstück),* a series of peri-
ods ending in the tonic (II, pp. 138–139). His discussion, part of a section on rhythm, defines these
segments with respect to length, cadence, and meter, and draws on examples by Sebastian and
Emanuel Bach. See also Putnam Aldrich, "'Rhythmic Harmony' as Taught by Johann Philipp

tions, a dance form results *(Versuch,* III, pp. 39–50).[11] If the period or group of periods, again usually in two parts, is successively repeated with elaborations in which one may discern the original melody, variation form results (pp. 52, 313–314). If the period is regularly alternated with contrasting periods, rondo form results (pp. 248–262). And if the periods are expanded into principal periods *(Hauptperioden),* "first-movement form" or, more familiarly, "sonata form" results (pp. 231–232).[12]

The first three forms use small periods, variously arranged, and ought to be called "small form," while the fourth differs more fundamentally in that expansion techniques are applied to the second level of structure, and ought to be considered "expanded form." Of course, there is a distinction to be made between a single small form, such as a two-reprise dance, variation theme, or rondo theme, and the composite small form resulting from the series of variations or episodes and refrains. Without forcing a proliferation of categories, I will maintain this distinction between "simple" and "composite" small form.[13] Because the theorists considered simple small forms to be models for the large ones, they began with small-form pieces, structuring phrases and periods harmonically and developing terminology according to the final cadence in each phrase. Yet their compositional instruction always referred principally to melody, and the regularity of short phrases in each section creates a symmetry of design and equality of function that even alternate cadence patterns and modulations cannot dislodge.

From small pieces, the theorists moved on to the expansion of melodic sections, so that the student could compose pieces with larger dimensions. In expansion techniques, Riepel and Koch are nearly identical, but the way they applied these techniques reveals the generational difference between them. Drawing largely on compositional practice before 1750, Riepel arrived at a generally symmetrical expansion, tending to treat each phrase equally. Koch, on the other hand, modeled his method on the practices of the 1760s through 1780s, constructing a proportional expansion, in which the function of a phrase determines the extent to which it will be expanded.[14]

Kirnberger," in *Studies in Eighteenth-Century Music,* ed. Landon, pp. 37–52; Floyd K. Grave, "'Rhythmic Harmony' in Mozart," *MR* 41 (1980), 88–90; Baker, "Heinrich Koch," pp. 8–11.

11. Different ways to combine these periods in the dance forms are illustrated in *Versuch,* III, pp. 57–152.

12. The construction of principal periods is then described in great detail, in "first-movement form" (pp. 304–313, 341–421), in aria (pp. 240–247), and in the concerto (pp. 327–339). I will use the anachronistic but convenient term "sonata form" instead of the more cumbersome "first-movement form."

13. Heartz, for example, notes the course of Attwood's studies with Mozart as progressing "from the simple exercises realizing a figured bass, through the writing of little minuets and other pieces of a periodic nature, species counterpoint, canon, fugue, orchestration, ending finally with more complicated minuets and larger pieces such as theme and variations, rondo, and sonata form"; see "Attwood's Lessons," pp. 175–176.

14. For a list of the composers from whom Koch chose his examples, see Gudrun Henneberg, "Heinrich Christoph Koch's Analysen von Instrumentalwerken Joseph Haydns," *HSt* 4 (1978),

Riepel explained that a piece may be made longer by repetitions *(Wiederholungen)* of all or part of a phrase, through expansion *(Ausdähnung)* by adding new notes and measures, especially to a contrasting harmonic progression, by insertion *(Einschiebsel)* of phrases or smaller units between or within phrases, and by the doubling of cadences *(Verdoppelung der Cadenzen).*[15] The first and last of these include varied repetition, for which the student may draw on the resources of melodic permutations *(Verwechselungskunst, ars combinatoria).*[16] He illuminated three stages in expanding a small form, but instead of simply presenting the smallest version first and expanding it twice in succession, he gave a two-part symphony Allegro, then showed the small form whose melodic and harmonic plan it elaborated, and finally expanded the original Allegro to more than twice its length, commenting on the expansion techniques used.[17] Example 4.1 allows us to compare the first sections of the three versions.

The melodic and harmonic plan in each version demonstrates the nearly symmetrical application of Riepel's expansion techniques. In the first section of the small form *(S),* there are four melodic-harmonic segments, each articulated by a rest, ending on the tonic, half-cadence in the tonic, half-cadence in the dominant, and dominant. The first expansion *(E1),* keeping the same harmonies, expands each of the four segments to exactly twice its original length. And in the second expansion *(E2),* the dimensions of both the opening triadic flourish and the concluding segment in the dominant are doubled again. Yet the modulatory segment in *E2* is as short as the corresponding passage in *S,* with its harmonies reversed so that it ends on the dominant; Riepel even described these measures as an insertion. This curious curtailment of what we would perceive as functionally important material is never explained. The second section of each expansion (not shown in Ex. 4.1) shows vestiges of an older style. For example, the second section of *E1* mirrors the first, creating the type of closed, two-part symphony Allegro described by Scheibe in 1739, and characteristic of Baroque binary form.[18] And that of *E2* is marked by a series of sequences, also typical of the earlier practice. In neither expansion does the open-

105. Haydn is the composer most often cited (seventeen times), with Mozart among the least, although Koch refers approvingly to the quartets Mozart dedicated to Haydn *(Versuch,* III, pp. 326–327).

15. Riepel, *Tonordnung,* pp. 54–63. *Wiederholung* is also discussed in *Tactordnung,* pp. 26–27.

16. Riepel, *Tactordnung,* pp. 12–13, 25–32.

17. Riepel, *Tonordnung,* pp. 64–65, 69–70. In offering a reduction, Riepel took an analytical approach not dissimilar to C. P. E. Bach's harmonic plan and realization of a fantasia (Bach, *Versuch,* II, chap. 7; *Essay,* pp. 442–445) and Vogler's later harmonic reductions (see Grave and Grave, *In Praise of Harmony,* chap. 2).

18. Scheibe, *Critischer Musicus,* pp. 623–624. The relevant passage is translated in Baker, "From *Teil* to *Tonstück*," pp. 255–257; translated somewhat differently and discussed in Immanuel Willheim, "Johann Adolph Scheibe: German Musical Thought in Transition" (Ph.D. diss., University of Illinois, 1963), pp. 200–202; and explained more fully in Fred Ritzel, *Die Entwicklung der "Sonatenform" im musiktheoretischen Schrifttum der 18. and 19. Jahrhunderts* (Wiesbaden, 1968), pp. 49–55.

Example 4.1. Riepel, small and expanded form.

ing theme return in the tonic, although Riepel later shows that such a return is usual, at least in a solo composition.[19]

Koch's three expansion techniques and their formal application more nearly reflect late eighteenth-century compositional practice. As in Riepel's treatise, the first technique is repetition *(Wiederholung)*, the simplest and most often used of the three.[20] In addition to repeating all or part of a phrase, one may also repeat melodic segments with different harmonies or with voice-exchange on the same harmony. Koch's methods of varied repetition were already recounted in Chapter 3.[21] His model is the Andante of Haydn's Symphony 42; although he did not spell this out, the exposition can be seen as a thirty-four-measure expansion of two eight-measure periods (mm. 1–8 and a period made up of mm. 17–20, 25–26, and 33–34); second group material may be seen as entirely an expansion or else based on an additional period (mm. 34–40 and 48–49, expanded to fill mm. 34–69). Example 4.2 shows the exposition of the Andante to the beginning of the second group, and its hypothetical small form. The first period of the small form is simply repeated, with variation, in its entirety, and resembles Bach's varied reprise; the progressively smaller units that are repeated in the second period (four measures varied once, then two measures varied thrice) create an entirely different sort of expansion. Thus, not only repetition but also the size and function of the model are the keys to this compositional and analytical method.

In Koch's second technique, the ends of phrases and of larger sections gain in emphasis and importance.[22] Called the multiplication of closing formulas and cadences *(der Vielfältigung der Absatzformeln und Cadenzen,* apparently an enrichment of Riepel's "doubled cadences"), it suggests the repeat of a final phrase segment *(Glied)*, often with decorative neighbor notes, or the addition of an unrelated appendix *(Anhang)* of several segments. This appendix is itself subject to expansion, through the repetition of its closing segment or the addition of still another closing phrase. It may be seen in the dramatic expansion of the end of Symphony 42's exposition (mm. 34–69).

Finally, Koch's third technique, the expansion of complete melodic sections *(die Erweiterung der vollständigen melodischen Theile)*, outlines three ways to expand from the center of the phrase.[23] The first method, involving internal repetition within a phrase, displaces a phrase segment to another step of the scale *(Versetzung)*; if modulation occurs, this is called a transposition *(Transposition)*; and if the displacement continues, and the segment is repeated several times on successive scale degrees, a sequence *(Progression)* results. Sequence and transposition may be combined. The second method expands a phrase by repeating a previously heard metric formula (a dotted rhythm, for example), or a me-

19. The violin sonata cited in *Tonordnung,* pp. 97–99, has such a return labeled the "third section."

20. Koch, *Versuch,* III, pp. 153–190; *Introductory Essay,* pp. 129–148.

21. See Chapter 3, n. 48.

22. Koch, *Versuch,* III, pp. 191–205; *Introductory Essay,* pp. 148–154.

23. Koch, *Versuch,* III, pp. 205–230; *Introductory Essay,* pp. 154–165.

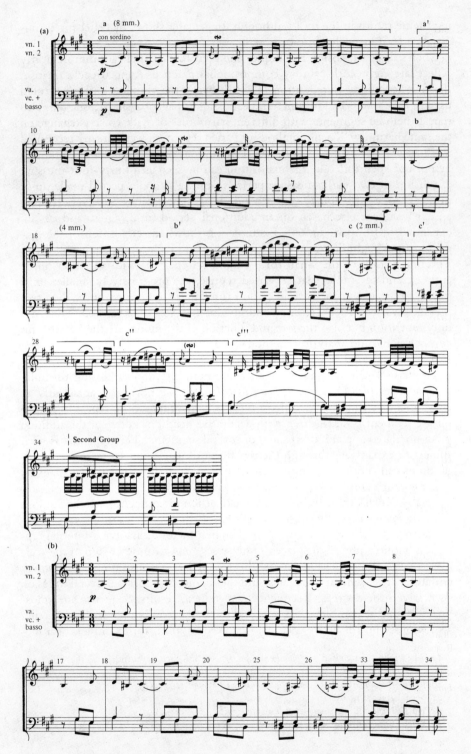

Example 4.2. Haydn, Symphony No. 42/ii: (a): exposition, first group; (b): hypothetical small form of exposition.

lodic figure *(Passagie)*. A series of sixteenth-note runs illustrates the latter, re-calling Riepel's discussion of rushing figures *(Rauscher)* and their importance in longer compositions.[24] Koch's last method of expansion here is parenthesis or interpolation *(Einschaltung)*, whereby melodic material may be inserted be-tween segments of a phrase or between a phrase and its repetition. This com-bination of techniques—interpolation and repetition—indicates that, just as with rhetorical figures, expansion techniques are interrelated and are used in conjunction with each other.[25]

Koch then demonstrated how these expansion techniques, applied to phrases and periods, create principal periods, that is, large sections ending in a strong cadence in the tonic or related key.[26] Within these principal periods, every phrase has a particular function; for example, in the first principal period of a larger composition, the most important functions are stating the main theme *(Hauptsatz)*, modulating, introducing a subsidiary melody *(melodische Neben-theil)*, and concluding. Although small forms have similar principles of design (they contain modulatory and cadential phrases), the difference in function be-tween small and principal periods is the difference between a closed, balanced unit and a concatenation of such units. Expanded forms are those that contain principal periods, which are in turn based on expansion techniques.

Principal Periods

Koch offered a single musical illustration to clarify the precise relationship be-tween small and expanded forms. By enlarging an eight-measure period into a thirty-two-measure principal period, and identifying the relevant techniques, he left us a convenient analysis of his own compositional practice (see Example 4.3).[27] Using the system of symbols that he had set up in the second volume of the *Versuch* (pp. 360–363), Koch marked every phrase but the closing one with a square and every incise—the interior point of rest in a phrase—with a tri-angle.[28] The original period is a succession of regular two-measure phrases, each with an incise. In addition, each concludes with the same cadence as did

24. Riepel, *Tonordnung*, pp. 97–100 and passim.

25. Expansion techniques were hardly ever discussed by other theorists. Kirnberger mentioned insertion *(Einschiebsel)* very briefly, referring only to the echo-like repetition of the second of two measures or the last two of four measures *(Die Kunst des reinen Satzes*, II, p. 143). And Daube claimed that "through frequent repetition and transposition of each figure, such a melody of one or two measures can then grow to a melody of one hundred or more measures, whose length cannot become vexing to the ear" *(Anleitung zur Erfindung der Melodie*, p. 9). An interesting discus-sion of phrase expansion that draws on eighteenth- and nineteenth-century theories is William Rothstein, *Phrase Rhythm in Tonal Music* (New York, 1989), chap. 3.

26. "By principal period, I mean the connection of several phrases, of which the last concludes with a formal cadence either in the tonic or in a closely related key" *(Versuch*, III, pp. 231–232; *Introductory Essay*, p. 166, n. 43). Baker translates *Hauptperiode* throughout as "main period."

27. Koch, *Versuch*, III, pp. 226–230; *Introductory Essay*, pp. 164–165.

28. He may have derived this idea from Riepel's use of a white square and a black square to designate phrases ending on the dominant and tonic, respectively (Riepel, *Tonordnung*, p. 41).

Example 4.3. Koch, small and expanded form.

Sequence (par. 65, p. 210); Tech. #3

Addition of segment ending
in a half-cadence (par. 56,
p. 195); Tech. #2

Repetition of second segment of closing phrase as
appendix (par. 61 fig. 1, p. 200); Tech. #2

Repetition of figuration (par. 69, p. 216); Tech. #3

Transposition (par. 64 fig. 3,
p. 207); Tech. #3

Addition of new closing segment
as appendix to closing phrase
(par. 61 fig. 2, p. 200); Tech. #2

Example 4.3   (continued)

the corresponding phrase of Riepel's small-form model: after two phrases in the tonic, the first ending on tonic harmony *(Grundabsatz)* and the second on a half-cadence *(Quintabsatz)*, the third phrase modulates to the dominant, ending on a half-cadence in that key. The final phrase *(Schlußsatz)* closes in the dominant. Riepel had indicated that successive phrases ought not to end with the same harmonic points of rest, a piece of advice strikingly similar to Quintilian: "It is a fault . . . to end a number of successive sentences with similar cadences, terminations, and inflexions."[29]

The principal period, Koch's most basic type,[30] maintains each of these points of rest. Two-measure phrases in the original become "punctuated principal sections" *(interpunctische Haupttheile)* in the expanded principal period, each ending on the same harmony as the smaller model. In this way, an exact correspondence obtains between the small period and the period to which expansion techniques have been applied. But each phrase is not simply quadrupled in size in order to retain the same proportion to the whole. Rather, the most expanded portions of the original are its third and fourth phrases, that is, the phrase that modulates and the phrase that concludes in the dominant. While each of the first two phrases becomes five measures long, the third and fourth phrases grow to thirteen and nine measures respectively. In fact, expansion techniques are applied at only four points in the first two phrases, but at ten points in the last two; the sole unexpanded measure is that of the half-cadence in the tonic (m. 4).

Moving away from the tonic and establishing a second key area require longer expansions not only because of the difficulty in obscuring the original tonic, but also because modulation assumes a role of almost unprecedented significance in this expanded form. Koch always emphasizes tonal events when he discusses "sonata form": its first section contains one principal period which modulates to the dominant, while its second section usually contains two principal periods, the first of which modulates continuously and closes in a related key, and the second of which begins and remains in the tonic.[31] That modulation begins less than halfway through the first principal period and continues

29. Quintilian, *Institutio oratoria,* IX.iv.42. Both Koch and Kirnberger distinguish between resting points of phrases, or caesuras *(Cäsur),* and cadences at the end of closing phrases *(Cadenz),* that is, the last phrase of a period (Kirnberger, *Kunst des reinen Satzes,* II, pp. 139, 141; Koch, *Versuch,* II, pp. 384ff. and 419ff.). On the importance of cadential structure to this form, see Dahlhaus, "Das rhetorische Formbegriff H. Chr. Kochs"; Karol Berger, "The First-Movement Punctuation Form in Mozart's Piano Concertos," in *Mozart's Piano Concertos: Text, Context, Interpretation,* ed. Neal Zaslaw (Ann Arbor, in press).

30. Later in the treatise, when Koch describes possible constructions for the first Allegro in the symphony, he refers back to this one as the most basic because it has no subsidiary melodic sections. He also introduces terms at that point to describe each of the expanded segments *(Versuch,* III, pp. 342–343; *Introductory Essay,* pp. 199–201).

31. See Ratner, "Harmonic Aspects of Classic Form," *JAMS* 2 (1949), 159–168, for evidence that late eighteenth-century theorists discussed form primarily in harmonic terms. For a theorist who discussed the thematic content of sonata form, see Bathia Churgin, "Francesco Galeazzi's Description (1796) of Sonata Form," *JAMS* 21 (1968), 181–199.

through the third clearly shows its central position, and in setting up the dramatic return to the tonic in the third principal period, it provides the largest forum for the use of expansion techniques. It thus also explains the necessity for lengthy concluding and "key-establishing" segments, in the guise of *Passagie* and multiple cadence formulas.

Koch finally pointed to the principal period as the hallmark of expanded form:

> This is . . . [the] form, with its most common variants, in which the first principal period of such pieces is fitted out, which is not used in the special form of rondo, or in the variations on a short air.
>
> At first appearance, e.g. in the first period of an aria, one often believes oneself to be hearing a form of this [first] period quite different from [that in] the symphony; however, this striking difference between the two aforementioned pieces is not caused by difference in the punctuated form; rather, it is caused partly through the inner character of the melodic sections, partly through the manner in which they are presented in this form, partly, however, also through their accompaniment; for the Adagio, e.g., is fitted out differently from the Allegro in this form. A piece which has only one principal voice arrives at this form differently from such a one where all voices have the right to let the most prominent ideas be heard.[32]

Thus, all forms using principal periods are essentially similar in construction. Despite the various ways in which Adagios and Allegros, symphony and sonata movements, instrumental pieces and arias differ from one another—and the differences are considerable, in the types of melodic sections, means of connecting them, and number of expansion techniques they use—their "punctuated form," the disposition of material in principal periods, remains the same.[33] Variation and rondo are therefore (composite) small forms because they do not contain principal periods, while sonata form is the paradigm for expanded forms.[34] By codifying techniques of connecting and expanding phrases within a general tonal plan, Koch has given us the means to make explicit the relationship between small forms and larger, expanded compositions.

Nicole Schwindt-Gross sets out a one-to-one correspondence between Koch's structural levels of phrases and periods and their equivalent verbal structures in the rhetoric treatise of Daniel Peucer (see n. 5). Koch's "basic phrase" *(enger Satz)*, "expanded phrase" *(erweiterte Satz)*, and "period" *(Periode)* correlate with Peucer's *propositio Logica, periodus simplex,* and *periodus composita,* respectively. More interesting are her final two identifications: *kleines Tonstück* with *chria,* and *großes Tonstück* with *ganze Rede.*[35] A *chria* is a moral or

32. Koch, *Versuch,* III, pp. 381–382. My translation differs from that by Baker in *Introductory Essay,* pp. 228–229.

33. Koch, *Versuch,* III, pp. 382–385; *Introductory Essay,* pp. 229–230.

34. According to Koch, rondos may have "amplified episodes" *(Introductory Essay,* p. 213), especially in concerto finales, but this does not imply principal periods. See also his discussion of the form on pp. 172–178.

35. Schwindt-Gross, *Drama und Diskurs,* p. 88.

ethical saying developed into a short essay, and practice in writing such essays was part of a Latin education; Peucer identified it as the "first and easiest exercise of eloquence."[36] In addition, Peucer described a *chria* as the result of joining several periods according to the guiding principle of a main theme. In Chapter 2, a *chria* was used as the example of *refining* or *expolitio* given in the [*Rhetorica*] *Ad Herrenium*. Since music was frequently held to have a moral component, this association has fascinating possibilities. Moreover, connecting a large-scale composition with a complete oration lends a certain substance to the attempts to find structural links between them.

The phrase-to-form models of eighteenth-century theorists clarify in a new way several crucial distinctions among forms. For example, it is precisely the disproportion within the different functional segments of a principal period that creates the drama and dramatic resolution of sonata form, far exceeding that of a theme *da capo* or melodic reprise in a set of variations. That disproportion partly results from repetition or varied repetition of asymmetrical elements. Because an entire variation is a repetition, it can never achieve that internal necessity for return or resolution without extraordinary measures to bring it about. Thus, even when expansion techniques are applied to variation themes or individual variations within a set, that set does not turn into an expanded form. And variation remains the only classical structure unable to expand into principal periods within the series, although, as Haydn showed, expansion was possible in a concluding segment. I will return to this point in the next section.

Haydn's Expansions

Haydn's expansions offer the closest possible analogy to Koch's model, as well as views of different genres and moments in the history of style: the divertimento-symphony pair of movements comes from the early 1760s, the piano-trio pair from about thirty years later. In the earlier expansion, the slow movement of Symphony 14 expands the theme of the slow variation-finale of Divertimento 11 ("Der Geburtstag"), which has the kind of walking bass typical of Haydn's early variation themes.[37] Example 4.4 shows the variation theme, which will be referred to as *S* (small), transposed from C to D major,

36. Ibid., p. 102.
37. This piece is discussed in more detail in my "Small and Expanded Forms," pp. 460–463. Landon dates Symphony 14 to c. 1762 on the basis of its date in the Göttweig catalogue (1764); see *Haydn: Chronicle and Works*, I: *Haydn: The Early Years 1732–1765* (Bloomington, 1980), p. 552. The date of the divertimento may be around 1760 (ibid., pp. 183–184, and edition in *Diletto musicale* 57 [Vienna, 1960]); there are also dated copies of the mid–1760s. Like the rest of Haydn's divertimenti, this one has no authentic sources and is simply assumed to be a pre-Esterházy work. (I am indebted to James Webster for this information.) The source of its title is unknown; the play of that name by Franz von Heufeld was not performed until 1767. In addition, many copies title the Andante "Mann und Weib." The transmission of not one but two nicknames for the divertimento suggests its popularity, and the symphony movement was likewise popular, printed in a keyboard version in Hiller's *Wöchentliche Nachrichten, die Musik betreffend* in 1767 (No. 32 [Leipzig, 3 February 1767]); Landon, *Haydn Chronicle*, I, p. 561.

Example 4.4. Haydn, Divertimento Hob. II:11/iv, "Der Geburtstag," theme.

the key of the symphony movement. The first period of *S* differs from Koch's small period in that it has two phrases instead of four, the first ending in the tonic, the second in the dominant, and it is in 2/4 rather than 4/4. Example 4.5 shows the first principal period of the expanded Andante *(E)*, which grows to four phrases, actually the four punctuated principal sections that Koch described. As in Koch's model, the greatest expansion takes place in the modulatory and closing sections. Two segments from the second period of *S*—phrase *4S*, the varied repetition of phrase *1S*, and the first incise of phrase *3S* (mm. 9–10)—are here included in the first section of *E*, and help set up the punctuated sections. Phrase *4S* now becomes phrase *2E*, acting as both a means of expansion (varied repetition) of the first phrase, and a phrase ending on a half-cadence. And the first incise of *3S* is used in *E* as a subsidiary melodic section in the dominant, establishing the new key and closing on its own dominant. Finally, Koch's second group of expansion techniques, the multiplication of closing formulas, explains the considerably expanded final phrase of *E*.

More important in this context is Haydn's second expansion, in the first movement of his Piano Trio No. 19 (Hob. XV:19/i, 1794), which has variations on two themes, one minor and one major.[38] After a single variation on

---

38. See Sisman, "Small and Expanded Forms," pp. 463–470; Rosen, *The Classical Style*, pp. 83–88. Rosen's conclusion, based on this expansion, that "sonata form is an immense melody, an expanded Classical phrase," is exactly Koch's point in the *Versuch*.

Example 4.5. Haydn, Symphony No. 14/ii, exposition.

each theme (ABA₁B₁), the concluding Presto expands the second (major) theme into a sonata-form-like finale. That the Presto is a literal expansion of the variation theme, and therefore directly comparable to Koch's model, is easily shown (Example 4.6); because the expansion is actually a variation, a high degree of resemblance with the theme is not only desirable but even obligatory.

Both the nature and the purpose of the expansion illuminate aspects of thematic relationship and cyclic design. The minor theme is atypically large, partly through affective repetitions of a measure or incise (as in the first phrase), and partly because each period has an appendix over a pedal. But far from being cadential filler, the appendix is actually the source for the melody of the B theme and thus for the Presto expansion itself. In addition, the first variation on A already has figuration in thirty-second notes and thus vitiates the following sixteenth-note B₁ section. Rhythmically speaking, there is nowhere to go at this point but to triplets (or to syncopations, which Haydn rarely invoked as a variation topic). Haydn, who virtually never changed meter and tempo at the end of his variation movements, here adopts Mozart's practice of a final coda-like variation—often fast and metrically altered—that emphatically asserts closure. Closure is achieved not only through the burst of energy of the new tempo and meter but also by the brilliant style of *Rauscher,* the modulatory and concluding runs and their repetitions. These "rushing figures" accelerate the figurations of A₁, the fastest to that point, and thus continue, in a sense, the alternation inherent in A and B. In fact, the final drive to cadence occurs on a tonic pedal, and thus derives from the appendix to the A theme (just as the B theme had drawn inspiration from the melody at that point). While skewing the movement toward the B theme at the close, the Presto actually subtly reinforces both the concept of alternation and the constructive and figural tactics of the A theme. As a rhetorical ploy, this resolution of antitheses is a fully realized example of *refining.*

VARIATION AND EXPANSION

Haydn only rarely used varied repetition as an expansion technique in the Presto of the piano trio, except in the extra concluding section. But in a number of his sonata-form movements, he systematically applied variation techniques either to expand or to interrelate thematic and other functional areas (modulatory passages, development). The presence of so much repetition and variation in these movements, by linking variation as expansion technique with variation as small form, pushes closer the concepts of small and expanded forms. An important locus for their interaction is the slow movement of a larger composition. Koch described the slow movement of a symphony as having three options, the second and third of which are rondo and variations. The first option is a kind of "sonata form"—that is, similar to the first movement in construction, but with this critical distinction: "In the andante the melodic ideas are less extended and not so often compounded; thus more formal phrase endings are used than in the allegro. This accords with the nature of the feelings

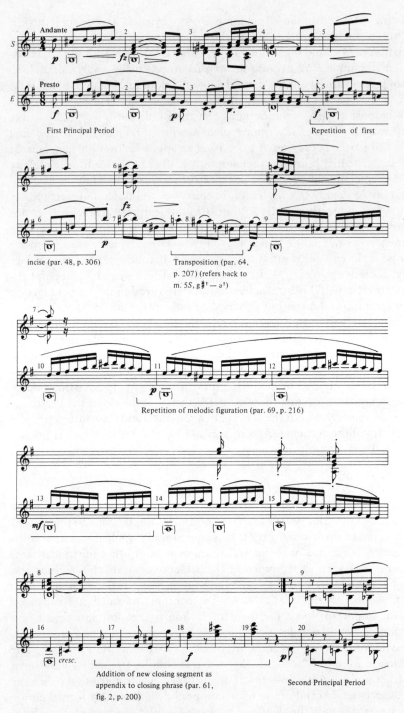

Andante

First Principal Period   Repetition of first

incise (par. 48, p. 306)   Transposition (par. 64,
                                  p. 207) (refers back to
                                  m. 5S, g♯¹ — a¹)

Repetition of melodic figuration (par. 69, p. 216)

Addition of new closing segment as
appendix to closing phrase (par. 61,   Second Principal Period
fig. 2, p. 200)

Example 4.6.   Haydn, Piano Trio Hob. XV:19/i.

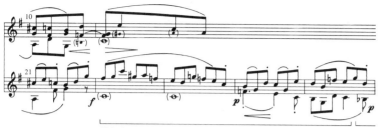

Main theme in related key (expansion of subdominant chord)

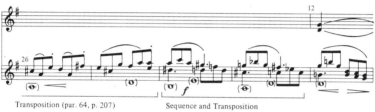

Transposition (par. 64, p. 207)

Sequence and Transposition
(par. 67, p. 213) (based on
preceding transposition,
mm. 26–27E)

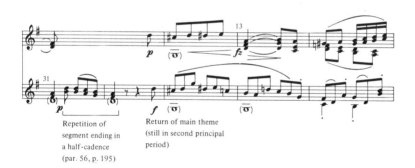

Repetition of
segment ending in
a half-cadence
(par. 56, p. 195)

Return of main theme
(still in second principal
period)

Example 4.6   (continued)

Repetition of melodic figuration (par. 69, p. 216)

Varied repetition of closing phrase
(par. 47, p. 156; par. 61, p. 200);
Reinterpret details of S, mm. 18–20
(cf. mm. 45–52E and mm. 18–19S)

Repetition of melodic
figuration (par. 69,
p. 216)

Addition of new closing segment
as appendix to closing phrase
(par. 61, fig. 2, p. 200);
Cf. m. 20S

Example 4.6 (continued)

which tend to be expressed in slow movements."[39] Affect and tempo lead to a form more concise in precisely the techniques differentiating small from expanded forms, that is, in extension and in nature of cadences, which are often elided in the allegro.

Haydn's earliest "sonatas with varied reprises" in the string quartets of Opp. 9, 17, and 20 may have induced him to take variation in slow movements still further. Several movements present a complete varied repetition of the theme—that is, the entire first period—immediately after its first appearance; examples are the slow movements of Symphony No. 44, Sonata Hob. XVI:46, and Quartets Opp. 20 No. 5, 33 No. 1, 50 No. 2, 54 No. 2. Ironically, it is the proximate position of the varied repetition that suggests a form other than theme and variations, since such pieces hardly ever contain varied repeats within their themes or have themes of a single period; only the self-contained first period and archaic style of the exquisite Db-major sonata movement just listed suggest that the movement might continue on its varied course to become a passacaglia. In Symphony 42, the piece given by Koch as a model of variation as expansion as well as a model of sonata form (Example 4.2a), the melodic segments to be varied become smaller and smaller, decreasing symmetrically from eight- to four- to two-measure segments that are repeated with variation. If the initial varying of an entire period is closer to the small-period construction of variation form, the successively smaller varied repetitions act like interpolations in the flow of melodic events, expanding phrases from their centers. Both sorts of variation, in stressing *repetition,* retain the underlying structural unit of period, phrase, or incise in a linking of paratactic and sequential structure far from Schoenberg's concept of "developing variation" and its "thematicist" progeny.[40] I will return to paratactic elements in Haydn's sonata forms at the end of this section.

The unifying tendencies of variation technique are evident in the slow movement of Symphony No. 87 (1785). Here a single theme prevails, an eight-measure period that is repeated with a flute countermelody, and returns in the dominant (m. 24) with new orchestration, the triplet accompaniment of the preceding modulatory passage, and some structural modifications. A beautiful wind cadenza serves as closing material. The entire second principal period (development section) comprises two successive modified repetitions of that theme in different tonalities (V and vi), followed by the newly reorchestrated theme in the tonic at the beginning of the third principal period (recapitulation). Two more appearances of the theme in this last section, the original dominant version now in the tonic, and as a coda over a tonic pedal, complete the sonata-form design. Not only is varied repetition used to expand the theme, but it also delineates the subsidiary melodic sections.

A comparison of this movement with the first movement of Symphony No.

39. Koch, *Introductory Essay,* p. 201.

40. See James Webster, *Haydn's Farewell Symphony,* pp. 194–204, for a discussion of the skeins of thematic relationships known as thematicism and developing variation, especially between movements, citing much literature on the subject.

85 ("La Reine," probably 1785) allows the relationship between Haydn's variation technique in fast and in slow movements to emerge. In No. 85 the opening theme, a twelve-measure period, is repeated with new orchestration and accompaniment, but only after eight bars of contrasting *tutti*. Again, the theme highlighting the second key is another version of this theme, now with the melodic line in the oboe and an extended final phrase. And varied returns of the theme, in different tonalities, occupy much of the second principal period.[41] As Koch would lead us to expect, there are many more melodic segments between each new variation of the theme in the Allegro, some of which are themselves treated with varied repetition.

Haydn used the same primary variation techniques—reorchestration and countermelody—in the set of variations in the second movement of the same symphony, as if to call attention to the precise difference between variation as a technique in an expanded form and as a form itself. Other aspects of the variations also recall the first movement. For example, the first variation emphasizes its own modulation to the dominant with a sudden change in dynamics, orchestration, figuration, and rhythmic activity. And the central minor variation, unusual among Haydn's *minores* in its close adherence to the theme melody, echoes the first movement, where the theme returns in minor in the second principal period. Yet the variations retain all the property of small form in their repetitions of small periods, whereas the first movement modifies the theme structurally and links it with other expanded sections into principal periods. This last point is true of Symphony 87's slow movement as well, even though it has more consecutive varying. The difference in types of variation, then, lies in the nature of expansion itself: not only does it make dimensions increase, but it causes proportions to change. Variation is most effective as an expansion technique when it works at the level of phrase and incise, hence in conjunction with interpolation and cadence extensions so that it can alter phrases, periods, and larger sections proportionally. Otherwise, varied repetitions of entire periods, if they are not to function as the consecutive repetitions of variation form, must occur in a piece with different intervening melodic segments so that they actually become varied returns.

In these senses, variation as expansion technique (as in Symphony 42/ii or 87/ii) has an entirely different rhetorical stance from a varied repetition in which the second theme is a variation of the first (Symphony 85/i). The former seems to exemplify the sententious figures of Puttenham—serving both the ear and the understanding, enlarging the whole with copious amplifications—because these expansions depend on as well as contribute to the formal and syntactic meaning of the model. A varied return of the main theme in some functionally different part of the movement, however, requires a mental effort at comparison and recognition (especially when the variation is disguised, as in

41. Jens Peter Larsen discussed this movement in "Sonata Form Problems," *Handel, Haydn, and the Viennese Classical Style*, trans. Ulrich Krämer (Ann Arbor, 1988), pp. 269–279.

the first movement of Haydn's Quartet Op. 77 No. 2), and thus calls on Put-tenham's "sensable" figures, which give "efficacie to sence."

The variation principle in Haydn's sonata-form movements is not limited to these two types, however, nor were they necessarily mutually exclusive. In the two late piano sonatas in C major and Eb major, Hob. XVI:50 and 52, for example, successive varied restatements of the theme during the first group and modulatory passage set up later varied returns while exploiting a broad sweep of pianistic resources. In the C-major Sonata, No. 50, variations of the opening theme—figural, textural, registral, harmonic—even come to domi-nate the exposition and development. These pieces suggest a paratactic ap-proach to sonata form in Haydn's works. In a little noticed but brilliant article of 1982, Rudolf Klein made a distinction between the parataxis of Haydn's symphonic sonata forms and the hypotaxis of Mozart's.[42] The correlation be-tween parataxis and variation remained unexplored, however, and, I believe, deserves to be underscored. A particularly striking example is the first move-ment of Symphony No. 88, where there is a rhythmic similarity among the principal thematic areas as well as rhythmic differentiation among successive segments that is strikingly reminiscent of the progressive diminution *(gradatio)* in strophic variations. Each of the four functional areas of the exposition (tonic [main theme], bridge [modulation], second key [subsidiary melodic section], closing) is built on the opening eighth-note theme with its characteristic up-beat. Moreover, each continues with that eighth-note theme accompanied by a counterfigure in sixteenth notes. If one labels the eighth-note themes *a* and the more rhythmically active passage with sixteenths and eighths *b,* the paratactic outline of the movement emerges as:

1. First group: *a* (m. 16)   *b* (m. 25)

2. Bridge: *a* (m. 44)   *b* (m. 51)

3. Second group: *a* (m. 61)   *b* (m. 71)

4. Closing: *a* (m. 77)   *b* (m. 85)

Example 4.7 shows the beginnings of each *a* and *b* segment. The continuation of the *b* section in the first group reverses this process on its way to the bridge: an active passage in sixteenths (m. 32) becomes more thematic (m. 36), calling attention to the sixteenth notes as embellishments of the underlying eighth-note patterns.

Variation and Expanded Forms

In 1780 and 1781, Haydn wrote several hybrid slow movements in which the boundaries between small and expanded forms are called into question: Sym-

---

42. Rudolf Klein, "Wo kann die Analysen von Haydns Symphonik ansetzen?" *ÖMz* 37 (1982), 234–241.

Example 4.7. Haydn, Symphony No. 88/i.

phony No. 74 and four string quartets in Op. 33 (Nos. 2, 4, 5, and 6). Indeed, rather than considering formal hybrids to be *Mischformen* of conventional structures—binary, rondo, variation, sonata—we might approach them as the outcomes of fruitful interactions between small and expanded form. Such an approach confirms the observation of Leo Treitler that

> The apprehension of a musical work depends . . . on two intertwined processes: on the one hand the underlying patterns of conventional genres and implicit constraints arising from the grammar of style (harmony, voice-leading, and so on), and on the other the progressive interpretation of these determinants through the

unfolding of the work in time . . . The first dimension constrains the second, the second interprets the first.[43]

Especially innovative among these pieces is the Largo e sostenuto third movement of the E♭-major string quartet Op. 33/2 (1781), which appears to combine sonata form without development (Rosen's "slow-movement sonata form"),[44] variation, and rondo in its design (Example 4.8). Its opening theme *(a)*, a tonally closed duet of eight measures for viola and cello, is immediately repeated an octave higher *(a₁)* in the violins, with the addition at midpoint of a slow written-out trill in the cello to embellish the dominant. At the end of the theme that slow trill asserts itself as the principal agent of transition, a position it will occupy for the remainder of the movement. Two groups of fortissimo chords *(b)* initiate a modulation to the dominant (via G minor), and the trill (on V/V) leads to a chordal contrasting phrase *(c)* based on the descending half-step motive of *b*. The third particle of this theme turns into a figured line returning to the trill, as a closing passage *(d)*, now exposing the trill figure as the precursor of the descending half-step. The motives are thus labeled separately as *x* (trill), *y* (descending half-step in *b*), *y′* (descending half-step in *c*), and *y″* (descending half-step in *d*). To this point, and despite the closed first period, the movement traces a principal period with a doubled cadence formula (at m. 28), in the reduced dimensions of a slow movement.

A return to the opening theme *(a₂)* in the tonic with the figured line *(x)* on top is now a fuller three-part texture with expanded range. Were this movement to be a sonata form without development we would hear *b, c,* and *d* in the tonic, but *b* is missing, *c* appears in the subdominant, and *d* starts in C minor (ii, the relative minor of IV, just as *b* was originally heard in the relative minor, g). Instead of acting as the closing phrase, *d* seems slightly developmental, shortening and harmonically reinterpreting the related earlier passage. It thus motivates a return to *a* yet again, in four-part texture *(a₃)*, ending in a deceptive cadence. The missing particles now come back. First, *b* returns in a coda-like subdominant gesture that echoes the previous appearance of *c* in m. 40 and resolves the original appearance of *b* (mm. 19–20 in V, mm. 62–63 in I). Finally, a shortened version of *a* is elided with a short coda that conflates the *x* accompaniment with the cadential patterns of the first *d;* the final chords echo the *y* motive.

Because the main theme returns intact three times, the movement suggests rondo. Because its texture is varied each time, with an increasing fullness and registral diffusion, variation form is also present. But the brief modulatory, thematic, and closing areas in the dominant, abetted by motivic interrelationships, also indicate the presence of an expanded form. This movement exists in the interstices of several structures, both small and expanded; its only constant,

43. Treitler, "Mozart and the Idea of Absolute Music," in his *Music and the Historical Imagination* (Cambridge, Mass., 1989), p. 190.
44. Rosen, *Classical Style,* p. 100.

Example 4.8. Haydn, String Quartet Op. 33/2/iii.

Example 4.8   (continued)

paradoxically, is the recurrence of varied repetition. Haydn found such varied repetitions indispensable in hybrid structures.

Koch ultimately ignored the question of formal expansion after a closed binary main theme. For rondos and sonata rondos he merely indicated that the episodes may be "amplified," as in concerto-finales.[45] Certainly rondos and

45. Koch, *Introductory Essay,* p. 213. See also Malcolm S. Cole, "Sonata-Rondo, the Formulation of a Theoretical Concept in the 18th and 19th Centuries," *MQ* 55 (1969), 180–192. Stephen Fisher takes up the rondo-sonata relationship in "Sonata Procedures in Haydn's Symphonic Rondo Finales of the 1770s," *Haydn Studies,* ed. Larsen et al., pp. 481–487.

rondo-variations will include episodes that modulate to the dominant and sub-sequently resolve to the tonic (Symphony 74/ii) or that "open out" into devel-opmental episodes (Symphony 55/iv). Even the set of variations on a Scottish air that forms the slow movement of Johann Christian Bach's piano concerto Op. 13 No. 2 (1777) has a modulation to and theme in the dominant after the first variation; followed by a tutti theme reprise and figured variation, the dominant theme never returns, and the modulation seems motivated entirely by the brevity of the song.[46] Yet there appears to be no theory in the eighteenth century to account for a small form with two reprises, itself entirely bounded, participating in a fully expanded and polarized musical structure, as in the fi-nale of Mozart's Symphony No. 40 or the slow movement of his Symphony No. 39.[47]

Eighteenth-century concepts of phrase and form can aid in assessing the question of how variation technique participates in the proportionate expan-sions of sonata form. But can they elucidate the idea, widely held, that varia-tion forms aspire to and finally arrive at sonata-like designs themselves?[48] Pos-iting the sonata aesthetic as the key to classical style derogates everything that does not fit—as the variations of Haydn and Mozart patently do not. Charles Rosen's otherwise compelling discussion of Beethoven's variations includes this assertion: "Essentially static and decorative, almost always in one key so that the interplay between harmonic tension and general texture could only be on the level of small details, variations presented a problem to the dramatically conceived classical style. Even the rigidly fixed proportions of the form were alien to it."[49] Yet Haydn voluntarily inserted many of these alien bodies into his symphonies, string quartets, and sonatas despite their apparent violation of his dramatically conceived sense of style.

Sonata form must have principal periods, no matter how narrowly defined; a variation theme will never be part of one. Hence, to see variations as influ-enced by the sonata aesthetic is to adopt a value judgment—they are better than earlier non-sonata-form-like variations—masquerading as a simile. The irony is that this view has to do with precisely that aspect of variation that is least like sonata form: its reliance on unmediated repetition. As suggested in Chapter 1, repetition is somewhat unstable and seeks another kind of organization. Con-sequently, changes in key or mode, or elision of linking segments, or clustering of particular character-giving elements, lead to an ostensible relationship with

46. Johann Christian Bach, *Piano Concertos,* ed. Ludwig Landshoff (Frankfurt, 1931).

47. See Leo Treitler's vivid account of the latter piece in "Mozart and the Idea of Absolute Mu-sic," pp. 191–213. There are, of course, many other movements with closed first themes and sonata-form-like structures, such as the sonata-rondo finales of Haydn's London symphonies, and slow movements often have closed first themes, though more often without repeats, as in the slow movement of Mozart's Symphony No. 40.

48. Rosen persuasively expresses this idea in *The Classical Style,* p. 437. See also William Kin-derman, "Tonality and Form in the Variation Movements of Beethoven's Late Quartets," in *Beiträge zu Beethovens Kammermusik,* ed. Sieghard Brandenburg and Helmut Loos (Munich, 1987), pp. 135–151.

49. Rosen, *The Classical Style,* p. 437.

the dramatic process of divergence, development, and return of which sonata form claims itself the privileged embodiment. The assumption that return after contrast, even a melodic/tonal return after tonal contrast, is indicative of sonata style strikes me as biased and unwarranted. Now it is perfectly possible to view certain kinds of sonata designs as the repetition of large modulating periods. For example, the Andantino of Mozart's Eb-major Piano Concerto K. 449 (1784) consists, broadly speaking, of five sections, in which concerto-sonata-form elements mingle with strophic design; the principal melodic sections of the opening tutti are *a* (mm. 1–10), *b* (mm. 11–14), and *c* (mm. 15–22, a variant of *a*), while those of the first solo section (A₁) replace *b* and *c* with *d* (mm. 31–40, a rhythmic variant of *b*) and *e* (mm. 41–52).[50] The plan of the movement is as follows:

A: Bb major, segments *a-b-c* [tutti]

A₁: Bb–F major, m. 23, segments *a-d-e* [solo + tutti]

A₂: Ab–Eb major, m. 52, segments *a-d-e*

A₃: Bb major, m. 80, segments *a-b-e* (in which *b* and *e* are varied)

A₄: (coda), m. 112, segment *c*

Of course, Mozart's varied slow-movement forms are never clear of (or at least are not as ambivalent about) principal periods the way Haydn's are; hypotactic structure—that is, in this case, the hierarchical principal period—is as natural to Mozart as paratactic is to Haydn. This is one reason why Mozart's variation forms are more goal-oriented and conscious of shape, while Haydn's luxuriate in successive details. In a piece like the *Eroica* finale, on the other hand, every one of the variations remains a small-form conception linked by transitions and developed in fugatos. Our willingness to read sonata form into such a piece reflects the enormous prestige of the form and the consequent stake in identifying its organic character wherever possible. Yet both the key scheme and the formal design of a central set of shortened variations in different keys reflect not sonata form, but the ternary designs of so many of Haydn's slow movements.[51] The transformation of the relative weight and purpose of each theme, as well as the progressively enacted drama of the return over three segments of the movement, is an entirely new symphonic outgrowth of the alternating-variation tradition of Haydn, as Chapter 8 will make clear, and has little to do with the sonata aesthetic.

A critical approach that can take "sonata-like features" into account without being beholden to them ought thus to be developed from within the variation tradition and its own rhetorical, structural, and aesthetic components. A good

50. For a sensitive voice-leading analysis of this movement, see Carl Schachter, "Idiosyncratic Features of Three Mozart Slow Movements: K. 449, K. 453, and K. 467," in *Mozart's Piano Concertos: Text, Context, Interpretation,* ed. Neal Zaslaw (Ann Arbor, in press).

51. The slow movement of the *Eroica* itself is a ternary form expanded into a rondo by means of a developmental fugato that interrupts the first return of the theme.

opportunity is afforded by the slow movement of Beethoven's "Appassionata" sonata, Op. 57, which has been compellingly analyzed by both Rosen and Lawrence Kramer in terms of its satisfyingly sonata-like shape and sense of resolution, caused by the rise of register and increase in speed of figuration before the final reprise-variation.[52] But there are senses of resolution outside the sonata model, I believe, that are here generated by paratactic details. What accounts for this movement's power are the sources of the transcendental beauty of the hymn theme: first, its extraordinarily repetitive nature, which violates the eighteenth-century rules of syntax by closing not only every phrase but even every *incise* with the same tonic harmony, and second, the rhythmic acceleration, registral ascent, and more action-oriented harmonies—no more ethereal subdominants—in its second period. The course of the movement, with its ecstatic trajectory, is thus entirely adumbrated by the theme. It is the first variation movement known to me to combine the *gradatio* of rhythm with that of register:[53] eighth-note syncopations in the low register, where the melody stays squarely on the beat and the accompaniment is syncopated, in contrast to the usual practice of late eighteenth-century composers, sixteenths in the middle register and thirty-seconds in the high register with written-out varied repeats.[54] Moreover, the variations have two points of return: the modified melodic reprise in var. 3 over varied accompaniment, and the modified theme reprise in the original low register but with higher consequent phrases and an embellished bass line. The variations thus fulfill each of the registral and rhythmic promises of the theme and then return to it for final approving comparison in a theme reprise, suitably shaded with the registers thus far encountered. What is new about this movement, then, is not a metaphorical association with sonata style, but a rhetorical synthesis of *inventio* and *dispositio* in which the nature and characteristics of the main idea generate the entire chain of argumentation. Indeed, this movement is the belated essence of the eighteenth-century theorists' insistence on models of structure that grow from phrase to piece: here, repetition on the smallest scale, within incises, is what enables the theme to grow into a small form itself subjected, in the course of the variations, to repetition and return.

52. Rosen, *Classical Style,* p. 438; Lawrence Kramer, *Music and Poetry: The Nineteenth Century and After* (Berkeley and Los Angeles, 1984), pp. 43–45.

53. Beethoven was to return to this technique in the first three variations of the Seventh Symphony; the last variation is similarly a quasi-reprise in different registers. The opening contrapuntal variations of the *Eroica* also increase rhythmic velocity and register, but culminate in the second theme; see Chapter 8. And in the last variation of the E-major Sonata, Op. 109, the progressive acceleration of rhythm and register becomes a force for closure, yielding, as in Op. 57, to a theme reprise.

54. The thirty-seconds remain at first in the middle register while the melody ascends an octave; at the varied repeat, the parts are reversed. The rhythmic doubling thus occurs in a register already won. Only the second variation breaks new registral ground with an ornamented line, which partly explains the sheer poetry of its initial moment.

CHAPTER FIVE

Convention and Innovation in Haydn's Variations to 1780

In the late 1750s and 1760s, Haydn was one of a number of composers working in and around Vienna who occasionally included variations as first movements or finales in instrumental compositions. During the 1770s, however, Haydn emerged as the principal innovator in variations, demonstrating both their affective power as weightier slow-movement centerpieces and their formal versatility in hybrid designs. As Burney put it:

> About the middle of the last century, the musical world was overwhelmed with dull and unmeaning variations to old and new tunes, which consisted of nothing more than regular multiplication of notes, without fancy, taste, or harmonical resources; till Haydn, in the slow and graceful middle movements of his quartets and symphonies, by richness of imagination, by double counterpoint, and inexhaustible resources of melody and harmony, rendered variations the most ingenious, pleasing, and heart felt of his admirable production *a grand orchestra*.[1]

Indeed, Haydn's later works reveal that variation became more and more central to his style, especially in slow movements, where varied repetitions and recurrences shaped his structures and sharpened his musical utterances. In this chapter I will consider Haydn's sets of strophic variations of the 1750s, 1760s, and 1770s, as well as the variety of hybrid structures from 1767 on, resulting from his interest in varied reprises. The two compositions of 1772 that herald a new departure in the rhetoric of the variation—the slow movements of Symphony No. 47 and the D-major String Quartet, Op. 20 No. 4—are, I will argue, the first variation sets of greatness in the Classical style.

Early Variations

The striking correlation between theoretical description and Haydn's practice shows the extended stylistic development charted over a half-century by

---

1. Charles Burney, "Theme," in *The Cyclopedia: or Universal Dictionary of Arts, Sciences, and Literature,* ed. Abraham Rees, 45 vols. (1802–1820), quoted in Kerry S. Grant, *Dr. Burney as Critic and Historian of Music* (Ann Arbor, 1983), p. 215.

Scheibe, Schulz, and Koch, telescoped into the works of a single composer within a fifteen-year period. (Table A.1 in Appendix A lists all of Haydn's variations; the dates come from Georg Feder's worklist in *The New Grove*.) Over the fixed bass lines of the late 1750s and 1760s, Haydn wrote melodic lines in each variation that at first featured figurations and contours independent of the theme, but later came to include within each set more and more embellishments and figurations draped, as it were, over the original melodic outline of the theme. At times, the bass line itself was subject to variation, although with negligible effect on the harmony. All genres participated in this change, the gradual nature of which is evidenced only by the baryton trios, Haydn's most intensively and continuously cultivated instrumental genre in this period. The genres produced sporadically, on the other hand, made the turn to melodic-outline variation seem rather sudden, in that they leap-frogged over the baryton trios: compare the early string quartets (c. 1757–59) with Op. 9 (c. 1769–70) and Op. 17 (1771), to be discussed below, or the first independent keyboard sets in D major and A major (XVII:7 and 2, both c. 1765) with that in Eb (XVII:3, c. 1770–74). In the A-major set (XVII:2), Haydn aimed at a comprehensive survey of keyboard technique, with hand-crossings (var. 3), consecutive practice in right-hand and left-hand runs (vars. 5–6), repeated notes (var. 8), octaves (var. 20), and many other kinds of dexterity yoking together compositional and pedagogic interest and submerging the theme melody (except in var. 9).[2] In the Eb-major set (XVII:3), by contrast, the main notes of the theme's melody are recognizable, especially at the beginning, through the "superfluous" notes of a pleonastic cantabile style; only vars. 5, 6, and 8 significantly depart from it. Possibly the use of a pre-existent theme, the minuet from Op. 9 No. 2, inspired Haydn to maintain greater similarity to it than in the earlier movement.

All of Haydn's early strophic variation movements are first movements or finales, as are those of his contemporaries.[3] Slow or moderate tempos and duple meter predominate for first movements, while minuet tempo and meter prevail in finales.[4] The finale was by far the most common location for varia-

2. On the different versions and textual variants of XVII:2, which exists in a G-major and an A-major version with either twelve or twenty variations, see Brown, *Joseph Haydn's Keyboard Music*, pp. 88–92. I have used the Henle-Urtext edition of Haydn's *Klavierstücke*, ed. Sonja Gerlach (Munich, c. 1968).

3. I have turned up no variation movements in an interior position. Barry Brook lists a concerto by Michel Corrette (1709–1795) whose middle movement is "Aria Andante, Variazione 1, Variazione 2." (*La Symphonie française dans la seconde moitié du XVIIIe siècle* [Paris, 1962], II, 207). The date of this work, the fifth of Corrette's Op. 26 *(Sei Concerti a sei stromenti)* in F major, is dated "vers 1742" by Brook; David Fuller corrects it to 1756 in his article on Corrette in *The New Grove*, vol. 4, p. 802.

4. The exceptions are the divertimento- and symphony-finales in slow or moderate duple meter, and one string trio-finale in quick duple meter. The piano trio XV:C1 is a curious case, because although in triple meter, its finale is marked Adagio in the more authentic sources and Minuet Adagio in somewhat more peripheral sources. (See the *Kritischer Bericht* to *Klaviertrios, JHW* XVII/1 by Wolfgang Stockmeier [Munich, 1971].) The latter designation clearly fits in with Haydn's typical practice, but *JHW* has gone along with the more authentic sources. See also Mich-

tions in the mid-eighteenth century—Haydn was unusual in the sheer numbers of his first movements—probably because of the preponderance of Tempo di Menuet variations held over from the suite. Finale-variations were also appropriate conclusions to divertimenti for strings and winds, with a parade of *concertante* instruments each taking a star turn. Indeed, Tempo di Menuet and *concertante* make up, with two exceptions, Haydn's early variation finales. The Tempo di Menuet type serves as finale to all six of the violin-viola duos (Hob. VI), two string trios (V:8 and 11), as well as the triple-meter finale to the piano trio XV:C1, whose authentic tempo designation is in doubt. The *concertante* type appeared in two divertimenti (Hob. II:1 ["La Fantasy"] and 11 ["Der Geburtstag"]) and two symphonies (31, 72); the finale of II:1 is a *concertante* minuet. Even after the so-called early period, variation finales predominate among the sonatas *anno 776* (five of the six, XVI:27, 28, 29, 30, 31), and then are never used again, outside the rondo-variation finale.

Haydn's theme-types often differed from those of his contemporaries: melodies of disjunct, consistently moving eighth notes that might be termed "walking melodies" appeared in duple movements, sometimes together with a partially walking bass as well (Example 5.1), as did a type of melody with short-note upbeat followed by eighths or longer notes. These theme-types are not found in variations by his contemporaries. Haydn also wrote themes with upbeats in far greater numbers than they did, in both duple and minuet movements, although his earliest variations in first movements all lack upbeats (Quartet Op. 2 No. 6, String Trios V:D3 and V:8, Sonata XVII:D1). On the other hand, Haydn never wrote the cut-time moderato themes in long notes favored by Gassmann and Ordonez (see the following section), nor did that type appeal to later composers. Yet Haydn's early theme-types are not easily reducible to a few stereotypes, offering more profiles than the few that scholars have found in his slow movements.[5] For instance, despite the outward similarity of the variation movements in the baryton trios—all twenty-one are first movements in duple meter, mostly Adagio or Andante, and all but one have an upbeat[6]—the rhythmic values and melodic contours of the opening phrases of each theme can be placed in nearly a dozen different categories. The themes are thus diverse.

Nor is there a correlation between the type of theme melody and the technique by which it is varied. Disjunct eighth-note melodies, for example, ap-

---

elle Fillion, "Eine bisher unbekannte Quelle für Haydns frühes Klaviertrio Hob. XV:C1," *HSt* 5 (1982), 59–63. The Andante marking in Hoboken probably comes from the later Hummel edition or Berlin copy. With a Moderato marking we are on surer ground: the finale of divertimento II:1 ("Moderato. La Fantasy") is a Tempo di Menuet in all but name.

5. See Georg Feder, "Bemerkungen über die Ausbildung in der klassischen Tonsprache in der Instrumentalmusik Haydns," *International Musicological Society, Report of the Eighth Congress, New York, 1961* (Kassel, 1961), p. 306; James Webster, "When Did Haydn Begin to Write 'Beautiful' Melodies?" in *Haydn Studies,* ed. Larsen et al., p. 387.

6. Trios 2 and 116 are Allegretto, 41 and 106 are Moderato, and 95 is Allegro; Trio 6, in common time, has no upbeat.

TRIO 8

Example 5.1. Haydn, "walking melody" theme: Baryton trio XI:8/i.

pear appropriately in many early constant-bass sets, varied as a contrapuntal
projection of the bass line (Baryton Trio 8, Symphony No. 72), but are also
given melodic-outline treatment (Quartet Op. 9 No. 5, var. 1). And tuneful
theme melodies, on the other hand, may be ignored in constant-bass variations, as in Baryton Trio 29, which began life as an aria in *La Canterina.* Thus,
a theme for variations may not necessarily imply a particular treatment, but
must merely be, in Koch's vague words, "a somewhat simple but flowing melody, capable of many variations."[7] Indeed, Haydn occasionally varied a theme
in a manner so at odds with the nature of that theme, as in Symphony 47 and
Quartet Op. 76 No. 6, that deliberate disparity becomes a topic for the movement. Such ironic treatments reveal Haydn's fascination with rhetorical notions
of the idea and its elaboration.[8] This novel approach will be elucidated below.

Part of the problem is the concept of "theme" itself in a variation work: what
precisely is the matter, the *res,* of the movement; what is to be varied? The
answer is a paradox: although a theme is clearly stated at the outset, its features
considered essential to the composer—whether this is primarily melody, harmony, bass line, phrase structure, or some combination—can become clear
only in the variations. In constant-harmony variations the theme is really the
succession of harmonies and the phrase structure, as J. A. P. Schulz suggested;
the melody heard with the theme is merely one possible treble line that fits the
chords. The harmonic background is presented with a plausible melodic and
rhythmic foreground, and in succeeding variations new foregrounds are pro-
jected against that background. In melodic-outline variations, on the other
hand, the theme is a melody associated with a set of harmonies, as Koch made
clear, and then that melody is elaborated into ever more detailed foreground
configurations. Finally, in contrapuntal variations, the meaning of the theme
may include both or neither of these features. Thus, the frequent appearance of
disjunct eighth-note melodies in Haydn's early constant-bass variations, as in
Example 5.1, reflects their function not as tunes but as contrapuntal projections
of the harmony and bass line.

7. Koch, *Versuch,* III, p. 52; *Introductory Essay,* p. 83.
8. On "idea," see Jürgen Neubacher, "'Idee' und 'Ausführung.' Zum Kompositionsprozeß bei
Joseph Haydn," *AfMw* 41 (1984), 187–207.

Significant in the works of Haydn's contemporaries working in and around Vienna is the comparatively tiny number of variation movements from the 1760s and, in particular, the almost total absence of variation movements in their symphonies; I have located only two symphonies with variations, neither of which has previously been identified by modern scholars. One of these is the misnamed "Rondo" finale of Gassmann's Symphony No. 65 in A♭ Major, dated 1768 in the holograph manuscript (Example 5.2).[9] When Albrechtsberger copied this symphony in 1792, he labeled the last movement "Rondo," presumably as a synonym for "finale"; the modern edition by László Somfai draws on this source.[10] But the movement in question is a set of variations on a nearly unchanging bass, with instrumental figuration of a sometimes *concertante* nature given to a different instrument in each variation. This approach is similar to Haydn's *concertante* finales in symphonies of the mid–1760s (Nos. 31 and 72). The finale of Ordonez's Symphony D6 in D major has also not been recognized as variations, perhaps because this composer, like Gassmann, wrote very few variation movements (one string quartet and one string trio), and did not label the variations. It is by no means uncommon to find variation movements without explicitly labeled variations, and composers were rarely consistent in this regard. A. Peter Brown describes the finale as "a series of five closed chain couplets" and coda.[11] Not only is the theme an unusual one for variations by virtue of its string tremolo and lack of melody, but the beautiful ascending suspensions in the second variation are of a kind never written by Haydn. Example 5.3 shows theme and var. 2.

Equally far from Haydn's style is the theme of the finale of Ordonez's G-major Quartet Op. 2 No. 6; indeed, the preponderance of root-position chords and frequent cadences does not make the quartet theme a promising one for variations (Example 5.4).[12] Yet as the conclusion to a piece that began with a slow movement in minor followed by a fugue, the sweetly affirmative full sonorities are not inappropriate. Thus context may override technical criteria. The quartet movements by Haydn's Preßburg colleague Anton Zimmermann (1741–1781) have either less rhythmic motion or greater contrast within the theme than works by Haydn, as Zimmermann's F-major String Quartet

9. George R. Hill, *A Thematic Catalog of the Instrumental Music of Florian Leopold Gassmann* (Hackensack, 1976), pp. ix, 15–16. Nomenclature is a problem when composers often did not label their variations. See Elaine R. Sisman, "Haydn's Variations" (Ph.D. diss., Princeton University, 1978), pp. 145–153.

10. *Musica Rinata* 18 (Budapest, 1972).

11. A. Peter Brown, "The Symphonies of Carlo d'Ordonez: A Contribution to the History of Viennese Instrumental Music during the Second Half of the Eighteenth Century, *HYb* 12 (1981), 117; see also idem, "The Chamber Music with Strings of Carlos d'Ordonez: A Bibliographic and Stylistic Study," *AM* 46 (1974), 222–272, and *Carlo d'Ordonez 1734–1786: A Thematic Catalog* (Detroit, 1978). Brown dates Symphony D6 to the 1770s.

12. In its repetitive phrase stressing the subdominant, however, the quartet theme resembles the theme of a keyboard piece attributed to Haydn, Hob. XVII:7*, published in the appendix to Gerlach's edition of Haydn's *Klavierstücke*.

Example 5.2.   Gassmann, Symphony no. 65 in Ab major, finale: *concertante* variations on a constant bass.

shows (Example 5.5 taken from manuscript copy in A-Wn S.m. 12518). Albrechtsberger's early D-major quartet, attributed to Haydn (Hob. III:D3) until the autograph was identified in Budapest,[13] has more rhythmic contrast in the

13. László Somfai, "Albrechtsberger-Eigenschriften in der Nationalbibliothek Széchény, Budapest," *SM* 2 (1961), 201, Ms. mus. 2395, no. 39 in the catalogue. There is a copy in Göttweig dated 1763 (Hoboken, *Haydn-Verzeichnis,* I, p. 446). On the other hand, a Melk copy is inscribed "Composui 10. Octobris 767" (Hoboken, *Haydn-Verzeichnis,* III, p. 305). The style of the piece is similar to Haydn's Quartet Op. 2 No. 6. See also Georg Feder, "Apokryphe 'Haydn'-Streichquartette," *HSt* 4 (1974), 135–136.

Example 5.3. Ordonez, Symphony D6 in D major, finale: theme and var. 2.

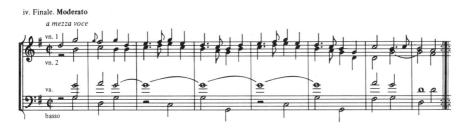

Example 5.4. Ordonez, String Quartet in G major, Op. 2/6/iv: theme.

theme than is typical of Haydn from this or indeed any period. It also features a strikingly chromatic—for this period—deceptive cadence on an augmented sixth chord in both its first and second sections (Example 5.6). A curious co-incidence is that the variation theme of another string quartet wrongly attrib-uted to Haydn, the "Fantasia con variazioni" first movement of Op. 3 No. 2, now thought to be probably by Romanus Hofstetter, also contains an aug-mented sixth chord, although somewhat more conventionally deployed in the second period as part of a varied repetition of a two-measure incise ending

Example 5.5.   Zimmermann, String Quartet in F major, first mvt.: theme.

Example 5.6.   Albrechtsberger, String Quartet in D major (Hob. III:D3), first mvt.: theme.

on a half-cadence. The ballet-composer Franz Aspelmayr's undistinguished Eb-major Quartet, listed in the Breitkopf Supplement of 1768 (A-Wgm IX 1116), has a rather stiff, repetitive theme with both phrases in the first period ending on the nearly identical cadence (V/V-V); the variations that follow trade off phrase by phrase *concertante* roles for the two violins, a pattern used by Haydn only in his Horn Trio, Hob. IV:5 (1767).

Gassmann's divertimenti for oboe and strings have two variation finales with constant bass, and as noted in Chapter 3, composers like Dittersdorf, Gassmann, Aspelmayr, Albrechtsberger, and Vanhal wrote many minuet finales with constant-bass variation in sonatas for violin and bass (or another combination of two strings).[14] Most of these works have stereotyped figurative patterns, usually including one variation each of triplets, sixteenth-notes, syncopations, and double-stops. Haydn's own set of six violin-viola duos, published in 1775 but possibly written in the late 1760s for Luigi Tomasini, is a striking exception in sometimes altering the viola line and allowing occasional participation.[15] And Haydn goes much farther in variation procedures than his contemporaries, since two of the slow movements have varied reprises (Hob. VI:3 and 6, both *sicilianas*), and one has a first movement in variation form as well; VI:3 in Bb major thus has three movements in which variation is the dominating principle. As is typical of Haydn throughout his career, the variations themselves contain "varied reprises," in the form of occasional returns of the unvaried theme followed by a varied repeat. Haydn's Viennese contemporaries hardly ever used this technique.

Interestingly, very few of Haydn's contemporaries in and around Vienna appear to have written variations for keyboard or keyboard ensemble during the 1750s, 1760s, and 1770s.[16] Wenzel Raimund Birck's *Trattenimenti per Clavicembalo*, published in Vienna in 1757, contains in its first "Trattenimento" an "Aria con sei variazioni" in which the melody is always recognizable and the rhythmic patterns of the figurations increase in speed and complexity in such a way as to imply progressive graded exercises for keyboard students, probably Birck's own: the title page identifies Birck as "Maestro di Tre Sereniβimi Arciduchi," the sons of Maria Theresia.[17] Many of the aforementioned works can-

---

14. On the genre of works for two stringed instruments, see Ulrich Masurowicz, *Das Streichduett in Wien von 1760 bis zum Tode Joseph Haydns* (Tutzing, 1982).

15. Gerber asserted that he had seen two of the duets already in 1769 *(Neues historisch-biographisches Lexicon der Tonkünstler,* II [1812], p. 580), but Larsen finds no reason to accept this *(Die Haydn-Überlieferung* [Copenhagen, 1939], p. 226). Pohl originally suggested the connection to Tomasini (Carl Ferdinand Pohl, *Joseph Haydn* [Leipzig, 1878–1882], I, p. 262); Landon considers it to be "generally accepted" *(Haydn Chronicle,* II, pp. 346–347), and suggests moreover a date of c. 1766–1768, to make them "studies" for the quartets.

16. Carla Pollock does not mention any, other than the ones given here, in her thorough dissertation "Viennese Solo Keyboard Music, 1740–1770: A Study in the Evolution of the Classical Style" (Ph.D. diss., Brandeis University, 1984). She kindly shared some of her material on Steffan with me.

17. Copy in A-Wgm VII 15208. An excerpt from this movement appears in Brown, *Haydn's Keyboard Music,* p. 187. Birck also wrote a "Passacaile où Passagaglio" as the finale to a trio ("à 3", Nr. XIII) for two violins and bass; manuscript in A-Wgm IX 31817. The eleven variations of the five-measure theme consist of six in major and five in minor, in that order.

not be dated with precision, but share certain clichés of mid-century style, especially in cadence patterns. Constant-bass variations are also a sure sign of composition prior to about 1770. None of Wagenseil's published sets of sonatas contains variations and only one of Steffan's does, a minuet finale (Op. 2/6, 1760) that alternates major and minor variations on the theme.[18] Vanhal wrote a single keyboard trio with constant-bass variations, and even Haydn included only one in an early sonata (Hob. XVII:D1/i) and two in trios (Hob. XV:C1 and XV:2, both finales).

The following discussion will focus on Haydn's strophic variations up to the mid-1770s, considering characteristic features of his constant-harmony variations against the background of contemporary practice, as well as the impact of adding more and more melodic-outline variations to a set. Haydn developed several ways to create motivic connections between variations and the theme, even in the absence of direct melodic correspondences. Comparisons of motivically-oriented variations with those that present a new melody and with those that modify the theme melody will clarify Haydn's contributions to a mid-century variation aesthetic, as well as to rhetorical notions of the theme and its treatment.

CHAMBER MUSIC FOR STRINGS

Haydn's early chamber music for strings is bedeviled by various problems—chronology and authenticity in the string trios, the nature of genre in the first ten string quartets (or "quartet-divertimenti," as Landon calls them), and musical weight in the baryton trios. The ten quartets of "Op. 1" and "Op. 2" most probably date from the mid or late 1750s, when Haydn provided music for the informal quartet parties at Baron von Fürnberg's estate at Weinzierl.[19] The string trios, completed by the mid-1760s, may date in part from the 1750s as well.[20] And covering over half of the first Esterházy decade are the baryton trios. The relationships among these genres are problematic. Oliver Strunk and H. C. Robbins Landon have suggested that all the trios were "practice pieces" for quartets, and that the results of experimentation can be seen in the quartets of Op. 9 (c. 1769–70) and Op. 17 (1771).[21] Georg Feder, on the other

18. This set of six sonatas was dedicated to the Archduke (and future Emperor) Joseph (A-Wgm Q11490), and was advertised in 1760.

19. See James Webster, "The Chronology of Haydn's String Quartets," *MQ* 61 (1975), 35–44, for a suggested dating of 1755–1759. (The earlier part of that period now seems most likely.) Albrechtsberger's early quartets, written at Melk, may have been used there as well. But the authentic manuscripts of the Bb-major quartet, Op. 2/6 (Hob. III: 12), show the spelling of "Menuet" used by Haydn somewhat later (c. 1760–62). See Georg Feder, "Zur Datierung Haydnscher Werke," in *Anthony van Hoboken. Festschrift zum 75. Geburtstag,* ed. Joseph Schmidt-Görg (Mainz, 1962), pp. 50–54.

20. Landon, *Haydn Chronicle* I, pp. 219–224, 259–260; Barry Brook and Bruce MacIntyre, foreword to *Streichtrios: JHW IX/1* (Munich, 1987), pp. vii-viii.

21. See Oliver Strunk, "Haydn's Divertimenti for Baryton, Viola, and Bass," *MQ* 18 (1932), 216–251, rpt. in *Essays on Music in the Western World* (New York, 1974), pp. 160–161; Landon, *Haydn Chronicle,* II, p. 351. This point of view goes back to Haydn's imaginative early biographer Carpani *(Le Haydine* [Milan, 1812]) and the more sober C. F. Pohl *(Joseph Haydn,* I, p. 256).

hand, has posited a division of Haydn's early genres into "serious" and "light," which suggests little cross-fertilization: string trios and string quartets beginning with Opus 9 are considered serious and thus a world apart from the earliest quartets and baryton trios, the lighter genres.[22] The fundamental problem of establishing a canon of string trios has hampered stylistic assessments,[23] while discussions of the baryton trios, ever since Strunk first laid the groundwork for their study, have tended to focus on single elements, like the fugues, rather than on a full survey.[24]

An examination of the variation movements in all three genres of chamber music with strings will clarify aspects of their differing compositional procedures. For example, although all of the earliest variations in quartets and trios retain the bass line of the theme, their treatment of the theme's melody is strikingly more complex and motivically connected in the string-quartet variations than in the string-trio variations, while the string trios, in turn, are more motivic than most of the melodic substitutions in the baryton-trio variation movements. The degree of difference in motivic treatment is especially pertinent in the quartet and string-trio movements in Bb major, Op. 2 No. 6 and Hob. V:8 (both first movements), because of the unusual similarity in the contour of their themes, about which a short digression is in order.[25]

VARIATIONS ON SIMILAR THEMES

The two Bb-major variation movements just cited form the first of four groups of pieces which vary similar themes in related ways; the others are, second, baryton trio XI:38/i (c. 1767) and keyboard variations for four hands XVIIa:1 ("Il maestro e lo scolare," 1768); third, string trio V:7/ii (before about 1765), string duo VI:2/iii (before about 1769), and possibly sonata XVI:30/iii (1776); and fourth, sonatas XVI:36/ii (c. 1770–75) and 39/i (before 1780).[26] We might be inclined to discount such resemblances as being within typical or normal

22. See Georg Feder, "Die beiden Pole im Instrumentalschaffen des jungen Haydns," in *Der junge Haydn,* ed. Vera Schwarz (Graz, 1972), pp. 192–201. For a partial refinement of this view, see Elaine R. Sisman, "Haydn's Baryton Pieces and His Serious Genres," in *Internationaler Joseph Haydn Kongress Wien 1982,* ed. Eva Badura-Skoda (Munich, 1986), pp. 426–435.

23. Publication of the eighteen authentic string trios in *Joseph Haydn Werke,* edited by Barry Brook and Bruce MacIntyre (Munich, 1987), has rectified the situation. Hubert Unverricht's study of string trios *(Das Streichtrio* [Tutzing, 1969]) discusses only Haydn's baryton trios, not the rest of his string trio output. My thanks to Barry Brook and Bruce MacIntyre for providing me with copies of the string trios before publication of their edition.

24. See Warren Kirkendale, *Fugue and Fugato in Rococo and Classical Chamber Music,* 2nd ed., rev. and trans. Margaret Bent and the author (Durham, N.C., 1979), pp. 140–141; Susan Wollenberg, "Haydn's Baryton Trios and the *Gradus,*" *ML* 54 (1973), 170–180.

25. A nearly identical pattern also appears at the beginning of the Divertimento Hob. II:11, "Der Geburtstag," first movement; the variations in the finale are not affected.

26. For more details about the string trio and string duo, see Sisman, "Haydn's Variations," pp. 198–200. Another not fully analogous pair are the sonata-form slow movements of Piano Trio XV:26 (?1794) and Symphony 102 (1795); in the symphony movement, the exposition is given a varied reprise, primarily changing the tone color. For other occasions of Haydn reusing material, see Georg Feder, "Similarities in the Works of Haydn," in *Studies in Eighteenth-Century Music,* ed. Landon, pp. 186–197.

ranges within a narrow chronological spectrum in the works of a single composer, but for the fact that Haydn himself called attention to the third such group in a defensive letter to his publisher. The facts of this third situation suggest that Haydn's operating procedures in the earlier movements were similar, but took place out of the public eye, that is, without the spotlight of publication.

Haydn's by-now familiar letter to Artaria of 25 February 1780 explained the near-identity of two movements in the set of sonatas dedicated to the Auenbrugger sisters, the Scherzando/Allegro con brio middle movement of the C#-minor sonata (Hob. XVI:36) and the Allegro con brio first movement of the G-major sonata (Hob. XVI:39):

> Incidentally, I consider it necessary, in order to forestall the criticisms of any would-be wits [*Witzlinge*], to print on the reverse side of the title page the following sentence, here underlined:
>
> Avertissement:
>
> *Among these 6 Sonatas there are two single movements in which the same idea occurs through several bars: the author has done this intentionally, to show different methods of realization [Ausführung].* For of course I could have chosen a hundred other ideas instead of this one; but so that the whole opus will not be exposed to blame on account of this one intentional detail (which the critics and especially my enemies might interpret wrongly), I think that this avertissement or something like it must be appended, otherwise the sale might be hindered thereby.[27]

The term *Ausführung*, which might also be translated "elaboration" or "execution" (or "treatment," as Landon has it), frequently appeared in discussions of both compositional process and rhetoric, as one stage of organizing musical or verbal material.[28] Haydn's use of the word *Idee* recalls what he told his biographers about his method of composing: "I sat down [at the clavier], began to improvise, sad or happy according to my mood, serious or trifling. Once I had seized upon an idea, my whole endeavor was to develop and sustain it in keeping with the rules of art."[29] The association made here between Haydn's "mood" and the musical idea he found is made explicit by the notice that Artaria actually included in the edition of the Auenbrugger sonatas: the "Avertimento" referred to two pieces with the same "sentimento" and to the working out of that idea as the "Continuazione del Sentimento."[30] It is also worth noting that when Griesinger questioned Haydn on the "motives [from which] he wrote his compositions, as well as the feelings and ideas he had in mind and that he strove to express through musical language," Haydn conceded that he

27. H. C. Robbins Landon, trans. and ed., *The Complete Correspondence and London Notebooks of Joseph Haydn* [hereafter *CCLN*], p. 25 (translation slightly altered); Haydn, *Gesammelte Briefe und Aufzeichnungen* [hereafter *Briefe*], ed. Dénes Bartha (Kassel, 1965), pp. 90–91. See Sisman, "Haydn's Hybrid Variations," in *Haydn Studies*, ed. Larsen et al., pp. 510–512; Neubacher, "'Idee' und 'Ausführung'"; and A. Peter Brown, *Haydn's Keyboard Music*, p. 320.

28. See Chapter 2.

29. Griesinger, *Notizen*, p. 114; Gotwals, *Haydn*, p. 61.

30. Haydn, *Briefe*, p. 91.

had sought to portray "moral characters" in his symphonies, giving the celebrated example of a Symphony adagio in which the "reigning idea" was of God
remonstrating with an unrepentant sinner.[31] The word "idea," then, could refer
to the musical thought or to its attendant affect, character, or "meaning." Thus,
the source of Haydn's ideas, his *inventio,* is intimately bound up with affective
quality.

The influence of movement-position on these works also accounts for some
of their differences. The G-major movement is an opener: its theme features
the assertive dotted rhythms that Haydn favored for so many first movements
in the sonatas. The A-major movement is a middle movement, softened both
by the "Scherzando" designation and by its sunny aspect after the brooding
C♯-minor first movement. Perhaps because a Scherzando is part of the dance-
movement convention, the contrasting episodes are both in the tonic minor, as
would be likely in a scherzo and trio; in the G-major movement, on the other
hand, a higher degree of contrast is sustained by unrelated episodes in tonic and
relative minors. Precedents are the finale of the D-major sonata XVI:19 (a
rondo-variation with episodes in tonic minor and dominant) and the Tempo di
Menuetto finale of the E-major sonata XVI:22 (an alternating rondo-variation
with episodes in tonic minor). Yet the A-major movement seems curiously out
of place, because it is an Allegro con brio *followed* by the minuet; Haydn here
reverses the plan of his slightly earlier B-minor sonata Hob. XVI:32.

The notion that Haydn used similar themes "intentionally, to show different
methods of realization" is equally significant in the A-major baryton trio and
"Il maestro e lo scolare." In the former, the melodic contour of the theme is all
but obliterated in the variations, while the keyboard set decorates the melody
of the theme, with only a few substitutions of its principal notes (Example
5.7). And this manner of embellishment is driven home by the gambit of the
latter piece: everything the master says, the student repeats in a higher octave.
It is plausible that Haydn envisioned a different type of amateur audience for
the four-hand set, one to whom progressive melodic decoration meant greater
intelligibility.[32]

QUARTET OP. 2 NO. 6 AND STRING TRIO HOB. V:8

To return to the early chamber music: the *Hauptnoten* of the theme melody in
these pieces are generally to be found at cadences only. For the rest of the
phrase—or for the entire phrase, when even the cadence pattern is not observed—the variation may focus on one or more motives from the theme, on
new motives, on a new melody entirely, or on a neutral projection of the harmonies. The first of these techniques characterizes the Quartet Op. 2 No. 6,

31. Griesinger, *Notizen,* p. 117; Gotwals, *Haydn,* p. 63. See Sisman, "Haydn's Theater Symphonies," *JAMS* 42 (1990), 336–339; Webster, *Haydn's "Farewell" Symphony,* pp. 234–235, 244.

32. Two of the other "groups" of variation movements share key, movement-position, and technique. The early chamber-music variations are both B♭-major first movements and employ similar
motivic treatments (see below), while the A-major grouping consists exclusively of Tempo di
Menuetto finales with frequent melodic reprises in different registers.

(a) Trio 38

Un poco Andante

Var. 1

Example 5.7. (a): Haydn, Baryton Trio XI:38/i. Theme and var. 1; (b): Haydn, Sonata for keyboard four-hands, Hob. XVIIa: 1/i ("Il Maestro e lo scolare"). Theme and var. 1.

the second the Trio Hob. V:8, and the last two the vast majority of the baryton-trio variations. At issue is the level of "density" of the variations, referring both to the level of activity and to the quality of that activity vis-à-vis the theme. A set with a preponderance of motivically saturated or texturally complex variations exhibits the "heaping-up" tendency of the word-figure *congeries,* a rhetorical strategy intensified by *comparison.* The baryton trios never achieve this level of saturation. In this respect, perhaps, Feder's designation of the baryton trios as "light" takes on a literal meaning.

Haydn's ten early string quartets contain just the one set of variations already mentioned, the first movement of the Bb-major quartet, Op. 2 No. 6 (Hob. III:12), the sophisticated motivic and textural organization of which reveals Haydn as a master already in his twenties.[33] In each of its three variations, motivic fragments of the theme are reconfigured, placed in different textural contexts over the unchanging bass. The melody, so prominent in the treble-dominated theme, seems simply to disappear. Yet during the theme reprise, pleonastic melodic-outline technique animates the varied repeats of each section of the theme, proving the resurgence of the theme melody to be a convincing method for ending the movement. The Adagio theme (Example 5.8), one of Haydn's earliest with a markedly cantabile character, is almost numbing in its initial regularity: each of the first three phrases constitutes an embellished descent from f² with a dotted rhythm on the first beat. A new rhythm introduced in m. 10 provides interest as the basis of a transitional incise (mm. 13–14). Most unusual for a variation theme is the "scrambled" tonic reprise in the second period (mm. 15–20), with the original first measure now displaced into

33. Webster convincingly argues for a reassessment of Haydn's works of the 1750s and 1760s, describing them as unfairly denigrated by the notion that Haydn reached musical "maturity" in the 1770s or even 1780s. See *Haydn's "Farewell" Symphony,* pp. 334–366.

Example 5.7   (*continued*)

Example 5.8.   Haydn, String Quartet Op. 2/6/i (Hob. III:12) and String Trio Hob. V:8/i, themes compared; (a) Quartet, (b) Trio.

Example 5.8 (*continued*)

the second, the new rhythm replacing the simple repeated notes, and the ordering into six measures a complication of earlier constructions.[34] The structure of the Adagio theme of the Bb-major String Trio, on the other hand, contains irregular phrases right from the start, with a melodic appendix to the first three-bar phrase—perhaps Haydn's earliest "redundant" tonic cadence—and imitation at the beginning of the second period. But the six-bar return eliding the first three bars of the first phrase with the second three bars of the second phrase (mm. 1–3 and 6–8) resembles that six-bar returning phrase of the Quartet. Example 5.8 compares the themes of the quartet and the Bb-major String Trio by bracketing the similar and recurring elements in corresponding measures.

Every variation in Op. 2 No. 6 pits the first violin against a paired second violin and viola, a texture perhaps forecast by their parallel thirds in m. 4 of the theme (Example 5.9a). While the first violin in var. 1 projects the opening melodic interval of the theme (an ascending fourth) over a two-bar span, the inner voices create a pervasive sixteenth-note pattern by diminishing and transforming the theme's second bar. In the second variation, two different rhythmic motives are similarly exploited, the dotted figures of the first violin deriving from m. 7, and the "answering" sixteenths in the inner voices a smoother version of the theme's melodic contour (ultimately also deriving from m. 4). The constant give-and-take of the upper voices increases the disjunction of phrase rhythm: each original phrase is now separable into half-measure units. Var. 3 enlarges that to full-measure units, but now it is the first violin which answers the central violin 2/viola pair.

The contrast between variations of the entire theme and embellished reprise of the theme *within* each statement completes the case for free motivic treatment as distinct from melodic-outline technique. Each of the variations thus far has manifested a kind of part-for-whole relationship to the theme, or the figure *synecdoche,* while the decorations in the reprise, in the guise of varied repeats, are pleonastic (Example 5.9b). Almost every note of the theme melody is present in the same part of the measure in which it originally appeared, with the addition of those pleonastic figurations. Haydn thus distinguishes starkly between treating a theme as a compound of harmony, melody, and rhythm—a conception that leads to motivic variations—and treating it as a melody only. The circular function of the theme reprise now refers to the act of varying itself.

A very different kind of motivic organization animates the first movement of the Bb-major String Trio Hob. V:8, Haydn's only trio in the "modern" scoring of violin, viola, and bass (cello) instead of two violins over the bass, vaguely reminiscent of the trio sonata. Here the rhythmic motives dominating each variation are not clearly derived from the theme, and thus sound "generic"

34. Other examples of unconventional arrangements in Haydn's music of this period are offered in James Webster, "Freedom of Form in Haydn's Early String Quartets," in *Haydn Studies,* ed. Larsen et al., pp. 522–530.

(b) Varied Repeat of Theme Reprise in Var. 4

Example 5.9. Haydn, Op. 2/6/i. (a): motives; (b): var. 4, varied repeat (mm. 89ff.).

(Example 5.10).[35] The progression from larger to smaller note values is twice interrupted, first by the more cantabile third variation, and then by the slower syncopations in the fifth. Haydn rarely sustained syncopation throughout an entire variation, and its effect here, especially given the viola partly doubling

35. These motives are similar to Haydn's only other set of variations in the first movement of a string trio, Hob. V:D3, especially in the sixteenth-note and syncopated variation. The D-major piece, however, varies the bass in every variation, Haydn's earliest set to do so.

Example 5.10. Haydn, String Trio Hob. V:8/i, motives.

the cello (and varying the bass line), is to turn the bass line into a cantus firmus with species counterpoint. And var. 3 departs most strikingly from the structure of the theme, yet it is the only variation to retain the descending stepwise figures of the theme and its counterpoint. As the center of the six-variation set, this third variation is at once the structural point of furthest remove and the melodic point of thematic reference.[36]

A third type of free treatment over a constant bass is more characteristic of the baryton trios than other early genres. A representative example is Trio 29 (Hob. XI:29), written in 1766 or 1768 on a tune from Haydn's 1766 opera-intermezzo *La Canterina* (no. 1, "Che visino delicato"). Unlike either the quartet or the string trio, the melodies are new counterpoints to the bass, retaining only the cadence formulas of the theme. Rarely, a motive from the theme appears:

Var. 1:   "neutral" projection of the bass line
Var. 2:   figuration without individual profile

36. The expression "point of furthest remove" is taken from Leonard Ratner's description of the harmonic progress of the development section *(Classic Music,* pp. 225–227). I use it by broad structural analogy, rather than in a precise correspondence.

Var. 3:   more interesting revision of melodic line, with dotted rhythm at different part of the measure
Var. 4:   sixteenth-triplets
Var. 5:   written-out theme *da capo*

Example 5.11 shows the theme and first phrases of vars. 1–3. The variations diverge most from the contour of the theme melody when the harmonic rhythm is most stable, usually in the first phrase, while melodic similarity between theme and variation tends to increase in sequential passages after the double bar. These sequential passages are often strikingly similar to the harmonic-motion strategies for transitions that Riepel whimsically described and named *Monte* (mountain, an ascending sequence), *Ponte* (bridge, for a kind of horizontal "holding" passage on V), and *Fonte* (fountain, a descending sequence).[37] In Trio 29, the sequence (mm. 9–11) is sufficiently memorable to recall the theme regardless of melodic content, while the succeeding parallel-tenth construction (mm. 12–14) precludes deviations in voice-leading. Within the notion of free melodic treatment, then, resemblance to the theme's melody finds a place. I have suggested that the rhetorical figure *synonymy* best describes the introduction of new melodies to the harmonies of the theme.[38]

BARYTON TRIOS

The baryton trios do more than merely furnish us with representative samples of Haydn's variation technique. In fact, they now take up a major portion of the remaining stylistic history of Haydn's early strophic variations.[39] As the most intensively cultivated genre of Haydn's early career, the trios occupy the period between the early quartets and string trios and the next phase of quartet writing beginning around 1770, as well as the introduction of sustained symphonic variation-writing in the early 1770s. And in fulfilling Prince Nikolaus Esterházy's constant demands for new works, Haydn had first to invent a new genre, much as he had done with his earlier chamber works, one moreover circumscribed by the Prince's limited technical ability and the tenor range of his instrument. One wonders how widespread was Burney's disgusted assessment of the baryton as an "ungrateful instrument, with the additional embarrassment of base [*sic*] strings at the back of the neck . . . an admirable expedient in a desert, or even in a house, where there is but one musician; but to be at the trouble of accompanying yourself in a great concert, surrounded by idle performers who could take the trouble off your hands . . ."[40] After the Prince made official his demands for baryton works in the *Regulatio Chori Kissmarton-*

---

37. Riepel, *Tonordnung*, pp. 57–58, and passim. Examples are given in Ratner, "*Ars combinatoria,*" p. 351, and Landon, "Riepel and *Absatz,*" pp. 511–512.

38. See Chapter 2. For other examples of free melodic treatment, see Sisman, "Haydn's Variations," pp. 164–197.

39. See Sisman, "Haydn's Baryton Pieces." One of the most serious flaws in Ernst Reichert's dissertation on Haydn's variations is that the baryton pieces were unknown to him ("Die Variation-Arbeit bei Haydn," Ph.D. diss., Vienna, 1926).

40. Burney, *A General History of Music,* II, p. 1020.

Example 5.11. Haydn, Baryton Trio Hob. XI:29/i.

iensis of 1765,[41] Haydn not only began to produce trios and other ensemble music for the baryton (including solos, duos, and concertos listed in Hob. X–XIV), but he also had the trios richly bound in leather and gold each time another twenty-four were completed.[42] We know nothing of the Prince's possible predilection for variation movements. That the predilection is Haydn's and not his patron's is suggested by the complete absence of variations in the many baryton trios written for the Prince by Luigi Tomasini, the Esterházy concertmaster; unlike Haydn, Tomasini included rondo finales as a matter of course.[43]

41. The document is translated in Landon, *Haydn Chronicle,* I, 420; the relevant passage appears at the end: "Finally, said *Capelmeister* [*sic*] Haydn is urgently enjoined to apply himself to composition more diligently than heretofore, and especially to write such pieces as can be played on the gamba [baryton], of which pieces we have seen very few up to now; and to be able to judge his diligence, he shall at times send us the first copy, cleanly and carefully written, of each and every composition."

42. The dates of completion of the five volumes are 1766, 1767, 1768, the end of 1771, and 1778; the last of these included pieces composed a good deal earlier, probably around 1772, by which time the Prince had lost interest in the instrument. See Sonja Gerlach, *Vorwort* to *Barytontrios 1–24. Joseph Haydn Werke XIV/1,* ed. Sonja Gerlach and Jürgen Braun, pp. vii–viii. Documentation on the binding of the volumes appears in Ulrich Tank, "Die Dokumente der Esterházy-Archive zur fürstlichen Hofkapelle in der Zeit von 1761 bis 1770," *HSt* 4 (1980), passim.

43. Tomasini did include variation movements in his other string chamber music, especially quartets and violin duos, sometimes in slow movements. See Friedrich Korcak, "Luigi Tomasini

Just as each volume represents a different stage in the stylistic history of the genre, the variation sets within each volume show an evolving conception of technique and structure. In examining the works on their own terms and in comparison with earlier and later string chamber music, we ought to hold temporarily in abeyance the tendency to trivialize them that is almost inevitably aroused by their origin in princely idiosyncrasy and their ostensible role as practice pieces. (The relevant movements are included in Table A.1.) The variations of the first book reveal greater variety than other movements among these tiny pieces in which Haydn was still testing the ranges and balance of the instruments. Here we find Haydn's first variation theme with five-measure periods (phrases of $3 + 2$, $2 + 3$ in Trio 6, which is also the only set in common time). Theme reprises, normally in last position and different from the literal da capos identified in the table, often reconfigure the texture or accompaniment without changing the bass line. All of the earliest sets are of the constant-bass type, and Haydn alternates variations showing new or neutral melodies, usually with a figured viola line, with those that feature figuration only. This alternation, which recurs throughout the baryton trios, occurs nowhere else among Haydn's early variations; its importance to Haydn's later style suggests a larger role of the baryton trios in shaping its development than has heretofore been recognized.

The second and third volumes expanded textural and thematic possibilities. In particular, Haydn focused on the unique sonorous capabilities of the baryton, exploiting not only its sympathetic plucked strings in variation movements of Trios 41, 45, 50, 60, and 69, but also its soloistic potential in *concertante* passages and cadenzas, especially in Trio 60. At the same time, he allowed the bass to participate in thematic play, a general departure in his chamber music; this appears for the first time in Trio 41, where viola and cello imitate each other to the quaint sounds of the plucked baryton strings. In thematic structure too, Haydn introduced new features, such as a second-period contrast in minor as well as an appendix over a tonic pedal, both in Trio 50.[44] That sort of appendix became important to his later variation style, and can be found even among works of the 1790s, as in the first-movement themes of the G-minor Piano Trio Hob. XV:19 and Eb-major Quartet Op. 76 No. 6.

Trio 60 embodies a tale of progressive abandonment of the theme melody, while projecting its harmony more and more forcefully. Both features are paradoxically embodied in the theme itself (Example 5.12). First, the disjunct melodic line contains the seeds of its dissolution in its incorporation of a plucked bass note and in its stuttering stop in the fourth phrase (mm. 14–15), unable to resolve until rescued by a cadenza. And second, the full-triad accompaniment to the baryton found at the beginning of the theme (double-stops in the viola) immediately stands apart from every other baryton-trio variation movement.

(1741–1808). Konzertmeister der fürstlich Esterhazyschen Kapelle in Eisenstadt unter Joseph Haydn" (Ph.D. diss., Vienna, 1952).

44. First reprise: eight bars ending in the tonic; second reprise: four bars in tonic minor, return of first reprise, then four-bar appendix.

Example 5.12. Haydn, Baryton Trio Hob. XI:60/i.

In the first variation a melodic-outline treatment pleonastically fills in some of the leaps, and then, as if sensing the futility of trying to do anything with that melody, the second variation replaces it with a higher, more neutral, and slower-moving melody over broken-chord accompaniment in the viola. By var. 3, a presentation of the theme harmony with varied bass line and double- and even triple-stops in the baryton itself, there is no melodic line at all, and even the written-out cadenza is avoided.[45] Rounding off the narrative is the laconic *da capo.*

45. Most of Haydn's cadenzas in ensemble pieces are simply notated with a *ferma,* so the presence of written-out cadenzas in vars. 1 and 2 is rather more unusual.

The fourth volume of trios, longer in the making, contained pieces with greater pretensions and affective richness, including the only two trios in minor. The theme reprise of Trio 73 in G major has its entire first reprise in tonic minor, just as the recapitulation of the G-major symphony, No. 47 (1772), begins the recapitulation in G minor; Haydn's first true *minore* variations appeared in keyboard sonatas of 1774–1776. The second period of Trio 81 has harmonies never followed in the variations. And Trio 95 has the only first-movement variation set with an Allegro theme; its walking bass is fully varied in sixteenth notes during the last variation, a partial theme reprise which wittily changes the theme melody in midstream.[46] Thus, formally, contrapuntally, and texturally, the form has reached a new level. Only the specific soloistic features of the baryton recede somewhat, mirroring in microcosm Haydn's decreasing interest in *concertante* spotlights generally by the early 1770s. Finally, the greater length of the trios in Volume 5 cannot hide that only some of them aspire to continue the deepened expressive content of the previous volumes. Yet in their coordination of elements, the trios of the final volume approach the polish of the string quartets written around 1770, though on a much more superficial level: every variation movement contains varied bass lines, and some have bass participation in motivic play (105, 106, 116); the viola is given greater solo prominence in at least one variation of every set; and in every movement melodic-outline technique predominates.

QUARTETS OP. 9 AND OP. 17

The two variation movements in the Quartets Op. 9 and Op. 17 (No. 5 and No. 3, respectively) are recognizably derived from techniques first used in the baryton trios, and refer as well to types of figuration used earlier in the Bb-major quartet Op. 2/6. The turn to minor after the double bar, the active if sporadic participation of the bass, a new melodic contour over fast-moving accompaniment, all are prefigured in the trios.[47] The principal "advances" are, first, inherent in the string quartet genre itself. Compared with the baryton, a metallic-sounding middle-range instrument, the violin exhibits tremendous versatility and range, which in a four-part texture leads inevitably to new compositional possibilities. Not until Op. 20 are these possibilities fully realized in variations, however. And second, the themes of the two quartet movements are simply more inventive in Op. 9—the return beginning in the "wrong" key, for example—and more profound in Op. 17, with its chain of suspensions and

46. Haydn's gradual varying of the bass line is discussed in Ludwig Finscher, *Studien zur Geschichte des Streichquartetts. I: Die Entstehung des klassischen Streichquartetts: Von den Vorformen zur Grundlegung durch Joseph Haydn* (Kassel, 1974), pp. 172–173; see also Sisman, "Haydn's Variations," chap. 4.

47. Strunk and Finscher have called attention to Haydn's intensification of the latest baryton-trio variation techniques in the string quartets of Opp. 9 and 17: freer use of the theme in a non-reprise variation in Op. 9 No. 5, and varied bass in the reprise of Op. 17 No. 3 (as well as the assignment of the bass line to an instrument other than the cello in Op. 20 No. 4). See Strunk, "Haydn's Baryton Trios," pp. 148–149; Finscher, *Geschichte des Streichquartetts*, p. 174.

phrase-expansion in the second reprise. The most imaginative variation in the two quartets is the second one of Op. 9 No. 5, which juxtaposes free and melodic-outline treatment, and combines constant motivic play with intermittent melodic reprise; in these senses it unites Op. 2 No. 6 and the baryton trios. Otherwise, the Op. 9 variations have a garden-variety plan of progressive diminution (sixteenths to sixteenth-triplets to thirty-seconds) and a theme reprise with decorated repeats.

The true significance of Op. 9 and Op. 17 for Haydn's variation procedures lies less in the strophic variations *per se* than in the varied reprise movements, the "only art-form Haydn owes to [C. P. E.] Bach," as Tovey put it.[48] Bach's sonatas circulated in Vienna in 1767, 1769, and 1773; Haydn's quartets were written between 1769 and 1771.[49] (Haydn had already written a tiny, binary slow movement with varied reprises in a divertimento [Hob. II:23/iii]; for that matter, the third of Porpora's twelve sonatas for violin and bass concluded with a Vivace with varied reprises, and these works were published in Vienna in 1754, probably the period of Haydn's studies with him.)[50] Unlike Bach, Haydn repeats only the exposition in varied form. These three movements mark the first systematic permeation of a slow movement by variation, and thus lay the foundation not only for the variation slow movement of Op. 20 No. 4, but also for Haydn's extraordinary varied slow movements in quartets, symphonies, and sonatas, far into the 1780s and 1790s. And not just the fact of varied reprise but the choice of movement—the hyper-expressive C-minor Adagio of Op. 9 No. 2 with an introductory recitative—suggests that Haydn chose variation as an intensifier of affect rather than as a signpost of the trivially *galant,* as some modern writers have supposed.[51] The vocal element of Op. 9 No. 2, heightened by the apparent recitative-aria pairing, also lends itself to embellishment (Example 5.13).[52] Indeed, the varied reprise so overbalances the movement that the second reprise not only has no repeat, it barely contains a return, only a tiny retransition and partial resolution of the final phrases.

48. Donald Francis Tovey, "Haydn's Chamber Music," rpt. in *The Main Stream of Music and Other Essays* (Cleveland and New York, 1959), p. 27. A. Peter Brown disputes Bach's influence in *Haydn's Keyboard Music,* pp. 220–221.

49. See Hannelore Gericke, *Der Wiener Musikalienhandel von 1700 bis 1778* (Graz, 1960), pp. 61, 72. On the dating of Op. 9 (c. 1769–1770), see Webster, "The Chronology of Haydn's String Quartets," pp. 30–34. The autograph of the Op. 17 quartets is dated 1771.

50. Copy in A-Wst MH 9887; the first movement includes a fugue. These pieces are full of interesting features.

51. László Somfai, in an otherwise convincing study, asserts that the opening variation movement in a quartet opus represented the "point of exhaustion" *(Ermüdungsmoment),* the flagging of the inspiration that, if strong, would have produced a sonata-form movement. See "Opus-Planung und Neuerung bei Joseph Haydn," *SM* 22 (1980), 93.

52. The only instrumental recitative I have found that actually forms part of a variation movement is the fifth variation of Michael Haydn's Divertimento in F major, No. 105, fourth movement; the variation is marked "Adagio senza rigor di tempo." See Reimund Hess, "Serenade, Cassation, Notturno und Divertimento bei Michael Haydn" (Ph.D. diss., Mainz, 1963), pp. 97–101 and ex. 29.

Example 5.13. Haydn, String Quartet Op. 9/2/ii: (a): opening recitative; (b): exposition, at second phrase; (c): varied repeat of second phrase.

The Watershed of 1772: Symphony in G major (No. 47)
and Quartet in D Major (Op. 20 No. 4)

After writing roughly four dozen sets of strophic variations, Haydn created a dramatic change in the weight of his variation movements. Perhaps the greater number of fixed elements prompted this, but perhaps also, to use Abbé Vogler's terminology, he had exhausted one set of rhetorical analogies and was seeking a new kind of unity in diversity. In 1772 Haydn moved the variation set into the interior slow movement, the first known to me. He would not have taken such a step lightly. He had always carefully crafted the overall construction of a multi-movement work, and in variations he had distinguished among the styles of duple first-movement variations in slow tempo, slow *concertante*-finale variations, and Menuet-finale variations. Symphony and string quartet were the most serious instrumental genres of the time.[53] The importance of two movements to Haydn's variation style—in Quartet Op. 20 No. 4 and Symphony No. 47—cannot be overestimated.

While the theme of the Adagio of Symphony 47 is as delicate and muted as other symphonic slow movements of the early 1770s, it is unprecedented in structure and texture among Haydn's variation themes. A true ternary form, its self-contained first section in two-part counterpoint returns in its entirety as the third section with the parts inverted. And this emphasis on the contrapuntal extends to the nature of that first section which, while balanced, is more linear than truly melodic: its two lines are counterpoises, similar in rhythm and melodic motion, the bass line lacking only the upward octave thrust of the melody (Example 5.14).[54]

Despite—or perhaps because of—the ambiguous status of the melody, Haydn varies it with a relentlessly melody-centered technique, that of progressive diminution, a rhythmic *gradatio*. During the inverted passage, the figured line moves to the bottom, while the bass, now in the upper register, remains the same. Haydn thus calls attention to a paradoxical combination of melodic-outline and constant-bass variation, each now in the "wrong" register. The result is a twofold "irony," because the theme does not lend itself to the treatment it gets, and because even that treatment turns a conventional technique into a comment on varying.[55]

But the plan of the movement has another dimension as well. The contrasting middle section of the theme, in adding winds and horns, achieves the fullest

53. See Feder, "Die beiden Pole," for a general discussion of this concept.

54. James Webster considers the theme to be a "beautiful melody" according to the criteria he outlines in "When Did Haydn Begin to Write 'Beautiful' Melodies?", pp. 385–388, at 387. Gretchen Wheelock, on the other hand, in discussing its appropriation as a song, describes it as an "unpromising choice" because it is a "skeletal duo"; see "Marriage à la Mode: Haydn's Instrumental Works 'Englished' for Voice and Piano," *JM* 8 (1990), 385. I am fundamentally in agreement with her description.

55. This sense of irony is similar to the ideas of "ironic distance" and consciousness of the composer's craft discussed in Mark Evan Bonds, "Haydn, Laurence Sterne, and the Origins of Musical Irony," *JAMS* 44 (1991), 57–91.

Example 5.14.   Haydn, Symphony No. 47/ii.

Var. 1

Var. 2

Var. 3

Example 5.14   (continued)

sonority in a variation theme to that time—indeed among all symphonic slow movements not overtly programmatic, theater-directed, or in first position—softening the bare counterpoint of the outer sections. It also forecasts the fully orchestrated theme reprise and coda at the end. And in presenting two new phrase structures (4 + 6, after the 5 + 5 of the opening), it fulfills the dual function of a local contrast between the first and third sections, and a harbinger of the phrase extensions in the coda, in which the movement's plan culminates. Finally, in leaving the bass register entirely, its chain of descending first-inversion triads—usually a signpost of heightened affect, of rhetorical intensification as the parts join together—makes a purely emotional appeal. In numerous ways, then, this piece is a departure for Haydn: the structure, texture, and orchestration of the theme, the nature of the melody and its incongruous treatment, and the overall organization in which each of these elements participates.

A panoply of rhetorical elements color this work, none acting in isolation. Of these the most obvious is progressive diminution acting as a rhythmic *gradatio,* or intensification, which recalls the similar procedure in the first movement of the symphony: martial first group succeeded by eighth-note triplets in the second group and sixteenths in the closing. More important than the increasing speed of figuration, however, is the role of the bass as *synecdoche* when it moves to the treble, standing in not only for the theme's melody but for its rhythmic values in countering the increasingly heavy-footed figuration in the bass. The continuing *ironic* tension between the nature of the melody and its treatment is thus exacerbated by the special incongruity of melodic-outline technique and *gradatio* applied in this way to the bass register. Ultimately, the rhythmic and melodic equivalence of melody and bass is made clear by the passage over a dominant pedal in the expressive coda, from which the final reprise of the theme arises (Example 5.15). Dominant pedals are quite rare in variations. The pedal here may be traced not only to the contrapuntal nature of the movement but also to the need for a final blurring of distinctions between

Example 5.15. Haydn, Symphony No. 47/ii, coda.

melody and bass: by extending each phrase to six measures from five (mm. 159–164, 165–170, to a deceptive cadence), the melody line starts to meander down the scale just as the bass does, and, to underscore their similarity, both phrases give the bass line above the melody. Finally, after all of the full cadences contained in the theme and variations, neither the reprise nor the final-period reprise in the coda is able to cadence in the tonic. The last phrase of the coda replaces the oft-repeated gesture to V with one to IV in order ultimately to attain closure.

The slow movement of the D-major String Quartet, Op. 20 No. 4, has several unusual features: its minor mode, Haydn's only set completely in minor;

its cello variation, part of the greater participation of the cello in this opus; and its long coda. Yet the most important aspects of the set are its large-scale planning together with a new sense of variations as comments on the theme, explorations of the different paths it suggests. This type of varying opened up a new realm to Haydn.

That the theme will have a heightened expressive character is already suggested by the tempo designation, Un poco Adagio e affettuoso. Its melody exploits the affective intensity of B♭, the sixth degree: it is the first melodic point of arrival, it is stressed during the modulation to F major, and it is the prolonged bass in the second section's climax (Example 5.16). The B♭ always resolves to A, in both melody and bass, as part of chord progressions such as vii^7–i, V^7/III–vi/III, IV$^{\sharp 6}_5$–V, or IV$^{\sharp 6}_5$–i$^6_4$. Most of these stressed B♭s are lost or less exposed in the variations, undermined by figurations or displaced in the measure. This temporary submergence of the B♭ is important to the large-scale design, as is the supporting role given to the first violin. The "filigree" texture of the first variation eliminates the single main voice of the theme by dividing figuration and syncopation between second violin and viola; in addition, the figuration type, rhythm, and participating voices change frequently. Left out of the main material, the first violin joins the bass in its supporting rhythmic role. Var. 2 continues the descent of the melody into the lower voices with a cello melody, although the cello is free to serve as both melody and bass instrument. In addition, it switches back and forth between a new, unfigured melodic contour and rapid sixteenth-note and sixteenth-triplet figuration. Var. 3 is then, in a sense, the opposite of var. 2, in its treble-dominated texture: it is the standard pleonastic solo-violin variation, normally found in first position, in which subtle bowing changes emphasize the melody notes of the theme. Not merely a return to the texture of the theme, the third variation is rather a coalescing of tendencies in figuration in the earlier variations: each was heading toward full figuration, which has now arrived. By waiting until this point, Haydn reinterprets the meaning of conventional gestures in variation form.

The theme reprise, like that in Symphony 47 but unlike any earlier variation sets, is elided with the coda in its penultimate measure (Example 5.17). In practical terms this means that the reprise is cut off on an unresolved I$^6_4$ chord, the traditional cadenza harmony, and enables us to perceive the entire coda as a cadenza-like prolongation of the dominant, an impression heightened by its chord progression with no melody, its skirting the dominant with both lower and upper neighbors while resolving neither of them (especially in mm. 106–111), and its final trill cadence. Significantly, the coda is bounded by B♭–A cadences, which are unresolved or deceptive until the last three measures. And the coda's harmonic focus replaces the melodic focus of the variations, offering yet another comment on the theme, reinterpreting all of its leading-tone and other half-step neighbor figures (that is, mm. 2, 7, 10, 12, and the final ascent in mm. 13–15) in compressed and enriched harmonic form. Given special rhetorical prominence are the *digression* from the expected resolution (at *a* in Ex. 5.17), the sudden fortissimo *arousal* and *apostrophe* in mm. 105–106 (at *b*), and

Example 5.16.   Haydn, String Quartet Op. 20/4/ii.

Example 5.17. Haydn, Op. 20/4/ii, coda, m. 89 replacing m. 16 of theme reprise, after B♭ unresolved in bass.

the pathetic peroration on the Neapolitan (m. 116, at *c*), which recasts both the arousal-apostrophe and the context of the pitch B♭. The deceptive resolution to the trill cadence (V–VI or A–B♭ in the bass) reverses the harmonic and bass motion at the beginning of the coda and calls forth the poignant *pathopoeia* motive, the descending diminished seventh from B♭ to C♯, forecast both in m. 2 of the theme (vln 1–2) and more recently at the close of the apostrophe in m. 106. It is remarkable how similar this is to the coda of the F-minor piano variations (1793): both redistribute the emotional weight of the piece.

Just at the point when the requirements of a variation movement were at their most restrictive, then, Haydn's first slow-movement variations show him reconceiving his variation aesthetic. Several new directions are evident. Symphony 47 points the way to themes with unusual structures, to the anomalous treatment of themes, and to extensive counterpoint in variations. A paradigmatic late example of the first two of these aspects is the opening movement of the E♭-major Quartet, Op. 76 No. 6, whose unusually long theme (36 mm., the last 9 mm. a tonic pedal) is highly repetitive and unrelievedly homophonic. Yet Haydn chooses to treat it as a cantus firmus, moving it from voice to voice, changing the texture around it, providing countermelodies and imitations, changing the topic to Baroque overture (var. 2), even adding an Allegro fugue on it in what may be the first fugal conclusion to a variation movement.[56] Invertible counterpoint also returns in Symphony 70, in the minor theme which alternates with major sections (discussed toward the end of this chapter).

The D-minor quartet movement opened up another direction, with the variations exploring aspects suggested by the theme, redefining the analogies it presented, creating new characters through new figurations that look backward to the theme and forward to the plan of the movement—in effect merging two rhetorical models, copious language and exegeses of a theme. This development resonates throughout Haydn's later strophic variations.

In Symphony No. 57 (1774), for example, the witty, reticent theme begins with an epigrammatic gesture, a pizzicato final cadence that is full of holes.[57] Rests between measures and larger syntactic units emphasize distinctions between textures: plucked versus bowed strings, chords versus ornamented lines. At the end of the theme, the longest and harmonically most complex phrase has a full cadence a measure "too early," so the opening pizzicato returns as a frame, an *epanalepsis*. In Example 5.18, individual gestures are labeled: *x* and its variants for the pizzicato measure in mm. 1, 3, and 12, as well as its modified reappearance in m. 7; *y* and its variants for the *arco* consequent to *x* in mm. 2, 4, 8, and 9–11; *z* for the embellished cadence measures of the first period, mm. 5–6. The longest unit is thus the three-bar extension of *y* in mm. 9–11. In all but the final variation, Haydn refines the theme by finding ways to connect the

56. Of course, fugues had already appeared within or at the end of independent sets of variations, including Beethoven's variations on "Là ci darem la mano" for two oboes and English horn, WoO 28 (?1795). See Chapter 6 for a fuller discussion of Op. 76 No. 6.

57. Before Beethoven, Haydn appears to be the only composer who wrote variation themes with so many rests.

Example 5.18. Haydn, Symphony No. 57/ii: (a): theme; (b): vars. 1–4; (c) var. 4, expansion in second period.

Example 5.18 (continued)

atomized first two measures into a continuous incise, *arco,* thereby transforming the closing pizzicato measure into an *epistrophe* (the use of the same figure
to open and close).[58] In order to avoid figuration stopping in the middle of a
measure, each variation fills in a different pause of the theme. Var. 1 still has
rests in its second measure, as well as the last appearance of the medial *x* motive
in its third, while in var. 2 those rests are filled by the horns and in var. 3 by the
second violin and viola. The first variation is pleonastic, the second periphrastic in figuration; the third combines both of these types. When the opening
pizzicato measure bursts forth in a climactic, wind-reinforced, *arco* return in
the fourth variation, it has the air of a summing up, a theme reprise calling
attention to the artificiality of its own gaps.

58. Only in var. 1 is the pizzicato third measure retained.

Haydn is also at his phraseological best when he comments on the unusual double final cadence of the theme by amplification: expanding variations 3 and 4 before the final cadential measure of their second periods. In the third variation this is accomplished by substituting a deceptive cadence for the first full one in the second period (m. 47), then adding a varied repeat of the previous three measures, while in var. 4 no deceptive cadence interrupts the varied repetition (voices inverted, beginning in m. 63), to a further extension of the dominant. Three measures become six, and then eight. Thus, in the larger design of the movement, we see a composing out of the small textural distinctions within the theme itself, copiously filling holes with a "sweet, fluent" sound, as Cicero said of open figurative display in the epideictic oration.[59] Each of these expansions also continues a change of character resulting from different figurations and orchestrations. In this regard the sweet chromaticism of m. 8 in the last two variations recalls the change of character embodied in "la dolcezza" from Mozart's "Madamina."[60]

In the serene Poco Adagio of Symphony No. 75 (?1779), Haydn introduced the hymn as a theme-type for variations, which was to have profound consequences for Mozart and Beethoven. (The theme is given in Example 7.5.) The two central variations interpret the celestial connotations of the hymn in unprecedented ways: in var. 2, a martial motive of judgment is played forte by the winds and horns, while in var. 3 a solo string trio sounds like an angel choir set against ripieno strings playing pizzicato. Such imagery resonates with Haydn's anecdote about the English clergyman who heard in this movement a premonition of his own death, and, moreoever, died within a short time.[61] Yet the nature of the hymn itself contributes to these dramatic musical reassessments, especially since it returns, nearly intact in every variation but the first. Indeed, the fourth and final variation conflates the full scoring of the second with the rapid accompaniment pattern of the third, as accompaniment to a melodic reprise.

In 1772, then, Haydn responded to the challenge of the mid-century variation aesthetic—the relationship between constant and changing elements which neutrally maintained the paratactic nature of the form—by changing that aesthetic. In order to overcome the loose arrangement of constant-harmony variations with melodic-outline technique, he introduced interpretation into the variation movement, as a "style" of variation composition and also as a way of creating and perceiving order. The variations were now understood to comment upon the theme in a way that would reflect back upon the theme itself but also forward into the ongoing repetitive pattern. Each variation, in mediating between the first segment and the whole, redefined the relationship among all the components. Haydn extracted as much significance as

---

59. Cicero, *Orator*, xiii.42.337, cited in Chapter 2.
60. The same contour is found in Mozart's Minuet K. 355 (576b).
61. The performance in question took place in London in 1792, and Haydn noted down the event in his diary; Landon, *Haydn Chronicle*, III, p. 152.

possible from a theme, just as he did in his sonata works, but the events follow a different logic: one based not on dramatic unfolding, but on the constant reinterpretation of bounded segments, whose boundaries are both necessary and permeable.

The year 1772 was, of course, a watershed year in other respects as well. Aside from marking Haydn's fortieth birthday, it saw the "Farewell" Symphony and Symphony No. 46 in B major, the beginning of Haydn's intensive collaboration with the theater troupe of Karl Wahr, the extraordinary series of quartets, Op. 20, with their fugal finales, and the Missa Sancti Nicolai.[62] It may also have marked a period of general compositional reevaluation. When J. A. P. Schulz visited Haydn in Eszterháza in 1770, according to Reichardt, he found him much occupied with the works of Bach and Handel, a report hitherto unnoticed in the Haydn literature: "Haydn, whose overwhelming modesty initially set Schulz in a state of embarrassment, had also done him the favor to show him and play for him still unknown works, which not only strengthened Schulz's high opinion of Haydn's original genius, but also revealed him to be a diligent composer—for which Haydn was at that time not yet known—who devotedly studied the masterworks of Bach and Handel."[63] While the validity of Reichardt's chronology and reportage cannot be ascertained, the plausibility of this account, together with the musical evidence, suggests that the period around 1772 forged a crucial reconsideration of compositional givens, and prompts an inquiry into the way that year is assessed in overviews of Haydn's creative life.

Haydn's "Creative Periods"

Modern attempts at "periodization" of Haydn's creative life typically do not single out 1772, nor are they kind to the rest of the 1770s, during which time Haydn developed new hybrid designs for variations, discussed in the next section. Indeed, the stinging critique by James Webster of all previous periodizations, in which he detects their hidden agenda of pinpointing the moment when Haydn's style became "mature" and, not coincidentally, the Classical

62. On the significance of the "Farewell" Symphony, and on the idea of Symphonies 45 and 46 as a pair, see James Webster, *Haydn's "Farewell" Symphony;* on Haydn and Wahr, see Sisman, "Haydn's Theater Symphonies." There is one dated baryton trio (105) from 1772; many works of the period are, of course, difficult to date.

63. J. F. Reichardt, "J. A. P. Schulz," *AMZ* 3 (1800), col. 176: "Haydn, dessen übergrosse Bescheidenheit Schulzen anfänglich in nicht geringe Verlegenheit sezte, hatte auch die Gefälligkeit für ihn gehabt, ihm noch unbekannte Arbeiten zu zeigen und vorzuspielen, die nicht nur Schulzens hohen Begriff von Haydns Originalgenie bekräftigen, sondern auch von einem fleissigen Künstler zeugten—für den man Haydn damals noch nicht hielt—der die Meisterwerke Bachs und Händels mit Andacht studierte." Mark Evan Bonds has found striking evidence that Haydn embarked on a self-described "complete course of composition" at about this time; see "Haydn's *Cours complet de la composition* and the Keyboard Sonatas of the *Sturm und Drang,*" paper presented at the Conference and Festival of Haydn's Piano Sonatas, Westfield Center for Early Keyboard Studies, Smith College, March 1990.

style became "fully developed," avoids all such identifying of stylistic goal points. Concluding that Haydn's unceasing experimentation was a "fundamental aspect of his musical personality" and that "all his works are mature,"[64] Webster nonetheless sees the period between 1773 and 1779 as less intense than the previous seven years. His own periodization of Haydn's Esterházy years (1761–1790) characterizes each group of years by both "external turning points" and "changes of genre and style"; in simplified outline, as follows: (1) 1761–1765/66, the Vice-Kapellmeister years, "courtly-expressive" style; (2) 1765/66–1772, the new Kapellmeister, "personally expressive" style; (3) 1773–c.1779, the opera years, "'light'" and "'theatrical'" style; (4) c.1779–1784, "compositional independence" (a new contract and publications), style of "'popular artistry'" and "modest scale"; and (5) c.1785–1790, foreign commissions, "large-scale, more deeply felt" style.[65]

Influential earlier periodizations maintain the teleological approach opposed by Webster. For example, Wilhelm Fischer, who saw the canonical three periods, identified a "preclassical" phase before Eisenstadt (to 1761); a middle period, 1761–1781, showing Haydn's gradual mastery of voice-leading, development, and phrase structure, until the thorough permeation of "thematische Arbeit" with the Op. 33 quartets; and the final period of "highest mastery," including his greatest works.[66] That 1781 marked a point of arrival for Haydn had already been proposed by Adolf Sandberger in 1900, who glorified Op. 33; Fischer incorporated Sandberger's persuasive view of the growing motivic mastery of the 1770s.[67] In 1931, Ernst Bücken postulated a different three-part division, pushing back Fischer's turning points by ten years each.[68] It was but a short step, therefore, from these overlapping claims to Karl Geiringer's five-part division by decades, proposed by him in 1932 and retained in later editions of his biography.[69] Geiringer gave each decade a name: Youth, Transition, Storm and Stress, Maturity, and Consummate Mastery. Assimilating the two earlier versions of Bücken and Fischer, Geiringer was also the first to propose "Sturm und Drang" as a replacement for the "crise romantique" first postulated by Théodore de Wyzewa in 1909.[70] Geiringer's synthesis has been disparaged by other writers because the decade division appears arbitrary

64. Webster, *Haydn's "Farewell" Symphony*, pp. 364–366.

65. This summarizes Webster's table 9.1 in ibid., p. 362.

66. Wilhelm Fischer, "Stilkritische Anhang" to Adolf Schnerich, *Joseph Haydn und seine Sendung* (Zürich, Leipzig, and Vienna, 1926), p. 248. On the idea of "three periods" and for valuable discussion of periodization, see Maynard Solomon, "The Creative Periods of Beethoven," in *Beethoven Essays* (Cambridge, Mass., 1988), pp. 116–125.

67. Adolf Sandberger, "Zur Geschichte des Haydnschen Streichquartetts," rpt. in *Ausgewählte Aufsätze zur Musikgeschichte*, 2 vols. (Munich, 1924), I, pp. 224–265.

68. Thus, the "middle period" is 1770–1790; Ernst Bücken, *Musik des Rokokos und der Klassik* (Potsdam, 1931), pp. 191–205.

69. Karl Geiringer, *Joseph Haydn* (Potsdam, 1932), trans. as *Joseph Haydn: A Creative Life in Music*, 3rd ed. (Berkeley and Los Angeles, 1982).

70. Théodore de Wyzewa, "La crise romantique dans l'oeuvre de Joseph Haydn," *Revue des deux mondes* 79th year/vol. 51 (15 June 1909), 935–946.

and too reminiscent of modern media attention given to the "character" of each decade.

With Geiringer, the handwriting was on the wall: the complexity of Haydn's development required revision of the previously sacrosanct three periods. The next attempt, by Jens Peter Larsen and H. C. Robbins Landon in *Die Musik im Geschichte und Gegenwart,* went to eight periods. Most significant here is the breakdown of the years of Esterházy employment, which begins with Haydn's "second period": the first half of the 1760s, which saw a trend toward the classical multi-movement cycle in instrumental works; a deepening of expression between 1765 and 1772; a period of less significant production (1773–1778/79) followed by a return to experimentation (1779–1784); and the final clarification of style before the London period (1784–1790). This complex periodization was further discussed by Larsen in an article of the same year, in which he drew the essential but problematic distinction between internal and external criteria in the development of a composer's style.[71] The former, or inner creative development, Larsen claimed, is exemplified by Beethoven's three periods, where actual musical style is the only determinant.[72] External criteria, on the other hand, have to do with the circumstances of a composer's career, such as Bach working in Weimar or Leipzig, or Haydn traveling to London. In Haydn's case, Larsen argues that internal and external criteria must be combined for a valid picture to emerge. One concludes that the most persuasive turning points would be those in which biographical and stylistic changes occurred at the same time.

Later assessments by Landon (in *Haydn Chronicle)* and Larsen (in *New Grove)* modified their earlier periodizations in analogous ways. Both now cite the year 1776 as crucial based on the enormous expansion of operatic life at Eszterháza and its attendant pressures on Haydn starting in that year. The greater number of subdivisions put forward by Landon is based on the "Chronicle and Works" approach, but the judgments are identical to those from his earlier symphony monograph. Larsen, on the other hand, considerably altered his earlier approach. The division into seven periods is entirely based on biographical events: after the early period come Eisenstadt (1761–1766), the years of expansion at Eszterháza (1766–1775), the years of operatic activity (1776–1784), foreign commissions (1785–1790), and finally London and the late Vienna years. Yet Larsen finds that each period, no matter how demarcated, shows a unified approach to style. He implies, therefore, not only that external events have internal results, but that these stylistic features remain constant until the next change in circumstance. This view suggests that Haydn's approach to composition was entirely reactive.

71. Jens Peter Larsen, "Zu Haydns künstlerischer Entwicklung," *Festschrift Wilhelm Fischer* (Innsbruck, 1956), pp. 123–129, trans. by Ulrich Krämer in *Essays on Handel, Haydn, and the Viennese Classical Style* (Ann Arbor, 1988), pp. 109–115.

72. Of course, this is not so for Beethoven: the crises of deafness toward the end of the first period, and the crisis with his nephew toward the end of the second, serve as biographical turning points roughly correlated with stylistic turning points.

Studies of individual genres have also come up with disparate periodizations. The symphonies have been plotted by Rywosch into four periods and into seven by Landon, including his notorious "trivial" phase in the later 1770s and early 1780s.[73] A. Peter Brown more recently proposed five periods for the keyboard sonatas and trios, optimistically suggesting that the keyboard pieces "divide themselves" in this way.[74] James Webster argued that the string quartets, rather than culminating in Op. 33, may more fruitfully be perceived in two large groups: the first made up of three widely separated stages in quartet composition, the second representing sustained quartet production, beginning with Op. 50 in 1787.[75] Finally, other specialized studies have taken an interest in stylistic inflections of a given instrument (as Paul Bryan's five periods of horn usage in Haydn), of a given set of years (as László Somfai's study of the London revision of Haydn's style), or as an aid to determining chronology (as Sonja Gerlach's work on the symphonies of 1774–1782).[76] Occasionally a new creative period is identified, as in A. Peter Brown's claim that the years 1787–1790 were overlooked "critical years."[77]

In thus addressing 1772 as a "critical year," I am aware not only of the problematic realm of periodization but also of the limited phenomenon to which I am calling attention: strophic variation movements. But because considerations of Haydn's style have never taken account of his variation procedures, some of the more controversial aspects of his creative life—for example, whether the symphonies of the later 1770s are light or trivial, whether 1781 and the Op. 33 quartets were really the arrival of the high Classical style—have not received their fullest accounting. Part of this accounting concerns the relative weight of slow movements, which have traditionally been subjected to less scrutiny than first movements, finales, and even minuets. Yet whenever Haydn makes a statement about variation and its importance, it occurs after a "tryout" period in another position and is then moved to the slow movement. Only in the late 1780s and 1790s do weighty variation movements appear in first position (Quartets Op. 55 No. 2, Op. 76 No. 6; Piano Trios XV:13, 19, 23; Sonata XVI:48). By that time, however, variation permeated the slow movement, in sonata-type movements, ABAs, and rondos.

The slow variation movements of 1772 thus reverberated in Haydn's works

73. Bernhard Rywosch, *Beiträge zur Entwicklung in Joseph Haydns Symphonik* (Turbenthal, 1934), p. 25: (1) 1759–1771 (Rationalismus und Rokoko); (2) 1771–1774 (Sturm und Drang); (3) 1774–1781 (Organisierungsprozeß); (4) 1781–1795 (Klassik, Meisterschaft); Landon, *The Symphonies of Joseph Haydn* (London, 1955), pp. 171–173: (1) beginning–c.1761/1762; (2) 1761–1765; (3) 1766–1770; (4) 1771–1774; (5) 1774–1784; (6) 1785–1788; (7) Salomon symphonies, 1791–1795.
74. A. Peter Brown, "The Structure of the Exposition in Haydn's Keyboard Sonatas," *MR* 36 (1975), 102–129.
75. Webster, "Chronology of Haydn's String Quartets," 44–46.
76. Paul Robey Bryan, "The Horn in the Works of Mozart and Haydn," *HYb* 9 (1975), 213: (1) before 1761; (2) 1761–c.1776; (3) c.1777–1785; (4) c.1785–1792; (5) 1793–1809; László Somfai, "The London Revision of Haydn's Style," *PRMA* 100 (1974), 159–174; Gerlach, "Die chronologische Ordnung von Haydns Sinfonien zwischen 1774 und 1782," *HSt* 2 (1969–1970), 34–66.
77. A. Peter Brown, "Critical Years for Haydn's Instrumental Music," *MQ* 62 (1976), 374–394.

for the rest of his career. Among their aftereffects were closer relationships between the theme of a variation set and its treatment; codas as expressively constituted perorations outside the variation series; the idea of coda as cadenza (most notably in Symphonies 71 and 84) or as reinterpretation of the theme (Symphony 94); the exploration of contrapuntal textures in variations (as in the invertible counterpoint of Symphony 70 and cantus firmus technique in later quartets); and the play of registers. Haydn also began to modify, sometimes strongly, the structure of one or more variations in a set, especially toward the end. And he explored the idea of alternation, of recurrence, perhaps as a consequence of his thinking about hybrid structures entirely based on those principles. I turn now to the development of those hybrids in Haydn's music of the late 1760s and 1770s, when he developed formal stereotypes that were ever after to be associated with him.

Hybrid Variations: Principles and Development

Haydn's interest in combining variation procedures with forms based on contrast and recurrence, like rondo and ternary forms, may be interpreted on several different levels beyond his obvious attraction to variation *per se*. The first concerns *concertante* instrumentation, the highlighting of individual instruments in an ensemble texture, often by means of register and figuration in addition to timbre. The idea of alternating those elements was part of Haydn's wide-ranging approach to *concertante* techniques throughout the 1760s. For example, his first rondo-variation movement, the finale of Sonata XVI:19 (1767), follows a concerto-style slow movement in which an upper-register ritornello introduces a tenor-range "solo."[78] The finale ($ABA_1CA_2A_3$) similarly distinguishes between an upper-register theme and its variations, and the lower-register episodes. Only in the last variation, a "rescored" reprise, are the registers united. Haydn's purely *concertante* variation movements, in two symphonic and two divertimento finales, join in a different tradition, unrelated to alternation except in the "turn-taking" sense.[79] I prefer the term "rondo-variation" to "variation rondo" because of Koch's remark that finales could take the form of variations with inserted episodes "nach Art des Rondo," rather than the other way around.[80] "Variation rondo" works well only for fast finales with incidental figurations, as Haydn's symphonic finales indeed became later in the 1770s: Symphonies 61/iv, 66/iv, 68/iv, 69/iv, and 75/iv belong here, as do Sonata XVI:43/iii and three baryton octets (X:2, 3, 5). Many composers wrote variation rondos, but only a few wrote true rondo-variations. I also use the term "alternating variation" instead of "double variation" for two reasons: first, the

78. I have already discussed the concerto elements in the slow movement, suggesting its similarity to a baryton concerto, in "Haydn's Baryton Pieces," pp. 429–430.

79. Symphonies 31 (1765) and 72 (before 1765) are both *concertante* symphonies with four horns and other solo instruments. The divertimentos are II:1 and 11. Many of Haydn's contemporaries wrote such *concertante* variations in that period.

80. Koch, *Versuch*, III, p. 314; see Chapter 3.

idea of a double theme is frequently given the lie by the many such pieces which end with a variation of the first theme (that is, the second does not alternate fully, thus resembling rondo), and second, because of the frequent and continuing use of "double variation," especially by music theorists, to mean written-out varied repeats within variations.

Hybrid variations may also be seen as Haydn's response to melodic-outline technique, which ensures easy recognition of the theme when it is varied after intervening material. Indeed, his earliest varied recurrences always appeared as the varied repeats of literal reprises, as in the minuet finales of Sonatas XVI:44 (c. 1771–73) and 22 (1773). They may thus be part of Haydn's general debt to C. P. E. Bach's varied-reprise principle. But an equally significant feature of these early alternating variations is their origin in the minuet, as the continuation not only of the minuet-trio alternation into a second trio and third minuet, but more particularly in the essential principle of mode alternation.[81]

Alternating tonic major and minor takes two principal forms in multi-movement cycles of the later eighteenth century: (1) the opposite mode of the first-movement tonic chosen for the slow movement, and (2) the alternation of mode within minuet and trio, with the minuet in the first-movement tonic and the trio typically in the opposite mode. Sometimes these two approaches are combined in a single-tonic cycle, and sometimes a piece whose opening movement is minor then moves to the major, remaining and ending in major. (More rarely a piece begins in major and has a last movement that begins in minor, as in Quartets Op. 76 No. 1, which goes back to major at the recapitulation, and Op. 76 No. 3, which does not become major until the second group in the recapitulation.) It ought also to be noted that single-tonic cycles are generally considered to be "regressive" in that they resemble Baroque suite movements in sticking to major and minor versions of the same tonic. Yet Haydn never fully gave them up, and none of these mature works could be considered regressive in the sense that the term implies about mid-century symphonies: his latest single-tonic cycles with mode alternation include Symphony 63 (c. 1778–79), Sonata XVI:37 (1780), Piano Trio XV:6 (1784), and Quartet Op. 76 No. 2 (1797). Only the last of these discloses elements of a consciously recalled earlier style.[82]

Of Haydn's symphonies, nearly one-third (thirty-two) have at least one movement or the trio in the parallel major or minor: sixteen are single-tonic with a movement or trio in the opposite mode, another six have two or three keys, and another ten have only a trio in the opposite mode. There is a preponderance of such pieces during the late 1760s and early 1770s. Of the string quartets, ten are single-tonic, another ten have movements in different keys and modes, and a full sixteen have an opposite-mode trio; the total, thirty-six, is

81. Georg Feder discusses some aspects of mode alternation in Haydn and its influence on Beethoven in "Stilelemente Haydns in Beethovens Werken," *Bericht über den internationalen musikwissenschaftlichen Kongress Bonn 1970,* ed. Carl Dahlhaus et al. (Kassel, 1971), pp. 65–70.

82. See László Somfai, "'Learned Style' in Two Late String Quartet Movements of Haydn," *SM* 28 (1986), 336–349.

over 50 percent. The single-tonic pieces begin with Op. 17 in 1771 and continue sporadically (two in Op. 20, one in nearly every remaining opus). The genres with piano—trios and sonatas—are strikingly single-tonic in orientation among the pieces with mode-alternation: twelve of the thirteen trios and eighteen of twenty-three sonatas. The remaining five sonatas all have opposite-mode trios. Of the early genres, four of six string duos feature mode alternation, all with a single tonic, while the string trios, which are overwhelmingly single-tonic pieces generally, have four with an opposite-mode trio; baryton trios, with sixty-four single-tonic members (over 50 percent), all featured opposite-mode trios, and one (No. 97) has both kinds of mode change.

ALTERNATING VARIATIONS

The single-tonic mode-alternating cycle with a variation movement appears to have its origins in a relatively humble piece, the G-major Baryton Trio No. 73, from the fourth volume (1768–71). Not only is the trio of the minuet in G minor, but the theme reprise at the end of the opening variation movement begins with its entire first period in G minor as well.[83] That the first period ends in the tonic only serves to accentuate the importance of this extensive (and repeated) segment in minor. Haydn's two other mode-alternating variations appear in single-tonic keyboard sonatas of a few years later, in the minuet-style finales. In the earlier of these, the G-minor Sonata XVI:44 (c. 1771–73), the idea of alternation is not fully played out. Here the open-ended *maggiore* that follows the minor theme is almost a variation of it, with identical rhythmic and motivic patterns and similar structures. A varied return to the minor theme puts the segments out of order, and the final appearance of the *maggiore* is partial:

A (G minor): ||: a_v :||: b a_I :||
B (G major): c_I | d retrans.
A_1 (G minor): a_v $a_I{}^1$ | b^1 $a_I{}^2$
B_1 (G major): c_I appendix

The finale of Sonata 22 (1773) expands on the idea of alternation in a second trio and second and third minuet varying the first. The movement is otherwise unadventurous. Indeed, the variations on the two returns of the E-major minuet are always presented as varied repeats. Yet the brief, open-ended *minore* returns with its parts inverted, a contrapuntal ploy perhaps stemming from the invertible counterpoint of Symphony 47; the minuet *al rovescio* of that symphony appears in another sonata of the 1773 set, the A-major No. 26. The resemblance between alternating variations and minuet and trio form is suggested again much later in Beethoven's early sketches for the slow movements of his Fifth and Ninth Symphonies: he labeled the first and second themes of the former "Andante quasi Menuetto" and "quasi Trio," and the second theme

83. The similarity to the G-minor beginning of the recapitulation of Symphony 47/i of 1772, mentioned above, suggests another connection between Haydn's procedures in sonata forms and variation form.

of the latter "alla Menuetto."[84] Even Haydn's earliest *minore* "variation" is the unlabeled *alla zoppa* trio of the Tempo di Menuetto finale to Sonata 29 (1774); from this movement (ABA_1A_2) it was but a short step to actual minor-mode variations, as in the single-tonic Sonata in E major, Hob. XVI:31. The minor reprise-variations of Sonatas 27 and 28 possibly descend from Baryton Trio 73.

Sonatas 44 and 22 point to the future in the predisposition for a major ending to variations beginning in minor, and for alternating variations to inscribe a thematic resemblance between A and B sections. Later single-tonic works with alternating variations are the D-major Sonata 33, with a slow movement in tonic minor and final Tempo di Menuetto in alternating rondo-variation form, the F-minor String Quartet Op. 55 No. 2, with an opening alternating strophic-variation movement and minuet in tonic major, and the two-movement piano trios in C minor (13) and G minor (19).

At about the same time in the early 1770s, Haydn explored further the rondo-variation principles of Sonata 19, together with the *concertante* elements of movements from the 1760s, in the finales of Symphonies 42 (1771), 51 (c. 1771–74)—with its extraordinary horn-writing—and 55 (1774). The slow variation movement in No. 55 as well as the variation-permeated slow movement of No. 42, taken together with systematically varied refrains in the finales, mark this as a period of intense preoccupation with variation applied to all formal contexts. Haydn contravened the "rule" of melodic-outline variation in hybrid forms with interesting results in Symphony 51: the "B section" appears to be an episode even though actually a variation because its constant-harmony technique and contrasting scoring disguise it in this context.

The most important predecessor for Haydn's alternating procedures is the one-movement Sonata in C minor by C. P. E. Bach, the sixth in his set of *Sonaten mit veränderten Reprisen* (W. 50 No. 6, H. 140), published in 1760. Its first theme, in C minor, recurs twice, after the C-major *Gegensatz* and after its variation, with the whole piece concluding in minor (Example 5.19). In keeping with the varied reprise idea, the melody is constantly varied, not only upon returns of sections but also during repetitions of individual phrases and periods:

A (C min.): $a\ a_1\ b\ b_1$
B (C maj.): $c\ c_1\ d\ d_1$
A_1: $a_2\ a_3\ b_2\ b_3$
B_1: $c_2\ c_3\ d_2\ d_3$
A_2: $a_4\ a_5\ b_4\ b_5$

As noted earlier, this set of sonatas was advertised in Vienna several times in the period in which Haydn wrote his first hybrid variations in sonatas (and also

---

84. See Gustav Nottebohm, *Beethoveniana* (Leipzig, 1872), p. 14, and *Zweite Beethoveniana* (Leipzig, 1887), p. 173, respectively.

Example 5.19. C. P. E. Bach, Sonata in C minor, H. 140, W. 50/6.

his first varied-reprise movements in quartets).[85] In these and many other hybrid sets by Haydn, the melody returns intact after intervening episodes or second themes and their variations, and is then given a varied repetition. The influence of C. P. E. Bach in these works by Haydn, although controversial, seems more than merely plausible.[86]

Less well known are the other very few precedents for the alternating format, all of them (at least those that I have found) in keyboard music. These pieces regularly alternated mode, beginning with the major, but the *minores* did not vary a different minor theme, but rather were variations on the major theme simply altered in mode. They include the finale of a C-major sonata by Padre Martini, published in Amsterdam in 1742, an A-major set in the notebook Leopold Mozart compiled for his daughter Nannerl in 1759, and the finale of the sixth sonata in Joseph Anton Steffan's Op. 2, published in Vienna in 1760 (Example 5.20a, b, and c, respectively).[87] The sources of the variation set

85. See above, n. 49. The bizarre triple coincidence of the dates for Haydn's first hybrids suggests that he must have purchased or at least known Bach's set. See Sisman, "Haydn's Hybrid Variations," pp. 509–515.

86. Tovey was perhaps the first to note that Haydn owed his varied reprise format to Bach, but Tovey meant only the sonata with varied reprises, not the alternating variation that Haydn seems also to have picked up from Bach's sixth Sonata. See Tovey, "Haydn's Chamber Music," pp. 27–29. More recently, A. Peter Brown has questioned the specific influence of Bach on Haydn's varied reprise; see "Joseph Haydn and C. P. E. Bach: The Question of Influence," in *Haydn Studies,* ed. Larsen et al., p. 164. David Schulenberg discusses the broader question of variation in C. P. E. Bach's style in "Composition as Variation," where he takes pains to distance it from Viennese music generally.

87. G. B. Martini, [*12*] *Sonate d'Intavolatura per l'organo e 'l Cembalo* (Amsterdam, [1742]; New York, 1967), no. 4; mod. ed. of Aria with variations in Kurt von Fischer, *The Variation;* four variations, nos. 1 and 3 in minor. Leopold Mozart, *Nannerls Notenbuch,* ed. E. Valentin (Munich, 1956), no. 35; also ed. W. Plath, *Neue Mozart Ausgabe* IX/27/1 (Kassel, 1982); twelve variations, nos. 2, 4,

(a) Aria

Var. 1

Var. 2

Var. 3

Var. 4

Example 5.20. (a): Martini, Aria with variations from C-major Sonata; (b): Arietta con Variationi in *Nannerl Notenbuch* (elsewhere attrib. Wagenseil); (c): Steffan, Sonata in C major, Op. 2/6/v.

(b)

Var. 1ᵐᵃ   Var. 2ᵈᵃ

Var. 3ⁱⁿ   Var. 4ᵗᵃ
                          6

Example 5.20   (continued)

in the *Nannerl Notenbuch* reveal so many conflicting attributions and structural arrangements that the alternating format might well have been put together by Leopold Mozart himself, working with a copy of what appear to be pasticcio variations.[88] Haydn also wrote two unusual mode-alternating movements whose *minore* variations are based on the melody of the major theme (C-major Sonata, Hob. XVI:48/i [1789], and E♭-major Quartet, Op. 71 No. 3/ii [1793]),

---

6, 8 in minor. J. A. Steffan (Josef Antonín Štěpán), *VI Sonate* (Vienna, [1760], A-Wgm VII 14297), no. 6; twelve variations, nos. 2, 4, 6, 8, 11 in minor. A modern edition of the Steffan, as a theme with variations without mention of the sonata, is in *Ceské Variace XVIII. století. Böhmische Variationen des XVIII. Jahrhunderts,* ed. Dana Šetková, *Musica Viva Historica* 15 (Prague, n.d.).

88. Plath attributed the set to C. P. E. Bach (pp. xvi–xviii) based on the near-identity of several of its variations with a set published in the *Musikalisches Allerley* in 1762 (W. 118 No. 2, H. 155). In that publication, however, only vars. 13, 14, and 17 are attributed to Bach, while 12, 15, and 16 are given to C. F. C. Fasch. Moreover, in a manuscript copy of the variations (B-Bc 5899), Bach's reliable admirer J. J. H. Westphal identified the authors as Steffan (vars. 1, 3, 4, 6), Fasch (12, 15, 16), Bach (13, 14, 17–22, including a few published later in the *Musikalisches Vielerley* of 1770), and anonymous (nos. 2, 5, 7–11), while the theme itself was by Agricola! (See *The Collected Works for Solo Keyboard of Carl Philipp Emanuel Bach,* ed. Darrell Berg [New York, 1985], V, p. xx.) My thanks to Professor E. Eugene Helm for his materials on W. 118 No. 2. Kurt von Fischer was evidently unaware of more than the Fasch attribution ("C. Ph. E. Bachs Variationenwerke," *Revue*

(c) XII. Variazioni in tempo di Menuet

Example 5.20 (*continued*)

but each *minore* is harmonically very different from the major theme and from each other. Mozart's *minore* variations, on the other hand, tend to be much more similar to the major theme than Haydn's.

Haydn's alternating variations found few imitators among composers of his

---

Belge de Musicologie 6 [1952], 190–218, and "Arietta variata," in *Studies in Eighteenth-Century Music,* ed. Landon, pp. 224–235). Plath dismisses the attribution to Wagenseil transmitted in one source destroyed during the Second World War, given in Helga Scholz-Michelitsch, *Das Klavierwerk von Georg Christoph Wagenseil: thematischer Katalog* (Vienna, 1966), no. 96. The published "Bach" set offers as minor variations only nos. 2, 5, 8, 13, and 16, while of the *Musikalisches Vielerley,* nos. 2 and 4 of the five variations are in minor.

own or of the next two generations. Mozart wrote no alternating variations. Vanhal included two rondo movements in his keyboard capriccios in which episodes in the tonic major alternated with identical returns of the minor theme.[89] Steffan returned to the idea of alternating major and minor variations of the same theme, not systematically carried out, in a piano piece of 1786, and a sonata movement by Kozeluch alternated minor and major variations between the middle and the end of the variation movement.[90] Of Haydn's younger contemporaries, only the Viennese Kapellmeister Anton Teiber (1756–1822) wrote an alternating movement, in a Notturno for two pianos with three variations on each theme, and only the indefatigable variation-writer Abbé Josef Gelinek wrote an independent set for piano.[91] Rondo-variations became much more common, while ABA variations, with their more conventional associations of *da capo* decorations, appear in the works of Mozart and Johann Baptist Schenk, doubtless among others. Three of Schenk's four variation movements in his symphonies of the late 1780s–1790s are of the ABA type.[92] Beethoven was thus unusual in his attraction to the alternating form: he adapted it for all of his slow symphonic variation movements, and several other movements as well.

It is reasonable to ask, then, what elements of the alternating variation made it so appealing to Haydn. Perhaps most significant is the often close relationship between the two themes: when they share melodic contour or rhythmic pattern, the second takes on the aspect of a reaction to or interpretation of the first, and the two seem welded into a single musical unit. That the unit embodies a dichotomy of character—the most obvious result of mode change—en-

89. Trois Caprises [*sic*], Op. 35 (Vienna, 1783), No. 2. For dating, see Milan Poštolka, "Vanhal," in *New Grove*, vol. 19, p. 524; Margarethe von Dewitz, *Jean Baptiste Vanhal, Leben und Klavierwerke. Ein Beitrag zur Wiener Klassik* (Munich, 1933), p. 125; Weinmann, *Verlagsverzeichnis Artaria*, p. 20. In another set of capriccios, Vanhal wrote a set of variations on a G-major theme also used by C. P. E. Bach for a rondo; the Vanhal is apparently the earlier of the two: Trois Caprices, Op. 36, No. 1 (Speyer, 1784) was originally published as Op. 15 (Berlin, 1778), while the Bach rondo (H. 271, W. 57/3), published in the third volume of *Sonaten fürs Kenner und Liebhaber* (Leipzig, 1781), was written in 1780. See E. Eugene Helm, *Thematic Catalogue of the Works of Carl Philipp Emanuel Bach* (New Haven, 1989), p. 61.

90. Steffan, "25 Variationi per il Cembalo di Forte Piano scritti e dedicati al publico favorevole" (Vienna, c. 1786; A-Wgm Q15544), with *minores* in both parallel (nos. 4, 14, 16, 22) and relative (7, 11, 19) minors; Kozeluch, A-major Piano Trio/ii, Andantino con Variazioni, vars. 1–3, 5, 7 in A minor, vars. 4 and 6 in A major (A-Wgm Q17402).

91. Teiber's Notturno for two pianos appears in manuscript in A-Wgm (VII 15285); its format resembles the alternating plan described in Reicha's treatise (see Chapter 3). Gelinek's set on "Les Allemandes Saxones" (Op. 67, published in Vienna by the Magasin de l'Imprimerie Chimique, n.d.) alternates variations on the "Thema" and "Trio," listing subsequent numbers as "Variation I," "Variation II Trio," "Variation III," "Variation IV Trio," and so on. Teiber studied in Bologna for nine years with Padre Martini, and thus might also have had access to his mode-alternating variations. See Herbert Vogg, "Franz Tuma (1704–1774) als Instrumentalkomponist nebst Beiträgen zur Wiener Musikgeschichte des 18. Jahrhunderts (Die Hofkapelle der Kaiserin-Witwe Elisabeth Christine)" (Ph.D. diss., Vienna, 1951), p. 74.

92. Copies in A-Wgm: XIII 17666, XIII 17670, XIII 17671; the first and third of these are Romances. Schenk, of course, was one of Beethoven's teachers in the 1790s.

abled Haydn to explore the ways in which reconciliation could be effected or avoided toward the end of the movement.[93] The least-studied aspect of Haydn's recycling of themes in sonata form is the change in character of the main theme when it returns in a revised version in the second key area. In alternating variations such character changes are elevated to a formal principle.

Broadly speaking, these movements use melodic-outline technique almost exclusively, tend to vary the second theme more lightly than the first while changing texture or scoring, and almost always end in the major mode.[94] Full, partial, or melodic reprises punctuate the sets now and then. Haydn also unified and gave direction to some of these pieces by altering structure or harmony toward the end of the set: the resulting forward drive again transcends the alternations, as well as "mere" decoration. And the occasional lengthy coda sometimes brings back elements of both themes. The alternating form itself, then, as Haydn developed it, was flexible, and offered many opportunities to overcome an enforced melodic resemblance, even as the very notion of alternation exploited that resemblance. The standard diagrammatic representations, shown in Table A.1, of his two types of alternating variations—$ABA_1B_1A_2$ and $ABA_1B_1A_2B_2$ for alternating rondo-variations and alternating strophic-variations, respectively—do not adequately reflect that flexibility.

The rhetoric of the alternating variation enables us to fill in the picture. Proceeding by *antitheses,* the alternating set opposes a major and a minor theme, often very similar in melodic contour or rhythm, which may share or exchange other elements, such as instrumentation or accompaniment pattern, toward the close of the movement. Indeed, an arrangement by antithesis was a sanctioned option in classical rhetoric.[95] As a figure, antithesis *(contrapositum, contentio)* produces a style "built on contraries,"[96] which may occur between words, between phrases, or between sentences.[97] In those sets with related themes, one may also speak of the figure *contrarium,* or *reasoning by contraries,* which uses one of two opposing statements to prove the other.[98] This figure also explains the unusual arrangement $(ABA_1B_1A_2A_{[3]})$ of the slow movement of Symphony 53. The A-theme (A major) is followed by a slightly more poignant version of itself in the B-section (A minor), decorated with a faster accompaniment pattern in sixteenths. Even the chord progression after the double bar is similar, a rare occurrence (each half has V/ii–ii–V, though after the double bar the first two of these chords are in the mediant and the third is in the tonic: [III:] V/ii–ii–[i:] V). The last variation is a theme reprise of A with the identical

93. A disappointing treatment of this subject is found in Gottfried Scholz, "Der dialektische Prozess in Haydns Doppelvariationen," *Musicologica Austriaca* 2 (1979), 97–107.

94. Only three end in minor: the slow movement of Symphony 70, the atypically rondo-like finale of the E-minor Sonata, Hob. XVI:34, and the F-minor variations for piano.

95. Gerd Uehding and Bernd Steinbrink, *Grundriß der Rhetorik: Geschichte, Technik, Methode* (Stuttgart, 1986), p. 198.

96. [*Rhetorica*] *Ad Herennium*, IV.xv.21, p. 283.

97. Quintilian, *Institutio oratoria*, IX.iii.81.

98. *Ad Herennium*, IV.xviii.26, p. 293.

decorative accompaniment of the B theme: in one stroke Haydn has synthesized the themes and enabled the movement to end in the preferred major mode.[99]

Two other slow movements of the late 1770s, in Symphonies 63 and 70, traverse the remaining issues of the alternating variation. Both have mode contrast, but No. 63 has closely related themes while those of No. 70 contrast strongly; both begin in minor but the former has six sections, the latter five; and the former becomes more complex while the latter has so much complexity within the theme that its "progress" is quite different. In addition, each is obliquely connected to the theater. The slow movement of Symphony 63 (c. 1779) is titled "Die Roxelana" on Esterházy and other manuscript parts, probably referring to the heroine of Favart's popular play *Soliman II ou Les trois sultanes (Soliman der zweyte)*, which was performed in Vienna throughout the 1770s and brought to Eszterháza in 1777 by the Karl Wahr troupe in its last season in residence.[100] Landon assumes that Symphony 63 originated as incidental music, despite the discrepancy in dates—the symphony was likely assembled (with the overture to *Il mondo della luna* [1777] as first movement) toward the end of 1779—while Stephen Fisher suggests that the slow movement may simply be a "character piece" about Roxelane.[101] And Symphony 70 was performed at the festivities surrounding the laying of the cornerstone for a new theater on 18 December 1779 to replace the one destroyed by fire one month previously; Landon even hears in the finale a depiction of the terrifying fire.[102]

The slow movement of No. 63, which became widely known in its arrangement for piano, perfectly encapsulates opposing characters—or a single character under circumstances now more sinister, now more optimistic—in its minor and major themes. The circumstances are partly elucidated by the scoring, with the C-minor theme played by muted strings and the brightly-colored C-major theme calling on oboes to double the violins and bassoon and horn to replace the string bass line. In addition, the major theme is more rhythmically differentiated and immediately uses a new sixteenth-note pattern to ascend to a high G (m. 3) rather than repeat the low G of the second measure in A. The B-theme is also simpler harmonically. Whether these elements of character actually link up with features of Roxelane that manipulate the heart of Soliman more successfully than her rivals cannot be known.

Each section will take on features of the other as the movement proceeds. In A_1, for example, the highest register is occupied by a flute, the only instrument

99. Sonja Gerlach assumes that this structure is a more "primitive" version of the six-part alternating variation of Symphony 63, and she suggests that it was written first; "Die chronologische Ordnung Haydns Sinfonien," p. 63.

100. See Sisman, "Haydn's Theater Symphonies." Wahr had also performed it in Vienna in 1770 before becoming principal of his own company.

101. Landon, *Haydn Chronicle,* II, pp. 403, 561; Stephen C. Fisher, "Haydn's Overtures and Their Adaptations as Concert Orchestral Works" (Ph.D. diss., University of Pennsylvania, 1985), pp. 187, 307–309. On the dating of Symphony 63, see Gerlach, "Die chronologische Ordnung Haydns Sinfonien," 34–66.

102. An Esterházy copy is dated "18. Xbris 779": Landon, *Haydn Chronicle,* II, p. 421.

in the ensemble not yet heard from but a wind sonority already associated with the B theme; the principal tension in the variation comes from the split between the flute and violin in the second half of each period. B_1 inaugurates the structural changes, in addition to adopting the string band: it modulates to the dominant instead of hovering on it, increases in harmonic complexity after the double bar, and contains two strikingly different modes of expression within each period. The initial melodic reprise of A_2 is belied by its own modulation to the (minor) dominant, while the recasting and expansion of the second period lead to the strongest statement yet of the A-theme, in unison. Thus, despite its apparently regular alternations of thematic materials, the movement gradually changes each of its components: the second theme, originally a simple foil to the first, sets in motion a series of harmonic and structural changes that engulfs the final A-section and creates its own culminating tutti (B_2), containing not two but three consecutive periods ending in the tonic.

Symphony 70 is a profound work all in D major and D minor, alternating the galant, predominantly major, first and third movements with the learned-style, predominantly minor, second and fourth. This alternating plan is a larger projection of the Andante, which opposes a deeply serious, contrapuntal A-theme in D minor with a gently lyrical B-theme in D major (Example 5.21). The cello part of the Andante is headed "Specie d'un canone in contrapunto doppio," the canon actually a "rule" for the inversion of treble and bass at the repeat of the first period. When the treble goes into the bass, it is labeled *canto fermo,* while at a' the original bass line, now in the second violin, is called *contrapunto.*[103] The effect of the muted violins and heavy-tread staccatos is austere at the outset, then curiously ominous as the flute doubles the violin's contrapuntal voice in a higher register. As in Symphony 47, the similarity of the two voices renders the bass fully "melodic" when it appears in the upper register, and only the "canto fermo"—the theme melody—is pleonastically varied, but the fuller orchestration in No. 70 creates an immediate reinterpretation within each variation. The playful major theme seems to come from a different world. Yet it plots, over four measures, the melodic contour of the first two measures of A; and both themes are nearly identical in scoring and dynamics, each with a fully orchestrated return. Such similarities are more covert than those of Symphony 82, whose themes are related by rhythm but contrast starkly in scoring and dynamics, and require a coda to unite their disparate elements.

The pattern of repeats and varied repeats of the A-theme in Symphony 70 and subsequent variations somewhat mitigates the pure alternations of the five-part form:

A: ‖ a | a_{inv} ‖: b a_1 :‖
B: ‖: c :‖: d_1 :‖
A_1: ‖ $a_{refrain}$ (4m) | a_{var} | a_{inv} ‖: b a_1 :‖
B_1: ‖ $c_{refrain}$ | c_{var} ‖: d c_1 :‖
A_2: ‖ $a_{refrain}$ ‖ b_{var} a_1 ‖

103. Landon points out that these headings are in Haydn's hand in the Esterházy-parts; cf. *Joseph Haydn. Sämtliche Symphonien* (Vienna, 1967), VII, p. lxxxi.

Example 5.21. Haydn, Symphony No. 70/ii.

Thus, the second period in every variation has a literal repeat except for A$_2$; only B has literal repetitions and only A$_2$ has no repetitions, while A, A$_1$, and B$_1$ include varied repetitions; of these only A$_1$ has both a refrain and varied repetitions. The A-theme has both the longest (A$_1$) and the shortest (A$_2$) segments, while B is influenced by its refrain idea. Haydn always sought to ensure recognition of the theme after intervening material, but this practice has significant formal consequences: even an apparently static symmetry like the five-part alternating rondo-variation can change the shape and balances of its components as it proceeds.

Although variations with a single *minore* ought not to be considered hybrid variations, Haydn's treatment of the *minore* leads his works of the later 1770s to adopt an important component of hybrids: frequent reprises of the theme's melody. And because Haydn's variation movements after 1776 never have more than four variations, a *minore* has the power to reorganize the whole set whether perceived as an episode or as a variation. Rarely decorative, Haydn's *minores* normally do not retain the harmonic structure of the theme, tending instead toward a simple first period moving to the relative major, and then an intensified second period. A commonplace in variations by Mozart, Beethoven, and most composers of the period, *minores* appeared in four of the five variation finales in Haydn's set of sonatas *anno 776,* each handled somewhat differently. In the first two sonatas, Hob. XVI:27 and 28, the *minore* is part of a theme reprise, while in the third, XVI:29, it is, in effect, a trio. The most interesting of these finales is that of the E-major sonata, XVI:31, because the *minore,* which bears no melodic resemblance to the theme, intensifies a move away from the theme already begun in the altered harmonies of the previous (second) variation.[104]

From the finales of sonatas, Haydn next brought the strophic variation with *minore* into the slow movements of symphonies in the 1780s. Indeed, Symphonies 71 (c. 1778/79) and 75 (c. 1779) are his last symphonic variations without a *minore;* thereafter only string-quartet and piano-trio variations of the 1790s sometimes omit *minores.* And those without *minores* tend to offer a special texture or theme type best explored in a single mode. But the *minore* has another vital consequence in Haydn's later slow movements: it provides the impetus for his masterly ternary forms with variations, those ABA-structures in which B is in the parallel minor and often varies or develops material from A, while individual segments of A are subject to varied repetitions, refrains and varied reprises, and other elaborative restatements. Variation and varied reprises now indeed became indispensable—C. P. E. Bach's term—to Haydn.

104. On Haydn's *minores,* see Sisman, "Haydn's Variations," pp. 218–230.

CHAPTER SIX

Synthesis: Haydn's Variations in the 1780s and 1790s

By 1780, Haydn had developed to a very high degree nearly all of the principal variation formats—strophic variations, varied-reprise sonata, rondo-variation, alternating variation. After this point he began to infuse variation into his ternary movements as well and, indeed, into most of his slow movements. It does not go far enough to say that Haydn's later works showed a tendency to vary returning phrases: the variation became essential to the flow of the movement. And his special development of the 1790s—the cantus-firmus or constant-melody variation in string quartets—confirmed two new interests: the fruitful interaction of variation and counterpoint, and the idea of repetition without decoration—that is, elaborating the environment in which the melody appears, not the melody itself. In Haydn's piano music, on the other hand, figured melody, especially in the more improvisatory-sounding pieces, had profound rhetorical consequences. By examining how deeply into Haydn's later music the variation penetrated, this chapter will outline a new view of his stylistic development.

Profondeur, the missing quality in variations lamented by Momigny in his encyclopedia article of 1818, generally does not characterize the variation movements of Haydn's and Mozart's contemporaries during the 1780s and 1790s, when the numbers of such pieces increased dramatically.[1] Largely but not exclusively limited to independent sets, the vogue for variations included slow-movement or finale variations, sometimes with a *minore* (or *maggiore*) and coda, in chamber works and piano sonatas by Gyrowetz, Hoffmeister, Kozeluch, Pichl, Pleyel, Teiber, and Vanhal, among others. Most of the composers of independent sets are almost entirely unfamiliar today. Works entitled "Fantasie" or "Capriccio" also might contain a set of variations;[2] Beethoven's

1. Momigny, "Variations," p. 551. After quoting Rousseau's definition of the term, he went on to deplore not only the lack of a successor in variations to J. S. Bach, Haydn, and Mozart, claiming that Beethoven was a talent "more bizarre than original," but also the very fad for variations itself. See Chapter 3.

2. For example, Vanhal, *Due Fantasie per il forte-piano, La 1ma con un Rondò e la 2da con Variazioni* (Milan, n.d.).

G-major Fantasy for piano, Op. 77 (1809), is part of this tradition. Some of Haydn's more easily imitated features also turned up regularly—the hymn theme or the reharmonizing coda in Pleyel's music, for example.[3] While variation movements tended generally to be of higher quality than independent sets of variations, the keyboard seemed to attract a lowest-common-denominator approach: variations in piano sonatas were often themselves based on popular melodies, to trivial effect. And in the 1790s, the multitude of variations by the Abbé Gelinek and Daniel Steibelt helped to decrease further the respectability of the form: as Momigny said of Gelinek, his variations may be brilliant, effective, even elegant, but they have no depth, no true understanding of the art: "his talent is in his fingers rather than in his head or in his heart."[4] To bring variations into the realm of the showman-musician, these composers added elaborate flourish-filled but unrelated introductions which compromised the rhetorical effectiveness of the form.

Attractive lyricism occasionally characterizes variation movements by Leopold Kozeluch (1747–1818), a composer celebrated for his keyboard style and virtuosity; indeed, in 1796 he was credited with the ascendancy of the fortepiano over the harpsichord.[5] Momigny even mourned his loss to the world of variations. The middle movement of Kozeluch's F-major sonata, "La Chasse" (Vienna, 1781), varies its already highly detailed theme with rhythmic figures carried through an entire variation (Example 6.1), much in the way praised by Vogler in his little book devoted to improving Forkel's variations on "God Save the King."[6] After four variations, a slightly embellished theme reprise leads to an interesting written-out cadenza. Kozeluch's original themes were generally of a higher quality than those of many of his contemporaries. For example, even the pleasant conceit of Vanhal's "Theme avec VII Variations caracteristiques" (Vienna, c. 1805), which employs the different rhythms, meters, and tempos of national dances, cannot overcome the fundamentally tedious theme (Example 6.2).[7] In addition to transitional passages connecting the fourth, fifth, and sixth variations and a written-out "Ferma" between the sixth and seventh, the theme is preceded by a "Cadenza" of eight primarily chordal measures, presumably intended to stimulate the creation of figuration appropriate to its "intrada"-like aspect. A record of comparable formal and technical characteristics, together with an index of the charm or tedium of such variations or variation movements by Haydn's and Mozart's contemporaries of the 1780s, 1790s, and beyond, will not be attempted here.

3. See Julius Zsako, "The String Quartets of Ignace J. Pleyel" (Ph.D. diss., Columbia University, 1975).

4. Momigny, "Variations," p. 551.

5. Johann Ferdinand von Schönfeld, *Jahrbuch der Tonkunst von Wien und Prag* (Vienna, 1796; facs. Munich, 1976), pp. 34–35.

6. See Chapter 2, n. 32. The numbering of Kozeluch's works comes from the thematic catalogue by Milan Poštolka in *Leopold Koželuh: život a díló* (Prague, 1964). A copy of the Artaria edition is in A-Wst M 10883.

7. A copy of the Traeg edition is in A-Wgm Q15895.

Example 6.1. Kozeluch, "La Chasse," Sonata XIII:2/ii, Andante con Variazioni.

Example 6.2.   Vanhal, "Theme avec VII Variations caracteristiques."

Symphonies

From about 1780 on, nearly every slow movement in Haydn's symphonies is saturated with variation. Outside of theme-and-variations movements, these include ternary (ABA) variations; rondo-variations; sonata forms to which variation or its paratactic repetition is extensively applied; even lyrical and inventive combinations of three structures simultaneously. Of the symphonies from the Paris set on, only Nos. 83, 98, and 99 are without significant variation. Haydn's reliance on variation was partly a function of his preference for the binary-form theme, whose implied or actual double bars and repeats impelled him to act on his apparent dislike of literal repetition. As a thematic model it virtually cries out for varied-reprise treatment, even when its first period ends in the tonic. The Adagio cantabile theme of Symphony No. 74 (?1780)—an aba form without repeats, the first section ending in the tonic (|| a || ba ||)—will be varied twice in the course of the movement.[8] But first, a tutti version of the theme immediately initiates a modulation to the dominant (2 + 2), followed by a vigorous, repeated cadential passage ($6_v + 6_I$). The varied theme returns, as does a short episode based on the original dominant material, now more or less resolved to the tonic. In this rondo-variation with a strong sonata element, variation provides the *raison d'être*.[9]

Haydn's later strophic variations in the symphonies also contain varied reprises; indeed, the frequent literal recurrences of sections of the theme recall figures of repetition such as *anaphora* (for repetition at the beginning) and *epistrophe* (for repetition at the end), but transferred to a higher structural level. These movements also invariably have a *minore,* with its rich possibilities for recalibrating the pattern. Most often the second variation out of four (out of three in Nos. 84 and 97), these *minores* sometimes seem like a shorthand reference to the more leisurely unfoldings of the B-sections in ternary movements. Within the variation movements they tend to resonate with the coda. And in Nos. 85, 94, and 95 the *minore* includes a transition back to the *maggiore,* a reduction of paratactic articulation in the series that imparts to the succeeding *maggiore* the rhetorical effect of refuting an argument or returning to the point after a comparison by negation.

Of Haydn's many combinations of variation, sonata, and rondo, the Largo of Symphony 88, one of his most celebrated and beautiful works, deserves consideration. Shocking in its delay of trumpets and timpani (seen but not heard during the first movement) until their fortissimo blasts in the slow movement—where Haydn had never before put them—the Largo also suggests itself as the successor to the Poco Adagio of Symphony 75 in the hymn-like

8. This movement, both in its two-voice theme in a lower register with "Alberti" accompaniment and in its sonata and rondo elements, looks forward to Haydn's last variation movement, in the Quartet Op. 77 No. 2.

9. The other slow movements of the early 1780s include rondo-variations (Symphonies 73, 76), ternary variations (No. 77), and a curious movement (No. 79) that varies a theme once and then moves on to a binary-form Allegro (un poco Allegro), the first period of which is a variation of the melodic contour of the original theme.

nature of the theme and its orchestration.[10] Beginning as a binary form with a varied repeat of the first section (Example 6.3), the theme is given over to solo cello and solo oboe, playing in octaves; the varied repetition adds pizzicato violins. The second period adds a full wind and horn complement on the dominant-pedal phrase (c_V), then enriches the accompaniment for the return yet again, this time adding descending two-note figures that anticipate the slow movement of Mozart's G-minor symphony, No. 40 (K. 550), written the following year. Because the principal melody is an eight-measure period ending in the tonic, and is varied already within the theme, the formal boundaries within that theme are not so clear-cut: the complete first period (‖ :ab: ‖), after all, contains within it a symmetrical, tonally closed aba (mm. 1–20).

The first half of the theme has a varied reprise, while the second half has a varied return; the rest of the movement is essentially a series of such varied returns after digressions in related keys. But those digressions always include a statement of the *a* theme in that key, played by the first violins, followed each time by a return to the second period in the tonic with newly varied accompaniment. Because the first of these keys is the dominant, the ghost of a principal period seems to emerge, especially since Haydn's sonata forms often include a restatement of the first theme in the dominant. The second digression goes to F major, the relative major of the tonic minor. An overall plan of the movement, using the letters given in Example 6.3, would look like this; double bars have been added to the diagram to clarify the structure:

[Theme:]	‖ a b_V | a^1 b_V	‖ c_V	a^2 b_I ‖
ff-chords [+ mod. to V]	$a_{in\ V}$	‖ c_V	a^3 b_I ‖
ff-chords [i–III]	$a_{in\ III–i}$	*ff*-chords	a^4 b_I
ff-chords (coda)			

The fortissimo chords, a string tremolo/trumpet/drum passage, first occur immediately after the theme, announcing a disruption in the smoothly flowing cantabile of the movement. Apparently without reference to any of the formal categories with which the piece is associated (variation, sonata, binary, ABA), this fortissimo passage always signals a change in tonal direction. Only once is it actually integrated into the thematic substance of the movement, when it substitutes for c_V, the dominant pedal passage of the second period of the theme just before the theme's last return. And for the last return, the first violins join the solo cello and oboe in stating the melody, uniting all of its previous statements by "resolving" tonality and orchestration simultaneously. The thread of variation thus runs through a rondo-like and sonata-like series of keys and returns. That the variation principle dominates is in part a tribute to the memorable qualities of one of Haydn's most eloquent melodies.

10. See Example 7.5. Haydn then uses trumpets and drums in every slow movement from Symphony 92 on, with the exceptions of 95 and 98. Mozart had used them only in the "Linz" symphony, K. 425. Like No. 88, Symphony 100 ("Military") saves orchestral surprises for the slow movement, in the latter case the "Turkish" percussion.

Example 6.3. Haydn, Symphony 88/ii: theme.

Undoubtedly the happy commingling of Haydn's deepest compositional proclivities with the taste of his audiences, variation technique is the principal constant in Haydn's later symphonic slow movements, outside of the big sonata-form slow movement of Symphonies 98 and 99. Several movements adopt an ABA design with central *minore* (Nos. 89, 92, 93, 96, 100, and 104); one is a varied-reprise movement (No. 102); two are alternating variations (No. 91 in five parts, No. 103 in six); four are strophic variations with a *minore* (Nos. 91, 94, 95, 97); and one is a kind of rondo-variation (No. 101). Techniques of orchestration and melodic treatment make the slow movement of the "Drumroll" Symphony, No. 103 (1795), the richest variation movement in Haydn's symphonies, and among the best-known to his posterity. Both melodies in the alternating structure are based on Croatian folk tunes,[11] and in the course of the movement, each takes on some aspects of the other (Example 6.4). The second theme is based on the dotted rhythm and pitches of m. 3 of A, itself a varied version of m. 1; the greater propulsion of the first theme comes from the diminution of the dotted rhythm in m. 4, which displaces the slower version (in mm. 6, 7) and generates the host of rapid rhythms in the final phrases. In the

11. The evidence for folk origin is summarized by Landon, *Haydn Chronicle,* III, pp. 597–599.

Example 6.4.   Haydn, Symphony 103/ii: themes A and B.

second theme, on the other hand, the dotted rhythm and a related trill figure sit squarely on the first beats of most measures.

As in Symphony No. 63, wind color is first associated with the major theme, and the minor theme is typically scored for strings alone. When A_1 introduces solo flute and oboe (in motivic imitation with bassoons), B_1 counters with a solo violin in a florid variation and B_2 brings back solo flute and bassoon; brass and timpani, present together only in B, join again in A_2. After the figured melody in B_1, the final A variation also dissolves its melodic line, in contrast to the melodic reprise with countermotives in A_1. Finally, the lengthy coda (mm. 160–198), based on the second theme, alludes to the first in a passage in E♭ major that touches on F minor (mm. 174–186), and in the martial cadence's sly suggestion of the fanfare accompaniment in A_2 (mm. 196–198). Thus, although the similarities between the themes make it difficult to speak of reconciling opposites, the discrete shapes of individual sections gradually become more fluid.

In the Andante of his last symphony, No. 104 ("London"), Haydn adapts a ternary variation form that he had introduced in piano sonatas and trios of 1784 (the finales of XVI:40 and 42 and XV:6).[12] Marked in its earlier stages by varied reprises and a binary B-section, the form loosened up in the 1790s to include a more continuous or contrapuntal B-section, although it never gave up

---

12. The quasi-ternary, quasi-rondo-variation slow movement of Symphony No. 77 is an exception to these, because the B section is actually a development of A, which returns partially in the varied repeat of the second period in A_1:

A ‖ a | a ‖ b a | b_{var} a_{var} ‖

B dev. of A, incl. a in B♭ maj.; imitation on a;

A_1 ‖ a_{var} | a'_{var} ‖ b_{var} a | imitation on a; a_{var} ‖ ext

the varied reprise, especially in the return of A.[13] For Symphony No. 104, Haydn explores a rhetoric of variation founded on the flexibility of classical phrase structures and expansions, within a ternary design. Expansion techniques are applied in the first A section, particularly to the return of *a* in the second period: the first model is expanded by inserting and then extending a subdominant chord (mm. 23–25), while the second is given a deceptive cadence (m. 29), and a tonic-pedal appendix introduces figuration and concludes the whole (Example 6.5a). The *minore* B-section, beginning with a wind choir in G minor, sounds like a variation until a passage without clear directional phrase structure—the tutti sequence on a rhythm similar to the theme (mm. 42–55)—identifies it as part of a segment more expanded than a variation. The same process repeats with a string version of *d* (in B♭ major, m. 57), but the tutti sequence, now on the head of the theme itself, again points to development rather than variation: it uses the affective Baroque minor-key circle-of-fifths sequence with suspensions and imitation, more often associated with Mozart, that is simply never used in variations: B♭-F-c-g-d-[a deflected], in mm. 60–65. Varied reprise accompanies the return (m. 74), with sweeping dotted-rhythmic tutti gestures. The return of *a* in the second period of A₁ (m. 98, Example 6.5b) is decorated further before the subdominant-chord expansion turns into a ten-measure excursion to ♭VI (D♭), followed by a wind cadenza based on *a* (mm. 104–113, 114–117). Instead of picking up where it left off before the expansion, the second period goes back to the beginning of *a* to continue the variation, which thus has the last word.

The movement does not simply set side by side the small-scale expansion of the A section, the developmental topics of B, and the greater, more colorful expansions of A₁. By adding varied passages to A₁ and thus implying a connection to the ornate minor sequences of B, the form acquires both a rounded and a progressively expanding element. There is nothing "symmetrical" about this ABA movement, nor is sonata form its process, nor parataxis. It takes its cue from the expansion of the first A section, and is able to expand further in A₁ precisely because of the new figuration that the variation has added. The vividness of that expansion, together with the meditative wind cadenza to which it gives rise, then motivates the final, fully varied return. At the end, the horn fifths perform a gesture not just of closure but of farewell.

Quartets

One of the long-running controversies in Haydn scholarship concerns the significance of Haydn's set of six string quartets, Op. 33 (1781), which Haydn claimed were written in an "entirely new and special manner" *(Neu, gantz besonderer Art)*. An examination of variation procedures and forms in these quartets reveals an expanded role for variation in general: in the intricate hybrid

13. These include Quartets Opp. 64 Nos. 4–6, 71 No. 2, and 76 No. 5 and Piano Trios Hob. XV:27, 29, 30, and 31.

Example 6.5. Haydn, Symphony 104/ii. (a): A theme, return of a in second period, to deceptive cadence (mm. 17–29); (b): A₁, same spot (mm. 98–113).

Example 6.5   (continued)

slow movements of Nos. 2 and 4; in the strophic finale of No. 5 and alternating rondo-variation finale of No. 6; in the varied-reprise slow movement of No. 3; in the related episodes in the rondo finales of Nos. 2 and 3 (for example, AB_xAB_yA); and in the decorated refrains in the rondo finale of No. 4. This far exceeds the single strophic slow movement of Op. 20 No. 4 and varied reprise of Op. 20 No. 6. Yet as we have seen, the Op. 20 No. 4 variations are intense, concentrated, interpretive, while the Op. 33 No. 5 variations are light decorations of the melodic outline of the graceful *siciliana* theme, and generally reflect the popular style of the other finales in the opus. And the alternating rondo-variations in Op. 33/6 use a "walking" melody type of the 1760s, and offer none of the profundity of Symphonies 63 and 70. In an important sense, then, Haydn has "relegated" variations to the finale, even as he has deepened the expressive possibilities of varied returns in a slow movement. Other than as a source for Mozart's variations (for example, the *siciliana* theme with Allegro coda adopted for the finale of K. 421; see Chapter 7), then, Haydn's Op. 33 quartets do not represent an "advance" in his theme and variations, but mark the increased presence of variation in slow movements and hybrids with sonata form. By incorporating variation into different formal and affective contexts, the quartets of Op. 33 illustrated how far variation had permeated Haydn's assumptions. After Op. 33, nearly every quartet has extensive variation. A new level of expressive detail emerged in the late 1780s,[14] with the finely worked thematic contrast of the slow movement of the F#-minor Quartet, Op. 50 No. 4, revising and deepening the registral opposition of the A and B themes first outlined in Op. 33 No. 6 (Example 6.6).

The string quartets of the 1790s include some of Haydn's profoundest works. From the simple but transcendentally lovely strophic slow movement of Op. 64 No. 2 to the complex syntheses of variation and counterpoint in Op. 76 and Op. 77, Haydn revealed in quartets more than in any other genre the relationship between variation and contrapuntal development and thus the centrality of variation to his compositional thinking. Nearly every slow movement is permeated by variation techniques. In fact, the quartets of the 1790s offer facets of the form not previously introduced by other composers, and integrate variation movements into the rest of the work in entirely new ways. The slow movement of the B-minor Quartet, Op. 64 No. 2, one of Haydn's few variation Adagios (here ma non troppo), immediately announces itself as something special, partly because themes in this period rarely move in measure-filling notes (and Haydn's variation themes rarely sing in sustained notes above the middle register), and partly because its first four measures define harmonic stability and centering, through four root-position chords (I–IV–V–I), after the tense and harmonically ambiguous first movement. Even though every subsequent phrase speeds up the harmonic rhythm and has a deceptive cadence, the feeling of rootedness remains (Example 6.7).

Rhetorical power in the movement derives from its style of simple sublimity, an elevated mode of expression that renders superfluous the decorative aspects of the movement. Indeed, this piece seems the embodiment of Longinus's assertion that periphrasis contributes to the sublime if not overused. The elevated style of the first-period cadence (m. 8), with its powerful suspension, relatively rare in Haydn, remains in every variation. When Rosen describes the scale-based melody as a "cantus firmus on which a florid and expressive decoration is draped," he is correct in every way but the literal one, in that whenever Haydn treats a theme as a cantus firmus he moves it, virtually unchanged, from voice to voice in the texture.[15] Here the theme is an essence, a scale figure, and what moves from voice to voice is the arpeggiated accompaniment given to the second violin at the outset: in the theme it appears also in viola and cello at the ends of phrases; in the second reprise of var. 1 it decorates the melody in the first violin; it moves to the cello in var. 2, where it accompanies the purest

14. One of these, the Adagio cantabile of Op. 55 No. 1, resembles a smaller version of the Largo of Symphony 88: a rondo-variation with restatements of the theme in the dominant and then the tonic minor. Indeed, the contrast between these two movements suggests that distinction between "sonata style" and "symphony style" discussed by the theorists. See Michael Broyles, "The Two Instrumental Styles of Classicism," *JAMS* 36 (1983), 210–242.

15. Rosen, *The Classical Style*, p. 140.

Example 6.6. Haydn, String Quartets. (a): Op. 33/6/iv, themes A and B; (b): Op. 50/4/ii, themes A and B.

form of the theme; and it is diminished into sixteenth-note broken chords in the final variation, again moving from voice to voice.

CANTUS-FIRMUS OR CONSTANT-MELODY VARIATION: QUARTET OP. 76 NO. 6

Haydn's cantus firmus principle, or constant-melody variation, manifests itself in four string-quartet movements of the 1790s, each of which has a striking theme: the scherzando Op. 64 No. 1 (third movement), the hymn Op. 76

Example 6.7. Haydn, String Quartet, Op. 64/2/ii.

No. 3 (second movement), and the strangely repetitive Op. 76 No. 6 (first movement) and Op. 77 No. 2 (third movement).[16] The most celebrated of these movements is of course the slow movement of Op. 76 No. 3, whose theme, Haydn's newly composed melody for the Austrian national anthem— "Gott erhalte Franz den Kaiser"—caused the entire quartet to be nicknamed the *Kaiserquartett,* and may have given rise to topical political references in the

16. The term "cantus firmus" was still in use at the time: Vogler criticizes Forkel's handling of the *canto fermo* in one of his "God Save the King" variations *(Verbesserung,* p. 10).

first movement as well.[17] Its crystal-clear structure (‖ :a: ‖ b ‖ :c: ‖) and preponderance of unambiguous root-position chords make it outstandingly suited to its treatment, the only theme of the four cantus-firmus pieces able to be so described: its clarity and beauty make it capable of many repetitions.

The rhetoric of the cantus-firmus variation is problematic on the face of it, because the inevitable presence of both theme and countermelody epitomizes simultaneity, the single biggest textural distinction between music and speech. A running spoken obbligato to a speech would render both unintelligible. And depending upon the contour and character of the musical theme, its deployment in different voices may or may not be instantly recognizable. But Haydn makes it a rewarding topic in that he can dwell on the melody and dissemble at the same time. Because the melody is always present, the techniques by which it is varied are all the more exposed; instead of hearing a relationship with the theme retrospectively, the listener is made aware of simultaneous comparison.

The first movement of Op. 76 No. 6, as mentioned in Chapter 5, is a *locus classicus* of the ironic treatment of a variation theme. In this case, the theme is treated in a way utterly at odds with its melodic character. A long, rhythmically repetitive, m lodically somewhat dull theme—it sounds like an outline of a theme—is, paradoxically, preserved intact in every variation, moved from voice to voice, used as the basis for an elaborate set of comparisons. The irony is heightened because the *Kaiserhymn,* which everyone knew as a melody and as a piano arrangement, received the same treatment yet is lyrical, beautiful, noble. In Op. 76 No. 6, all four incises of its first reprise have the identical rhythm (Example 6.8). That rhythm continues in the second reprise, which moves briefly to the supertonic (F minor), then generates a dotted-rhythm passage as a diminution of the original rhythm; after the partial thematic return, the upbeat pattern alone is duplicated, with the faster dotted rhythms relegated to the lengthy appendix (mm. 28–36) over a tonic pedal at the end.

As a variation theme, this Allegretto is unpromisingly repetitive, hesitant, even enervating, and harmonically circular. Yet as in the *Kaiser* variations, var. 1 begins with two-part counterpoint between the violins. Unlike the flowing sixteenth-notes of that other quartet, however, and in contrast to the homogeneous theme, here heterogeneity reigns: syncopations at the outset give way to sixteenths after the double bar, then yield to full texture in which the first violin gives up its heightened level of rhythmic activity in favor of a different kind of assertiveness, in more sustained lines (mm. 53–56, 62–64), amusing rejoinders (mm. 59–61, ascending dotted figures to counter the descending ones of the theme melody), and even a measure taking over the melody (mm. 57–58¹). In var. 2, the theme moves to the bass, where it supports an exaggerated Baroque overture, complete with dotted rhythms and trills, all pauses of the theme now filled in. Var. 3 deliberately mimics and mocks the first violin's theme in the

17. See Somfai's recent provocative interpretation of the entire piece as a "Quartetto in tempore belli" ("'Learned Style' in Two Late String Quartet Movements of Haydn," pp. 326–336). He sees the opening of the first theme, G-E-F-D-C, as an acronym for the title of the hymn, with C substituting for the nonmusical K in Kaiser.

Example 6.8.   Haydn, String Quartet, Op. 76/6/i.

Var. 1

Var. 2

Var. 3

Var. 3, second period

117

Allegro

145

Example 6.8 (*continued*)

lower register; goaded by this, the melody line finally takes on pleonastic figuration, the main notes now part of an agitated sixteenth-note line. Not only does the first violin thus return to the sixteenth-note motion of its countermelody in var. 1, but it forces the theme melody, at the return, back into the second violin (mm. 125–136) so that it is free to embellish and extend its contrary-motion echoes (the "amusing rejoinders") of the earlier variation (mm. 131–136).

Haydn's masterstroke in the movement is the Allegro fugue, whose aim is both to recapitulate textures and keys, and to invigorate the cycle. The subject taps into the energy of the running sixteenths of var. 3 while the countersubject, typically heard together with the theme, temporarily moves to the subdominant, as did the theme in its second reprise. The countersubject must have struck Beethoven forcibly, because he used it in the *Eroica* finale, as counterpoise to the bass theme at the beginning and as the countersubject in the first (C-minor) fugato.[18] In its recapitulatory aspect, Haydn's fugato first recalls the two-part texture of var. 1 and the sixteenths of var. 3, in addition to harmonies of the theme. Arriving on a dominant pedal in m. 185, it also refers to the overture version of the theme (var. 2) with its trill, then returns literally to the figuration of var. 3 in its second reprise. (Beethoven's piano variations on the *Eroica* theme, Op. 35, similarly end with a fugato that merges with variations.) The reappearance of that variation in the new Allegro tempo brings the fugal "finale" into the variation-series and reveals the fugue to have been another in the succession of textures recasting the theme.

The treatment of the fugue and final variation also binds it to the second movement, an Adagio Fantasia of great beauty and strangeness.[19] The Adagio consists of an eight-measure period in B major (with no key signature, and with two parallel phrases) which, at its repetition, sets in motion a series of statements in ever more remote keys, each connected by a sequential, scalar passage which brings the next statement to yet another key (Example 6.9). The second statement diverges in its antepenultimate measure to cadence in C♯ minor. Subsequent returns are in E major/E minor, cadencing in G major; B♭ major/B♭ minor, cadencing in B major (!), and initiating an imitative and sequential transition through C♯ minor to a cadence suggesting G♯ minor, enharmonically recast as V⁷/A♭. The ensuing subject in A♭ major, the only eight-measure period since the first to begin and end in the same key, prepares the return home, where the B-major statement (now *with* key signature) gives way to a series of quasi-fugal entries on the subject, first in B/F♯, then in g♯/E. The

18. See Example 8.5. Wulf Konold suggests that the countersubject of Haydn's fugato returns in augmented form as a transitional passage in the second movement, mm. 39–42; cf. Example 6.9(b). See his "Normerfüllung und Normverweigerung beim späten Haydn—am Beispiel des Streichquartetts op. 76 Nr. 6," in *Joseph Haydn: Tradition und Rezeption,* ed. Georg Feder, Heinrich Hüschen, and Ulrich Tank (Regensburg, 1985), p. 63. The piece is also discussed in Kirkendale, *Fugue and Fugato,* pp. 147–149.

19. For a Schenkerian analysis, see Felix Salzer, "Haydn's Fantasia from the String Quartet, Opus 76, No. 6," *Music Forum* 4 (1976), 161–194.

Example 6.9. Haydn, Op. 76/6/ii: (a): theme; (b): transition, B♭ statement, imitative transition; (c): fugal passage, m. 64.

counterpoint itself yields to insistent sixteenth-note figuration—maintaining the shadow of A♮ from the E-major entries—as the preferred mode of closure borrowed from the first movement. That this figuration descends through the four instruments also resembles the texture of the first movement, as well as the linking transitions. Thus, the movement's plan—a repetitive series of thematic statements followed by a fugue, ending with figuration—is not dissimilar to the first movement; but its key scheme supports the "fantasia" label. This plan may be outlined as follows:

A/A$_1$	trans	A$_2$	trans	A$_3$	trans	A$_4$	trans	A$_5$/fugue
B/B–C♯m	(vn)	E–G	(vc)	B♭–B	(imit.)	A♭	(vc)	B

Indeed, repetition seems to be one important strand of the capriccio-fantasia tradition in the later eighteenth century, especially repetition of a theme in distant keys. Haydn's early keyboard Capriccio in G major (Hob. XVII:1) repeats its folk-song subject ("Acht Sauschneider müssen seyn") in a variety of keys, changing the accompaniment and adding transitional and figured passages between statements. Two more ambiguous capriccio movements also include considerable repetition of their opening ideas: the slow movement of the Quartet Op. 20 No. 2, a dramatic *scena* beginning with an oddly declamatory opening section with several repetitions of an arioso melody, and the slow movement of Symphony No. 86, a sonata-form hybrid. A striking corroboration of this idea comes from Beethoven's four-hand variations in C major on a theme of Count Waldstein (WoO 67, c. 1792): toward the close of the eighth variation, a *minore,* a passage beginning with unexpected restatements of the theme in D♭ and A♭ major is marked *Capriccio.* And reverse confirmation comes from Steffan's piano capriccios, in which short passages of varied restatements in the *same* key are marked *variaz.*

Returning to repetition as a structuring device is the *Alternativo* of the Menuet in the third movement of Op. 76 No. 6. A series of unheralded cantus-firmus variations, the piece is based on the E♭-major scale, which each instrument plays in turn from cello to first violin or the reverse, and either ascending or descending (Example 6.10). Scalar motives, prominent in the transitions of the Fantasia, also came to the fore in the Menuet, a Presto movement featuring Haydn's trademark of metric displacement; scales in contrary motion articulated its final cadence. Structured as six groups of four statements each, the *alternativo* is more finely ordered into three groups of two: A-section: four descending scales ascending in register from bottom to top, then four ascending statements from bottom to top; B-section: four descending statements from top to bottom, then four ascending statements from top to bottom; A$_1$-section: same ordering as the first.[20]

20. Kirkendale's attractive diagram of this movement, in *Fugue and Fugato,* p. 148, does not point out this ABA construction. He notes that Beethoven adopted the scalar theme for the Menuet of his First Symphony.

Example 6.10. Haydn, Op. 76/6/iii: (a): *Alternativo,* first set of entries; (b): dance-like countersubject; (c): fugal-style countersubject.

	A			B			A₁	
1		2	3		4	5		6
desc.		asc.	desc.		asc.	desc.		asc.
vc–va–v2–v1			v1–v2–va–vc			vc–va–v2–v1		

But every single one of these scalar statements has different counterpoints, and every one grows gradually from one voice to four. Mixing textures, harmonies, and styles, from dance-like galant (mm. 113–116, Example 6.10b) to the fugal learned style (the countersubject in mm. 128ff, Example 6.10c), the *alternativo* is thus a congeries of varied repetition.

Where the scales in the *alternativo* proceed logically and inexorably, the scalar motives of the helter-skelter finale are subject not only to repetition but also to frequent metric displacements in imitative stretto passages. Moreover, the descending direction of the principal five-note motive in the first group (beginning with $\hat5\ \hat4\ \hat3\ |\ \hat2\ \hat1$ in eighths) directly counters both the final ascending statement of the *alternativo* and the final flourish of the Menuet. As in the first movement and *alternativo,* register and direction enhance the effect of repetition. After the main theme in the treble (vn. 1), and two eight-measure periods of metric displacement based on it (mm. 13–20, 21–28, both of which are omitted in the recapitulation), the leading voice in two-part stretto is in a lower register (va. and vc., m. 28²). The second theme (m. 42), a variant of the first, unites registers and directions: the scale motive still descends, but the descending arpeggio that introduces it in the cello is then inverted in the first violin's much higher register. Agreement among the voices is underscored in the very first rests observed by all instruments, however briefly, in mm. 47–49. An unusual feature of the development section suggests another link with the first three non-sonata movements: tonally, the development acts like a "middle section" in that, lacking only a final cadence (as did the exposition itself), it begins and ends in the same key (C minor), modulating to its own submediant (Ab) for a restatement of the main theme (a "false recapitulation," m. 94). In addition, the development uses register more or less symmetrically: it begins with the theme in the cello, now as a response to the chords that originally answered it (compare the first theme with mm. 66–70), moves the principal action to the first violin, then returns to the middle and low registers in the learned-style modulation back to C minor (mm. 100–106). The imitative stretto passage starting with the cello (m. 111; cf. m. 28) that both resolves to C minor and leads back to Eb for the recapitulation concludes this open-ended, quasi-paratactic middle section.

The real subject of this quartet, I believe, is repetition itself and, moreover, repetition without decoration. That each movement contains both varied repetition and a fugue or other older form of complex repetition supports this contention. Even the finale uses a kind of rhythmically displaced repetition of figures in both first and second groups of the sonata form. In fact, the unit to be repeated gets smaller and smaller in successive movements: a thirty-six-bar theme of variations; an eight-bar fantasia theme; a four-bar *alternativo* theme; and a scalar motive of less than a full bar in the finale. Thus the variations move beyond the first movement to play a rhetorical part in the entire quartet, introducing a concept that becomes progressively richer and more varied throughout the piece.

Keyboard Works

Beginning with the Piano Trio Hob. XV:5 (1784), nearly every trio has significant varying, although there is only one variation movement in slow-movement position, on a theme for left hand alone (XV:20). The slow movements and even some of the finales (and one first movement) tend to be ABA types, while the first movements are most often alternating strophic-variations using dotted rhythms in the first themes.[21] The two themes of the D-minor Piano Trio, Hob. XV:23, first movement (1795), show an especially subtle relationship, given their surface opposition in melody, sonority, and affect (Example 6.11). Part of the power of the sinuous first theme derives from the sforzandos in the unison opening phrase, Bb and G♯. As neighbors to the dominant or as part of the augmented-sixth chord, they later help to articulate every cadence in the second period. When the theme melody returns in the bass (m. 13), the upper line is a contrary-motion counterpoint recalling Symphony No. 70. After the last brooding dotted rhythms in the bass on the D-minor triad, the violin sings out the second theme's radiant affirmation of D major. Yet the second period of this theme is marked by a return to the rhetoric of the first theme: tonic minor, dotted rhythm, lines in contrary motion with the melody in the bass, dominant pedal, and half cadences introduced by the augmented sixth. Even the final cadence of the *maggiore* is shadowed by an augmented-sixth chord (m. 41). Not only does the second theme acquire this essential part of its structure from the first theme, but it also picks up and continues to the end of the movement the progressive diminution of the first *minore* variation, while the *minore* itself subsides, at its second variation, into a melodic reprise enriched with a syncopated contrapuntal answer. Indeed, the *minore*'s preoccupations with counterpoint, dotted rhythms, and the pitch Bb make it a highly ornate descendant of Haydn's other D-minor variations, Quartet Op. 20/4 and Symphony 70.

SONATAS

Haydn's keyboard sonatas are the only genre with no real variations in slow-movement position, and thus on the surface appear not to have weighty variations. But even the lighter sonatas have their eloquent side. For example, Sonata XVI:40, the first of the three two-movement sonatas for Princess Marie Esterházy, is paradigmatic of the attractive, light, amateur style in sonatas of the period,[22] as evidenced by its "Allegretto e innocente" heading and the swaying 6/8 meter, rarely used either in opening movements or in variations (only Nos. 47, first movement, and 34, third movement, respectively). Yet an examination of the relationship between the major and minor themes, and particularly in the figures used to vary them, reveals a rhetorical framework, utilizing progressive refining but cast in the tone of an argument, with its connotation of forcefulness in performance (Example 6.12). The alternating

21. Only the G-minor Trio, Hob. XV:19, is unusual in structure: its Presto "finale," after a single variation of each theme, turns out to be a sonata-like expansion of the second theme. See Chapter 4 for a discussion of this movement. An additional similarity among the trio movements is that both the first and second themes are patterned the same way, with a return to the opening melody in their second sections, sometimes in the bass. This is also true of Symphony 103 and the contrapuntally organized theme of Symphony 70, which in turn recalls that of the strophic variation set in Symphony 47. It is not uncommon in Haydn's two-reprise structures in general.

22. For an interesting categorization of Haydn's sonatas, including the idea of *Damensonaten* for this set of pieces, see László Somfai, "Stilfragen der Klaviersonaten von Haydn," *ÖMz* 37 (1982), 147–153.

Example 6.11. Haydn, Piano Trio XV:23/i: themes A and B.

Example 6.12.   Haydn, Piano Sonata XVI:40/i: themes A and B, motives.

scheme, with its series of large-scale antitheses, provides the framework within which the drama of two motives is enacted.

In the context of the swaying pattern of the A theme, the motives that artic-ulate its first two feminine cadences seem unproblematic: the first, marked as x in m. 2, is staccato repeated notes, while the second, marked as y in m. 4, has a slurred appoggiatura on the downbeat. The first of these is the source of the waiting passage on the dominant in the second reprise (first right hand, then left hand), marked x' in mm. 12–13. The B theme is clearly derived from the latter passage (x''), but then recasts y as the affective half-steps of the third and fourth bars (y'), offering a corrective to the innocence of the A theme. When A_1 returns, the half-steps find their way into the figured accompaniment, a combination of x and y now defused and galant in expressive orientation. In B_1, the half-step becomes an appoggiatura decorating even the opening re-peated notes (y''), recasting the terms of that *minore*'s relationship to the *mag-giore,* insisting on its own contribution. And the accented half-step passage now becomes an improvisatory outburst in the second period, the first such unrestrained activity in the piece. The last two repeated notes, mid-measure, are a subdued recognition of relationship. In the final variation, A_2, the half-steps are again neutralized, and the repeated notes are fully drawn out, true *Schwärmer* (Marpurg's repeated-note figures), intensifying rhythmically and expanding structurally in the second period. The original relationship between themes and motives is now convincingly emphasized. It is left to the A theme only to take on the improvisatory chord-and-scale outburst of B, but now as a stabilizing cadential force (m. 94). The major theme has changed from gentle remonstrance to violent enthusiasm, whose German term is, tellingly, *Schwär-merei.*

The first movement of XVI:42, from the same set of sonatas, has a highly ornate surface. Indeed, its rests are among its most significant features: they make the theme seem to be caught in the act of its own invention (Example 6.13), as befits one of only two movements in the sonatas to be marked "con espressione" (the other being the first-movement quasi-improvisatory varia-tion movement, Hob. XVI:48).[23] After a simple pleonastic variation, the *minore* seems to unite Forkel's two classes of rhetorical figures: figures for the under-standing, which are contrapuntal, and figures for the imagination, which con-cern affective musical "painting." The contrapuntal, suspension-laden opening actually generates an astonishing climax at the moment the opening passage should return (m. 53), its first three measures compressed in the bass *(abridge-ment)* together with powerful figuration. This seems to me a clear instance of *hyperbole (superlatio),* an exaggeration for the sake of magnifying a point,

23. Other con espressione movements: Hob. IV:10/i (similarly with rests in melodic line, scored for vn. 1 or flute, vn. 2, and vc.); *Philemon und Baucis* (Hob. XXIXb Nr. 2), Ouverture (D minor) and Zwischenspiel, Nr. 10, taken from the ballet at the end of Act I of Gluck's *Paride ed Elena;* 31 Scottish songs (Hob. XXXIa); 8 Welsh songs (Hob. XXXIb); and the well-known Lied with Piano (Hob. XXVIa:34), from 6 English canzonettas (1794/95) 4, "She never told her love" (Shake-speare), Largo assai e con espressione (A♭ major).

Example 6.13. Haydn, Piano Sonata XVI:42/i: (a): theme; (b): var. 2, second period.

which is a form of *emphasis (significatio).*[24] Part of the point it magnifies is the topical disparity between the theme hesitantly creating itself, and the overture or preludial style in the *minore;* the *minore*'s first-period figuration seems tightly controlled, not improvisatory, but the return sheds this control. After this outburst, the final variation begins with a theme reprise, but the subsequent figurations during this last *maggiore* turn to a more virtuosic version of self-creation, in effect uniting the rhetorical modes of both theme and *minore.*

The intersection of rhetoric and improvisation may again be located in the first movement of Sonata XVI:48 (1789), also Andante con espressione. An unusual five-part construction in which the B-sections are both parallel-minor variants of A, the piece alternates in mode yet is not an alternating variation *per se.* Rather, the piece explores the ramifications of its idea in different registers,

24. *Ad Herrenium,* cited by Murphy, *Rhetoric in the Middle Ages,* pp. 370–373.

directions, and modes. Each successive segment takes as its starting point some aspect of the most recent version of A (Example 6.14). In the first *minore,* the opening recasts the opening of A in the minor, but, to distance it from the minor phrase after the double bar in A (mm. 11–17), now features imitative entries, forceful display (m. 32), and a varied reprise. The returning *maggiore* (A$_1$) has two varied reprises, and what A. Peter Brown calls the "pure form" of the theme, that is, its simplest melodic outline.[25] The next *minore* (B$_2$) continues with the pure form, develops the rhythm of its second measure, and instead of a varied reprise returns to the original format of the theme in Ab major. A return to A$_2$ rounds off the movement.

Sonata No. 48 is, like XVI:42, a work inventing itself as it goes along, one of the very few works by Haydn that seems literally to exemplify the stories of his composing at the keyboard, cited in Chapter 5: "I sat down, began to improvise, sad or happy according to my mood, serious or playful. Once I had seized upon an idea, my whole endeavor was to develop and sustain it in keeping with the rules of art."[26] The delight in keeping this particular idea going can be seen in the constant reworkings of the opening two-bar unit, as well as the manifold performance indications. Many of the dynamic inflections seem counterintuitive—for example, the soft closing chords in mm. 9–10, especially the *pp* on the fullest sonority in the theme—and probably were a palpable part of the piece's creation. It is conceivable that the rhetorical approach to performance style, especially the ever-varied presentation of small cells, represents Haydn's conscious attempt to please a north-German audience: this sonata was commissioned by Breitkopf in Leipzig, "probably his first commissioned work for Germany."[27]

As a piece whose varied repetitions have often been singled out as unusually extensive, the slow movement of the Eb-major Sonata, Hob. XVI:49, composed the following year for Haydn's Viennese friend Marianne von Genzinger, affords an interesting comparison in its approach to that technique. An ABA form in which the turn to minor in the second period of A increases the density of minor mode even before the contrasting B section (as in No. 48), the slow movement of Sonata No. 49 is as "decorative" as No. 48 in its elaborations of the opening phrase, but every aspect of the melodic contour is smoother and more controlled. And its B-section, far from intensifying the varying of A, is a completely new *Gestalt:* in fact, its subject is a variant of the principal two-bar unit of No. 48! (See Example 6.15.) What the A sections of No. 49 have, and what No. 48 lacks, is a smooth foundation for its copious language. That is why No. 49 must have an *abruptio* before the coda (m. 108–109), to tear it away from its rounded style, and, by contrast, why the deceptive cadence that inaugurates the brief close in No. 48 (m. 129) blends in with its surroundings. Brown aptly refers to No. 48 as "fantasy-variation"; what is especially appro-

25. Brown, *Haydn's Keyboard Music,* pp. 340–344.
26. Griesinger, *Biographische Notizen,* p. 114; Gotwals, *Haydn,* p. 61.
27. Landon, *Haydn Chronicle,* II, p. 643.

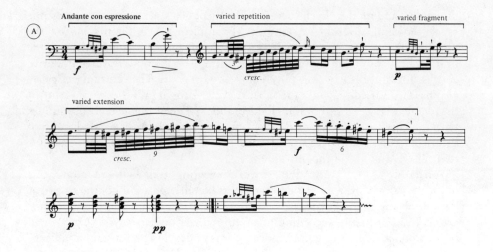

Example 6.14. Haydn, Piano Sonata XVI:48/i.

priate about this term is that the rhetoric of fantasy involved engaging the imagination by creating a mental image, for which the different versions and dynamics of the piece seem well suited.[28] This type of forcefulness of expression (as Quintilian categorized it) is appropriate to first-movement position.

VARIATIONS IN F MINOR
The most intensely moving of Haydn's keyboard variations, indeed one of his greatest works in any genre, is the famous Andante in F minor for piano, Hob. XVII:6 (1793). Its lengthy and finely etched minor theme enters the realm of the *Charakterstück* with the first plaintive notes of the melody, whose dotted rhythms dominate the melancholy proceedings. The major theme, in contrast,

---

28. On *phantasia,* see Quintilian, VIII.iii.888, p. 261 ("phantasia or imagination, which assists us to form mental pictures of things") and Gregory Butler, "The Fantasia as Musical Image," *MQ* 60 (1974), 602–615.

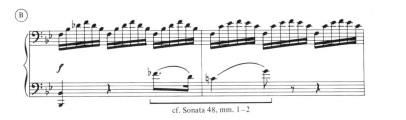

cf. Sonata 48, mm. 1–2

Example 6.15. Haydn, Piano Sonata XVI:49/ii: theme and B section.

is an idyll, more delicately figured and thinner in texture than the *minore* (Example 6.16). Every variation employs simple figures of the kind described by mid-century writers like Marpurg as *Setzmanieren,* but the syncopation of A_1 with accented offbeat appoggiaturas increases the theme's evocative qualities. Thus, as in the Mozart piano concertos (see Chapter 7), the rhetorically rich theme may call forth "mechanical" variations without losing affective resonance.

Titled "Sonate" on the autograph, in an Elβler copy signed by Haydn and in his London works list, and "un piccolo divertimento" on an authentic copy dedicated to Barbara Ployer, the work underwent several revisions that affected its structure and level of expression.[29] The original format was an alternating strophic-variation set in six parts, at which point Haydn may well have intended to write more movements to make a sonata.[30] (The second title is likely part of Haydn's sometimes excessive modesty, of the kind that Schulz found "embarrassing" when he visited Haydn in 1770.)[31] But the addition of a theme

29. See my "Haydn's Hybrid Variations," p. 512. The autograph is in US-NYpL; the Ployer copy is in A-Wn, ms. 18820; and the Elβler copy, hitherto believed lost, was recently acquired by A-Wgm, where it is catalogued as A158a. In all three of these, the original five-measure ending in F major was never crossed out, and appears before the theme reprise and coda. (For the original ending, see Anthony van Hoboken, *Haydn: Thematisch-Bibliographisches Werk-Verzeichnis,* 3 vols. [Mainz, 1957–1971], I, p. 792.) The London works list is reproduced in Haydn, *CCLN* and *Briefe,* p. 556: "1 Sonate in F Minore." The revisions in the autograph and copies are given a new account in an article by Leon Plantinga and Glenn Pierr Johnson, "Haydn's *Andante con variazioni*: Compositional Process, Text, and Genre," in *The Creative Process,* Studies in the History of Music, 3 (New York and Williamstown, in press).

30. The first-movement precedents to that time for alternating strophic variations include the C-minor Piano Trio, Hob. XV:13, and the F-minor String Quartet, Op. 55 No. 2.

31. See Chapter 5, n. 63.

Example 6.16.   Haydn, Variations in F minor, Hob. XVII:6: themes A and B.

reprise and coda did more than simply create a unique seven-part alternating set. Instead, these additions, especially the coda, at first match and then surpass the minor theme in intensity. Arising as an emotion-filled interruption of the reprise, the coda gains in power until it propels itself into a cadenza-like outburst, and yields to the close of the reprise, now transfigured.

What makes the coda special, beyond its obvious and unprecedented chromaticism, is that it concentrates on the dotted motive of the theme, the single most rhetorically powerful gesture of the piece. Indeed, the extraordinary repetition, in dotted rhythm, of the tonic pitch during the theme is one of the very few instances of a word-figure of immediate repetition in a variation theme *(epizeuxis)*. Part of the tension in the relationship between minor and major themes is that this tolling tonic pitch at the beginning of the A theme is airily disregarded by B. Yet at the same time, the B theme appropriates elements of A: the successive thirds of B are made into a more lush and closely written variation of the *minore*'s left-hand accompaniment; and B shares a similarly strong directional opening evolving into more complicated figures. B is necessary as a digression from A, however, not as its antithesis. The meaning of B is made clear in the five-measure codetta in major after B_2 that Haydn never actually canceled (it appears in the authentic copies corrected by Haydn): to reiterate the cadence flourish of A_2 and thus temporarily to bring those themes onto common ground, before safely abandoning B entirely.[32] If a strophic variation set presents the same meaning in different guises, then a piece like this raises the level of rhetoric threefold. In thus yoking together the more expressive with the more galant modes of the classical style, Haydn achieved his most intimate voice in variations.

32. Plantinga and Johnson argue that the crayon marking in the autograph inserting the theme da capo and coda directly after B_2 is not in fact in Haydn's handwriting.

In his instrumental music of the 1780s and 1790s, Haydn broadened the role of variation far beyond the specific formal types he had developed in all movement positions in the 1770s. Now variation was also a nearly ubiquitous presence in slow movements of symphonies and quartets; it was a rhetorical agent in keyboard works; and, as explored in Chapter 4, it was an underlying paratactic principle in sonata-form movements. The idea of varied reprise continued to imply, even require, decoration, while in the late quartets the idea of repetition grew less hospitable to it; a highly figured variation might be "bracketed off" from the rest. For Haydn's last variation movement, the Andante of the F-major Quartet, Op. 77 No. 2 (1799), no simple description of form nor phrase structure nor texture is possible. To call it a conflation of monothematic rondo-variation (the episodes vary the main theme in V and i respectively) and cantus-firmus technique (the melody migrates from first violin to second violin to cello, and recurs in the episodes) does not tell the whole story, because it omits the character of the strangely repetitive and circular theme, its deadpan opening in widely-spaced two-part texture and subsequent harmonization, and its inability to achieve closure except by fiat: the three full-measure chords of mm. 18–20 that never quite return. Every episode and variation has a seamless, sequential transition leading to a pause on V_7.[33] But only the second variation returns to the double bars of the theme for its fanciful violin figuration over the theme melody in the cello: a "true" variation of soloistic display, even ending with a cadenza. The double bars act almost like quotation marks, referring to that earlier tradition. Thus, conventional decoration is contained and made self-referential, while the repetitive motives of the theme, far from being static, serve to generate the rest of the movement.[34]

33. The format of the movement is AB[on A]A₁C[on A]A₂A₃[= A].
33. The format of the movement is AB[on A]A$_1$C[on A]A$_2$A$_3$[= A].
34. Var. 2 stands doubly apart in being the only section without the obsessive dotted rhythms of the theme (similar to those in the theme of Op. 76 No. 6/i).

CHAPTER SEVEN

Mozart's Variations

Mozart's approach to writing variations reflected the different facets of his career: the performing pianist who improvised and published independent sets, the serious composer who incorporated variations into weightier chamber genres like the string quartet, the serious composer *as* performing pianist including variations in piano concertos, and finally the writer of occasional, *concertante*-style music like wind serenades.[1] Of his sixteen variation sets and movements written primarily for Salzburg and Paris between 1766 and 1779, half were independent sets for keyboard, and one-quarter of them divertimenti in mixed scoring;[2] three of the remaining four were piano sonatas or piano-violin sonatas, and only one was for string quartet. During the Vienna years, his thirty-two variation sets and movements consisted primarily of piano genres, with the six piano-concerto movements epitomizing his new performing opportunities in large public concerts. Indeed, fully twenty-five of the variation sets were written between 1781 and 1786, the years of Mozart's greatest popularity. Reflecting both audience approval and compositional choice, the piano concertos thus have the largest critical mass of his variations in any multimovement genre.[3] In contrast to the earlier period, among his most significant contributions of the 1780s were variation movements in string chamber music

1. Mozart's arrangement of the C-minor Wind Serenade K. 388 as a string quintet (K. 406), a more serious genre, suggests that the "serious" wind serenade was a contemporary anomaly that might be rectified. The relative "weight" of instrumental genres in the later eighteenth century has been discussed by Georg Feder, "Die beiden Pole," and in my "Haydn's Baryton Pieces." See Chapter 5, n. 22.

2. On the divertimenti, see James Webster, "The Scoring of Mozart's Chamber Music for Strings," in *Music in the Classical Period. Essays in Honor of Barry Brook,* ed. Allan W. Atlas (New York, 1985), pp. 259–296.

3. The concerto-variations are rarely given the attention they deserve. Recent studies include Kimbell, "Variation Form in the Piano Concertos of Mozart"; Cavett-Dunsby, *Mozart's Variations Reconsidered,* which includes a "case study" of K. 491. General older studies of Mozart's variations include Herbert Viecenz, "Über die allgemeinen Grundlagen der Variationskunst, mit besonderer Berücksichtigung Mozarts," *MJb* 2 (1924), 185–232, and Paul Mies, "W. A. Mozarts Variationenwerke und ihre Formungen," *Archiv für Musikforschung* 2 (1937), 466–495.

and wind divertimenti. Table A.2 in Appendix A lists Mozart's variations and variation movements.

The external differences between Mozart's and Haydn's variation *oeuvres* seem at first glance to arise from these career differences. After all, Mozart wrote seventeen independent sets of variations for piano (including one for piano four-hands and two for piano and violin) compared to four for Haydn, and six in piano concertos compared to none in that genre for Haydn. Haydn, for his part, included variation movements in nearly one-quarter of his 107 symphonies, not even including ABA movements, while Mozart wrote no symphonic variations at all. Yet both included variation movements in about one-quarter of their chamber music with piano (trios for Haydn and sonatas and trios for Mozart), while Haydn had substantially more variation movements in piano sonatas (nearly one-third, excluding ABA variations, to only about one-tenth, or two sonatas, for Mozart). A comparison of the genres in which both men wrote reveals a high degree of coincidence: both wrote serious quartet-variations, both wrote in occasional genres prompted by their circumstances of employment (Esterházy-influenced baryton trios for Haydn, Salzburg-influenced divertimenti for strings and winds for Mozart), both wrote chamber music with piano. Only in their orchestral genres was the difference absolute.

More subtle distinctions emerge on different levels of comparison. Haydn's divertimenti and string trios are early, and are not comparable in pretension or quality to Mozart's mature Divertimento for violin, viola, and cello K. 563, wind serenades K. 388 and K. 361, and Clarinet Quintet K. 581. Mozart wrote no alternating variations and few rondo- and ABA-variations. He also wrote variation finales throughout his life, a placement Haydn abandoned after 1781 (Op. 33) in favor of slow-movement variations and rondo-variation finales. Haydn was sparing in the number of variations in a set, Mozart prolix. And their themes for variations show considerable differences in phrase structure as well as expressive stance. Thus, aside from gross differences in genre and chronology, the main rhetorical thrust of variation—the *inventio, dispositio,* and *elaboratio*—strikingly diverges in Mozart from the Haydn model that he apparently tried at times to emulate rather precisely.

In this chapter I will evaluate Mozart's approaches to these rhetorical and aesthetic issues in works of several different genres. My aim will not be to provide a complete descriptive survey, as has already been attempted by Paul Mies and Esther Cavett-Dunsby.[4] Instead, I will explore the special qualities that Mozart imparted to a set of variations both on their own terms and in relation to Haydn. Some of these characteristics justify Schoenberg's comment that Mozart had the "unique capacity of combining heterogeneous elements in the smallest space."[5]

4. See n. 3. Cavett-Dunsby, in chap. 2, also briefly summarizes the current state of knowledge about sources and authenticity of Mozart's piano variations.

5. Arnold Schoenberg, "Bach" (1950), reprinted in *Style and Idea,* ed. Leon Stein (Berkeley and Los Angeles, 1975; rpt. 1984), p. 395.

Inventio: Choice and Adaptation of Themes

"Variations are a kind of musical rhetoric, in which the given meaning is presented in different guises."[6] The choice of musical materials that creates the theme, the first "meaning," falls under the heading of *inventio,* that elusive but essential first step in producing any speech (or piece of music): finding a suitable subject. Given the overwhelming importance of the theme to a set of variations upon it, *inventio* is thus crucial.[7] The focus of the first part of this chapter will be the sources, characters, and rhetorical stances of Mozart's variation themes, the ways in which these are constrained by movement-position, and implications for their subsequent treatment.

A broad view of Mozart's variation themes takes in characteristics shared with most other variations of the period: that is, they are usually two-reprise structures, borrowed from popular vocal or instrumental tunes when used for independent sets, but are newly composed for variation movements.[8] Also surprising, at least in comparison with Haydn and other composers, is the very high percentage of themes for variations whose first reprises end in the tonic. Of Mozart's variation movements, nearly one-third (nine, or 31 percent) have first periods ending in the tonic, including all three of the movements in D minor; the percentage in independent sets is more like two-thirds (65 percent, or 11 of 17). The consequences are an increased sense of circularity, as well as larger second periods, which must pick up the slack in harmonic interest.

Some of Mozart's themes also embody changes of texture that are radical in the context of the rather uniform variation themes of the period, Haydn's included. In K. 421, the nervously repeating high As in the first violin bring the chromatic second-violin line to prominence—the ear is suddenly caught between simultaneous and disparate motives and registers. This complexity is particularly unusual in a *siciliana*-type theme. At the same point in K. 464, on the other hand, the texture apparently simplifies, changing from a conventional melody-plus-accompaniment to parallel first-inversion triads in the fourth measure. This shift of focus reverberates in every variation and motivates some of the most sublime moments in the movement.

In choice of topic, Mozart's original themes stay within a conventional orbit. That he only rarely varies a minuet (for example, K. 573), however, suggests that the ubiquitous minuet-variations of the 1760s and 1770s were no longer in fashion. A newer fashion, the triple-meter hymn theme introduced by Haydn in the 1770s, appears in two movements by Mozart, the slow movements of the piano concerto K. 450 (1784) and the piano trio K. 564 (1788). That the

6. Vogler, *Verbesserung der Forkel'schen Veränderungen,* p. 5.

7. Tovey famously asserted that variation composers may be divided into those who know their theme and those who do not *(Beethoven* [Oxford, 1944; rpt., 1971], p. 124). *Inventio* also included finding appropriate arguments.

8. There are but few exceptions to each category: themes without repeats or in ternary form, the two independent sets on an original theme, and the variation movements whose themes have a melodic source or model in another work, by Mozart himself or by Haydn, as we shall see.

hymn might somehow replace the minuet as a favored topic for variation is suggested by the source of the latter movement: the piano-trio theme takes its cue from the canonic trio of the minuet in Mozart's C-minor wind serenade, K. 388, that he had rescored as a string quintet the previous year (K. 406) (Example 7.1).

The reason for choosing a particular theme is sometimes obvious: in a concert at the Burgtheater on 23 March 1783, Mozart varied a theme by Gluck, who, having recently praised him, was probably in the audience. Also present was the Emperor. Homage to Gluck, in the form of variations on a tune from his comic opera *Die Pilgrime von Mekka (La rencontre imprévue)*, resulted in a composition published over a year later. More interesting than this mere fact, however, is the difference between this work, K. 455, and the other variation set, on a theme of Paisiello, improvised by Mozart at the same concert and published later that year (K. 398). Of course, we do not know how the published versions compare to the improvisation, but the differences between the sets are suggestive. First, the Paisiello theme has several heterogeneous elements arranged almost arbitrarily and with little internal repetition. The Gluck theme, on the other hand, has tiny dimensions and considerable repetition, both rhythmic and sequential. And the method by which these themes are varied, at least in their published versions, shows the difference between improvisatory exuberance and musical profundity. The Paisiello melody is almost al-

Example 7.1. Mozart, Wind Serenade, K. 388/iii Trio; Piano Trio, K. 564/ii.

ways present during the variations, and these in turn are showy in their
virtuosity, and have fully three improvisatory passages—two shorter connecting *Eingänge* and one full-fledged cadenza—between the last four variations, all
of which also change the theme's structure. Although the Gluck set appears
more superficially conventional for having an Adagio-Allegro pair, the sim-
plicities of the theme are turned on their head in a display of compositional skill
likely to be appreciated by the older composer. For example, its most recognizable yet ordinary feature—the scalar descent from tonic to dominant that opens
the theme—is consistently reharmonized or else negated in the fourth variation, inverted and made chromatic in the fifth variation (a *minore*), and reharmonized and given affective sigh-motives in the sixth. Example 7.2 shows the
fourth variation, which offers, in place of the bracketed notes in mm. 2–3 of
the theme (V–IV^6), V^7–IV^6 (mm. 50–51), V$^4_3$/IV–IV^6 (mm. 54–55), V$^6_5$/vi–VI^6/
vi (=IV^6, now a deceptive cadence, mm. 62–63), and finally V$^6_5$/V–V^7 (mm.
70–71). At the two points marked by arrows, striking cross relations highlight
harmonic change. The Emperor and the audience were more likely to have
responded favorably to the Paisiello, which might account for its almost immediate publication.

The Gluck theme also provides a good example of Mozart's skill in adapt-
ing a vocal model for variations. Gluck's original number is rondo-like
(ab$_1$b$_2$ab$_2$aca with further orchestral reiteration of b$_2$ and a; Example 7.3); Mozart reduced this to a small ab$_2$a with repeats, omitting b$_1$ and c entirely. But he
retained the memorable first phrase and a subsequent sequential phrase. It is
possible that Mozart simply used what he remembered of the piece. More
likely is that he consciously omitted precisely those segments that lacked a
sharp profile (b$_1$) or already contained triplet—that is, variation-like—figuration (c).

Example 7.2.   Mozart, Variations on a Theme of Gluck, K. 455.

Example 7.2 (continued)

Example 7.3.   Gluck, "Unser dummer Pöbel meint."

THE Bb–MAJOR PIANO CONCERTO, K. 450

A more complicated situation is that of a theme which appears to be modeled on that of another work. One such work, in my view, is one that has never been discussed from this point of view. The Bb-major Concerto, K. 450, completed according to Mozart's catalogue on 15 March 1784, contains Mozart's first set of slow-movement variations in the piano concertos. Its hymn-like theme is occasionally described as being profound and spiritual, but the variations themselves are generally relegated to a decorative category in which the melody has features of a cantus firmus.[9]

Recent attention to K. 450 has focused on alterations in the autograph which show that Mozart changed most of the first reprise of the theme and half of the second, as well as the corresponding parts in varied reprises and variation 1. Example 7.4 shows the original version (a) and the altered version (b), omitting the repeats varied by the soloist (the bar numbers of the second period reflect the intervening eight measures). Karl-Heinz Köhler suggests, from the layout of the autograph, that Mozart wrote two separate and equal versions and then (before the final variation?) simply made an arbitrary choice.[10] Jutta Ruile-Dronke, on the other hand, values the revision more highly, claiming that its voice-leading is superior.[11] I would propose an entirely different reason for Mozart's alteration of these measures, one hinging on the source of the theme itself, and thus on the notion of *inventio*.

Mozart wrote down the themes of three Haydn symphonies in 1784, Nos. 75, 47, and 62, and it seems plausible that he considered them for inclusion on his concerts. (The leaf containing these themes includes an unidentified incipit and an *Eingang* for concerto K. 415.)[12] He also wrote to his father on 15 May 1784 to be extremely careful in having his latest four concertos copied since copyists were well known to be thieves; Haydn had many symphonies pirated this way, he warned, then boasted that he actually owned copies of Haydn's three latest symphonies.[13] These may have been the symphonies Joseph Haydn wrote for England, Nos. 76–78, advertised by Torricella in Vienna in July 1784; Mozart might have gotten hold of an advance manuscript copy of them. It is also possible that Mozart had a copy of Hummel's 1781 edition of six Haydn symphonies (issued in three parts), including Nos. 75, 62, and 63. On the other hand, in the context of a discussion of Salzburg copyists, Mozart might well have meant *Michael* Haydn.[14]

As we have seen, Joseph Haydn was identified by contemporary writers as

9. Théodore de Wyzewa and Georges de Saint-Foix note both the spirituality and the decoration; *W.-A. Mozart: Sa vie musicale et son oeuvre* (rpt. New York, 1980), II, p. 460. See also Girdlestone, *Mozart and His Piano Concertos*, pp. 202–204; Donald F. Tovey, *Essays in Musical Analysis*, III: *Concertos* (Oxford, 1936), p. 32; and Arthur Hutchings, *A Companion to Mozart's Piano Concertos* (Oxford, 1948), pp. 40–41. Reinhard Strohm noted that the melody resembles a setting of an Italian verse-form, the *Quinario*, or five-syllable line: his example sets the following text to it: "Sento pietade, non son crudele, ma son legata d'un altro amore"; "Merkmale italienischer Versvertonung in Mozarts Klavierkonzerten," *Analecta musicologica* 18 (1974), 221.

10. Karl-Heinz Köhler, "Zur Bewertung der Korrekturen und Provenienznachweise im Autograph zum Klavierkonzert KV 450: Ein Beitrag zu Mozarts Kompositionsweise 1784," *MJb 1984/85*, 52–61.

11. Jutta Ruile-Dronke, *Ritornell und Solo in Mozarts Klavierkonzerte* (Tutzing, 1978), pp. 197–220.

12. Köchel, *Chronologisch-thematisches Verzeichnis sämtlicher Tonwerke Wolfgang Amadé Mozart*, 7th ed. (Wiesbaden, 1965), pp. 763–764 (K.Anh.A59).

13. Anderson no. 513, pp. 876–877.

14. Neal Zaslaw, *Mozart's Symphonies: Context, Performance Practice, Reception* (Oxford, 1989), pp. 395–396.

(a) Version 1, first period

(b) Version 2, first period

(a) Version 1, second period

(b) Version 2, second period

Example 7.4. Mozart, Piano Concerto K. 450, Andante: (a): first version of orchestral theme (autograph); (b): second version; varied repeats omitted.

both a pioneer and a consummate master in writing variations in the slow movements of symphonies,[15] beginning with Symphony 47 (1772). Not only is Haydn's Symphony No. 75 (written probably at the end of 1779) the first symphony to feature a hymn-like theme for variations in this period, but its rhythmic pattern, texture, and triple meter are exactly the same as in Mozart's slow movement (Example 7.5). I believe that Haydn's movement served Mozart as a model. Furthermore, I suggest that Mozart changed his theme when

15. Contemporary writers who noted his preeminence in this genre included Koch, *Versuch,* III, p. 314, and Vogler, *Verbesserung,* p. 8.

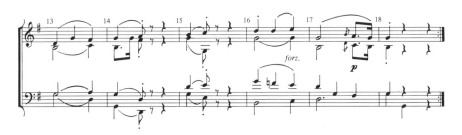

Example 7.5.   Haydn, Symphony 75, Poco Adagio.

he realized that the phrase beginning in m. 17 (after the double bar, so to speak) was nearly identical to Haydn's m. 9; in fact, in the Kees copy of this symphony in the Gesellschaft der Musikfreunde, the first notes after the double bar even use the chromatic descent from D.[16] Mozart may well have intended resemblance but not outright copying; this was not, after all, a set of independent variations on a borrowed theme. Thus, he needed to modify the offending phrase. And in order to change it, he also had to change the earlier ones; otherwise each of the first three phrases would begin with a nearly identical descending pattern. The repeated-note measure now appears in m. 5.

16. *Joseph Haydn sämtliche Symphonien,* ed. Landon, VIII, p. liii (variant reading given in score, p. 69).

To continue the argument: If the model were a symphony, Mozart would be at pains to emphasize the different characteristics of the concerto genre. K. 450 is the only variation movement in the piano concertos in which the repeats are varied by the soloist already in the theme itself. This miniature tutti-solo format, while contributing to the overall shape of the movement, nonetheless intrudes on the essential identity of the theme: it is shown to be "wanting" right away, its hymn-like frame nothing more than a scaffold for figuration. In every other concerto-variation, the theme as an entity is stated by the orchestra, in most cases with repeats; the first variation is an embellishment by the piano.[17] In rondo movements, on the other hand, whether in slow movements or finales, the theme is usually shared between solo and tutti. In addition, Haydn's symphony movement is marked Poco Adagio, while Mozart's concerto is Andante. That the distinction is significant is suggested by Mozart's letter to his father of 9 June 1784: "Please tell my sister that there is no adagio in any of these concertos [the first four of 1784, including K. 450]—only andantes."[18] The character of tempo was perhaps another way to distance himself from Haydn.[19]

The relationship of K. 450/ii to the Haydn model extends even to the first three phrases ending on or in the dominant. Mozart's intricate mirror-image patterns in the bass, however, add greater complexity and chromaticism: in both versions, the cadential measures 23–24 virtually retrograde mm. 1–2; in the revised version, the ascending chromatic line of mm. 5–6 descends in mm. 17–19 and the coda begins by extending the ascending bass pattern that retrogrades mm. 17–18. The original, diatonic version proceeds through the piano part until the varied reprises of the second variation, where the writing becomes extensively chromatic; it was at this point, I speculate, that Mozart saw a way out of the excessive reliance on Haydn, and revised the theme accordingly.

K. 450 was Mozart's first self-described *großes Konzert,* in orchestration and pretension; its every movement was conceived in such a way as to showcase the relationship among its three instrumental groups (winds, strings, and piano).[20] The layering effect of the second movement, then, can be seen in response to this overall conception. The theme sets up a varied-repeat pattern from which

17. In only one other variation movement by Mozart, the Divertimento for String Trio K. 563, does the theme have written-out varied repeats, and these also forecast the shape of the movement; in the violin sonata K. 377, the D-minor variation movement "reorchestrates" the repeat by giving the melody to the violin, but this has no effect on later variations, each of which has two double bars.

18. Anderson no. 515, p. 880. Landon points out that several copies of Haydn's Symphony 75 were marked Andante in the slow movement (see n. 15).

19. On the other hand, only a single piano-concerto slow movement of any form, that of K. 488, is marked Adagio.

20. Christoph Wolff suggests that the Wind Quintet K. 452 was the model for the integration of wind instruments into K. 450, in "Mozart 1784: Biographische und stilgeschichtliche Überlegungen," *MJb 1986,* 8. Alan Tyson has shown that Mozart might have begun sketching K. 452 in 1783; see *Mozart: Studies of the Autograph Scores* (Cambridge, Mass., 1987), pp. 77, 79.

the variations themselves do not diverge. Each variation has a two-fold layering, with the rhythm (actually speed of figuration) disposed by orchestration: in var. 1, the strings' melodic reprise is embellished by the piano, while in var. 2, the winds, entering for the first time, have the melody, the pizzicato strings have a sixteenth-note variation, and the piano has a 32nd-triplet variation.[21] Mozart did not take over Haydn's interesting orchestral layout, but some of the procedures are similar; Haydn tended toward alternation, rather than the building-up and spreading-out qualities of Mozart's movement. Following Haydn's theme is a variation for strings lightly embellishing the theme melody. The rest of the variations present a melodic reprise with varied accompaniment, but this takes three different forms: var. 2 has a martial fanfare motive in winds and horn, var. 3 offers the surprising spectacle of a *concertante* for solo string trio with a figured cello line and pizzicato ripieno strings, and the final variation is a fully orchestrated melodic reprise with an embellished inner voice. Mozart's last three concerto-variation movements (K. 456, 482, 491) did take on this alternating aspect, however.

A final point in support of Mozart's modeling procedures is that Mozart makes overt and thus apparently deliberate melodic references to no fewer than three variation movements by Haydn during the early 1780s, two of them from Haydn's symphonies (one from Mozart's jotted list and one from the Hummel print) and one from a string quartet. The variation movement of the Wind Serenade K. 361 (Example 7.6a) employs a theme remarkably like that in Haydn's Symphony No. 47 (Ex. 7.6b, transposed to B♭ from D major), a resemblance noted by Charles Rosen;[22] the minor variation of the same serenade (Ex. 7.6c) plays with the opening of the minor variation theme in Haydn's Symphony 63, called "La Roxelane" (Ex. 7.6d, transposed to B♭ minor from C minor). And the siciliana variation-finale of Mozart's D-minor Quartet dedicated to Haydn, K. 421, alludes as much to Haydn's G-major Quartet, Op. 33 No. 5, as to Mozart's own earlier D-minor variations in the Violin Sonata K. 377 (Example 7.7). In these cases, the resemblances are strengthened by striking "eye-rhymes," that is, the same pitches harmonized differently: in the K. 361 *minore,* the clarinet has the melody, and the clarinet reads in C minor, the same key as the model, while in K. 421, the same basic pitches as in Op. 33 No. 5 are harmonized in D minor instead of G major. One could also point, of course, to the striking resemblance between the opening Presto of Symphony 75 and the *Don Giovanni* overture, as Rosen has, and between the slow movement of Symphony 77 and Don Ottavio's aria "Il mio tesoro," to show the extent to which Mozart mined Haydn's symphonies for material.[23] Mozart might well have been acknowledging his older contemporary's preeminence in the world of orchestral variations, while at the same time consciously looking

21. The layout is somewhat more complex than this because of the varied repeats.

22. Rosen, *The Classical Style*, p. 152. The first variation of K. 361 even employs the same kind of triplet figuration found in var. 2 of the Haydn.

23. It is possible that these latter examples are "family relationships" between pieces rather than conscious intertextuality.

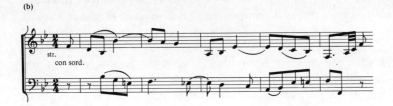

Example 7.6. Mozart's references to Haydn's variations: (a): Mozart, Serenade for winds, K. 361/vi, Andante; (b): Haydn, Symphony No. 47/ii, Un poco Adagio, cantabile (transposed); (c): Mozart, K. 361, var. 4; (d): Haydn, Symphony No. 63/ii, Allegretto (transposed).

(a)

Allegretto

staccato

(b)

(c)

Var. VI
Siciliana

p

(d)

Allegro ma non troppo

Example 7.7. Sources of Mozart's theme of String Quartet in D minor, K. 421/iv: (a): Haydn, String Quartet in G major, Op. 33 No. 5/iv; (b): Mozart, Violin Sonata in F major, K. 377/ii; (c): Mozart, K. 377/ii, var. 6; (d): Mozart, String Quartet in D minor, K. 421/iv.

to surpass him. And since one classic locus for the *inventio* of a theme is in imitation of the theme of another, or *imitatio,* this kind of homage is especially appropriate to variations.[24]

24. Mozart's variation set on Gluck's *Die Pilgrime von Mekka* improvised in Gluck's presence may also reflect his combination of homage and surpassing his models. On *imitatio,* see Howard Mayer

Dispositio: Ordering of Variations

Mozart's methods for organizing sets of strophic variations differ in nearly every particular from Haydn's. Because Mozart included so many more numbers in a set, and because he favored a few strategies of placement, commentators have usually referred to these methods as "stereotyped" or "conventional." But it is one thing to catalogue certain manifest similarities, and quite another to account for some of the profoundly different ends served by these similar means. Examples include cadenzas in keyboard sets, opposite-mode variations, especially *minores,* and the Adagio or Adagio-Allegro pair.

As Table A.2 shows, slightly more than half of Mozart's variation movements, including all the piano chamber music and divertimenti in mixed scoring, have six variations (15 of 29), with the next highest number (5) having five variations. Of the twenty-nine movements, fully twenty have opposite-mode variations, and three of these (all in C minor, K. 388, 482, and 491) have two. Excluding those last C-minor movements cited—each has both a traditional *maggiore* and one in the mediant or submediant major—ten of the remaining movements have an opposite-mode variation in fourth position, four have it in fifth position, and three put it third. Seven movements have a penultimate Adagio variation, and eleven (including six of the Adagio sets) conclude with a faster and often metrically altered variation (K. 424 has two faster numbers, Allegretto and then Allegro).

THE A-MAJOR STRING QUARTET, K. 464

One of the most persuasive documents in support of the idea of a consciously imposed plan is the autograph of the slow movement of Mozart's A-major Quartet K. 464. After completing five variations, Mozart decided that the subsequent coda should incorporate the cello figuration of the fourth variation, and thus reversed the order of the last two variations.[25] The coda (mm. 145–186) followed the original fifth variation in the manuscript. At that point the *minore* was added and given the number 4, and the original fourth variation was renumbered 6. Since *minores* are the rule rather than the exception in Mozart's variations, especially in the fourth-position spot, its addition seems uncontroversial. More curious is its initial omission. And here we come to an issue not heretofore discussed in the Mozart literature: the rationale behind the original plan of the movement.

Brown, "Emulation, Competition, and Homage: Imitation and Theories of Imitation in the Renaissance," *JAMS* 35 (1982), 1–48.

25. See the facsimile in *Wolfgang Amadeus Mozart, The Six "Haydn" Quartets: Facsimile of the Autograph Manuscripts in the British Library, Add. MS 37763,* introduction by Alan Tyson, British Library Music Facsimiles 4 (London: The British Library, 1985). Other variation movements made use of an earlier variation or episode in devising the coda, notably the Divertimento K. 287 (reiterating the horn motto of the third variation), Piano Concerto K. 482 (the first episode in the relative major comes back in the tonic), and Piano Trio K. 496 (the *minore* returns in the coda, now in major). Thus, Mozart might not have actually needed to put the cello variation right before the coda other than for reasons of continuity.

The original version of K. 464 had, in fact, a beautiful logic of its own: the most highly figured line in each variation descends gradually through the parts, from first violin to cello, followed by a contrapuntal epitome. Hardly any figuration appears in the theme outside of the upbeat and cadences (Example 7.8a); the parallel first-inversion chords phrased over the barline are especially noteworthy (mm. 4–6, 12–14), and play an important role in the movement. The 32nd-note first-violin ornamentation of the theme melody in var. 1 descends to 32nd-note accompaniment in the second violin with a new first-violin melody in var. 2, strikingly punctuated by an unmistakable refer-

Example 7.8. Mozart, String Quartet, K. 464/iii: (a): theme; (b): end of var. 2.

ence to the final cadence in "Che farò senza Euridice" from Gluck's *Orfeo* (mm. 42–44, Example 7.8b). The third variation breaks up the figuration with a dialogue between violins and lower strings, turning the parallel ⁶₃ chords into imitative entries of the motive and syncopated counterpoints to it. The original fourth variation (sixth in the final version) brings figuration down to the cello. And after every register has had its say, the contrapuntal fifth variation acts as a summation. Obviously intended as the final variation, it contains varied repeats (almost always saved for last or for the end of a principal subgroup), a revelation of the motivic connection between dotted-rhythm upbeat and parallel-chord motive, a reharmonization of the theme in the varied repeats, and conscious *stile antico* plainness (no figuration beyond the dotted rhythm of the upbeat). The contrapuntal major variation thus obviated the need for a *minore,* and even took over the *minore*'s prerogative of altering the phrase structure of the theme (here, shortening the second period). Example 7.9 gives the incipits of the original variations, according to this plan:

var. 1: vln. 1, melodic figuration in 32nd-notes
var. 2: vln. 1, new melody; vln. 2, accompaniment figuration in 32nd-notes
var. 3: paired violins with upbeat motive, viola with consequent incise, including 32nd-notes; in second phrase, the melodic pattern of the theme's parallel chords introduced as contrapuntal subject
var. 4 (present var. 6): vln. 1, new melody; vc, accompaniment figure in new, repeating rhythmic pattern
var. 5: imitative, contrapuntal with subjects derived from parallel chords

The coda begins with the ♩♪♪♪♪ motive of the cello variation, migrating back up the instruments and registers from viola to second to first violin, until a cadenza-like arpeggiated sweep downward yields to a partial theme reprise. Neither mere "rounding-off" nor weighted "recapitulation," this reprise conflates several previously disparate elements: it opens with the reharmonized version of var. 5 (mm. 164–165); it moves directly from the parallel first-inversion passage of the first reprise to that of the second reprise (that is, combining the theme's mm. 4–5 and 13–14) in order to compress the entire theme into ten bars; it literally quotes a cadential phrase from var. 5 (mm. 174–177), and then repeats it with the cello figuration of the original penultimate variation (now var. 6). The final measures of the coda return to the melodic pattern of the coda's beginning, with the figuration heard there in the viola now restored to the cello. Thus, the coda emphasizes both the role of the fifth variation in creating the expectation of imminent closure, and the common substratum of all the variations. The "sense of an ending" in a set of variations is, as we have seen, one of its most problematic aspects, and Mozart's maneuvers in K. 464 stem from his proposing a dual ending: the contrapuntal culmination to a set of variations and the coda as a more conventional end to a slow movement were ideas actually in conflict with each other. In fact, contrapuntal endings are

Example 7.9.   Mozart, K. 464/iii, original plan.

Example 7.9   (*continued*)

invariably mitigated in Mozart's instrumental works, reintegrated with galant-style themes and cadences. This is true of the finales of the G-major Quartet K. 387, the F-major Piano Concerto K. 459, and the "Jupiter" Symphony K. 551. It may be that Mozart painted himself into a corner with his luminous fifth variation, and needed to change its position in the movement to create a convincing, even if more conventional, close.

THE DIVERTIMENTO FOR STRINGS, K. 563

One other movement seeks to articulate its imminent close with a contrapuntal study, the slow movement of the Divertimento for violin, viola, and cello, K. 563, which has four variations and coda.[26] Instead of imitation, however, the counterpoint takes the unusual form of a layered species exercise in which the chorale-like cantus firmus, played by the viola, itself includes two different note values (quarters and halves). The cello in sixteenths creates a largely third-species relationship to the viola, while the violin in thirty-second notes maintains a constant second-species relationship to the cello.[27] As a cantus firmus, the theme melody has been stripped down to a scale, the ultimate projection of the bareness of the theme (Example 7.10; asterisks identify notes of the theme that appear in the scalar version in var. 4). Indeed, the combination of busyness and bareness suggests that Var. 4 is the goal of several earlier elements in the movement. It reveals the distinctions between a rapidly-moving contrapuntal line and pure melodic "figuration" (var. 1, repeats) and between rhythmically differentiated lines in contrapuntal and obbligato (var. 2) textures. It is also the only section of the movement with no repeats, an unusual feature in chamber genres and especially in a piece with so many written-out varied repeats; perhaps the simultaneous rhythmic levels obviate the necessity, so to speak, for such repeats.

The organization of K. 563 again works "toward" the final contrapuntal variation, but in entirely different terms from K. 464 because every one of its elements is anticipated. First of all, the contrapuntal aspect emerges strongly in

---

26. For a detailed voice-leading analysis of the individual variations in this movement, see Felix Salzer, "The Variation Movement of Mozart's Divertimento K. 563," *Music Forum* 5 (1980), 257–315.

27. These are rhythmic relationships, and do not embody Fuxian dissonance treatments.

(a)

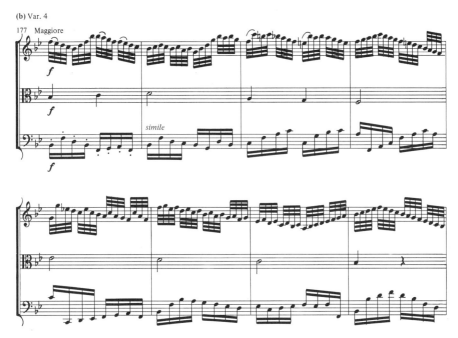

(b) Var. 4

Example 7.10. Mozart, Divertimento, K. 563/iv: (a): theme; (b): var. 4 (upbeat omitted).

the penultimate variation—the *minore*—in invertible counterpoint, with the leading voice alternating between violin and cello with each repeat. Second, the layering effect in the final variation occurs strikingly in var. 1 with, simultaneously, a melodic reprise in the viola, a soaring new melody in the violin, and a cello line that becomes motivic in the fifth and sixth measure. Finally, each of the variations confronts the polarity set up by the theme between bare two-part texture in the first reprise and richer three-part writing with motivic interactions among voices in its varied repetition.

This last point suggests the role of the theme in forecasting the structure of the movement. As in K. 450, the varied repeats of the theme continue into the body of the movement, affecting all but the final variation.[28] But this is not the total picture. The two-part version of the theme is rudimentary, skeletal, a kind of "pre-theme," giving way to the "true theme," its realized self. Indeed, the melody is at first not unlike a bass line, corresponding in particular to Mozart's own early string quartet in F major, K. 170 (1770; Example 7.11). As if to underscore the neutral quality of the opening in K. 563, the first two variations recast it, beginning instead on the higher F, which becomes especially noticeable because the second periods begin on the same pitch. In Mozart's rhythmic reduction of the melody in the last variation, the beginning is its most fragmented portion.

As in the theme, the varied repeats of the first and second variations represent a kind of arrival, in sonority, texture, and dynamics. The first half of var. 1 continues the textural complexity of the three-part version of the theme (in which the viola had achieved independence in m. 37), with the reprise, countermelody, and cello motive just mentioned. At the varied repeat, the violin confidently emerges as a *concertante* instrument to lush, sustained, root-position chords in viola and cello, forte. In effect, this reverses the direction of textural complexity. And reversing it again are the two repeats of the third variation, initially simpler (a new melody plus figured accompaniment) and at the repeat more complex (an imitative constant-harmony variation with repeated chords, forte).

The *minore,* var. 3, represents a continuation of the imitative mode, now made mysterious by the sudden pianissimo, suspensions, overlapping of phrases: a learned-style mood-piece. This entire third variation functions as the quiet forerunner to the final one, just as the first halves of vars. 1 and 2 were superseded by their varied repetitions. In the fourth variation, all previous modes of musical discourse are united synchronically: counterpoint, figuration, melodic outline, melody beginning from both Bb (viola) and F (violin). No repetition is needed. The coda (mm. 201–213) restores the one rhythmic value missing from var. 4: eighth notes, the prevailing values of the theme, first in a bit of fourth-species syncopation in the violin (mm. 203, 207 with viola), then in a final return to the opening measures of the theme. This last statement is a gentle summation: F is treated as a melodic goal, the tune is imitated by the cello, and the sixteenth-note accompaniment is a gentle reminder of previous figuration.

In format, the movement resembles the ubiquitous figure of *refining (expolitio)* as described in the [*Rhetorica*] *Ad Herennium* (see Chapter 2), in which the model speech included the Theme expressed simply, the Theme expressed in a new form, arguments from Comparison, Contrary, and Example, and a Conclusion which restates the theme. As a concise formal description of K. 563, *refining* works admirably: the three-part version casts the theme in a new form;

---

28. Salzer tries to make a distinction between "varied repeats," in which the theme melody is usually present, and a true contrasting variation of a given reprise. The latter, he claims, leads to "double variation." While wary of this term, Salzer is not aware of its frequent use as a synonym for alternating variations, and he thus muddies the waters further.

Example 7.11.   Mozart, String Quartet, K. 170/i.

vars. 1–2 present comparisons, var. 3 the contrary, and var. 4 the example—
simultaneous figured and unfigured layers—with the theme returning at the
end. Also germane is the way Mozart seems to unite Forkel's types of rhetorical
figures, figures for the imagination (painting the landscape of feelings) and figures for the understanding (intellectual pleasure through counterpoint).[29] Not
only is the *minore* full of affective intervals and suspensions that are made more
poignant by the counterpoint, but it introduces the cantus firmus of var. 4 with
its upbeat and quarter-note motion. Significant in all of Mozart's compositions
with learned-style *Mischformen* is their placement at the close: the intellect is
addressed only after passions have been raised.

VARIATION AND RONDO

Mozart referred to K. 382 as a "Variazion rondeau" or, simply, "rondeau," as
noted in Chapter 2. The form of the movement, a theme and variations in
which the first reprise returns periodically like a ritornello or rondo refrain,
appears again in Mozart's last solo-piano variation set, K. 613; Haydn had already used it—and perhaps was Mozart's source—in two of his sonatas for the
Auenbrugger sisters, Hob. XVI:36/ii and 39/i, published in Vienna in 1780 (see
Chapter 5). It is also similar to a type of variation described by Koch in 1793.[30]
And if this was the concerto Mozart referred to in a letter of 22 January 1783,
then he also improvised extensively when performing it; the invariant ritornello can be seen as a springboard to further flights of fancy.[31]

   After K. 382, the concertos of 1782–1784 show a heightened role for variation in rondo- and sonata-rondo finales. In K. 413, for example, one of Mozart's three subscription concertos of 1782, both refrains contain varied repetition, while in K. 415, the exceptionally long finale contains two tonic-minor
Adagio episodes, in which the second is a variation of the first. More pro-

---

29. See Chapter 2.

   30. Koch, *Versuch*, III, pp. 313–314; *Introductory Essay*, p. 202; see Chapter 3. Koch refers to the
"appendix" *(Anhang)* of the theme returning as a ritornello, especially in Andante movements of
symphonies; in K. 382, the first reprise returns intact at the close of the theme. In concertos, Koch
mentions variations with rondo-like episodes.

   31. Anderson no. 479, p. 837. The letter perhaps suggests K. 415, which has more opportunities
for *Eingänge* than K. 382. The only fermata in the latter piece appears just before the Adagio variation; Mozart need not have restricted himself to that.

foundly varied are the hybrid finales of K. 449 and K. 451 (1784), which combine rondo, sonata, and variation. Not only is each refrain a variation, but the final refrain in each concerto changes meter, in the manner of the Allegro variation in K. 382.[32] K. 451 resembles K. 382 not only in theme type, expressive orientation, and meter change (2/4 to 3/8), it also has the identical scoring and a similar deployment of trumpets and timpani, which are associated first with the pendant to the theme (mm. 17–20) and, except for two measures (mm. 212–213, the V^7 before the final refrain), occur only in refrains and the pendant.

In the alla breve finale of K. 449, Mozart developed a formal hybrid—sonata rondo-variation—of great textural complexity. The contrapuntal opening theme (a) dominates the tutti "ritornello" ($a_V\ a_I\ b\ [a]$), and is immediately varied in the soloist's entrance ($a_1\ a_2$ ext/mod $b_{in\ V}$). Instead of the second theme of sonata-rondo, Mozart brings back the first in the dominant, now shared between tutti and solo in a contrapuntal variation. In the first refrain, the tutti takes over the piano's figuration at its consequent phrase (a_I). An episode beginning in C minor leads to an extensive contrapuntal passage in the three-part invention style favored by Haydn in his piano sonatas, and offers a surprising twist in the often-revised conventions of sonata rondo: the C-minor theme returns in the tonic after the next refrain, in the manner of a resolved second theme. And the final refrain in 6/8 offers the return of the b theme in the tonic, now varied for the first time. An outline of the movement looks like this:

[Exp]	A: $a_V\ a_I\ b$ closing on a (tutti)
	A_1: $a_V\ a_I$ ext/mod to V $b_{in\ V}$ sequences (solo, m. 33)
	B (in V): a, sequences, V pedal (m. 91)
	A_2: $a_V\ a_I$ (m. 136)
[Dev]	C (c minor): c, dev of a (m. 152)
[Recap]	A_3 (in I): $a_V\ a_I\ c_{in\ I}$ [ferma] (m. 221)
	A_4 (6/8): $a_V\ a_I\ b_{in\ I}$ (m. 269)
[Coda]	coda (m. 308)

It is worth calling attention to Mozart's description of this movement: he distinguished it from the *grosse Konzerte* with winds, namely K. 450, K. 451,

---

32. On the forms of these movements, see Malcolm S. Cole, "Mozart Rondo Finales with Changes of Meter and Tempo," *SM* 16 (1974), 25–53; Hans Tischler, *A Structural Analysis of Mozart's Piano Concertos* (Brooklyn, 1966). Cole identifies as part of the coda what I have called the final refrain, presumably because he defines as coda everything that appears after the cadenza; Tischler describes K. 451 as "ritornello-variations," although unlike K. 382 the varied segments are not really ritornellos in the concerto sense, but rather refrains entirely in the rondo sense (that is, tutti and solo share material).

and K. 453, all suitable for big subscription concerts in the theater, by stressing its *à quattro* performance possibility; it was, as Alan Tyson has shown, begun together with the other *à quattro* concertos of 1782–1783.[33] Mozart described it as a concerto of "ganz besonderer Art" ("an entirely special manner"), almost exactly the same formulation used by Haydn to announce his Op. 33 quartets ("Neu, gantz besonderer Art"); Emily Anderson's translation of this passage as "concerto of a peculiar kind" has tended to obscure Mozart's claim.[34] The nature of K. 449 suggests that not only was its smaller scoring at issue, but also its intricate contrapuntal and motivic textures and the taut connections between thematic segments.[35] Its similarity to Haydn's Op. 33 in these respects, as in its tendency to make variation an essential component of formal hybrids, offers a linkage both between chamber and orchestral genres and between Mozart and Haydn.

The tendency toward greater contrast in the brilliant rondo-finales—from the *Variazion rondeau* of K. 382, to the monothematic and varied sonata-rondo of K. 449, to the bithematic and varied sonata-rondo of K. 451 ($ABA_1CA_2BA_3$)—finally results in the disappearance of systematic embellishment from the concerto finales. Of the nine later rondo finales, only four (K. 459, K. 467, K. 482, and K. 503) have any embellishments of the main theme, and these are all relatively local phenomena, far from the pervasive varying of the finales of 1782–1784. Mozart's most extraordinary rondo-finale, from the point of view of its combination of different structural and technical models, is K. 459, which synthesizes learned counterpoint, variation, elements of first-movement form, and rondo.

It would be wrong to see the "after-life" of K. 382 entirely in rondo movements, however, because Mozart derived the organization of all but one (K. 450) of his subsequent variation movements in the concertos from its layout: the solo-piano variation is always first, after the tutti theme; the second variation featur᾿s wind-band scoring with a theme reprise (in K. 482 the wind-band has an episᴗde [B] in that slot); piano figuration most often accompanies a theme reprise; and the opposite-mode variation is invariably fourth (in K. 491, the two opposite-mode variations are fourth and sixth). The element of K. 382 closest to his independent piano variations—the Adagio variation—never appears again, however. Mozart chose well from the work, and it resonated throughout the concertos of the mid–1780s.

We have already seen how Mozart articulates the close of a variation movement in a coda that quotes from the theme, recasting its phrase structure; both K. 464 and K. 563 end this way, although the coda in K. 464 is more extensive and

33. Tyson, *Mozart: Studies of the Autograph Scores*, p. 153.

34. Bauer-Deutsch, III, p. 315; Anderson no. 514, p. 877; Haydn's claim appeared in a letter of 3 December 1781 to Lavater, in *Briefe*, p. 106.

35. See Chapter 4 for an outline of the slow movement, an unusual hybrid of sonata design and strophic form.

refers to a variation as well. In many of Mozart's variations with very short codas or none at all, the convention of changing meter and increasing tempo for the final variation lends it the aspect of a "finale," so that closure is obtained naturally from within the variation series. This effect is heightened when the finale is preceded by an Adagio, so that the last two variations suggest the artificial traversal of an entire multi-movement cycle. Yet the effect of an Adagio-Allegro pair at the end of a variation movement must surely be different from that concluding an independent set of variations, and even among variation movements must differ at different positions in the cycle.[36]

In Mozart's independent sets, an Adagio-Allegro pair (so-called despite the variety of tempo designations for the faster segment) appears in fully two-thirds, but the majority of these will return to tempo primo for a brief recall or even full *da capo* of the theme. In variation movements, on the other hand, only one-fifth have the Adagio-Allegro pair, although the total rises to more than one-quarter if movements with just a concluding Allegro are added. In general, Allegro variations, most of which also change the meter, are theme *da capos* with a bit more energy. In one of these cases, Mozart models himself directly on Haydn. In his D-minor string quartet, K. 421, Mozart borrowed the *siciliana* topic from Haydn's Op. 33 No. 5, as we have already seen. At the conclusion, he also takes over from the same source the idea of a fast, slightly altered theme reprise that goes on for only one period before yielding to a coda. These are one-time occurrences in the *oeuvres* of both composers. In fact, Haydn, who never decreased the tempo in a variation set, wrote only a few concluding Allegros outside of this one: the two early *concertante* symphonies, Nos. 31 ("Hornsignal") and 72 (an unrelated coda to the symphony as a whole, in No. 31 bringing back the horn signal), the final variation in the London flute trio in G major Hob. IV:2, the alternating variation set in Piano Trio XV:19 (the Presto sonata-form, discussed in Chapter 4), the Allegro fugue-*cum*-variation in Op. 76 No. 6, and the concluding section of the ABA variation movement that opens Op. 76 No. 5.

A unique peroration is that of the finale of the G-major piano concerto K. 453 (1785), which has its own finale, labeled as such. Table 7.1 shows the organization of the movement, Example 7.12 its main musical ideas. The order of events of the theme and five variations resembles the other variation movements in the piano concertos (to be discussed in the following section): after the tutti theme, a more chromatic solo variation (var. 1), a wind-band melodic reprise with piano figuration (var. 2), a *concertante* wind trio with solo repeats (var. 3), a learned-style *minore* with imitation and syncopation (var. 4), and a symphonic-style tutti (var. 5, first reprise). The last two of these articulate a closing pair, in that the *minore,* among Mozart's most mysterious utterances, is

36. In her interesting article, "Mozart's Codas" *(MusA* 7 [1988], 31–51), Esther Cavett-Dunsby remarks: "If a coda comes at the end of a multi-movement work, we assume that it summarizes earlier events. But one at the end of a first movement seems to anticipate what follows. So how do we deal with works whose movements have at some stage been reordered or replaced? . . . Position in analysis is at its most crushingly obvious in a study of codas" (p. 47).

Table 7.1 Mozart, Piano Concerto K. 453/iii: Organization

VARIATIONS:
Theme (tutti)
A₁: Solo (+ str.), m. 17
A₂: Wind-band with melodic reprise, solo triplets (RH), m. 33;
  Repeats: piano/string melodic reprise, triplets (LH).
A₃: Cantabile melody for *concertante* winds (+ str.), m. 65;
  Repeats: piano and strings.
A₄: *Minore;* syncopated, imitative, mysterious, m. 97;
  Repeats: piano.
A₅: Tutti flourishes, fortissimo, m. 129;
  Repeats: piano trill (RH), melodic reprise (LH).
extension

FINALE:
Finale theme, Presto, m. 171 (tutti) (23mm.) (to V)
1. Finale theme, m. 194 (solo) (28mm.) (to V)
2. Two attempts at resolution (28mm.)
  a. *Ombra* parenthesis, m. 222 (12mm. to I, elided)
  b. ascending imitative progression to cadential passage,
    m. 233 (16mm. to I)
3. Return of Variation theme, m. 249 (24mm.)
  a. Theme (16mm.) (solo to V, tutti to V)
  b. transition (8mm.) (to V)
4. Two attempts at resolution (33mm.); Variation for soloist (25mm.)
  a. *Ombra* parenthesis, m. 273 (12mm. to I, elided)
  b. ascending imitative progression, m. 284, extended
    with repetition of cadential passage (23mm. to I)
  b₁. soloist's variation of (b), to resemble variation theme
    (25mm. to I)
5. Variation theme, m. 331 (solo, offset by tutti) (16mm.)

---

a sudden pianissimo; when the piano enters the pace of syncopation quickens, and the smoothly conjunct chromatic melody gives way to dissonant leaps. This variation contains the only extensive corrections in the autograph: in both of the piano's varied repeats, Mozart changed the left hand to increase the amount of syncopation.[37] The final variation, with its jolly fortissimo and flourishes, seems almost indecently relieved, and the solo's repeats introduce trills and passage work that could lead to a cadenza.

The great surprising stroke, then, after an extension, is that Mozart chose to conclude not with cadenza and coda, to "round off" the series, but rather with another set of quasi-paratactic segments in its (labeled) *Finale,* the accelerated

---

37. A copy of the relevant pages of the autograph was kindly supplied by David Rosen. Charles Rosen finds this *minore* to be "so heavily chromatic that it has the modulatory effect of a 'development' section"; *The Classical Style*, p. 226. It resembles the *minore* in K. 563.

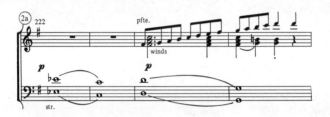

Example 7.12. Mozart, Piano Concerto, K. 453/iii: (a): variation theme; (b): finale theme, and segments 2a and 2b.

character of which is characteristic of opera buffa finales.[38] Supplanting the variations is an exciting five-part series of sometimes discontinuous events, all of which contain repeated and occasionally varied material. The mock-serious *ombra* passages emphasize the discontinuities by delaying resolutions; indeed, the finale seems to reverse the inevitable full cadences in the variations by giving thematic passages (the finale-theme and variation-theme sections) half ca-

38. For a comparison of the structure of K. 453's finale with that of operatic finales, see Marius Flothuis, "Bühne und Konzert," *MJb 1986,* 50–52.

dences only. As is well known, Mozart taught the theme's *Singspiel*-like melody to his pet starling, a detail which charmingly reinvigorates the vocal connotations of the movement.[39] Beyond the five-part division of material, some indicators of the paratactic quality of the finale are that it has practically the same number of measures as the theme and five variations, that it alludes to or quotes some of those earlier segments, and that a number of its segments could be rearranged. The finale theme and its piano reiteration resemble the theme and solo first variation; the *ombra* passage as well as the ascending imitative sequence with suspensions both refer, in character and counterpoint, to the *minore*. As a peroration, though, these features are transmuted into a seamless summation that aims to convince: we even hear an echo of Haydn's "Maestro e Scolare" variations in the trade-off of tutti and solo in different octaves in the final statement of the theme.

Elaboratio: Figures and Figurations

Rhetorical elements of music are often deeply embedded in its structure, and as such are not always separable from the "matter" of the piece, as verbal ornament may be separated from its matter. In variations, the association of musical and rhetorical figures works on three levels: the "intrinsic" figures embedded in the theme, the "extrinsic" figurations in the variations, and the "structural," in which an entire variation or series of variations works as a figure (as comparison, negation, antithesis, as part of the *gradatio* of progressive diminution, and so forth). The composer's strategy allows these types to intersect and interact in different ways. And just as verbal ornament makes a speech more expressive, so do intrinsic, extrinsic, and structural figures decorate, saturate, and exemplify the expressive values of a musical composition.

PIANO CONCERTOS

Although they share several aspects of layout with K. 382 and K. 450, Mozart's two remaining slow-movement variations in the piano concertos have such unusually long and profoundly expressive themes that they appear to be *sui generis*. Indeed, these minor-key movements from K. 456 (catalogued on 30 September 1784) and 482 (16 December 1785) are notable for their repeated expressive intervals, of the type sometimes found in discussions of musico-rhetorical figures as *pathopoeia* (affective minor seconds) and *saltus duriusculus* (larger chromatic intervals). These sorts of details in the theme, in my view, offer a way to bridge the gap perceived by eighteenth-century musical thinkers

39. In a fascinating study of the vocal and mimicking propensities of starlings, two scientists assert that Mozart's starling might have learned the tune almost at once (rather than Mozart learning it from the bird). They also hypothesize that Mozart's *Musical Joke* was a true Requiem for the bird, "bearing the vocal autograph of a starling." See Meredith J. West and Andrew P. King, "Mozart's Starling," *American Scientist* 78 (1990), 106–114. I am indebted to Siri von Reis for calling my attention to this article.

between the affective figures of rhetoric and the figures of passagework that were sometimes called *Setzmanieren*.[40]

The G-minor slow movement of K. 456 has a poignant gavotte theme suffused with rhetorical figures of interval and phrase (Example 7.13). Expressive intervals include the pathetic minor-second neighbor-note figure of 5–♭6–5 (a kind of *pathopoeia*), noted as *a* in the example, and the chromatic leaps of a diminished seventh or tritone *(saltus duriusculus)*, noted as *b*. Embedded in passages of ambiguous phrase rhythm and varying metric accents, these intervals take on heightened affective significance, and become "figures for the imagination," as Forkel termed such musico-rhetorical associations. In bars 4 and 5, for example, the melodic pattern of three eighth-notes in the first violin is echoed by the bass and by oboe and bassoon, each giving an accent to a different eighth-note at a different part of the measure; the most prominent of these patterns is the yearning neighbor-note figure given a plangent downbeat accent on the upper note by oboe and bassoon.

In phrase structure, the first reprise seems a model of regularity (two four-measure phrases, with parallel incise construction: 1 + 1 + 2 in each) compared to the second, where the rhythmic patterning changes in every incise. Its five consecutive two-measure and one expanded three-measure incises, marked with brackets and numbered in the example, are each strikingly different, and are attached in novel ways (shown with braces in the example): the arrangement, 2 + 2, 2, 2 + 2 + 3 (elided in m. 18), consists of a four-measure phrase (mm. 8^2–12^1) giving rise to a single incise (mm. 12^2–14^1), followed by a four-measure phrase (mm. 14^2–18^1) whose deceptive cadence sparks an expanded cadential repetition (mm. 18^2–21^1). The first sign of pressure to the system is the syncopated sforzando upbeat in m. 10^2, the first quarter-note upbeat, indeed, the first beat in the theme thus far that is not subdivided in any voice into smaller notes.[41] Emphatically reasserting the minor mode after a brief venture into the relative major, this second incise closes with a new sixteenth-note pattern (m. 11) which immediately generates the flute's sixteenth-note ascent in m. 12, as well as the third incise (mm. 12^2–14^1), a self-enclosed unit beginning and ending with the same sixteenth-note pattern: *anadiplosis* (noted as *c*) in its link to the previous incise, and *epanalepsis (d)* within the new incise. When the pattern closes the fifth incise as well, it forms an *epistrophe (e)*. The chromatic augmentation in the winds (m. 18, a *passus duriusculus, f*), imitated in the bass (mm. 18–19), links the last two incises and expands the second of them. Finally, the descending chromatic leaps as upbeats to the last two incises (diminished seventh, m. 16, and tritone, m. 18) create a more powerful echo of the last incise of the first period (mm. 6–8). Phrase construction and phrase-oriented "sentence-figures," both essential parts of musical rhetoric, are thus harnessed to the expressive function of intervallic figures.

This theme can hardly be improved upon in subsequent variations, and Mo-

40. These distinctions, made principally by Marpurg, were outlined in Chapter 2.

41. Only two more beats are not subdivided: the downbeat of m. 14, which concludes a harmonically static two-measure incise in the subdominant, and the downbeat of the final measure.

Example 7.13. Mozart, Piano Concerto, K. 456/ii, theme.

Example 7.13   (continued)

zart quotes it literally in var. 2 (twice) and var. 5, in the presence of "mechanical" piano figurations, the running, arpeggiated, and repeated-note *Setzmanieren*. His larger strategy is to alternate such variations with melodic variations for the piano (the pleonastic var. 1, and the partially periphrastic repeats of var. 3), and variations which substitute new melodies, textures, and topics (vars. 3, 4). Example 7.14 gives the incipits of vars. 1, 3, and 4. Unlike K. 450, in which the piano already had varied repeats in the theme, here the first piano variation (var. 1) acts as the second part of a dual exordium, relying on appoggiaturas as the personal coloring devices found almost exclusively in the piano concertos, familiar from K. 382. Mediating between the expressive figures of the theme and pure *Setzmanieren* in its first four measures, var. 1 varies the *pathopoeia* half-step in conjunction with repeated notes (mm. 1–2), and diminishes the chromatic ascending flute line of m. 18 (mm. 3–4), before turning into pure figuration. A single measure of harrowing dissonant voice-exchange in the second reprise (m. 15) intensifies the original wind answer. The solo, of course, is always able to *perform* expressively, performance being another aspect of rhetoric, and it is this interpretive quality that also softens the *Setzmanieren*.

After the concerto-generic identifier of the tutti theme and solo first variation, the next three variations (vars. 2–4) allude to other genres in both orchestration and characteristic motives; throughout, the piano continues its obligatory tissue of passagework but without essentially challenging the new interpretations of the orchestra. Var. 2 becomes a wind serenade, and introduces a chromatic descending line in the bass, an inversion and augmentation of the wind line in m. 18. The tutti-variation 3 refers to both symphonic and learned styles in its unfigured recasting of the theme melody, martial fanfares, and imitative running and leaping figures; its accented upbeats might derive from m. 10. Syncopations in the second reprise demolish the incise-structure

Example 7.14.   Mozart, K. 456/ii, vars. 1, 3, 4.

of the theme, in a passage reminiscent of some of the eccentric moments in
Wilhelm Friedemann Bach's F-major Symphony (F. 67/i).

   A *maggiore,* var. 4, restores the wind-band in an idyllic pastoral dialogue for
flute and oboe which both reverses and inverts the opening upbeat-downbeat
figure of the theme. And after the strikingly different varied repeats by the
piano in var. 3, here the varied repeat actually varies the first reprise of var. 4,
rather than the theme. Opposite-mode variations (as well as Adagio variations
in faster movements) often become a repository for expressive figures, but here
the *maggiore* relates to two variations outside itself: the juxtaposition of vigorous and far-ranging var. 3 with ethereal and self-contained var. 4 creates a rhe-

torical antithesis, while the wind scoring echoes var. 2. The ensuing *minore* (var. 5, the only variation without repeats) returns to the simpler mold of var. 2. Only in the coda does the piano play the unvaried and expressive opening motive of the theme, as consequent to the tutti and thus as the agent of closure. Its last gesture is as the counterpoise and answer to the affective neighbor-note motive.

Rhetorical figures densely populate the variation theme of Mozart's next concerto as well. At a subscription concert early in 1786, the C-minor Andante of the Eb-major Concerto, K. 482, was immediately recognized as something special and encored, to Mozart's surprise; Leopold noted in a letter to Nannerl that this was a quite unusual occurrence.[42] The plan of the movement is a rondo-variation:

A	A_1	B	A_2	C	A_3 ext.	Coda/B
C min.		Eb maj.		C maj.		
	pf	wind band	pf/str	fl-bsn	tutti/pf	
	m. 33	m. 65	m. 93	m. 125	m. 145	m. 186

The theme has no internal repeats, but in each period one or more motives turns into a rhetorical figure of repetition, until the theme seems virtually saturated with expressive motives (Example 7.15). As in K. 456, the upper-neighbor figure of 5-b6−5 is prominent (at *a*), and after an extra incise appears in mm. 5–6, traversing again the upper-neighbor figure of mm. 2–3, the figure is reinterpreted, repeated and expanded with new harmonies, like a *polyptoton* (repetition with a different grammatical function of the repeated word, at *b*). When the neighbor-figure returns toward the end of the theme (mm. 21–22), it is immediately repeated to greater effect a fourth higher (a *gradatio* of pitch, *c*), ushering in a sinuous passage in the learned style *(d)* to embellish its cadence. Another interval-figure derives from the opening upbeat of the movement, inverted in the first phrase after the Eb-major cadence (mm. 13–20) and extended into a gradually intensifying rising sequence *(gradatio* or *climax, e).*[43] And the final cadence is delayed by a repeated measure prolonging II_5^6 (mm. 28–29), and embellished by a sighing seventh *(exclamatio, f).*

The variations are much more figuratively neutral than the theme; indeed, the piano's A_2 is entirely a *setzmanierlich* accompaniment (left hand) to a theme reprise (right hand). After the obligatory solo variation, the same contrasts in scoring and genre-signals of K. 456 play their part—wind serenade, sym-

42. Letter of 13 January 1786; Anderson no. 536, p. 895.

43. The tension and increasing urgency in the semantic figure are mirrored in Mozart's ascending sequence in which the two-bar motive gives way to a shorter and quicker ascent, conveying something of the flavor of the verbal example given by Unger *(Die Beziehungen zwischen Rhetorik und Musik im 16.–18. Jahrhundert* [Würzburg, 1941], p. 7), from Goethe's play *Der Groß-Cophta* (1791): "Daß ich in dir, je länger ich dich kenne, immer den Bessern, den Größern, den Unbegreiflichen finde." Unger's source, significantly, is a work of 1839, Kehrein's *Beispielsammlung zu der Lehre von den Figuren und Tropen.*

Example 7.15. Mozart, Piano Concerto, K. 482/ii, theme.

phony, *maggiore* wind serenade with flute-bassoon *concertante*—this time with episodes in different keys, the relative and tonic majors, respectively, inter-mixed among the variations (Example 7.16). The form is thus a kind of rondo-variation, as described by Koch, with a coda harking back to the first episode, now in the tonic; the return of material in the tonic originally heard in the relative major suggests but does not enforce a similarity to sonata form.

Only the final variation (A$_3$) conflates different genres and modes of expression. In its vigorous, unfigured tutti, it recalls the symphonic gestures of K.

Example 7.16. Mozart, K. 482/ii, A₁, B, C, A₃.

456. But the quiet, embellished solo answers now come after each phrase or incise. More significant is the transformation of the redundant but expressive neighbor-note motive of mm. 5–6 (mm. 149–150), now an octave lower, made into a *forte* unison, and embellished with a trill. When the motive recurs in precisely this form, as a kind of ritornello, it becomes the source of two expansions in the second period, at the point of the second *gradatio* (mm. 21–24, here at mm. 165–170 and mm. 171–176). In addition, it is given a new counter-motive in the winds, which later generates the coda. A motive whose original stock in trade was intensified repetition thus reasserts its importance in a new interpretation in the final variation.

Lest it be thought that the expressive qualities in the themes of K. 456 and 482 derive principally from their minor mode, which was chosen infrequently for variations in this period, a brief comparison with Mozart's other minor-mode variation movements reveals that these two are unusual in nearly every respect. Only the Allegretto finale of the D-minor String Quartet K. 421 rivals them in length and expressive surface. The rest—the D-major Serenade for strings and horns, K. 334 (D-minor Andante), the F-major Violin Sonata K. 377 (D-minor Andante), and the C-minor finales of the Wind Serenade K. 388 (Allegro) and Piano Concerto K. 491 (Allegretto)—have short, rhythmically repetitive, nearly unfigured themes that are for these reasons more "neutral" in expressive character. And only in the finales are the variations figured in a rhetorically expressive as well as a *setzmanierlich* way. The relationship suggested here between rhetorical and compositional figures, then, is affected principally by genre and by movement-position, not by mode.

THE INTERSECTION OF *DISPOSITIO* AND *ELABORATIO*

Mozart's finale to the C-minor concerto, K. 491, his last set of variations in this genre, confirms that finale themes of variations contain less figurative detail than the slow-movement themes. It also supports the hypothesis that rhetorical figures come to the fore in the variations when they are not already present in the theme, a special feature of the piano concertos. The single expressive detail of the theme—the syncopation-triggered descending chromatic line in a higher register in mm. 11–12—cues the first solo variation A_1, which, unlike K. 456 and K. 482, is actually an intensification rather than a dilution of the expressive values of the theme (Example 7.17). Wholesale chromaticism in A_1 is also partly anticipated by the diminished seventh in m. 3 and the minor second of mm. 4–5 and 12–13 of the theme, while the measure of repeated quarter-notes following the minor second (mm. 5, 13) becomes an entire phrase of ascending repeated turning figures in A_1 (mm. 21–24), expanding the range of a theme in which three of four incises begin and end on the same note.

As a finale, this movement is longer and more intricately plotted than the slow movements, and Mozart's solution to the problem of organizing more than a few variations differs considerably from that of K. 382 (see Table 7.2 and Example 7.18; I use the lettering system [A, B] rather than labeling variations so the resemblance to the other multi-key piano-concerto variation (K. 482) will be clear). With the third variation (following the expected wind-band variation, A_2), Mozart begins a vast "middle section," in which variations refer to each other, and in which changes of character and generic allusion are more pronounced. The march-character of the theme is heightened in A_3 and A_5 by dotted rhythms, while variations in two other keys (A_4 in A♭ and A_6 in C, as quasi-B and quasi-C) continue the alternating wind-band scoring introduced in A_2, and thus more than casually recall the key-scheme and orchestration of K. 482, as well as those of the Larghetto slow movement of K. 491 itself. When repeated by the tutti, the first dotted-rhythmic variation (A_3) takes on the symphonic ritornello character already seen in K. 456 and 482. Then the wind-band

Example 7.17. Mozart, Piano Concerto, K. 491/iii, theme and A₁.

returns (A₄) in a paradoxical dual role as quasi-reprise (similar to the theme in rhythm and initial melody) and episode (submediant major). The important role of the wind-band in this concerto brings out some striking similarities with the wind-serenade in C minor, K. 388, which also concludes with a set of variations. Indeed, these are the only two variation sets by Mozart with eight variations, and, together with the rondo-like C-minor slow movement of K. 482, the only ones with the two opposite-mode variations (K. 388: A₅ in E♭, A₇ in C; K. 482: B-section in E♭, C-section in C; K. 491: A₄ in A♭, A₆ in C).

Table 7.2   Mozart, Piano Concerto K. 491/iii: Organization

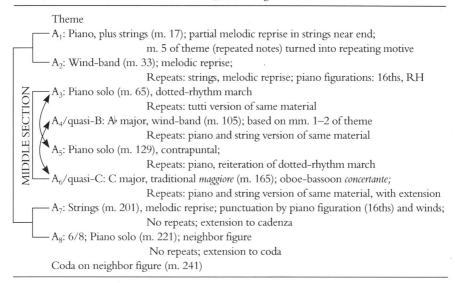

Theme

A₁: Piano, plus strings (m. 17); partial melodic reprise in strings near end;
    m. 5 of theme (repeated notes) turned into repeating motive

A₂: Wind-band (m. 33); melodic reprise;
    Repeats: strings, melodic reprise; piano figurations: 16ths, RH

A₃: Piano solo (m. 65), dotted-rhythm march
    Repeats: tutti version of same material

A₄/quasi-B: A♭ major, wind-band (m. 105); based on mm. 1–2 of theme
    Repeats: piano and string version of same material

A₅: Piano solo (m. 129), contrapuntal;
    Repeats: piano, reiteration of dotted-rhythm march

A₆/quasi-C: C major, traditional *maggiore* (m. 165); oboe-bassoon *concertante;*
    Repeats: piano and string version of same material, with extension

A₇: Strings (m. 201), melodic reprise; punctuation by piano figuration (16ths) and winds;
    No repeats; extension to cadenza

A₈: 6/8; Piano solo (m. 221); neighbor figure
    No repeats; extension to coda

Coda on neighbor figure (m. 241)

MIDDLE SECTION

The curious feature of A₅ is not its reiteration of the dotted-rhythmic march as varied and expanded repeats, but rather its chromatic counterpoint in the first reprises: this texture is usually reserved for the opposite-mode variation, the *minore* in an otherwise major variation set. Such an increase in expressivity between two major-key variations seems to relate this piece to the larger universe of Mozart's variations, emphasizing its intertextuality. And the second *maggiore,* A₆, a pastoral, imitative trio for *concertante* winds (the earlier slow movements had featured oboe-bassoon duets), introduces the descending bass line of an older style. The middle section, then, seems a compendium of characters, genres, topics, and styles, alluding to conventions that force a reappraisal of paratactic form.

The last two variations, both without repeats, balance the first two in the movement: a quasi-reprise uniting all the instrumental groups (A7) and the "finale-variation" in 6/8 that resembles the chromatic A₁ and also introduces a Neapolitan neighbor-note motive (a variant of the repeated-note measure 5, via the wind figure in A₇) and that merges with the coda. The expressive upgrading of a *Schwärmer*-figure of the theme to a *pathopoeia* minor-second motive in the last variation and coda provides final confirmation of the relationship between a neutral theme and more rhetorically detailed variations. Ultimately, the larger system of balances and symmetries in the movement turns it into a paradox: a paratactic form masquerading as the rounded *oratio periodica,* a structure in which final meaning is withheld until the last segment.

Mozart never moved into the realm of repetition without decoration envisioned by Haydn, nor was he attracted by alternation as a formal idea; he was

Example 7.18. Mozart, K. 491/iii, A₃, A₄, A₆, A₈, coda.

too involved in the endless figural possibilities, more attuned to the beauty of the surface. Yet he more assiduously cultivated the contrapuntal variation as a type, sometimes combining it with the *minore*. His best variations exhibit all the virtues of copiousness; as Vogler said of him, he "extravagantly endowed" his themes with variations and, as the autograph of the A-major string quartet shows, could continue even beyond the perfect end-point, in order to arrive at the perfect peroration.

CHAPTER EIGHT

Conclusion: Beethoven and the Transformation of the Classical Variation

When Haydn expressed impatience with the idea of following strict rules of composition—something of a sore point with him, to judge from comments sprinkled through his early biographies—his often-quoted rejoinder pointed the way to the future:

> Someone told Haydn that Albrechtsberger wished to see all ₁ourths banished from the purest style. "What does that mean?" replied Haydn. "Art is free, and will be limited by no pedestrian rules. The ear, assuming that it is trained, must decide, and I consider myself as competent as any to legislate here. Such affectations are worthless. I would rather someone tried to compose a really *new* minuet."[1]

Often taken to be a sanction for Beethoven's scherzos, the last sentence is also emblematic of the aged composer feeling the exhaustion of possibilities of a traditional form he had already taken so far. In both respects, Haydn's comment also forecasts the "really *new*" variations Beethoven was to produce, historically aided by the "wirklich gantz neue Manier" he claimed for his piano variations of 1802. The irony is that the "pedestrian rules" abhorred by Haydn are assumed by modern commentators to underlie those of his forms and genres later transformed by Beethoven.

The language of transformation, as of all conjurings with words like "freedom" and "liberation" in every context, inevitably casts down the thing transformed. Where Beethoven has been described as the true classic or the true innovator in variations, Haydn and Mozart have been tarred as insufficiently one or the other. Although there will be many occasions to speak of elements in Beethoven's variations that were simply not part of Haydn's and Mozart's stylistic or conceptual equipment, comparisons drawn in the following discussion will seek to be illuminating rather than invidious. In order to focus Beethoven's relationship to the classical variation, then, this concluding chapter will identify the works and assess the ways in which Beethoven first changed the rhetorical paradigm of the variation movement and independent variation.

---

1. Griesinger, *Notizen,* p. 114; trans. Gotwals, *Haydn,* p. 61.

The arguments will draw on decorum, on the nature of the theme, and on the shape of the movement.

Decorum

The association of "free" and "new" specifically in variations was drawn by C. F. Michaelis in an article of 1803 on repetition and variation.[2] The pretext of his remarks was a desire to transmit Neefe's views on repetition in the article "Ueber die musikalische Wiederholung" of 1776.[3] Agreeing with Neefe that repetition was necessary "according to psychological laws" to sharpen and to fix the impression made by a melodic or harmonic figure, but that the repetition had to be kept within limits, Michaelis argued that the goal of musical "Veränderung oder Variation" is to elevate and ennoble the pleasures of repetition:

> Variation forestalls the monotony, the triviality, in short, that void through which a melody simply becomes trite, overused, like a street ditty. But if the basic theme, the main melody, appears *clothed in a new manner,* under a delicate transparent cloak, so to speak, thus the soul of the listener obtains pleasure, in that it can automatically look through the veil, finding the known in the unknown, and can see it develop without effort.
>
> Variation demonstrates freedom of fantasy in treatment of the subject, excites pleasant astonishment in recognizing again in new forms the beauty, charm, or sublimity already known, attractively fusing the new with the old without creating a fantastic mixture of heterogeneous figures [*eine abentheuerliche Vermischung heterogener Manieren*]. [Variation] also concerns the freedom of reflection of the listener who now knows how to grasp hold of the main subject if he is given an inducement to hold on to it [when it appears] in different environments. Variation arouses admiration insofar as everything latent [*verborgen*] in the theme is gradually made manifest [*allmählich hervorruft*] and unfolds [into] the most attractive diversity.[4]

Obviously similar in some respects to the writers cited in Chapters 2 and 3—notably in the image of "clothing" the theme anew, and the admonition against "heterogeneous figures"—Michaelis nonetheless encapsulates several aspects of variation not discussed in quite these terms by any earlier writer. The principal topics of his discussion are particularly relevant to Beethoven—in fact precisely those features of Beethoven's style in the years 1799 to 1804 that he employed to distance himself from his predecessors.

Michaelis emphasized the pleasure of recognition, giving the metaphors of the transparent cloak or veil through which the familiar can be found out. But he clearly implied that the search was as necessary as the recognition itself

---

2. C[hristian] F[riedrich] Michaelis, "Ueber die musikalische Wiederholung und Veränderung," *Allgemeine musikalische Zeitung* 13 (1803), cols. 197–200. Michaelis was Beethoven's exact contemporary (1770–1834). A short biography appears in le Huray and Day, eds., *Music and Aesthetics in the Eighteenth and Early-Nineteenth Centuries,* p. 286.

3. See Chapter 1.

4. Michaelis, "Musikalische Wiederholung," col. 200.

for the pleasurable result to occur. After all, "freedom of fantasy" on the part of the composer in treating the theme will have its corresponding "freedom of reflection" in the listener in responding to that treatment. His last sentence, however, despite a conventional reference to "attractive diversity," reveals a bold new concept: that some things lie hidden or latent in the theme, awaiting expression; that all of these will gradually be revealed; and finally that, once revealed, they will be understood and admired.

Just as variation ennobles repetition, then, variation is in turn elevated by the yielding up of its secrets, gradually, so that the listener knows how to hear them, knows how to find the familiar amid the strange. The last point is crucial. At issue, in fact, is the rhetorical concept of decorum, or propriety. In *Orator,* Cicero outlines important guidelines for the orator, who must consider "what to say, in what order, and in what manner and style to say it."[5] As for the latter,

> In an oration, as in life, nothing is harder than to determine what is appropriate. The Greeks called it *prépon;* let us call it *decorum* or "propriety." . . . This depends on the subject under discussion, and on the character of both the speaker and the audience. . . . Moreover, in all cases the question must be "How far?" For although the limits of propriety differ for each subject, yet in general too much is more offensive than too little. . . . Since this is so important, let the orator consider what to do in the speech and its different divisions: it is certainly obvious that totally different styles must be used, not only in the different parts of the speech, but also that whole speeches must be now in one style, now in another.[6]

In works by Haydn and Mozart, the decorum of a variation movement—its traditional and hence normative technical and expressive limits—depended upon position in the work, upon genre, and upon the nature of the theme. In general, its implicit code included several different proprieties: a "propriety of ordering," in which simpler textures appeared early in a set while imitative polyphony never did, a "propriety of performance style," in which extremes of orchestration and dynamics would be introduced for local contrasts, rarely as the topic of an entire variation, and "propriety of contrast and return," in which distantly related or contrasting material would be followed by returns of the theme melody. Finally, the theme itself would observe a certain propriety, not only in its two-reprise structure with clearly delineated phrases, but also in the degree of repetition and contrast in its melodic segments, rhythms, and textures.

All of these proprieties devolve upon the concept of familiarity and recognition—without which, Koch said, "[the variations] give the impression of a group of arbitrarily related pieces which have nothing in common with each other, and for whose existence and ordering one can imagine no basis."[7] The key word in Michaelis's account is that the process of unfolding the secrets of

5. Cicero, *Orator,* xiv.43, p. 339.
6. Ibid., xxi.70–xxii.74, pp. 357–361.
7. Koch, *Musikalisches Lexikon,* s.v. "Variazionen, Variazioni," quoted in Chapter 3.

the theme happens "gradually." With this in mind, let us turn to Beethoven's first variation movement in the string quartets, Op. 18 No. 5.

STRING QUARTET IN A MAJOR, OP. 18 NO. 5

By the time Beethoven began work in 1799 on the fifth of his Op. 18 string quartets, he had already written at least twenty sets of variations, including six movements in larger works, although none in as "serious" a genre; Table A.3 lists all of Beethoven's variations.[8] It is possible that at least one of these earlier works was modeled on a work by Haydn: Douglas Johnson has suggested correlations between Beethoven's C-minor Piano Trio, Op. 1 No. 3, and Haydn's C-minor Symphony, No. 95, in their first movements and in the fact that both have Andante cantabile variation movements in E♭ major.[9] But the first work by Beethoven traditionally acknowledged to reveal modeling procedures in variations is the slow movement of Op. 18 No. 5: it is known that Beethoven copied out the last two movements of Mozart's A-major quartet K. 464, a work which also had a D-major variation movement after the minuet. In writing about the role of earlier models in the quartet, Joseph Kerman has suggested that, in choosing K. 464, Beethoven was also directly or indirectly referring to the variation model of that piece, namely Haydn's Op. 20 No. 4.[10] Kerman finds Mozart's quartet to be his "most serious and troubled work" and Haydn's quartet to be the most impressive composition of the 1770s; as a rationale for Beethoven's decision to model himself on the Mozart, he argues that writing a serious theme and variations as the center of gravity was an idea new and daunting to Beethoven.[11] And the result, although showing reasonably inventive and individual slants in the treatment of his theme, "stands inferior to the variations of Haydn and Mozart in practically every way."[12]

Yes and no. It is my contention that this movement radically breaks with the decorum of Classical variation movements, and that this is clearest in precisely those areas in which Beethoven appropriates earlier techniques. First, the "abstract construction" (Kerman's term) of the theme has a level of repetitiveness unusual in that it involves pitches as well as rhythms (Example 8.1); as we have seen, repetitive rhythmic patterns underlie the themes of Haydn's Op. 76 No. 6/i and Symphony No. 75/ii, as well as Mozart's B♭-major Piano Concerto K. 450/ii, while repetitive melodic patterns appeared in Haydn's Op. 77 No. 2, written the same year as Beethoven's Op. 18. As for the scalar element of the

8. All of the variation movements to this time are in genres that include piano, except for the Serenade, Op. 8, for string trio (1796–97).

9. Douglas Johnson, "1794–1795: Decisive Years in Beethoven's Early Development," in *Beethoven Studies* 3, ed. Alan Tyson (Cambridge, 1982), pp. 1–28. The coda of the Beethoven variations begins with a reharmonized theme, as in the codas of the variations in both the "Surprise" Symphony (No. 94) and No. 95.

10. Joseph Kerman, *The Beethoven Quartets* (New York, 1966), pp. 58–62.

11. Ibid., p. 60. Jeremy Yudkin frames Beethoven's engagement with Mozart's quartet in terms of Harold Bloom's theory of the "anxiety of influence"; see "Beethoven's 'Mozart' Quartet," *JAMS* 45 (1992), 30–74.

12. Kerman, *Beethoven Quartets*, p. 62.

pattern, Mozart had revealed the theme of his String Trio variations to be a scale in essence (in the final species-counterpoint variation), and Beethoven appears to be simply omitting the first step, offering the theme itself as a reduction. The harmonies are initially those of the Salieri and *Eroica* sets, I–V–V–I.

The first variation recasts the ordering of classical variations. Normally, a

Example 8.1.   Beethoven, Quartet Op. 18/5/iii: theme, vars. 1, 5, coda.

Example 8.1   (continued)

contrapuntal or fugal variation would be placed at or near the end of a set: here
the cello alone immediately sets out the terms of a gritty contrapuntal buildup,
with a crescendo to underscore the registral expansion and offbeat sforzandos
to deny a final coming together of the disparate voices and registers. The only
lyrical note reminiscent of the theme in the second period is an unexpectedly
serious minor subdominant, to replace the major IV of the theme. By virtue of
its prominent position, this variation becomes a manifesto, asserting control
over the language of the classical variation while challenging its decorum.

Variations 2 and 3 return to standard equipment: sixteenth-triplet figuration
in the first violin in the former and theme fragments accompanied by thirty-
second notes in the latter. Yet the texture is again unusual: the thirty-second-
note pattern is of slurred appoggiaturas instead of the customary broken-chord
or scalar patterns, and the theme fragments are themselves fragmented in instrumentation and register, ending the first period with viola and cello joined
at the octave in an odd feminine cadence.[13] The fourth variation draws on the
last one of Haydn's *Kaiserquartett,* reharmonizing the theme, but here by altering the melody itself in a strange borrowing of the melodic-minor scale in
B minor to end the first period in the mediant. As a *sempre pp* hymn, it corre-
sponds to the Corellian counterpoint in the Mozart quartet, except that here it
is the second of two variations to stand in for a *minore.* And it in no way prepares for the fifth and last variation, of which the high trill, offbeat accents, and
jumping cello line both balance the first variation and exceed the expressive
limits of allowable contrast; indeed, Kerman refers to its "unprecedented driv-
ing orchestral style."

13. The descending fifth of this cadence resonates in the variations in Brahms's B♭-major String
Sextet, Op. 18.

These novelties are surpassed by the coda, which begins as a deceptive cadence in ♭VI on the same disjunct cello figuration, Beethoven's only literal appropriation from the Mozart; we recall that Mozart had recast the last few variations in K. 464 in order to continue cello figuration into the coda. Rationalizing the harmonies of the first phrase of the theme—from I–V–V–I to I–V–I–V—Beethoven wittily inverts the theme in sixteenth notes as contrary-motion accompaniment to its original rhythm, stated first in B♭, then in D, then in G, with sequential connections between statements. Moreover, each statement reassigns the theme and counterpoint, beginning with a theme-counterpoint pairing of second violin/viola (B♭), then cello/first violin (D), then viola/second violin counterpoint (G). Moving the theme through the voices in this way seems to be a reference both to Mozart's treatment of figuration in K. 464 and to Haydn's cantus firmus technique in the quartets of Op. 76 published in the same year. Contrary motion becomes the logical development of the closing measures of the theme, while the sudden turn to B♭ at the beginning of the coda (exacerbated by its rattling uselessly for two measures in an egregiously unaccompanied Alberti-bass pattern in the cello) may correlate enharmonically with the single biggest earlier shock in the movement, the A♯ in the melody of var. 4.[14] Participating in a different sort of development, the strikingly similar passage in the opening ABA variation movement of Haydn's D-major Quartet Op. 76 No. 5, mm. 41–45, appeared in the contrapuntal D-minor middle section, where its key of B♭ had been fully prepared.

Beethoven breaks Classical decorum by calling into question every one of the proprieties mentioned above. His most radical step is his first, for it is here in var. 1, in the sudden eradication of harmony and conventional register in favor of the cello subject, that he defamiliarizes the theme. In a variation movement of 1799 one might diverge very widely from the theme, but a general propriety of familiarity asserted that the beginning was not the place for such a technique. The notion of "defamiliarization" or "making strange" as a component of artistic technique has long been known from the work of Russian Formalist critics.[15] By "making strange" the beginning of a variation work, Beethoven effectively violated Michaelis's context of the intelligible environment in which the *Grundthema* can be recognized. This is not to say, of course, that the listener of 1799 could not make sense of the resemblance between var-

14. In Beethoven's early Righini-variations, WoO 65 (1790–91), also in D major with a melodic descent from F♯ down to A, var. 21 *begins* with the minor passage and goes down to A♯, then reverts to A and a half-cadence in major.

15. Viktor Shklovsky wrote that "the technique of art is to make objects 'unfamiliar,' to make forms difficult, to increase the difficulty and length of perception because the process of perception itself is an aesthetic end in itself and must be prolonged." See Shklovsky, "Art as Technique," in *Russian Formalist Criticism: Four Essays,* trans. Lee T. Lemon and Marion J. Reis (Lincoln, Neb., 1965), p. 12. See also Victor Erlich, *Russian Formalism: History-Doctrine,* 3rd ed. (New Haven and London, 1965; preface, 1981); Fredric Jameson, *The Prison-House of Language: A Critical Account of Structuralism and Russian Formalism* (Princeton, 1972), pp. 50–60 and passim.

iation and theme. But by inserting a new level of difficulty into a previously more accessible form, Beethoven was staking his claim to a new decorum.[16]

STRING QUARTET IN E♭ MAJOR, OP. 74

Ten years later, Beethoven returned to the ground covered by this movement in the finale of his E♭-major quartet, Op. 74 ("Harp"), which similarly refers to antecedents in Haydn (Op. 76 No. 6) and Mozart.[17] Kerman's statement that "nothing about this work is problematic" prompted Nicholas Marston to probe its structure in Schenkerian terms and to arrive at a series of diagrams demonstrating its organicism.[18] In his convincing explorations of pitch structures, he also examines the prominent D♭ in movements 1 and 3 that emerges otherwise inexplicably in the last variation of the finale. However, both Marston and Kerman neglect the features of the finale that reveal its relationship to Haydn and Mozart as well as the ways in which the finale fits into the quartet as a whole.

The first new feature of these variations is the metric ambiguity of the motivic cells. No earlier variation movement known to me consistently obscures its downbeat by slurring over the bar, demanding heavy articulation at the upbeat part of the measure, ornamented by a dotted rhythm, and light articulation at the downbeat. That the period seems to have an extra measure is reinforced by the unusual move to V of C minor, a mediant relationship (Example 8.2).[19] In addition, the three-note motives each outline a third, and Beethoven uses both the filled-in and the hollow versions of the motives in subsequent variations.

Broadly speaking, the first three variations represent progressive diminution or simple *gradatio* from eighths to eighth-triplets to sixteenth-notes, while the second three offer a somewhat different, more layered version of the same idea, with quarters and eighths in var. 4, quarters, eighths, and sixteenths in var. 5, and, in a faster tempo (var. 6, *un poco più vivace*), eighths and triplets. More telling is that the dynamic levels, beginning with the *piano* theme, alternate from variation to variation, so that each piano-forte grouping is experienced as

16. Carl Dahlhaus discusses the phenomenon of Beethoven's contemporaries listening to difficult new works and experiencing them as "harboring a meaning which, with sufficient effort, could be made intelligible." See Dahlhaus, *Nineteenth-Century Music*, trans. J. Bradford Robinson (Berkeley and Los Angeles, 1989), pp. 10–11.

17. James Webster has pointed out some of the resemblances between the Beethoven and the Haydn in "Traditional Elements in Beethoven's Middle-Period Quartets," *Beethoven, Performers, and Critics: The International Beethoven Congress, Detroit, 1977,* ed. Robert Winter and Bruce Carr (Detroit, 1980), pp. 122–123.

18. Marston, "Analysing Variations: The Finale of Beethoven's String Quartet op. 74," *MusA* 8 (1989), 303–324. He might also be disturbed by Webster's assessment of the movement as "a plain set of variations exquisitely poised, perfectly articulated" (Webster, "Traditional Elements," p. 123).

19. Haydn had moved to the mediant or to V/vi three times in variation themes: in the Sonata XVI:31, in Quartet Op. 33 No. 5, and in the Quartet Op. 71 No. 3. The last two of these are also pointed out by Webster, "Traditional Elements," p. 122.

Example 8.2.   Beethoven, Quartet Op. 74/iv, theme.

an individual set of *Doubles:* theme–var. 1; vars. 2–3; vars. 4–5; var. 6–coda.[20]
The first of each pair is also the more oriented toward melody, the second
toward motive and figuration. This reading reveals the rationale for the two
threefold accelerations, each with its increase from piano to forte, that takes
place in the coda (Example 8.3). In the first of these, the melody of var. 6 moves
from viola to violins to cello with a progressive thickening of texture each
time. In the second, figurations reminiscent of the outline of the theme increase
in speed until the final Allegro. This final acceleration is not unlike the rhythmic acceleration in the climactic variation of the late Piano Sonata Op. 109.[21] It
also forecasts the extraordinary buildup at the beginning of the Allegretto of
the Seventh Symphony and the Finale of the Ninth: Beethoven's transformation of the *gradatio* of note values into an *incrementum,* expanding tone colors,
registers, and dynamics. The *incrementum,* part of Quintilian's model of amplifying the theme by "increasing its power by words and images,"[22] seems especially appropriate for those repetitions that embody an ascent into hyperbole.[23]

These features of the variations—alternating dynamic levels, alternating sets
of doubles, alternating models of acceleration—exemplify, unsurprisingly, different models of alternation. What is surprising is the extent to which these
models were forecast earlier in the quartet. The scherzo and trio alternate conventionally, in this case three of the former with two of the latter, but then a
final transitional section is added to close on the dominant of E♭, marked "attacca il Tema dei Variazioni."[24] The slow movement alternates refrains and episodes in its rondo-variation design, in which the melody remains intact during
the refrains but appears in the first violin one octave lower every time, while
the accompaniment figurations grow denser and more luxurious. The result is

20. On the idea of variations derived from each other as well as from the theme, see Edward T.
Cone, "On Derivation: Syntax and Rhetoric," *MusA* 6 (1987), 237–255.
21. Marston compares Op. 74 to Op. 109 but only in the nature of the motivic connections
between first movement and finale ("Analysing Variations," p. 321).
22. Quintilian, *Institutio Oratoria,* VIII.iv.3–8, pp. 265–267.
23. See Ellison's remark on repetition in Emerson cited in Chapter 1. Needless to say, Beethoven
used the incrementum in many different contexts, not least in the coda of the first movement of the
Eroica, at the final recasting of the main theme (mm. 630ff.).
24. The dominant cadence and attacca to a variation movement are typical of Haydn's piano
sonatas and trios that conclude with variations.

Example 8.3. Beethoven, Op. 74/iv, coda.

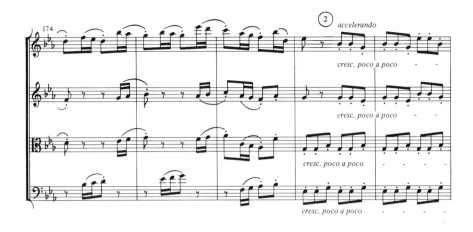

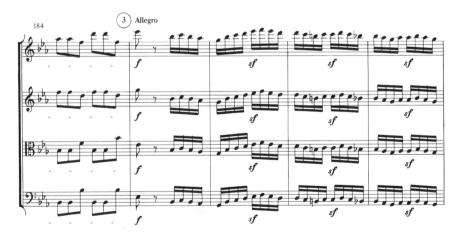

Example 8.3   *(continued)*

a kind of cantus-firmus variation that echoes in the variation techniques of the Allegretto, and seems to reflect Haydn's variation movements of Op. 76 and Op. 77.

Stranger still, in light of all these alternations, is the mode of presentation of the celebrated "harp-like" chordal and pizzicato passages in the first movement. Appearing as the pendant to the first theme, the coloristic four-measure phrase is presented twice, first high-string chords and low-string pizzicato, then the reverse (mm. 35–38, 39–42). During the retransition to the recapitulation, the pizzicato (now against sustained chords) accelerates from quarters to quarter-triplets to eighths to eighth-triplets (mm. 125–138). The recapitulation has a double statement (two sets of two four-measure phrases, mm. 153–168). But in the coda, the pizzicato appears against sixteenth-note figuration (m. 221) and, after three sets of ascending chords, gradually gives way to fragments of the main theme, *arco;* the figuration continues. In effect, then, the pizzicato texture is alternated with functional, thematic material in the movement, and increases each time either in length (exposition to recapitulation) or in speed of figuration (retransition to coda). And the increase in speed forecasts the successive *gradatios* of the finale.

The entire quartet, then, reflects a preoccupation with the idea of alternation, just as Haydn's comparable Eb-major quartet was "about" the idea of repetition.[25] Also at issue is embellishment: the gorgeous accompaniments of the slow rondo-variation, the different figural voices in the finale, and the decorative "harp" texture in the first movement. Here Haydn and Beethoven are on opposite sides because, as we have seen, Haydn's Op. 76 No. 6 epitomizes repetition without decoration. Thus, the finale of Beethoven's Op. 74 is neither unproblematic nor excessively problematized; it contributes another example of confronting the Classical models and, while overtly alluding to them, inventing its own decorum, essentially defamiliarizing one of the most basic accoutrements of earlier variation styles, the rhythmic *gradatio.*

PIANO TRIO IN Eb MAJOR, OP. 70 NO. 2
The impetus for such an idea might well have gone beyond the single Haydn model to a general meditation on Haydn-inspired issues. For example, the previous year Beethoven had written a Haydnesque alternating-variation movement in the Eb-major Piano Trio, Op. 70 No. 2. Indeed, in the trio Beethoven most closely approximated the theme-type, character, and form of Haydn's alternating strophic variations, in a work which quoted the slow movement of Haydn's Symphony 88 (as had the Trio of Op. 18 No. 5),[26] and which is worth

25. In Hugh Macdonald's provocative and polemical study "Fantasy and Order in Beethoven's Phantasie Op. 77" (in *Modern Musical Scholarship,* ed. Edward Olleson [Stocksfield, 1980], pp. 141–150], he suggests that the Phantasie is "about" disunity, that its "disunity, diversity, illogicality, inconsistencies and contradictions [are] themselves the principal idea of the piece" (p. 145).

26. For other movements by Beethoven that use the theme from Haydn's Symphony 88, see Georg Feder, "Stilelemente Haydns in Beethovens Werken," *Kongressbericht Bonn 1970,* p. 65. Another reference to Haydn in Op. 70 No. 2 might be the return of the slow introduction of the first

exploring here. E. T. A. Hoffmann noted the formal resemblance to Haydn in his 1813 review, and Czerny even strengthened the association by asserting that the major theme imitated a Croatian folksong.[27]

The themes of the Trio are in major and tonic minor, Haydn's standard practice (Example 8.4), but here with the modalities reversed so that the piece begins in major and ends in minor, a breach of decorum. These themes are closely related, the second theme arising from the playful upbeat of the first—a Lombard rhythm reversing Haydn's typical dotted rhythm in the piano trios—but because the second theme replaces the rhythmic accent with a dynamic one, and introduces thick chords and flat-sixth relationships, the affective difference between the themes is greater than in all of Haydn's sets but the D-minor Piano Trio and F-minor Andante, discussed in Chapter 6. The final phrase of the minor theme does not cadence: it ends on V/iv (a pun on the tonic) and brings back the Lombard rhythm to create a Haydnesque retransition, the unaccompanied repetition of a figure. Two variations on the major theme then follow consecutively. Beethoven here confounds our formal expectations and forces us to reassess our earlier interpretation: the *minore* might have been an episode or simply a darker variation of the C-major theme. But a return to the alternating plan shows that Beethoven plays with our expectations in much the same way that Haydn characteristically does.[28] Beethoven also used the time-honored devices of progressive diminution and melodic reprise after mode contrast.

Even the final segments of the movement, which appear to diverge from the Haydn model, are in fact firmly rooted in his practice. The last variation of the major theme (A_3) is little more than a reprise without repeats, emphasizing its tiny dimensions, while the final variation of the minor theme (B_2, Example 8.4) alters its harmonic structure so that all three phrases (each now with a varied repeat, like the major theme) end on the tonic. This heavy stress on the minor tonic forecasts the unusual minor ending for the movement, although the major theme coyly reappears once in a false reprise which joins the two themes into a single entity.[29] The plan of the movement might be schematized thus:

---

movement later in that movement, both Allegro and in the original slow tempo, almost exactly as in the first movement of the "Drumroll" Symphony, No. 103.

27. Hoffmann's unsigned review appeared in the *Allgemeine musikalische Zeitung* 15 (1813), cols. 141–154, here 150–151; he called the minores *Zwischensätze,* and claimed erroneously that the main theme always returns. Czerny's reminiscences are found in *On the Proper Performance of All Beethoven's Works for the Piano,* ed. Paul Badura-Skoda (Vienna, 1970), p. 12.

28. On this issue, see Edward T. Cone, "The Uses of Convention: Stravinsky and His Models," *MQ* 48 (1962), 288–290, rpt. in his *Music: A View from Delft,* ed. Robert P. Morgan (Chicago, 1989), pp. 281–284.

29. A second *minore* which similarly alters the harmonic structure of the first is strikingly exploited in four movements by Haydn: the rondo-style finale of Sonata 34, the first movement of Sonata 48, and the slow movements of Symphony 63 and Quartet Op. 71 No. 3. The quartet contains both a literal reprise of the major theme as the third section, and a structurally altered major variation before the partial final reprise.

Example 8.4.   Beethoven, Piano Trio Op. 70/2/iii: A, B, B$_2$.

A: C maj. a-a^1-b-b^1

B: C min. c$_V$-c$_{III}$-d-trans

A$_1$: melodic reprise in piano, counter-figuration in strings

A$_2$: *gradatio,* melodic-outline variation

B$_1$: melodic reprise, figured accompaniment (cf. A$_2$)

A$_3$: theme reprise, new cello figure in second period transition

B$_2$: melodically closer to A; new harmonic structure

coda: C major, to C minor, begins as reprise of A

Beethoven's E♭-major Trio, then, remains well within the boundaries established by Haydn. The collection of such details in a single work may be merely circumstantial evidence for a conscious recollection of Haydn, but it is tempt-

Example 8.4   (continued)

ing to speculate that the period of "consolidation" in Beethoven's later middle period may have been prompted by a reconsideration of Haydn's procedures during the older composer's last illness.[30]

Piano Variations and the "New Way"

But the String Quartet Op. 74 and Piano Trio Op. 70 No. 2 are works that appear after, and the Quartet Op. 18 No. 5 before, the self-advertised "Great

30. The relationship between Haydn and Beethoven has been thoroughly examined by James Webster, who has determined that "Haydn's and Beethoven's relationship was marred by mutual distrust and feelings of ambivalence, but only for the approximate period between 1800 and 1804." See Webster, "The Falling-out between Haydn and Beethoven: The Evidence of the Sources," in *Beethoven Essays: Studies in Honor of Elliot Forbes,* ed. Lewis Lockwood and Phyllis Benjamin (Cambridge, Mass., 1984), p. 28. Webster also describes a period of consolidation in "Traditional Elements," pp. 122–126.

Divide" in Beethoven's variations: the "wirklich gantz neue Manier" of Opp. 34 and 35 in 1802. It is my contention that, while the undeniably new features of these piano variations should not be downplayed (even if most of them were anticipated in earlier works), the *Eroica* finale more fully transforms Classical models. In this section I will sketch in some of the details of Beethoven's earlier independent sets, place the two sets of 1802 and their achievements in context, and conclude, in the last section of this chapter, with a consideration of the symphony.

Beethoven's first published work was an utterly ordinary set of variations on a minor-key march by Dressler (WoO 63); promoted by his teacher, Neefe, who hoped to attract attention and money to the twelve-year-old composer, the piece gave no indication of Beethoven's future direction.[31] Yet eight years later, with only two trivial variation movements intervening, he wrote the exceptional set of twenty-four variations on Righini's "Venni amore," WoO 65 (1790–91), which featured a highly imaginative array of both melodic-outline and constant-harmony techniques. Indeed, the variety of piano figurations and sonorities drew on the thicker and more contrast-oriented mode of writing for piano characteristic of northern German composers like Karl Friedrich Fasch (1736–1800), J. A. P. Schulz (1747–1800), and Johann Georg Müthel (1728–1788).[32]

The Viennese style in keyboard variations, seen in such disparate composers as Mozart and Vanhal, Steffan and Kozeluch, was thinner in texture. For his early Viennese sets, Beethoven generally adopted many of the common features of Mozart's keyboard sets—especially the *minore,* adagio, and finale-variations—which betray their common origin in improvised performance.[33] The finales to his variation sets take on a different form from Mozart's, however: they are normally rondos, with extended excursions into foreign keys, and do not feature written-out cadenzas. But the fine craftsmanship of the "Righini" variations is not again in evidence until the set on Salieri's "La stessa, la stessissima," WoO 73 (1799).[34] The conclusion of that set is an "alla Austriaca," a type of character piece especially popular, as seen in the "alla Po-

31. Maynard Solomon reports on a "devastating contemporary notice" of Beethoven's early publications in Forkel's *Musikalischer Almanach* of 1784 *(Beethoven* [New York, 1977], p. 28).

32. See the modern editions of some of these works: Fasch, "Ariette avec [14] Variations" (Berlin, 1782) and "Andantino con VII Variazioni" (Berlin, 1787), ed. Ludwig Landshoff, Nagels Musikarchiv 38 (Hanover, 1929); Müthel, "Zwei Ariosi mit zwölf Variationen" (Nüremberg, 1756), ed. Lothar Hoffmann-Erbrecht, Mitteldeutsches Musikarchiv 1/7 (Leipzig, 1954); Schulz, "Larghetto con Variazioni" in *Stücke für Klavier* (Amsterdam, 1776), ed. Willi Kahl, Deutsche Klaviermusik des 18. Jahrhunderts, 1 (Wolfenbüttel, 1935).

33. See Batta and Kovács, "Typbildung und Grossform," for an account of this repertory. Changes in mode, tempo, and time signature were more or less common currency anyway in independent piano variations of this period.

34. The long-held assumption that Beethoven revised WoO 65 for its 1802 publication has been convincingly refuted by Sieghard Brandenburg and Martin Staehelin, "Die 'erste Fassung' von Beethovens Righini-Variationen," *Festschrift Albi Rosenthal,* ed. Rudolf Elvers (Tutzing, 1984), pp. 43–66; the authors cite other literature on that piece. Both WoO 65 and WoO 73 are on "scaffold"-type themes, and the latter even begins with the I–V–V–I opening of the Op. 35 variations.

lonese," "alla Ungarese," and other dances in Vanhal's characteristic variations given in Example 6.2.[35] In the set on Süssmayr's "Tandeln und Scherzen" of 1799, Beethoven for the first time tried to link several variations tonally. The set is in F major, and vars. 5, 6, and 7, which run right into each other with no final cadence, are in D minor, B♭ major, and F major, respectively; var. 7 is the Adagio. Moreover, the final eighth variation is an Allegro fugue, which, after modulating to the dominant, goes into a series of third-related keys: F, A♭, B (= C♭), and D major. But these changes do not begin until the fifth variation.

This piece has significant consequences for the F-major variations, Op. 34. Beethoven's procedures must certainly have been regarded as original before this time, as is made clear in a letter he wrote to Eleonore von Breuning in 1794 that he had to begin publishing his variations because people were beginning to copy him:

> The v[ariations] will be rather difficult to play . . . I should never have written down this kind of piece, had I not already noticed fairly often how some people in Vienna after hearing me extemporize of an evening would note down on the following day several peculiarities of my style and palm them off with pride as their own. Well, as I foresaw that their pieces would soon be published, I resolved to forestall those people.[36]

But audience acclaim did not always translate into favorable reviews. In a review of 1799 of his variations for piano and cello on "Ein Mädchen oder Weibchen" (Op. 66) and for piano on "Une fièvre brûlante" (WoO 72), Beethoven was patronizingly treated; his talents as a pianist were praised but compositional ability was found to be wanting. The review made only one substantive critical remark about his modulations and then went on to deplore the torrent of terrible variations being published, offering this advice to the would-be composer of variations: first, learn from Haydn in choosing a theme, because his are simple and easy to grasp, beautifully rhythmic, and not common; second, read the little-known but important booklet by Vogler on Forkel's "God Save the King."[37] This no doubt would have enraged Beethoven, as would the laconic review in the June issue of that year: "gut zu variiren versteht er nicht."[38]

While it probably goes too far to say that bad reviews prompted a reexamination of style—although the same claim has been made for Haydn in his Op. 20 quartets—it is interesting that the areas of Beethoven's revisions in Op. 34 and Op. 35 start from their original themes, a fact to which Beethoven called attention in his letter to Breitkopf of December 1802: "I have included them in the proper numerical series *of my greater musical works,* the more so as

35. When Koch described a theme for variations as a piece with no particular character (see Chapter 3, n. 83), he did not of course preclude characteristic variations on that theme.

36. Emily Anderson, *The Letters of Beethoven,* 3rd ed. (New York, 1985), I, no. 9, pp. 14–15. Beethoven went on to say that he wanted to cause embarrassment to enemy pianists who would be called upon to play his music.

37. *AMZ* 1 (1799): cols. 366–368. The review is signed "M . . ." (Michaelis?).

38. Ibid., col. 607.

the themes have been composed by me."[39] On 18 October 1802, he made his biggest claim about the pieces:

> I have just composed two sets of variations, one consisting of eight variations and the other of thirty. Both sets are worked out in a *completely new manner,* and each in a *separate and different way.* . . . *Each theme is treated in its own way and in a different way from the other one.* Usually I have to wait for other people to tell me when I have new ideas, because I never know this myself. But this time—I myself can assure you that in both these works *the method is quite new so far as I am concerned—*[40]

Considerable scholarly attention has been paid to these claims.[41] Christopher Reynolds, in linking the variations in the violin sonata, Op. 30 No. 1, with these works, suggests that Beethoven felt greater freedom to modify the theme if he had composed it himself.[42] Part of Beethoven's claim is surely based on trying to distance himself from the relatively low status of a genre based on hit tunes and mass appeal. And he undoubtedly recognized that Haydn's high status in variations came down to his writing his own themes. When Haydn's F-minor variations were published in 1799, they needed no such announcement as Beethoven envisioned for himself. Indeed, Haydn's set had been given a glowing account—"varied as only a master can"—in the same journal that was so critical of Beethoven. Finally, he needed to establish himself as an entirely legitimate composer, perhaps especially to the prestigious Leipzig publisher Breitkopf & Härtel, which brought out the *Allgemeine musikalische Zeitung,* the source of all these reviews; indeed, Breitkopf's very first edition of a Beethoven work, the String Quintet, Op. 29, was only just appearing at the same time as these other letters announcing Op. 34 and Op. 35 (late 1802), and there might thus have been an ulterior motive in placing these piano works with that firm.[43]

The F-major set, the first free-standing Adagio with variations known to me, moves from F major to D, Bb, G, Eb, and C minor, before returning to F. It also notoriously changes the key-signatures and often the tempos as well:

39. Anderson, *Letters of Beethoven,* no. 67, pp. 83–84. Beethoven wanted that comment to be included at the front of the edition.

40. Ibid., no. 62, pp. 76–77.

41. The most recent of these are Stefan Kunze, "Die 'wirklich gantz neue Manier' in Beethovens Eroica-Variationen op. 35," *AfMw* 29 (1972), 124–149; Christopher Reynolds, "Beethoven's Sketches for the Variations in Eb, Op. 35," *Beethoven Studies* 3, ed. Tyson, pp. 47–84. See also Rudolf Flotzinger, "Die Barocke Doppelgerüst-Technik im Variationsschaffen Beethovens," *Beethoven-Studien. Festgabe der Österreichische Akademie der Wissenschaften zum 200. Geburtstag von Ludwig van Beethoven* (Vienna, 1970), pp. 159–194.

42. Reynolds, "Ends and Means in the Second Finale to Beethoven's Op. 30, no. 1," in *Beethoven Essays,* ed. Lockwood and Benjamin, p. 145.

43. Indeed, exactly sixty years later Brahms tried hard to place his "Variations on a Theme of Handel" with the same publisher, his first communication with them. And I have suggested in Chapter 6 that the unusual style of Haydn's Sonata XVI:48/i may be connected with its commission by Breitkopf.

Thema: Adagio Cantabile. F, 2/4

Var. 1: D, 2/4 (including 64th-note figurations)

Var. 2: Bb, 6/8, Allegro ma non troppo ("Chasse"-type)

Var. 3: G, C-time, Allegretto ("Bourrée"-type)

Var. 4: Eb, 3/4, Tempo di Menuetto

Var. 5: C minor, 2/4, Marcia, Allegretto (and trans. on dotted rhythm)

Var. 6: F, 6/8, Allegretto

Coda and Adagio molto, 2/4 (extravagantly ornamented reprise)

Op. 34 immediately gives a new perspective to techniques already becoming hackneyed: melodic decoration and characteristic changes of meter and tempo.[44] It does this by means of a technique already won in Op. 18 No. 5: a radical defamiliarization of the theme in the first variation above all. None of the other variations in Op. 34 can match this effect. If the key is so different that it takes some time to recognize where the functionally important notes in the key are before even trying to find the melody, then the pleonastic and periphrastic figurations truly dissemble—they cover the theme with foliage. The variation techniques themselves are simple; they need the conjurer's trick of key change to effect the break in decorum. In fact, the decorum is that of the extempore capriccio or fantasia in its harmonically colorful ways of recasting a theme.

Beethoven referred to the F-major set as "the small variations" and the Eb set as "the grand variations" in his correspondence with Breitkopf, and it is easy to see why. In an era when the technical level of every piano piece was the subject for comment in a review, the Eb variations are outstandingly difficult to play. And their contrapuntal pretensions are immediately apparent in the three cantus-firmus variations on the bass of the theme, the "canone all'ottava" and the "Finale. Alla Fuga." The Goldberg Variations were available in Vienna from different publishers between 1799 and 1803—note that Beethoven originally claimed that his piece had thirty variations—and in 1802 Handel's Chaconne with 62 variations appeared, as did variations on the Folies d'Espagne by C. P. E. Bach.[45]

Beethoven's self-conscious "Introduzione col Basso del Tema" not only announces the scope of the piece, but it carefully covers up the identity of the real theme, which was originally both a Contredanse and the Finale of Beethoven's

44. Much has been made of the fact that despite their outwardly revolutionary appearance, these variations stick rather closely to the *Hauptmelodie* of the theme. Rosen remarks that their solution to the problem of variations is purely "exterior" *(The Classical Style,* p. 437).

45. See Martin Zenck, "Rezeption von Geschichte in Beethovens 'Diabelli-Variationen,'" *AfMw* 37 (1980), 73–74; Walter Pass, "Beethoven und der Historismus," *Beethoven-Studien. Festgabe,* pp. 128–130. The Handel and C. P. E. Bach sets were reviewed not very favorably in the *AMZ* of 1803–1804 (vol. 6, cols. 242–244).

very popular ballet "The Creatures of Prometheus," Op. 42, which received twenty-three performances in 1801–1802.[46] He was thus deliberately withholding from his audience the real source of the theme—the piece was not, of course, titled "Variations on a Theme from Prometheus." The introduction also conceals the nature of the constant-harmony variations to come by stressing the "recognition factor" of a cantus firmus. Thus, Op. 35, like its companion, presented recognition of the familiar as a problem, not a solution.

Eroica: Transformation of the Alternating Variation

The piece that destroyed irrevocably the decorum of the *alternating* variation—that Haydnesque series of antitheses—was the finale of the *Eroica*. Technically speaking, Beethoven remained in control of Haydn's arsenal of devices for alternating variations: melodic-outline technique and a certain amount of constant-harmony technique with sufficient melodic reprise. What he modified instead was the nature of the themes and of the alternating plan itself.[47] This movement is related to, and departs from, the variation tradition in hitherto unrecognized ways.[48]

Every one of Beethoven's symphonic variation movements, except the Ninth Symphony finale, adopts some type of alternating-variation scheme.[49] And in each one, the succession of variations is made more or less continuous and fluid by the extensions and transitions that also occasionally marked Haydn's symphonic variations (after or within the *minores* of Nos. 85, 90, and 94, and in rondo-variations generally), and Mozart's piano-concerto variations.[50] The special character of the "symphony style" of Classicism, although most marked in opening Allegro movements, may have affected the overall configuration of variation movements as well: according to Koch, "in the sonata [including chamber music] the melodic sections are not connected as continuously as in the symphony, but more often are separated through formal phrase-

46. Solomon, *Beethoven*, p. 111.

47. For a discussion of the later alternating movements—the Fifth, Seventh, and Ninth Symphonies and the *Heiliger Dankgesang* of the A-minor String Quartet, Op. 132—see Elaine R. Sisman, "Tradition and Transformation in the Alternating Variations of Haydn and Beethoven," *AM* 62 (1990), 176–181.

48. Several recent studies include discussions of these movements from the standpoint of program and myth in the complete symphony, rather than of form. See, for example, Constantin Floros, *Beethovens Eroica und Prometheus-Musik. Sujet-Studien,* Veröffentlichungen zur Musikforschung 3 (Wilhelmshaven, 1978); Peter Schleuning, "Beethoven in alter Deutung: Der 'neue Weg' mit der 'Sinfonia eroica,'" *AfMw* 44 (1987), 165–194; and Maynard Solomon's extraordinary essay, "The Ninth Symphony: A Search for Order," *Beethoven Essays* (Cambridge, Mass., and London, 1988), pp. 3–32. Such considerations lie outside the scope of this study.

49. James Webster suggests that variation groups (instrumental and vocal) in the finale of the Ninth alternate with the introductory material and fugue, but that the through-composed, cumulative elements of the movement prevail after "Seid umschlungen"; see "The Form of the Finale of Beethoven's Ninth Symphony," *Beethoven Forum* 1 (1992), 25–62.

50. In Symphony No. 94 ("Surprise," 1791), the second period of the *minore* is completely open.

endings."[51] A different rhetoric therefore informed the shaping forces of the alternating variation at Beethoven's disposal, as he made the symphony the privileged locus for breaking the mold of the theme.

The *Eroica* finale has but rarely been recognized as alternating variations. The most accurate published descriptions, in my view, are those of Warren Kirkendale and Carl Dahlhaus, as "double variations"; Kirkendale points out their tonally arranged symmetrical (ABA′) design, Dahlhaus their sense of process.[52] Other views cover every structural possibility. Schenker first gave a plan showing alternating variations or segments on two themes. After noting that the Theme A-variations rely only on its first four measures, while Theme B is almost always fully varied, however, he concluded that the latter was the principal theme of the movement. Beethoven's goal, therefore, according to Schenker, was partly to avoid an unmediated series of variations on Theme B, and partly to create a "higher unity" in which variations subsequent to the initial presentation of Theme B consist of a "preluding" A section followed by a "main" B section.[53] Constantin Floros, in a provocative study of the *Eroica* and the *Prometheus* ballet, does not mention the alternating structure but believes that the bass theme (A) is given greater weight than the discant theme (B).[54] Paul Mies, Leonard Ratner, and Peter Schleuning identify the movement's overall form as rondo-like, but with different twists: to Mies, each "ritornello" is a variation of the bass theme and each "couplet" is a variation of the discant theme; to Ratner, the variations are arranged to form a suite; to Schleuning, purely formal considerations are less significant than an eloquent correlation of the piece with the libretto of the *Prometheus* ballet and its revolutionary and Napoleonic implications.[55] Kurt von Fischer views the plan as sonata-like, with the recapitulation located in the final Andante variation.[56] Most of these writers do not mention that the finale of the *Prometheus* ballet is a set of rondo-variations on the B theme. Finally, Lewis Lockwood's important recent study of the genesis of the *Eroica* finale argues that "the familiar sequential logic of the variation form is distorted by the unexpected juxtaposition of texturally dissimilar segments . . . The inner repetitions, the phrase symmetries, and the closed forms of even the most expanded strict variation set cannot

51. Koch, *Versuch*, III, p. 319; *Introductory Essay*, p. 204. On the distinctions between the sonata and symphony styles, see Broyles, "The Two Instrumental Styles of Classicism."

52. Kirkendale, *Fugue and Fugato*, p. 227; Dahlhaus, *Ludwig van Beethoven: Approaches to His Music*, trans. Mary Whittall (Oxford, 1991), pp. 27–29.

53. Heinrich Schenker, *Beethovens neunte Sinfonie* (Vienna, 1912; rpt. 1969), pp. 204–207. In his later work on the *Eroica*, however, Schenker differentiated only between the "bass sections" and variations on the "theme"; see Schenker, "Beethovens Dritte Sinfonie zum erstenmal in ihrem wahren Inhalt dargestellt," *Das Meisterwerk in der Musik. Ein Jahrbuch*, III (1930), pp. 74–84.

54. Floros, *Beethovens Eroica*, pp. 99–104.

55. Paul Mies, "Ludwig van Beethoven's Werke über seinen Kontretanz in Es-Dur," *Beethoven-Jahrbuch 1953/54*, 100 and 102; Leonard Ratner, *Classic Music*, pp. 258–259; Schleuning, "Beethoven in alter Deutung," pp. 174–176, 188–192.

56. Kurt von Fischer, "Eroica-Variationen op. 35 und Eroica-Finale," *Schweizerische Musikzeitung* 89 (1949), 282–286.

find a place." In emphasizing the unprecedented aspects of its structure, he points to three "phases: thematic creation [the introduction, variations on the bass, and melodic theme]; elaboration [the fugatos and variations that follow]; conclusion [coda]."[57]

I contend that the alternating-variation model provided Beethoven with the framework within which he could fashion a new kind of variation movement altogether, and one newly tailor-made for both symphony and finale position. Before the *Eroica,* variation finales had appeared infrequently in large orchestral compositions like symphonies or concerti. Although Haydn's *concertante* variation finales in Symphonies 72 and 31 of the mid–1760s are too slight to be true forerunners, Beethoven's earliest sketches for the *Eroica* finale show a *concertante* plan.[58] Mozart's G-major and C-minor piano-concerto finales and the finale of Haydn's "Clock" Symphony, No. 101 (1795), a masterly amalgamation of rondo, sonata, variation, and fugue, were pieces known to Beethoven, and might have encouraged his thinking about a large-scale hybrid variation finale. That his thinking might have been specifically rhetorical is shown by his use of the term *principio* over the G-minor introduction in his earliest sketches: Cicero's term for the most direct kind of exordium is *principium,* after which one might more "unobtrusively steal into the mind of the auditor" *(insinuatio).*[59]

Beethoven was clearly at pains to fashion no less than a variation finale that would entirely dwarf its predecessors, that would consciously both sum up and transcend the past. To these ends, he created a compendium of available variation techniques with a symmetrical harmonic plan, all within a progressively unfolding larger structure which redistributes the weight of its two themes as it proceeds. Although many specific features came from Op. 35, he now sought a seamless yet dramatic symphonic approach, making liberal use of modulations and transitions to link one section to the next.[60] For the overall plan, he drew not only on the alternating-variation format of Haydn, but partially also on Haydn's ABA variations with a quasi-developmental or contrapuntal middle section (for example, Symphony 104/ii, Quartet Op. 76 No. 5/ i), as well as on his own recent innovation in Op. 34 of a chain of variations in different keys. And by voluntary submission to the alternating pattern, he set out some of the limitations observed by the movement: that the second theme

57. Lewis Lockwood, "The Compositional Genesis of the *Eroica* Finale," in his *Beethoven: Studies in the Creative Process* (Cambridge, Mass., 1992), p. 165; a detailed table on p. 155 points out the symmetrical elements of the plan. He had earlier identified the first Andante variation as the "formal equivalent of a recapitulation"; "Beethoven's Earliest Sketches for the *Eroica* Symphony," *MQ* 67 (1981), rpt. in *Beethoven,* p. 148.

58. See the transcription in Lockwood, "Earliest Sketches," p. 147: markings for "Var. clarinetto solo corno solo," "Blasinstr.," and "Un poco Adagio. B. I. solo."

59. Cicero, *De inventione,* trans. H. M. Hubbell, Loeb Classical Library vol. 386 [Cicero vol. II] (Cambridge, Mass., 1949), I.xv.20, p. 43.

60. For a survey of some of the similarities between the two works, see Kurt von Fischer, "Eroica-Variationen op. 35 und Eroica-Finale"; Ludwig Misch, "Fugue and Fugato in Beethoven's Variation Form," *MQ* 42 (1956), 14–27; and Michael Broyles, *Beethoven: The Emergence and Evolution of Beethoven's Heroic Style* (New York, 1987), pp. 89–94.

is varied less than the first, that returning material should first resemble earlier statements, that key or mode contrast maintains tension between themes, and that the melodies of the themes are recognizable.[61]

That the first theme of the *Eroica* finale becomes the bass of the second theme—called *Basso del Tema* and *Tema* in Op. 35—has obscured the fact that they are always varied in turn, with their initial melodic contours nearly intact (see Example 8.5 and Table 8.1). The first theme (A) is always treated contrapuntally: the first two variations treat it as a cantus firmus; it becomes the subject of two fugatos (and is inverted in the second, as in Op. 35); and it is given an equally potent countermelody, the central march. In the example, the fugato sections appear as A_x and $A_{x'}$, because Beethoven commented in a letter to Breitkopf that "the Fugue [of Op. 35], of course, cannot be described as a variation."[62] He clearly thought of them as variations, however, because the occasion for his remark was Breitkopf's concern that Op. 35 did not have the thirty variations he had promised; he was trying to show that it had many variations that could not be labeled as such, among them written-out varied repeats (as in the Adagio) and fugue.

Beethoven's wholesale interest in contrapuntal variations and fugues in Op. 35 and the *Eroica* may stem from several sources. At the time when he studied Schulz's article on recitative in Sulzer's *Allgemeine Theorie der schönen Künste*,[63] he may also have read the one on variation, which extolled contrapuntal techniques. The fugues that Reicha published in Vienna in 1803 ("Thirty-Six Fugues," dedicated to Haydn) were already known to Beethoven in 1802, since they are presumably the fugues he disparaged in a letter to Breitkopf of December 1802.[64] Finally, a specific Haydn model is discernible here beyond the alternating-variation form itself, namely the cantus-firmus variations and fugue of Op. 76 No. 6. Beethoven's modeling procedures often took place in pieces with the same key as the model.[65]

The compendium of variation techniques in the *Eroica* finale continues with the rhythmic *gradatio* (progressive diminution) technique animating the cantus-

61. A multi-movement genre requires a greater degree of melodic resemblance between theme and variations than does an independent set, and in this Beethoven adhered to tradition. Tovey astutely observed that "all sonata form works through external melody . . . variations must stick to the melody of their theme if they are to form part of a sonata scheme"; see *Essays in Musical Analysis: Symphonies and Other Orchestral Works,* new ed. (London, 1981), p. 111.

62. Letter to Breitkopf & Härtel, 8 April 1803, Anderson no. 72, p. 89. Floros and Lockwood identify the fugatos as variations (*Beethovens Eroica,* p. 101, and "Genesis of the *Eroica* Finale," p. 155, respectively), while Schenker *(Beethovens neunte Sinfonie,* pp. 204–207) and Kirkendale *(Fugue and Fugato,* p. 225) merely include them as A-sections.

63. Kramer, "Beethoven and Carl Heinrich Graun."

64. Anderson no. 67. Peter Eliot Stone believes that changes in Beethoven's style in Op. 35 "may derive from Reicha's ideas on variation and fugue"; see his article on Reicha in the *New Grove,* vol. 15, p. 697. Actually connecting Beethoven's identification of a new way in variations with his criticism of Reicha is Hans-Werner Küthen, "Beethovens 'wirklich ganz neue Manier'—Eine Persiflage," in *Beiträge zu Beethovens Kammermusik,* ed. Brandenburg and Loos, pp. 216–224.

65. See Douglas Johnson, "Beethoven's Early Sketches in the 'Fischhof Miscellany'" (Ph.D. diss., University of California, Berkeley, 1978), pp. 923, 924, 926–939.

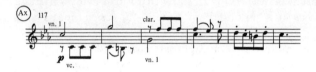

Example 8.5. Beethoven, Symphony No. 3, *Eroica,* Op. 55/iv: A, B, A$_x$, A$_3$, B$_3$.

firmus variations, as the accompaniment patterns of A$_1$, A$_2$, and B. Melodic reprise, typical treatment for a second theme, is always associated with the melodic theme. Constant-harmony technique appears in the highly figured second periods of the melodic-theme variation in D major (B$_1$) and in the first Andante variation (B$_3$). A march-like counter-melody, recalling both the turn-of-the-century characteristic variation and Mozart's C-minor piano concerto, K. 491, gives new interest to the simplified version of the bass theme in its third variation (A$_3$), marking the center of the set, and the return of the G minor of

Table 8.1   Beethoven, *Eroica* Finale: Organization

Introduction: G minor–E♭ major
A: E♭ major, varied repetitions
A₁: E♭ major, cantus-firmus variation with *gradatio,* strings only
A₂: E♭ major, same concept as A₁
B: E♭ major, with varied repetitions
transition
A$_x$: C minor, F minor etc., m. 117. Fugato, circle of fifths
B₁: B minor–D major, m. 175. First period: melodic reprise, varied repetitions;
                second period: constant-harmony variation
A₃: G minor–C minor, m. 211. New march melody added; extension
B₂: C major, m. 258. Melodic reprise; first period only
transition
A$_{x'}$: E♭ major, m. 277. Fugato, subject inverted; B appears (m. 292); A is diminished,
                then partially augmented in final statement
transition on V⁷
B₃: E♭ major, m. 349. Poco Andante. Hymnlike statement in winds, varied
                repetitions; second period: constant-harmony variation
B₄: E♭ major, m. 381. Melodic theme in bass, *ff*; climax of this theme, still Andante
Coda, m. 397: includes

                   B₅: A♭ major, m. 404, melodic-outline variation of first
                        period, still Andante
                   transition
                   Introduction: G minor, m. 431, Presto
                   B: E♭ major, m. 435.

the introduction.[66] This variation, in addition, provides the same sort of focal point as the central *minore* section in Haydn's ABA variations and as the *minore* variation in a strophic set. Melodic-outline technique appears in the D major variation (B₁, repeat of the first period, where both melody and accompanying bass are subjected to it) and in the coda, in the partial A♭-major variation of the melody (B₅).

The themes are far from being equal at the outset. While the melodic theme is treated as a point of arrival in rhythmic values and orchestration, the bass theme nonetheless outweighs it in frequency, in the prominence of its sharp intervallic profile, and in subsequent intensity of treatment: a fugue is always an intensification. But the progressive alternating principle of this movement is that the melodic theme gradually takes over in importance and relative weight. It is the last variation in a foreign key—the truncated C-major variation (B₂)—that begins the segment of the piece where the themes meet as equals for the first time, in the transition from B₂ to the second fugato in E♭.

This fugato, in the tonic and on the inverted bass theme, does less to reassert

66. Floros associates the G-minor section with the *danza eroica* of the *Prometheus* music (no. 8); see *Beethovens Eroica,* p. 103.

the primacy of that theme (or at least the level of intensity of the first fugato) than to forecast the ultimate triumph of the melodic theme. Two decisive events ensure this. First is the appearance of the melodic theme rhythmically transformed as a countersubject during the fugato (m. 292), the first time that B has invaded the turf of A. Second, the climactic nature of the partially augmented final statement of the bass—signaling the end of the fugato—is immediately superseded by the long dominant pedal which prepares the real climax of the movement, the two Andante variations of the melody (B$_3$, B$_4$). These, the first B variations in which A is not present even as a bass line, both balance and overcome the two bass variations at the beginning. And the return to the G minor flourish of the introduction, in the coda, now leads to the melody, underscoring its victory.[67]

Another apparently new feature of this movement is that the whirl of alternations from A$_x$ through A$_{x'}$ seems to proceed through a kind of dynamic, asymmetric middle section, framed by fugatos and marked by foreign keys, shortened variations, new phrase structures, and transitions. After the fugato in C minor, variations move around the circle of fifths from a sudden B minor/ D major to G minor (with the strongest cadence in this section) to C major and C minor; the second fugato then returns to the tonic. That such a middle section inevitably appears "developmental" reflects, on the one hand, the simultaneous and continuing changes of key and structure which lie outside the variation tradition to this time, and, on the other, the appearance of fugato, which had already been used for development in the first and second movements of the *Eroica*.[68] (In fact, all of Beethoven's symphonies that have variation movements also have fugatos.) But development goes much less far to explain the significance of this section than does repetition, specifically the transformation of the idea of repetition as an immutable model in a variation movement into something rather more malleable. All of the rhetorical structural models used in earlier variation movements—refining, dwelling on the point, *copia*—were in a sense predicated on the context of repetition. But in the *Eroica,* not only is the repetition less literal, but the inexorable pull of transitions and modulations makes the border of every variation permeable. In fact, Beethoven has voided the problem of the "white space" between stanzas by completely filling it up, and by changing the form of the stanzas as well; the paratactic form has become sequential in the service of the changing relationship of the two themes. And that the movement can have a "climax," as outlined above, indicates a rhetorical

67. On the possible meanings of the melody, see Schleuning, "Beethoven in alter Deutung," passim. Dahlhaus hears the triumph of the B theme as the "overthrow of the polyphonic principle by the homophonic"; *Beethoven,* p. 29.

68. The appearance of the countermotive in A$_1$ as the countersubject in the C-minor fugato enhances the notion of development. Development was not unknown in some of Haydn's ABA variations, as in the D-major Quartet, Op. 76 No. 5, and the slow movements of Symphonies 96 and 104. In these ternary pieces, the process of development continues into the return of the A section, in the Symphony, and in the coda, in the Quartet. The Allegretto of Beethoven's Seventh Symphony also contains a more developmental middle-section grouping of variations, complete with fugato; see my "Tradition and Transformation," pp. 176–177.

model of amplification in its totality, rather than within its separate elements, as seen in works by Haydn and Mozart.

Thus, both the external and internal aspects of the *Eroica* finale reveal how profoundly Beethoven had assimilated his models. He summed up the past by parading before us all of Haydn's variation techniques, only to shake off the past deliberately by transforming the formal and rhetorical context with which those techniques had been associated. He neither presented antitheses, nor did he refine a point or dwell on his theme. Nor, *pace* the many critics and scholars who locate in sonata recapitulations the source of emotional transcendence in an instrumental work, did he adapt a sonata model. Rather, he invented a "really *new*" kind of theme and subjected it to a different decorum, a teleological rhetoric. By the end of the work, both the alternating process and repetition itself have become something quite different. This was simply not part of Haydn's aesthetic. Moreover, Beethoven united, in a single movement, the two aspects of musical experience delineated by Milan Kundera as virtually incompatible, in *The Book of Laughter and Forgetting:*

> The symphony is a musical epic. We might compare it to a journey leading to the boundless reaches of the external world, on and on, farther and farther. Variations also constitute a journey, but not through the external world. You recall Pascal's *Pensée* about how man lives between the abyss of the infinitely large and the infinitely small. The journey of the variation form leads to that *second* infinity, the infinity of internal variety concealed in all things.
>
> What Beethoven discovered in his variations was another space and another direction. In that sense they are a challenge to undertake the journey, another *invitation au voyage*.
>
> The variation form is the form of maximum concentration. It enables the composer to limit himself to the matter at hand, to go straight to the heart of it . . . The journey to the second infinity is no less adventurous than the journey of the epic.[69]

In the *Eroica,* Beethoven radically conflates these seemingly contradictory destinations.

Profoundly transformed, then, is the status of the variation movement as a small or composite small form: as the series of variations becomes more seamless, as the complexity of the shape of the movement grows, I suggest, the small form becomes an *elaborated* form.[70] The nature of a given set of variations as small or elaborated—as well as the thickness of the "veiling" between theme and variation described by Michaelis—determines the approach to "reading" that piece, using the process of making sense of detective fiction that Edward

69. Milan Kundera, *The Book of Laughter and Forgetting* (New York, 1980), pp. 164–165. He is describing Beethoven's Sonata Op. 111, and concludes that the original theme "bears no more resemblance to the final variation than a flower to its image under the microscope."

70. In indirectly alluding to a rhetorical process—invention, arrangement, elaboration—Lockwood appears to suggest a conflation of process and product in the *Eroica* finale, stressing elaboration in particular; see his *Beethoven*, pp. 164–165.

T. Cone applies to understanding a piece of music, in a fascinating article called "Three Ways of Reading a Detective Story—Or a Brahms Intermezzo."[71] In the First Reading, according to Cone, we learn the story; in the Second Reading, we make structural sense of the whole; and in the Third Reading (the "ideal first reading"), we mediate between the modes of understanding of the first two, our thoughts running on a "double trajectory." An elaborated variation movement requires consideration of the whole for its structural secrets. But because of the special nature of varied repetition, that Third Reading in the case of a strophic variation movement might already be plausible by the time one arrives at the third segment of the piece, that is, the second variation: having already identified the form of the piece and the principal elements of the theme, the double trajectory takes over, allowing a simultaneous appreciation of ground and figure, of individual bounded segment and larger series, of recognition and interpretation of both the familiar and unfamiliar. In short, this aural mediation, whether in small or elaborated variations, whether through a transparent or opaque veil, is central to the immemorial pleasure of variation, and encourages a sense of the adventurous possibilities inherent in the theme's segmented journey.

71. Edward T. Cone, "Three Ways of Reading a Detective Story—Or a Brahms Intermezzo" (1977), reprinted in *Music: A View from Delft,* ed. Robert P. Morgan (Chicago, 1989), pp. 77–93.

Appendixes · Selected Bibliography · Index

Variations of Haydn, Mozart, and Beethoven

Table A.1   Haydn's Variations

Dating is based on *New Grove* worklist by Georg Feder (choosing the likely date instead of the terminus when possible for problematic cases); dating of early quartets is based on James Webster, "The Chronology of Haydn's String Quartets" (*MQ* 61 [1975], 35–44); order of genres follows Hoboken catalogue. A theme reprise is noted as "dc" (for da capo); if reorchestrated, it is noted as "o"; a *minore* is noted as "m"; a variation with altered structure is noted with an asterisk ($\star$); Tempo di Menuet is labelled TdiM; codas shorter than six bars are noted as "app" (for appendix).

I. Strophic Variations

Symphonies (Hob. I)

72/iv (? c. 1763–65)	6 vars. (A_6 = o) Presto coda
31/iv (1765)	7 vars. (A_6 = o) Presto coda
47/ii (1772)	4 vars. (A_4 = o) coda
55/ii (1774)	5 vars.
57/ii (1774)	4 vars. ($A_3\star$, $A_4\star$)
71/ii (?1778/79)	4 vars. (A_4 = dc) coda
75/ii (?1779)	4 vars. (A_4 = o) coda
81/ii (1784)	4 vars. (A_2 = m)
85/ii (?1785)	4 vars. (A_2 = m) coda
84/ii (1786)	3 vars. (A_1 = m) coda
91/ii (1788)	4 vars. (A_2 = m) coda
94/ii (1791)	4 vars. (A_2 = m$\star$) coda
95/ii (1791)	3 vars. (A_2 = m)
97/ii (1792)	3 vars. (A_2 = m)

Divertimenti (Hob. II)

11/iv (−1765)	8 vars. (A_8 = o)
1/iv (−1768)	6 vars. (A_6 = dc)

String Quartets (Hob. III)

Op. 2/6/i (c. 1755–59)	5 vars.
Op. 9/5/i (c. 1769–70)	4 vars. app

Op. 17/3/i (1771)	4 vars.
Op. 20/4/ii (1772)	4 vars. (A_4 = dc) coda
Op. 33/5/iv (1781)	3 vars. Presto/coda
Op. 50/1/ii (1787)	3 vars. (A_2 = m)
Op. 50/3/ii (1787)	4 vars. (A_1 = m) coda
Op. 55/3/ii (1788)	2 vars. ($A_2\star$) app
Op. 64/1/ii (1790)	2 vars.
Op. 64/2/ii (1790)	3 vars. coda
Op. 74/2/ii (1793)	3 vars. (A_2 = m) coda
Op. 76/3/ii (1797)	4 vars.
Op. 76/6/i (1797)	4 vars. Allegro/coda

Mixed Trios (Hob. IV)

5/i (1767)	3 vars.
2 (1794)	5 vars. (A_5 = Allegro) vars. on "The Lady's Looking-glass," Hob. XXXIc:17

String Trios (Hob. V)

7/ii (–1765)	3 vars.
8/i (–1765)	6 vars.
11/ii (–1765)	3 vars. (A_3 = dc)
18/ii (–1765)	2 vars.
D3/i (–1767)	3 vars.

String Duos (Hob. VI)

1/iii (–1775)	2 vars. app
2/iii (–1775)	4 vars.
3/i (–1775)	4 vars.
3/iii (–1775)	2 vars.
4/iii (–1775)	4 vars. (A_3 = dc) coda
5/iii (–1775)	4 vars.
6/iii (–1775)	4 vars.

Baryton Octets (Hob. X)

4/i (?1775)	5 vars.

Baryton Duos (Hob. XII)

4/i (c. 1764–69)	3 vars. (A_3 = dc)
(3 + 5)/i (c. 1764–69)	3 vars.

Baryton Trios (Hob. XI) (all first movements)

Vol. 1 (bound 1766)	2 (6 vars.)
	6 (4 vars.)
	8 (6 vars.)
	12 (4 vars.)
	17 (6 vars.)
Vol. 2 (bound 1767)	29 (5 vars.)
	38 (4 vars. and d.c.)

	41 (3 vars.)
	45 (3 vars.)
Vol. 3 (bound 1768)	50 (4 vars.)
	60 (3 vars. and d.c.)
	69 (4 vars.)
Vol. 4 (bound end 1771)	73 (4 vars.)
	78 (4 vars.)
	81 (3 vars.)
	95 (4 vars.)
Vol. 5 (bound 1778)	105 (4 vars.)
	106 (3 vars. and d.c.)
	111 (4 vars. and d.c.)
	116 (3 vars. and d.c.)
	126 (3 vars.)

Keyboard Trios (Hob. XV)

C1/iii (–?1760)	6 vars.
2/iii (?1767–71)	4 vars.
5/iii (1784)	1 var. coda
7/i (1785)	5 vars.
20/ii (1794)	3 vars. app

Keyboard Sonatas (Hob. XVI)

XVII:D1/i (?)	3 vars.
XVIIa:1/i (?c. 1768–70)	7 vars.
XVI:24/iii (?1773)	1 var. coda
29/iii (1774)	3 vars. (A$_2$ = m, or "trio"; TdiM)
27/iii (1776)	4 vars. (A$_3$ = m within dc)
28/iii (1776)	5 vars. (A$_3$ = m within dc)
30/iii (1776)	6 vars. (TdiM)
31/iii (1776)	4 vars. (A$_3$ = m)
42/i (1784)	3 vars. (A$_2$ = m)

Independent Sets

XVII:2 (?c. 1765)	solo keybd., A maj., 20 vars.
XVII:3 (c. 1770–74)	solo keybd., E♭ maj., 12 vars.
XVII:5 (1790)	solo keybd., C maj., 6 vars. (A$_5$ = m)
XVII:7★ (?c. 1750–55)	5 vars. (authentic?)
XXVIb:3 "Dr. Harington's Compliment" (1794), sop., chorus (SSTB), keybd.	A. maj., 4 vars. (A$_3$ = m)
XXXIa:176 "The Blue Bell[s] of Scotland" (1801/2), pf, vn, vc,	D maj., 3 vars. No. 1 of 6 "Scotch airs with vars." (Nos. 2–5 authentic?)

II. Alternating Variations

Symphonies (Hob. I)   *Themes related?*

53/ii (?1778/79)	A major	ABA$_1$B$_1$A$_2$A$_3$	Yes (mel)

70/ii (?1778/79)	D minor	ABA₁B₁A₂	No
63/ii (?1779)	C minor	ABA₁B₁A₂★B₂★	Yes (mel)
82/ii (1786)	F major	ABA₁B₁A₂ coda	Yes (rhyth)
90/ii (1788)	F major	ABA₁B₁A₂ coda	No
103/ii (1795)	C minor	ABA₁B₁A₂B₂ coda	Yes (mel)

String Quartets (Hob. III)

Op. 33/6/iv (1781)	D major	ABA₁B₁A₂	No
Op. 50/4/ii (1787)	A major	ABA₁B₁A₂	No
Op. 55/2/i (1788)	F minor	ABA₁B₁A₂B₂ coda	Yes (mel)
Op. 71/3/ii (1793)	B♭ major	ABAA₁B₁A₂ coda	Yes (Bs = var A)

Piano Trios (Hob. XV)

13/i (1789)	C minor	ABA₁B₁A₂B₂	Yes (mel)
19/i (1794)	G minor	ABA₁B₁B₂★ coda	No
23/i (1795)	D minor	ABA₁B₁A₂B₂ coda	Yes (details)

Piano Sonatas (Hob. XVI)

44/ii (c. 1771–3)	G minor	ABA₁★B₁★ coda (TdM)	Yes (rhyth)
22/iii (1773)	E major	ABA₁B₁A₂ (TdM)	Yes (mel)
33/iii (–1778)	D major	ABA₁B₁A₂ (TdM)	Yes (rhyth)
36/ii (1770–5?)	A major	ABAA₁B₁AA₂	No
34/iii (–1784)	E minor	ABA₁★B₁A₂ (rondo style)	Yes (mel)
40/i (1784)	G major	ABA₁B₁A₂	Yes (mel)
48/i (1789)	C major	ABA₁B₁★A₂★	Yes (Bs = var A)

Independent Set (Hob. XVII)

6 (1793)	F minor	ABA₁B₁A₂B₂A★ coda	No

III. Rondo-Variations

Symphonies (Hob. I)

42/iv (1771)	ABA₁CA₂ coda
51/iv (–1774)	AA₁BA₂CA₃ coda
55/iv (1774)	ABA₁CA₂ coda
74/ii (?1780)	ABA₁CA₂ coda
76/ii (?1782)	ABA₁CA₂ coda
101/ii (1794)	ABA₁CA₂ app.

String Quartets (Hob. III)

Op. 33/4/iv (1781)	ABA₁CA₂
Op. 55/1/ii (1787)	ABA₁CA₂
Op. 77/2/iii (1799)	ABA₁CA₂A₃ app.

Piano Trios (Hob. XV)

25/i (1795)	ABA₁CA₂
31/i (1795)	ABACA₁

Piano Sonatas (Hob. XVI)
19/iii (1767) $ABA_1CA_2A_3$
39/i (1780) $ABAA_1CAA_2$

IV. ABA Variations

Symphonies (Hob. I)

77/ii (?1782)	ext; B not *minore*
89/ii (1787)	coda
92/ii (1789)	coda
93/ii (1791)	coda
96/ii (1791)	coda
100/ii (1794)	coda
104/ii (1795)	coda

String Quartets (Hob. III)

Op. 64/3/ii (1790)	coda
Op. 64/4/iii (1790)	coda
Op. 64/5/ii (1790)	
Op. 64/6/iii (1790)	
Op. 71/2/iv (1793)	coda
Op. 74/3/ii (1793)	
Op. 76/2/ii (1797)	coda
Op. 76/5/i (1797)	ABA Allegro/coda

Piano Trios (Hob. XV)

6/ii (1784)	(TdiM)
8/ii (1785)	(TdiM) coda
11/ii (?1788)	(TdiM) coda; B not *minore*
15/iii (1790)	
18/ii (1794)	to V *attacca*
20/iii (1794)	coda
31/ii (1795)	B not *minore*
27/ii (?1795)	coda
29/i (?1795)	coda

Piano Sonatas (Hob. XVI)

40/ii (1784)	
41/ii (1784)	
49/ii (1789–90)	coda

V. Sonata Movements with Varied Reprises (all slow movements; varied reprise of exposition only unless noted)

Symphony No. 102/ii (1794)
Divertimento II:23/iii (small-form binary, both reprises varied) (?1760)
Quartet Op. 9/2/iii (c. 1769–70)
Quartet Op. 9/4/ii (c. 1769–70)
Quartet Op. 17/4/iii (1771)
Quartet Op. 20/6/ii (1772)

Table A.1   (continued)

Quartet Op. 33/3/iii (1781)
String Duo VI:3/ii (–1775)
String Duo VI:6/ii (–1775)
Sonata XVI:38/ii (?c. 1770–75)

VI. Other Hybrid Movements

Symphony 78/iv (?1782)   alternating rondo-variation style (ABA*[dev]B$_1$
                                      coda)
Symphony 79/ii (1784)   AA$_1$ Un poco allegro [quasi-A$_2$] coda
Symphony 88/ii (?1787)   variation, elements of rondo and sonata
Symphony 101/iv (1794)   sonata-rondo combined with variation and fugue
Quartet Op. 33/2/iii (1781)   rondo-variation combined with sonata
Quartet Op. 33/4/iii (1781)   rondo-variation combined with sonata

---

Table A.2   Mozart's Variations

Dating follows *New Grove* worklist by Stanley Sadie and Anthony Hicks. A theme reprise is noted as "dc"; a variation in the opposite mode (*minore or maggiore*) is noted as "m"; the presence of tempo and/or meter change[s] is noted with an asterisk (*); rondo-variation is noted as "rv."

Piano Concertos

K. 382 [=iii]	1782	7 vars. with ritornellos (A$_4$ = m): AA$_1$AA$_2$A$_3$AA$_4$A$_5$A$_6$AA$_7$ coda *
K. 450/ii	1784	3 vars.
K. 453/iii	1784	4 vars. (A$_3$ = m) Finale *
K. 456/ii	1784	5 vars. (A$_4$ = m) coda
K. 482/ii rv	1785	AA$_1$BA$_2$CA$_3$ (B, C = m) coda
K. 491/iii	1786	8 vars. (A$_4$ = m$_{VI}$, A$_6$ = m) coda *

Divertimenti (winds, and mixed scoring)

K. 251/iv	1776	3 vars. (dc after each)
K. 253/i	1776	6 vars. *
K. 287/271h/ii	1777	6 vars.
K. 334/320b/ii	1779–80	6 vars. (A$_4$ = m)
K. 361/370a/vi	1781/84	6 vars. (A$_4$ = m) *
K. 388/384a/iv	1782	8 vars. (A$_5$, A$_8$ = m)
K. 298/i	1786–87	4 vars.

Quintets
String Quintets:

K. 406/516b/iv (arr. of K. 388)	1788	8 vars. (A$_5$, A$_8'$ = m)
K. 614/ii rv	1791	ABA$_1$CA$_2$ coda

Clarinet Quintet:		
K. 581/iv	1789	6 vars.(A$_3$ = m) ★
String Quartets		
K. 170/i	1773	4 vars. + dc
K. 421/417b/iv	1783	5 vars. (A$_4$ = m) coda ★
K. 464/iii	1785	6 vars. (A$_4$ = m) coda
String Trio		
K. 563/iv	1788	4 vars. (A$_3$ = m) coda
String Duo		
K. 424/iii	1783?	7 vars. ★
Sonatas for Violin and Piano		
K. 31/ii	1766	6 vars.
K. 302/293b/ii	1778	ABA$_1$CA$_2$BA$_3$ coda
K. 305/293d/ii	1778	6 vars. (A$_5$ = m) ★
K. 379/373a/ii	1781	6 vars. (A$_4$ = m) ★
K. 377/374e/ii	1781	6 vars. (A$_5$ = m) ★
K. 481/ii	1785	ABA$_1$
K. 481/iii	1785	6 vars. ★
K. 547/iii	1788	6 vars. (A$_5$ = m)
Keyboard Trios		
K. 496/iii	1786	6 vars. (A$_4$ = m) ★
K. 498/iii rv	1786	ABA$_1$CA$_2$
K. 502/ii rv	1786	ABA$_1$CA$_2$ coda
K. 564/ii	1788	6 vars. (A$_5$ = m)
K. 564/iii rv	1788	ABA$_1$CA$_2$ (B, C = variants of A)
Sonatas for Piano		
K. 284/205b/ii rv	1775	ABA$_1$CBA$_2$ (As = varied consequent: a$_v$a$'_1$)
K. 284/205b/iii	1775	12 vars. (A$_7$ = m) ★
K. 331/300i/i	1781–83	6 vars. (A$_3$ = m) ★

Independent Sets
For piano (cadenzas noted as "c"):
8 Vars. in G major on "Laat ons Juichen Batavieren!", K. 24 (1766)   ★
7 Vars. in D major on "Willem van Nassau," K. 25 (1766)   ★
6 Vars. in G major on "Mio caro Adone," K. 180/173c (1773)   ★
12 Vars. in C major on a Menuet by Fischer, K. 179/189a (1774)   ★

12 Vars. in E♭ major on "Je suis Lindor," K. 354/299a (1778)	(A₉ = m) + dc c ★
12 Vars. in C major on "Ah, vous dirai-je Maman," K. 265/300e (1781–82)	(A₈ = m) ★
12 Vars. in E♭ major on "La belle Françoise," K. 353/300f (1781–82)	(A₉ = m) ★
12 Vars. in C major on "Lison dormait," K. 264/315d (1778)	(A₅ = m) c ★
8 Vars. in F major on "Dieu d'amour," K. 352/374c (1781)	(A₅ = m) ★
6 Vars. in F major on "Salve tu, Domine," K. 398/416e (1783)	(A₄ = m) + dc c ★
10 Vars. in G major on "Unser dummer Pöbel meint," K. 455 (1784)	(A₅ = m) + dc/coda c ★
Vars. on "Come un agnello," K. 460/454a (1784)	2 vars. in aut; 8-var. version doubtful
12 Vars. in B♭ major on an Allegretto, K. 500 (1786)	(A₇ = m) + dc c ★
9 Vars. in D major on a Menuet by Duport, K. 573 (1789)	(A₆ = m) + dc c ★
8 Vars. in F major on "Ein Weib ist das herrlichste Ding," K. 613 (1791)	(A₆ = m) coda ritornellos ★
For piano four-hands:	
5 Vars. in G major on an Andante, K. 501 (1786)	(A₄ = m)
For piano and violin:	
12 Vars. in G major on "La bergère Célimène," K. 359/374a (1781)	(A₇ = m)
6 Vars. in G minor on "Hélas, j'ai perdu mon amant," K. 360/374b (1781)	(A₅ = m)

Table A.3   Beethoven's Variations

Dating follows *New Grove* worklist by Alan Tyson. A theme reprise is noted as "dc"; variations in the opposite mode are noted as "m"; the presence of tempo and/or meter change[s] is noted with an asterisk (★); alternating variations are noted as "av"; rondo-variations are noted as "rv"; unusual key schemes are noted as "k"; transitions between variations are not noted.

A. *Orchestral*
1. *Solo and Orchestra*

Triple Concerto, Op. 56/ii (1802–1803)	1 var. (+ trans to V of finale)
Violin Concerto, Op. 61/ii (1806)	4 vars. (with 2 cadenza-type themes before and after A₄)
Fantasy (pfte., chor., orch.), Op. 80 (1808)	Intro 8 instrtl. vars. (6 = m) k, choral reiterations of theme ★

2. *Symphonies*

Symphony No. 3, Op. 55/iv (1803) av
Intro AA₁A₂B AₓB₁A₃B₂Aₓ. B₃B₄ coda/
(B₅, Intro, B) k ★

Symphony No. 4, Op. 60/ii (1806) rv
ABA₁CA₂B coda

Symphony No. 5, Op. 67/ii (1807–1808) av
ABA₁B₁ A₂B₂A₃ A₄ coda (A₃ = m) k ★

Symphony No. 7, Op. 92/ii (1811–1812) av
A [= AA₁A₂A₃] B A [= A₄A₅A₆] B
A₇/quasi-dc ★

Symphony No. 9, Op. 125/iii (1822–1824) av
ABA₁B₁ [ep] A₂ [ep₁] A₃ [ep₂] A₃ coda k ★

Symphony No. 9, Op. 125/iv (1822–1824)
Intro; *Freude*: instrtl. theme and 3 vars.;
intro; vocal theme and 4 vars. (+ dev);
(other segments, including *Seid
umschlungen* theme); final *Freude* var.
combined with *Seid* theme in double
fugue; finale

B. *Chamber Music*

1. *Strings*

Serenade (String Trio), Op. 8/viii (1796–1797)
5 vars. (3 = m; 5 = Allegro) coda ★

String Quartet, Op. 18/5/iii (1798–1800)
5 vars. coda

String Quartet, Op. 74/ii (1809) rv
ABA₁CA₂ B/coda

String Quartet, Op. 74/iv (1809)
6 vars. coda

String Quartet, Op. 127/ii (1823–1825)
5 vars. (with episode after 4) coda k ★

String Quartet, Op. 132/iii (1825) av
ABA₁B₁A₂ coda k ★

String Quartet, Op. 130/iv (1825–1826)
ABA₁ coda

String Quartet, Op. 131/iv (1826)
6 vars. coda k

String Quartet, Op. 135/iii (1826)
4 vars. k

2. *Winds or Strings/Winds*

Septet, Op. 20/iv (1799–1800)
5 vars. (4 = m) coda

Serenade (fl., vln., vla.), Op. 25/ii (1801)
3 vars. coda

3. *Piano and Strings or Strings/Winds*

Piano Quartet, WoO 36/1/ii (1785)
6 vars. + dc (5 = m, 3 = adagio)

Piano Trio, Op. 1/3/ii (1794–1795)
5 vars. (4 = m) (★)

Trio (pfte., cl., vc.), Op. 11/iii (1797), vars. on "Pria ch'io l'impegno"
9 vars. (4, 7 = m) coda ★

Piano Trio, Op. 70/2/ii (1808) av
ABA₁A₂B₁AB₂ coda

Piano Trio, Op. 97/ii ("Archduke") (1810–1811)
4 vars. + quasi-dc coda

Violin Sonata, Op. 12/1/ii (1797–1798)
4 vars. (3 = m)

Violin Sonata, Op. 30/1/iii (1801–1802)
6 vars. (5 = m) coda ★

Violin Sonata, Op. 30/2/ii (1801–1802)
ABA₁ coda

Violin Sonata, Op. 47/ii ("Kreutzer") (1802–1803)
4 vars. (3 = m) coda

Violin Sonata, Op. 96 (1812)
6 vars. + fugue + reprise/coda

C. *Piano Sonatas*

Kurfürsten sonata, WoO 47/3/ii (?1783)	6 vars. (5 = m)
Op. 14/2/ii (1799?)	3 vars. coda
Op. 26/i (1800–1801)	5 vars. (3 = m) coda
Op. 57/ii (1804–1805)	3 vars. + quasi-dc
Op. 109/iii (1820)	5 vars. + var./finale and dc
Op. 111/ii (1821–1822)	4 vars. + finale/var./coda

D. *Independent Sets*

1. *Chamber Ensemble*

12 vars. on "Se vuol ballare," pf, vn (WoO 40, 1792–1793)	(6-7 = m) coda
8 vars. on "Là ci darem la mano," 2 ob., Eng. hn (WoO 28, ?1795)	(6 = m) coda ★
12 vars. on "See the conquering hero comes," pf, vc (WoO 45, 1796)	(4, 8 = m) coda ★
12 vars. on "Ein Mädchen oder Weibchen," Op. 66, pf, vc (1796)	(10-11 = m) coda ★
7 vars. on "Bei Männern," pf, vc (WoO 46, 1801)	(4 = m) ★
14 vars. on original theme, Op. 44, pf trio (pub. 1804)	(13 = m) coda ★
10 vars. on "Ich bin der Schneider Kakadu," Op. 121a, pf trio (?1803, rev. 1816)	Intro (9 = m) coda
6 National Airs with Variations, Op. 105, pf, fl/vn (c. 1818)	no. 1: 3 vars. (3 = m) coda ★
	no. 2: 3 vars. (3 = m) quasi-dc ★
	no. 3: 6 vars. (5 = m) coda ★
	no. 4: 3 vars.
	no. 5: 3 vars. ★
	no. 6: 4 vars. k
10 National Airs with Variations, Op. 107, pf, fl/vn (c. 1818)	no. 1: 4 vars. (3 = m$_{,ii)}$ ★
	no. 2: 4 vars. + Allegro
	no. 3: 5 vars. + finale ★
	no. 4: 5 vars. (3 = m) ★
	no. 5: 3 vars. + finale ★
	no. 6: 4 vars. ★
	no. 7: 6 vars. + finale ★
	no. 8: 4 vars. coda ★
	no. 9: 5 vars. (4 = m) ★
	no. 10: 5 vars. (3 = m) ★

2. *Piano*

9 Vars. in C minor on March by Dressler (WoO 63, 1782)	(9 = m)
6 Vars. in F major on Swiss Song (WoO 64, before 1793)	(3 = m)

24 Vars. in D major on "Venni amore" (WoO 65, 1790–1791)	(12-13 = m) finale/coda ★
13 Vars. in A major on "Es war einmal ein alter Mann" (WoO 66, 1792)	(6 = m) ★
12 Vars. in C major on "Menuet à la Vigano" (WoO 68, 1795)	(4, 7 = m) finale/coda ★
9 Vars. in A major on "Quant' è più bello" (WoO 69, 1795)	(4 = m) coda ★
6 Vars. in G major on "Nel cor più non mi sento" (WoO 70, 1795)	(4 = m) coda
12 Vars. in A major on Russian Dance by Wranitzky (WoO 71, 1796–1797)	(3, 7, 11 = m) finale/coda ★
8 Vars. in C major on "Un fièvre brûlante" (WoO 72, ?1795)	(4 = m) coda ★
10 Vars. in B♭ major on "La stessa, la stessissima" (WoO 73, 1799)	(5 = m) finale/coda ★
7 Vars. in F major on "Kind willst du ruhig schlafen" (WoO 75, 1799)	(6 = m) finale/coda ★
6 Vars. in F major on "Tändeln und Scherzen" (WoO 76, 1799)	(5 = m_{vi}) finale/coda k ★
6 Vars. in G major on original theme (WoO 77, 1800)	(4 = m) coda
6 Vars. in F major on original theme, Op. 34 (1802)	(5 = m_v) coda k ★
15 Vars. and Fugue in E♭ major on original theme, Op. 35 (1802)	(6 = m_{vi}, 14 = m) coda, fugue, quasi-dc and var. ★
7 Vars. in C major on "God Save the King" (WoO 78, 1802/1803)	(5 = m) coda ★
5 Vars. in D major on "Rule Brittania" (WoO 79, 1803)	(4 = m_{vi}) coda
32 Vars. in C minor on original theme (WoO 80, 1806)	(12-16 = m) coda
6 Vars. in D major on original theme, Op. 76 (1809)	coda + dc
33 Vars. in C major on waltz by Diabelli, Op. 120 (1819–1823)	(9, 30-31 = m) coda k ★
3. Piano Four-Hands	
8 in C major on theme of Count Waldstein (WoO 67, ?1792)	(8 = m) coda ★
6 in D major on "Ich denke dein" (WoO 74, 1799, 1803)	(5 = m) coda ★
4. Miscellaneous Piano	
Fantasy in G major, Op. 77 (1809), concluding section in B major	7 vars. coda

APPENDIX B

Extended Original-Language Quotations

Chapter 1

At n. 67: Christian Gottlob Neefe, "Über die musikalische Wiederholung": "Es ist izt bey den Kritikern musikalischer Kompositionen, in Zeitungen, Journalen, Gesellschaften und Parterren sehr gewöhnlich, daβ sie den Komponisten Wiederholung vorrükken, und die wenigsten wissen wohl, was sie eigentlich damit sagen wollen. Es ist wahr, die Wiederholung kann auch in der Musik, wie in allen andern schönen Künsten und Wissenschaften zum Fehler werden, wenn sie ohne Grund; und Eckel bey den Zuhörern verursachen, wenn sie gar zu oft geschieht. Es kann aber auch eine musikalische Idee oft und vielleicht unmittelbar auf einander wiederholt wenden, und diese Wiederholung kann ein wahres Verdienst des Komponisten seyn. Ich will hier einige flüchtige Wörte über die musikalische Wiederholung aufsetzen . . .

"Die musikalische Wiederholung läβt sich in zwo Gattungen theilen: in die Wiederholung in Ansehung der Erfindung, und in die, in Absicht auf die Ausführung.

"Nach der erstern kann ein Komponist entweder seine eigenen, oder die Gedanken anderer wiederholen. Die Wiederholung von seinen eignen Gedanken entspringt aus verschiedenen Quellen. Entweder er ist wirklich arm an Erfindung, dann fehlts ihm freylich an einer der vorzüglichsten Eigenschaften eines Komponisten, und die daher entstandene Wiederholung ist allerdings strafbar . . . Oder sie hat ihren Enstehungsgrund in dem Mangel einer lebhaften Erinnerungskraft, so daβ ein Komponist sich die gegenwärtigen Gedanke, nicht als schon ehemals gehabte vorstellen kann. Oder sie entsteht aus der Nothwendigkeit, viel und geschwinde zu arbeiten. Dann ist es ein Fehler, der Nachsicht verdienst . . . Hasse und Graun selbst . . . sind von diesem Fehler nicht ganz frey gewesen . . . [example given from Hasse's *Il Rè Pastore*].

"Die Wiederholung, nach welcher ein Komponist die Gedanken Anderer an Tag bringt, kann aus eben den verschiedenen Ursachen entstehen, woraus die vorige Untergattung entstehen konnte. a) Aus Mangel der Erfindungskraft. Angehende Komponisten sind gemeiniglich diesem Fehler ausgesezt . . . Die Pergolesen, die jungen Genies, . . . sind selten. Philidor, . . . weis die Italiäner und andre trefflich zu nuzen . . . [example from *Jardinier de Sidon*]. b) Aus Übereilung. c) Aus einem schwachen Erinnerungsvermögen . . .

"Es gibt noch eine andere Gattung der Wiederholung, nämlich die, in Ansehung der Ausführung. Diese wird man doch nicht tadeln, und abgeschafft wissen wollen? Was würden wir dann für Ungeheuer von musikalischen Stücken bekommen, wenn man nur Ideen zu Ideen ohne Beziehung auf einander häufen, wenn man nur eine zügellose Phantasie und nicht zugleich Herz und Verstand arbeiten lassen wollte. Kein Zuhörer würde mehr eine Musik fassen und empfinden können. Alle Regel, die Periodologie des Gesanges, woran man seit so langer Zeit gearbeitet hat, ja so gar der wahre Ausdruck der Leidenschaft, der Situation des Karakters einen singenden Person würde verschwinden. Das Genie soll zwar nicht durch die Regel unterdrückt werden . . .

"Ich sagte vorhin, daβ wenn man diese zwote Gattung der Wiederholung vertilgen wollte, so würde oft der Ausdruck ganz verlohren gehen. Ich will diese durch ein Beyspiel belegen. Es gibt Fälle, wo der Komponist in der ersten Zeile seines Textes eine gewisse Leidenschaft auszudrucken hat. Er erfindet einen musikalischen Gedanken dazu. In den folgenden Zeilen steigt das Interesse eben derselben Leidenschaft. Soll er nun zu jeder folgenden Zeile einen neuen Gedanken erfinden? Oder soll er den ersten Gedanken verstärkt wiederholen? Ich meyne, das leztere . . . [example from Hasse, *Piramo e Tisbe*].

"Die Wiederholung wird aber auch noch aus einem andern Grunde oft nothwendig. Unsre Seele verlangt sich alles dessen, was ihr interessant ist; ganz zu bemächtigen. Darnach muβ sich der Komponist richten; er muβ einen interessanten, schmeichelhaften Gedanken wiederholen, damit die Seele ganz befriediget werde. In der Dichtkunst und Malerey ist diese Wiederholung nicht nöthig, weil ich eine vortrefliche Stelle in einem Gedicht mir selbst wiederholen, zwey- bis dreymal lesen, ein reizendes Gemälde lange hin und her, und her und hin betrachten kann. Dieβ kann der Zuhörer einer Musik nicht, die schnell nach einander fortgeht; er kann vieles verlieren, was er nicht gerne verlieren möchte, wenn ihn der Komponist nicht durch Wiederholung schadlos hält.

"Dieβ sind meine flüchtigen Ideen über diese Materie. Vielleicht sieht wenigstens mancher daraus, daβ er oft einen Komponisten der Wiederholung beschuldigt hat, ohne zu wissen, ob er sein voreiliges Urtheil verantworten könne, ohne zu wissen, ob er nicht durch seine Beschuldigung dem Komponisten unwissend ein Kompliment gemacht habe. Ich habe meine Gedanken auf die Singkomposition angewendet; sie lassen sich aber mit ein wenig mehre Einschränkung auch auf die Instrumentalkomposition anwenden."

Chapter 2

At n. 32 (Vogler): "Veränderungen sind eine Art musikalischer Rhetorik, wo der nämliche Sinn in mancherlei Wendungen vorkömmt, mit dem Unterschiede, daβ die Gränzlinien viel genauer in der Musik, als in der Redekunst bestimmt werden. Schon in der Prosa thut ein gewisser *numerus (un certo, non so, che; un, je ne sais, quoi)* die Wirkung einer Cäsur, eines mehr fühl- als bestimmbaren Rhythmus. Allein, nicht dieser Rhythmus, nicht einmal ein vorgeschriebener Einschnitt, auch selbst das Silbenmaasgereimt seyn sollender Verse, läβt sich noch lange nicht mit dem engen Pfade vergleichen, den uns das Thema ausgesteckt und eingezaumt hat . . .

"Diesem strengen Bezug aufs Thema, den man nie aus dem Gesichte verlieren darf, unbeschadet, öffnet sich doch auf der andern Seite eine Aussicht in das weiteste Feld, wenn von der Einkleidung die Rede ist. Um Variationen zu setzen, braucht der Kompositeur kein groβer Melopoet zu seyn, aber desto mehr Phraseologie muβ er inne haben. Eine Hauptverdienst ist, neue Spielarten erfinden, neue Formen, neue Figuren der Vorzeichnung anpassen: er muβ in der Analogie glücklich, d. i. im Stande seyn, dieselbe Analogie, die im Thema zwischen Harmonien und Harmonien, zwischen Melodien und Melodien herrscht, in den Veränderungen beizubehalten: kurz, jeden Karakter, den er dem ersten Takt anweist, durchaus fortzuführen."

Chapter 3

At n. 23 (Mattheson): "Gewisse langsame Bass-Noten, mit Beybehaltung ihres Ganges und Progressus, auf verschiedene Weise in kleinere Noten also zu verändern, dass zwar im Grunde der Satz sein Esse behalte; doch aber dahin diminuirt, zertheilt, und zergliedert werde, dass er mehr Leben, Stärke, Anmuth, und Zierrath bekomme. Was bey den Franzosen *double* (doppelt oder Verdopplung) heisset, solches nennt man bey uns, wiewohl nicht zum besten, eine Variation."

At n. 29 (Riedt): "1. Je mehr Mannigfaltiges durch den Ausführer in eine Melodie gebracht wird, je schöner ist die Ausführung. 2. Das Thema eines Stückes darf nur das erste und letztemal unverändert vorgetragen werden, ausserdem aber muss es dasselbe, so oft es sonst weiter vorkommt, auch jedesmal auf eine andere Art verändert werden. 3. Da die Musik eine freye Kunst ist, so hat ein jeder Ausführer auch die Freyheit, seine Veränderungen zu machen, wie es ihm gefällt. 4. Wenn man seine eigene Composition ausführt, kann man sie verändern wie man wolle, und sey man nicht daran gebunden, die Ordnung dabey so genau zu beobachten, als man wohl bey der Ausführung einer fremden Composition thun müssen."

At n. 30 (Riedt): "1. Eine jede Veränderungen muss niemalen mit derjenigen Harmonie streiten, welche in dem Gedanken zum Grunde lieget, dem man verändern will, und 2. Bey einer jeder Veränderungen muss ebenfalls die Bewegung des Gedankens beobachtet werden, damit auch in der Veränderung die Aehnlichkeit desselben erkannt werden könne."

At n. 40 (Bach): "Das Verändern beym Wiederholen ist heut zu Tage unentbehrlich. Man erwartet solches von jedem Ausführer. Einer meine Freunde giebt sich alle mögliche Mühe, ein Stück, so wie es gesetzt ist, rein und den Regeln des guten Vortrags gemäß herauszubringen; solte man ihm wol den Beyfall versagen können? Ein anderer, oft aus Noth gebrungen, ersetzt durch seine Kühnheit im Verändern, das, was ihm am Ausdruck der vorgeschriebenen Noten fehlet; nichts destoweniger erhebt ihn das Publicum vor jenem. Man will beynahe jeden Gedanken in der Wiederholung verändert wissen, ohne allezeit zu untersuchen, ob solches die Einrichtung des Stücks, und die Fähigkeit des Ausführers erlaubt. Bloß dieses Verändern, wenn es zumal mit einer langen und zuweilen gar zu sonderbar verzierten Cadenz begleitet ist, preßt oft den meisten Zuhörern das *Bravo* aus. Was entsteht nicht daher für ein Mißbrauch dieser zwo wirklichen Zierden der Ausführung! Man hat nicht mehr die Gedult, beym erstenmahle die vorgeschriebenen Noten zu spielen; das zu lange Ausbleiben des *Bravo* wird unerträglich. Oft sind diese unzeitigen Veränderungen wider den Satz, wider den Affect, und wider das Verhältnis des Gedanken unter sich; eine unangenehme Sache für manchen Componisten. Gesetzt aber, der Ausführer hat alle nöthige Eigenschaften, ein Stück so, wie es seyn soll, zu verändern: ist er auch allezeit dazu aufgelegt? Ereignen sich nicht bey unbekannten Sachen deswegen neue Schwierigkeiten? Ist nicht die Hauptabsicht beym verändern diese: daß der Ausführer sich und zugleich dem Stücke Ehre mache? Muß er nicht folglich beym zweytenmahle wenigstens eben so gute Gedanken vorbringen? Jedoch dieser Schwierigkeiten und des Mißbrauchs ohngeachtet, behalten die guten Veränderungen allezeit ihren Werth. Ich beziehe mich übrigens auf das, was ich am Ende des *ersten Theils meines Versuch* hiervon angeführt habe.

"Bey Verfertigung dieser Sonaten habe ich vornehmlich an Anfänger und solche Liebhaber gedacht, die wegen gewisser Jahre oder anderer Verrichtungen nicht mehr Gedult und Zeit genug haben, sich besonders stark zu üben. Ich habe ihnen bey der

Leichtigkeit zugleich auf eine bequeme Art das Vergnügen verschaffen wollen, sich mit Veränderungen hören zu lassen, ohne daß sie nöthig haben, solche entweder selbst zu erfinden, oder sich von andern vorschreiben zu lassen, und sie mit vieler Mühe auswendig zu lernen. Endlich habe ich alles, was zum guten Vortrage gehöret, ausdrücklich angedeutet, damit man diese Stücke, allenfalls auch bey einer nicht gar zu guten Disposition, mit aller Freyheit spielen könne.

"Ich freue mich, meines Wissens der erste zu seyn, der auf diese Art für den Nutzen und das Vergnügen seiner Gönner und Freunde gearbeitet hat. Wie glücklich bin ich, wenn man die besondere Lebhaftigkeit meiner Dienstgeflissenheit hieraus erkennet!"

At n. 63 (Schulz): "Man kann zu einer Folge von Harmonien, oder Accorden mehrere Melodien setzen, die alle nach den Regeln des harmonischen Satzes richtig sind. Wenn also eine Melodie von Sängern, oder Spielern wiederholt wird, so können sie das zweytemal vieles ganz anders, als das erstemal singen oder spielen, ohne die Regeln des Satzes zu verletzen; geübte Tonsetzer aber verfertigen bisweilen über einerley Harmonie mehrere Melodien, die mehr oder weniger den Charakter der ersten beybehalten: für beide Fälle braucht man das Wort Variation, das wir durch Veränderungen ausdrüken."

At n. 80 (Vogler): "Der erste Mann, der uns allgemeine Variationen gelehrt, der sie auf alle Instrumente verbreitet, der noch zum Verdienste Phraseologisch groß zu seyn, jenes, Gesänge und Themen selbst erfinden zu können, gesellet, ist der unnachahmliche Haydn. Er, ein wahrer Phöbus, dessen Arbeiten keiner fremden Wärme bedarfen, dessen Werke schon genug leuchten, ohne daß der von einem beliebten Satz geborgte Schimmer sie aufhelle, zeigte uns in Sinfonien, wie wir variiren sollen. Von keiner Vorliebe gehindert, durch keine Kurzsichtigkeit eingeschränkt war er gegen alle Instrumente gleich wohlthätig. Da er den Werth und die Würkung von allen genau kannte: so wies es jedem seinen Standpunkt an, um glänzen zu können, ohne je eines zu verdunkeln.

"Sein Schüler: Pleyel ahmte diesem großen Geist in Kleinen d.i. in Quartetten glüklich nach, selbst seine niedliche Klaviervariationen fanden Beifall. Doch konnte er keine solche Phraseologie aufstellen, wie der große Klavierspieler Mozart.

"Dieser Kraftmann, unerschöpflich in Wendungen, universel in Karakteren, pathetisch im *Adagio,* erschütternd im *Allegro,* der so viele Themen mit Veränderungen, fast darf ich sagen, verschwenderisch dotirt, zeigt in all diesen Geistesprodukten, wie man Einheit des aus- und fortzuführend Stofs mit der Mannichfaltigkeit in Phrasen verbinden könne; zeigt, wie abwechselnd im Karakter, wie eigenthümlich in der Spielart jede Veränderung seyn müsse, statt, daß H. F. [Herr Forkel] fast nie den ersten Takt strenge durchgeführt, keine einzige ungewöhnliche Spielart eingeführt und in manchen Veränderungen zu dreierlei, auch noch mehr Figuren seine Zuflucht ängstlich genommen hat."

At n. 90 (Koch): "Variationen, Variazioni. Man verstehet darunter einen mehrmalige unmittelbare Wiederholung eines kurzes Tonstücks, wobey die Melodie jedesmal durch Verschiedenheit der Zergliederungen ihrer Hauptnoten und der damit in Verbindung gebrachten durchgehenden und Nebennoten verändert wird, jedoch ohne dabey die Ähnlichkeit mit der Hauptmelodie ganz zu vermischen.

"Man bedient sich solcher Variationen sowohl als für sich verstehende Tonstücke zum Privat vergnügen, als auch in Verbindung mit andern Sätzen in grössern Tonstükken, wie z. B. in den Sonaten, Concerten, und Sinfonien.

"Sollen dergleichen Veränderungen gute Wirkung thun, so muß man 1) zu der zu variirenden Melodie einen cantabeln Gesang wählen, der schon an und für sich selbst Interesse hat, und der zugleich so beschaffen ist, daß er sich dem Gedächtnis leicht einprägt, 2) müssen die Veränderungen in Ansehung ihres besondern Characters abwechselnd seyn, das heisst, es dürfen nicht lauter schwärmende oder brillante Veränderungen unmittelbar aufeinander folgen, sondern zwischen zwey oder mehrere brillant muß immer wieder eine von sanftem Character eingeschoben werden, und 3) muß die Ähnlichkeit mit der Hauptmelodie in jeder Veränderung in so weit beybehalten werden, daß die Aufmerksamkeit des Zuhörers dadurch gefesselt wird; denn sobald diese Ähnlichkeit verloren gehet, sobald hört gemeiniglich auch das Interesse für die Veränderungen auf, und sie bekommen das Ansehen willkührlich an einander gereiheter Sätze, die nichts mit einander gemein haben, und von deren Daseyn und Folge man sich keinen Ursache denken kann."

Chapter 8

At n. 2 (Michaelis): "Die *Variation* kommt der Einförmigkeit, der Trivialität, kurz derjenigen Leere zuvor, durch welche eine Melodie leicht, wie man sagt, abgedroschen, abgenutzt oder zum Gassenhauer wird. Erscheint aber das Grundthema, die Hauptmelodie, *auf eine neue Art eingekleidet,* gleichsam unter einer zarten durchsichtigen Hülle, so gewinnt die Seele des Zuhörers an Vergnügen, indem sie selbstthätig durch den Schleier hindurchblickt, das Bekannte in den Unbekannten auffindet, und aus demselben ohne Anstrengung entwickelt.

"Die Variation beweist Freiheit der Phantasie in Behandlung des Gegenstandes, erregt angenehme Verwunderung, in neuen Formen die schon bekannte Schönheit, Anmuth oder Erhabenheit wieder zu erkennen, das Neue mit dem Alten reizend verschmolzen zu treffen, ohne dass jedoch hier eine abentheuerliche Vermischung heterogener Manieren Statt findet. Auch beschäftigt sie die Freiheit der Reflexion bey dem Zuhörer, der nun des Hauptgegenstandes sich erst recht bemächtigt zu haben weiss, wenn er denselben unter mancherley Umgebungen festzuhalten Anlass bekommt. Bewunderung erregt die Variation, in wiefern sie alles, was in einem Grundthema verborgen liegt, allmählich hervorruft und zur reizendsten Mannichfaltigkeit entfaltet."

Selected Bibliography

Omitted here are individual articles in The New Grove *(ed. Stanley Sadie, 20 vols. [London: Macmillan, 1980]); thematic catalogues; editions of music and their forewords and critical apparatus; and unpublished papers.*

Abert, Hermann. "Joseph Haydn's Klavierwerke." *ZfMw* 2 (1919–1920), 553–573; 3 (1920–1921), 535–552.

—— *W. A. Mozart.* 2 vols. Leipzig: Breitkopf & Härtel, 1919–1921.

Abrams, M. H. *The Mirror and the Lamp.* London: Oxford University Press, 1953.

Adlung, Jacob. *Anleitung zu der musikalischen Gelahrtheit.* Erfurt, 1758. Facsimile. Edited by Hans Joachim Moser. Kassel: Bärenreiter, 1953.

Adorno, Theodor. *Aesthetic Theory.* Translated by C. Lenhardt. Edited by Gretel Adorno and Rolf Tiedemann. London: Routledge and Kegan Paul, 1984.

Agawu, V. Kofi. "Concepts of Closure and Chopin's Opus 28." *Music Theory Spectrum* 9 (1987), 1–17.

—— *Playing with Signs: A Semiotic Interpretation of Classic Music.* Princeton: Princeton University Press, 1991.

Albrechtsberger, Johann Georg. *Gründliche Anweisung zur Composition.* Leipzig, 1790.

Aldrich, Putnam. "'Rhythmic Harmony' as Taught by Johann Philipp Kirnberger." In *Studies in Eighteenth-Century Music: A Tribute to Karl Geiringer on his Seventieth Birthday,* edited by H. C. Robbins Landon with Roger Chapman, pp. 37–52. New York: Oxford University Press, 1970.

Aristotle. *The "Art" of Rhetoric.* Translated by John Henry Freese. Loeb Classical Library. Cambridge, Mass.: Harvard University Press, 1925.

Arlt, Wulf. "Zur Handhabung der 'inventio' in der deutschen Musiklehre des frühen achtzehnten Jahrhunderts." In *New Mattheson Studies,* edited by George J. Buelow and Hans Joachim Marx, pp. 371–391. Cambridge: Cambridge University Press, 1983.

Arnold, F. T. *The Art of Accompaniment from a Thoroughbass as practiced in the XVIIth and XVIIIth Centuries.* London, 1931; New York: Dover, 1965.

Auerbach, Cornelia. *Die deutsche Clavichordkunst des 18. Jahrhunderts.* Leipzig: Universitätsverlag, 1930.

Auerbach, Erich. *Mimesis: The Representation of Reality in Western Literature.* Translated by Willard R. Trask. Princeton: Princeton University Press, 1953.

Bach, C. P. E. *Versuch über die wahre Art, das Clavier zu spielen.* 2 vols. Berlin, 1753–

1762. Facsimile. Leipzig: C. F. Kahnt Nachfolger, 1976. Translated and edited by William J. Mitchell as *Essay on the True Art of Playing Keyboard Instruments*. New York: W. W. Norton, 1949.

Baker, Nancy K. "From *Teil* to *Tonstück:* The Significance of the *Versuch einer Anleitung zur Composition* of Heinrich Christoph Koch." Ph.D. dissertation. Yale University, 1975.

———— "Heinrich Koch and the Theory of Melody." *JMT* 20 (1976), 1–48.

Barford, Philip. *The Keyboard Music of C. P. E. Bach.* London: Barrie and Rockliff, 1965.

———— "Some Afterthoughts by C. P. E. Bach." *MMR* 90 (1960), 94–98.

Barilli, Renato. *Rhetoric.* Translated by Giuliana Menozzi. Theory and History of Literature, vol. 63. Minneapolis: University of Minnesota Press, 1989.

Barthes, Roland. *The Semiotic Challenge,* translated by Richard Howard. New York: Hill and Wang, 1988.

Batta, Andréas, and Sandor Kovács. "Typbildung und Grossform in Beethovens frühen Klaviervariationen." *SM* 20 (1978), 125–156.

Beer, Johannes. *Musicalische Discurse.* Nuremberg, 1719. Facsimile. Leipzig: VEB Deutscher Verlag für Musik, 1982.

Beethoven, Ludwig van. *The Letters of Beethoven.* 3rd ed. Translated and edited by Emily Anderson. 3 vols. New York: W. W. Norton, 1985.

Benary, Peter. *Die deutsche Kompositionslehre des 18. Jahrhunderts.* Leipzig: Breitkopf & Härtel, 1961.

Bent, Ian. "Analytical Thinking in the First Half of the Nineteenth Century." In *Modern Musical Scholarship,* edited by Edward Olleson, pp. 151–166. Stocksfield, Northumberland: Oriel Press, 1980.

———— "The 'Compositional Process' in Music Theory, 1713–1850." *MusA* 3 (1984), 29–55.

Bent, Ian, with William Drabkin. *Analysis.* New York: W. W. Norton, 1987.

Berger, Karol. "The First-Movement Punctuation Form in Mozart's Piano Concertos." In *Mozart's Piano Concertos: Text, Context, Interpretation,* edited by Neal Zaslaw. Ann Arbor: University of Michigan Press, in press.

Bernhard, Christoph. *Tractatus compositionis augmentatus.* Edited by Joseph Müller-Blattau as *Die Kompositionslehre Heinrich Schützens in der Fassung seines Schülers Christoph Bernhard.* Kassel: Bärenreiter, 1926. Translated by Walter Hilse, "The Treatises of Christoph Bernhard." *MF* 3 (1973), 1–196.

Besseler, Heinrich. "Singstil und Instrumentalstil in der europäischen Musik." *Kongressbericht Bamberg 1953,* pp. 223–240. Kassel and Basel: Bärenreiter, 1954.

Beuermann, Erich H. "Die Reprisensonaten C. P. E. Bachs." *AfMw* 13 (1952), 168–179.

Black, Edwin. *Rhetorical Criticism: A Study in Method.* New York: Macmillan, 1965.

Blackall, Eric. *The Emergence of German as a Literary Language, 1700–1775.* 2nd ed. Ithaca, N.Y.: Cornell University Press, 1978.

Blair, Hugh. *Lectures on Rhetoric and Belles Lettres.* Rpt. New York, 1826.

Bonds, Mark Evan. "Haydn, Laurence Sterne, and the Origins of Musical Irony." *JAMS* 44 (1991), 57–91.

———— "Haydn's False Recapitulations and the Perception of Sonata Form in the Eighteenth Century." Ph.D. dissertation. Harvard University, 1988.

———— *Wordless Rhetoric: Musical Form and the Metaphor of the Oration.* Cambridge, Mass.: Harvard University Press, 1991.

Brandenburg, Sieghard. "Beethovens Skizzen zum zweiten Satz der 7. Symphonie op. 92." *Bericht über den internationalen musikwissenschaftlichen Kongress Bonn 1970,* edited by Carl Dahlhaus et al., pp. 355–357. Kassel: Bärenreiter, 1971.

Brandenburg, Sieghard, and Martin Staehelin. "Die 'erste Fassung' von Beethovens Righini-Variationen." In *Festschrift Albi Rosenthal,* edited by Rudolf Elvers, pp. 43–66. Tutzing: Hans Schneider, 1984.

Brandes, Heinz. *Studien zur musikalischen Figurenlehre im 16. Jahrhundert.* Berlin: Triltsch & Huther, 1935.

Braunbehrens, Volkmar. *Mozart in Vienna, 1781–1791.* Translated by Timothy Bell. New York: Grove Weidenfeld, 1989.

Brenet, Michel. *Les Concerts en France sous l'ancien régime.* Paris, 1900. Rpt. New York: Da Capo, 1970.

Brook, Barry S. *La Symphonie Française dans la seconde moitié du XVIIIe siècle.* 2 vols. Paris: Publications de l'institut de musicologie de l'université de Paris, 1962.

———— ed. *The Breitkopf Thematic Catalogue. The Six Parts and Sixteen Supplements, 1762–1787.* New York: Dover, 1966.

Brossard, Sebastien de. *Dictionaire de Musique.* 2nd ed. Paris, 1705. Facsimile. Hilversum: Fritz Knupf, 1966.

Brown, A. Peter. "Critical Years for Haydn's Instrumental Music." *MQ* 62 (1976), 374–394.

———— "Haydn and C. P. E. Bach: The Question of Influence." In *Haydn Studies,* edited by Jens Peter Larsen, Howard Serwer, and James Webster, pp. 158–164. New York: W. W. Norton, 1981.

———— *Joseph Haydn's Keyboard Music: Sources and Style.* Bloomington: Indiana University Press, 1986.

———— "The Chamber Music with Strings of Carlos d'Ordonez: A Bibliographic and Stylistic Study." *AM* 46 (1974), 222–72.

———— "The Structure of the Exposition in Haydn's Keyboard Sonatas." *MR* 36 (1975), 102–129.

———— "The Symphonies of Carlo d'Ordonez: A Contribution to the History of Viennese Instrumental Music during the Second Half of the Eighteenth Century." *HYb* 12 (1981), 5–121.

Brown, Howard Mayer. *Embellishing Sixteenth-Century Music.* London: Oxford University Press, 1976.

———— "Emulation, Competition, and Homage: Imitation and Theories of Imitation in the Renaissance." *JAMS* 35 (1982), 1–48.

Broyles, Michael. "The Two Instrumental Styles of Classicism." *JAMS* 36 (1983), 210–242.

Bryan, Paul Robey. "The Horn in the Works of Mozart and Haydn." *HYb* 9 (1975), 189–248.

Bücken, Ernst. *Musik des Rokokos und der Klassik.* Potsdam: Athenaion, 1931.

Budday, Wolfgang. *Grundlagen musikalischer Formen der Wiener Klassik: An Hand der zeitgenössischen Theorie von Joseph Riepel und Heinrich Christoph Koch dargestellt an Menuetten und Sonatensätze (1750–1790).* Kassel, Basel, and London: Bärenreiter, 1983.

Buelow, George J. "Music, Rhetoric, and the Concept of the Affections: A Selective Bibliography." *Notes* 30 (1973–74), 250–259.

———— "The Concept of 'Melodielehre': A Key to Classic Style." *MJb 1978/79,* 182–195.

——— "The *Loci Topici* and Affect in Late Baroque Music: Heinichen's Practical Demonstration." *MR* 27 (1966), 161–176.

Bukofzer, Manfred. "Allegory in Baroque Music." *Journal of the Warburg and Courtauld Institutes* 3 (1939–40), 1–21.

Burke, Edmund. *A Philosophical Enquiry into the Origin of our Ideas of the Sublime and Beautiful.* 2nd ed. (1759), edited by James T. Boulton. London, 1958; Notre Dame: Notre Dame University Press, 1968.

Burmeister, Joachim. *Musica poetica.* Rostock, 1606. Facsimile. Kassel: Bärenreiter, 1955.

Burney, Charles. *A General History of Music.* 4 vols. London, 1776–1789. Edited by Frank Mercer. 2nd ed. 2 vols. New York, 1935; rpt. New York: Dover, 1957.

Butler, Gregory G. "Fugue and Rhetoric." *JMT* 21 (1977), 49–109.

——— "Music and Rhetoric in Early Seventeenth-Century English Sources." *MQ* 66 (1980), 53–64.

——— "The Fantasia as Musical Image." *MQ* 60 (1974), 602–615.

Butt, John. "Improvised Vocal Ornamentation and German Baroque Compositional Theory: An Approach to 'Historical' Performance Practice." *JRMA* 116 (1991), 41–62.

Caplin, William E. "The 'Expanded Cadential Progression': A Category for the Analysis of Classical Form." *Journal of Musicological Research* 7 (1987), 215–257.

Carr, Thomas M., Jr. *Descartes and the Resilience of Rhetoric: Varieties of Cartesian Rhetorical Theory.* Carbondale and Edwardsville: University of Southern Illinois Press, 1990.

Cassirer, Ernst. *Kant's Life and Thought.* New Haven: Yale University Press, 1981; first pub. 1918.

Cavett-Dunsby, Esther. "Mozart's Codas." *MusA* 7 (1988), 31–51.

——— *Mozart's Variations Reconsidered: Four Case Studies (K. 613, K. 501, K. 421/417b, K. 491).* Ph.D. dissertation. University of London, 1985. New York: Garland, 1989.

Christmann, Johann Friedrich. *Elementarbuch der Tonkunst zum Unterricht beim Klavier für Lehrende und Lernende mit praktischen Beispielen. Eine musikalische Monatsschrift.* 2 vols. Speyer, 1782–1789.

Chrzanowski, Witold. *Das instrumentale Rondeau und die Rondoform im 18. Jahrhundert.* Leipzig, 1911.

Churgin, Bathia. "Francesco Galeazzi's Description (1796) of Sonata Form." *JAMS* 21 (1968), 181–199.

Cicero, *De inventione.* Translated by H. M. Hubbell. Loeb Classical Library, vol. 386 [Cicero vol. II]. Cambridge, Mass.: Harvard University Press, 1949.

——— *Orator.* Translated by H. M. Hubbell. Loeb Classical Library, vol. 342 [Cicero V]. Cambridge, Mass., and London: Harvard University Press, 1939.

Cole, Malcolm S. "Mozart Rondo Finales with Changes of Meter and Tempo." *SM* 16 (1974), 25–53.

——— "The Rondo Finale: Evidence for the Mozart-Haydn Exchange?" *MJb 1968/70,* 242–256.

——— "The Vogue of the Instrumental Rondo in the Late Eighteenth Century." *JAMS* 22 (1969), 425–455.

Cone, Edward T. *Music: A View from Delft. Selected Essays.* Edited by Robert P. Morgan. Chicago: University of Chicago Press, 1989.

——— "On Derivation: Syntax and Rhetoric." *MusA* 6 (1987), 237–255.

Cowart, Georgia. "Critical Language and Musical Thought in the Seventeenth and Eighteenth Centuries." *College Music Symposium* 27 (1987), 14–29.

———— The Origins of Modern Musical Criticism: French and Italian Music, 1600–1750. Ann Arbor: UMI Research Press, 1981.

Czerny, Carl. L'Art d'improviser. Paris [1836].

———— On the Proper Performance of All Beethoven's Works for the Piano. Edited by Paul Badura-Skoda. Vienna: Universal, 1970.

Dabney, J. P. The Musical Basis of Verse. New York: Longmans, Green, 1901.

Dahlhaus, Carl. Between Romanticism and Modernism: Four Studies in the Music of the Later Nineteenth Century. Translated by Mary Whittall. Berkeley and Los Angeles: University of California Press, 1980.

———— "Der rhetorische Formbegriff H. Chr. Kochs und die Theorie der Sonatenform." AfMw 35 (1978), 155–177.

———— Ludwig van Beethoven: Approaches to His Music. Translated by Mary Whittall. Oxford: Clarendon Press, 1991.

———— Nineteenth-Century Music. Translated by J. Bradford Robinson. Berkeley and Los Angeles: University of California Press, 1989.

Dammann, Rolf. Der Musikbegriff im deutschen Barock. Cologne: Arno Volk, 1967.

Daube, Johann Friedrich. Anleitung zur Erfindung der Melodie. Vienna, 1797–1798.

———— Der musikalische Dilettant. Eine Abhandlung der Komposition. Vienna, 1773.

Derr, Ellwood. "Beethoven's Long-Term Memory of C. P. E. Bach's Rondo in E Flat, W. 61/1 (1787), Manifest in the Variations in E Flat for Piano, Opus 35 (1802)." MQ 70 (1984), 45–76.

Dewitz, Margarethe von. Jean Baptiste Vanhal, Leben und Klavierwerke. Ein Beitrag zur Wiener Klassik. Munich: Salesinianischen Offizin, 1933.

Dies, Albert Christoph. Biographische Nachrichten von Joseph Haydn. Vienna, 1810. Edited by Horst Seeger. Berlin: Henschelverlag, 1959.

Dunsby, Jonathan. "The Formal Repeat." JRMA 112 (1986/87), 196–207.

Eitner, Lorenz. "Cages, Prisons, and Captives in Eighteenth-Century Art." In Images of Romanticism: Verbal and Visual Affinities, edited by Karl Kroeber and William Walling, pp. 13–38. New Haven: Yale University Press, 1978.

Ellison, Julie. Emerson's Romantic Style. Princeton: Princeton University Press, 1984.

Erasmus. De duplici copia rerum ac verborum commentarii duo. Paris, 1512–1534. Modern critical trans. and ed. by Betty I. Knott, Copia: Foundations of the Abundant Style, in Collected Works of Erasmus, Literary and Educational Writings 2, edited by Craig R. Thompson. Toronto: University of Toronto Press, 1978.

Erlich, Victor. Russian Formalism: History-Doctrine. 3rd ed. New Haven and London: Yale University Press, 1965; preface, 1981.

Espy, Willard R. The Garden of Eloquence: A Rhetorical Bestiary. New York: Harper & Row, 1983.

Feder, Georg. "Apokryphe 'Haydn'-Streichquartette." HSt 3 (1974), 125–150.

———— "Bemerkungen über die Ausbildung in der klassischen Tonsprache in der Instrumentalmusik Haydns." International Musicological Society, Report of the Eighth Congress, New York, 1961, pp. 305–313. Kassel: Bärenreiter, 1961.

———— "Die beiden Pole im Instrumentalschaffen des jungen Haydns." In Der junge Haydn, edited by Vera Schwarz, pp. 192–201. Graz: Akademische Druck- und Verlagsanstalt, 1972.

———— "Similarities in the Works of Haydn." In Studies in Eighteenth-Century Music: A Tribute to Karl Geiringer on His Seventieth Birthday, edited by H. C. Robbins Landon with Roger Chapman, pp. 186–197. New York: Oxford University Press, 1970.

———— "Stilelemente Haydns in Beethovens Werken." Bericht über den internationalen mu-

sikwissenschaftlichen Kongress Bonn 1970, edited by Carl Dahlhaus et al., pp. 65–70. Kassel: Bärenreiter, 1971.

——— "Zur Datierung Haydnscher Werke." In *Anthony van Hoboken. Festschrift zum 75. Geburtstag,* edited by Joseph Schmidt-Görg, pp. 50–54. Mainz: B. Schott's Söhne, 1962.

Federhofer, Hellmut. "Mozart als Schüler und Lehrer in der Musiktheorie." *MJb 1971/72,* 89–106.

——— "Mozart und die Musiktheorie seiner Zeit." *MJb 1978/79,* 172–175.

Fellinger, Imogen. "Mattheson als Begründer der ersten Musikzeitschrift *(Critica musica)."* In *New Mattheson Studies,* edited by George J. Buelow and Hans Joachim Marx, pp. 179–197. Cambridge: Cambridge University Press, 1983.

Ferand, Ernest R. "Didactic Embellishment Literature in the Late Renaissance: A Survey of Sources." In *Aspects of Medieval and Renaissance Music,* edited by Jan LaRue, pp. 154–172. New York: Norton, 1966.

Ferand, Ernest T. *Improvisation in Nine Centuries of Western Music.* Anthology of Music, vol. 12. Cologne: Arno Volk, 1961.

Fillion, Michelle. "Eine bisher unbekannte Quelle für Haydns frühes Klaviertrio Hob. XV:C1." *HSt* 5 (1982), 59–63.

——— "The Accompanied Keyboard Divertimenti of Haydn and his Viennese Contemporaries." Ph.D. dissertation. Cornell University, 1982.

Finscher, Ludwig. "Das Originalgenie und die Tradition. Zum Rolle der Tradition in der Entwicklungsgeschichte des Wiener klassischen Stils." In *Studien zur Tradition in der Musik. Kurt von Fischer zum 60. Geburtstag,* edited by Hans Heinrich Eggebrecht and Max Lütolf, pp. 165–176. Munich: Emil Katzbichler, 1973.

——— *Studien zur Geschichte des Streichquartetts. I: Die Entstehung des klassischen Streichquartetts: Von den Vorformen zur Grundlegung durch Joseph Haydn.* Kassel, 1974.

Fischer, Kurt von. "Arietta Variata." In *Studies in Eighteenth-Century Music: A Tribute to Karl Geiringer on His Seventieth Birthday,* edited by H. C. Robbins Landon with Roger Chapman, pp. 224–235. New York: Oxford University Press, 1970.

——— "Bemerkungen zu Beethovens Variationenwerken." *International Musicological Society, Report of the Fourth Congress, Basel 1949,* pp. 111–113. Basel: Bärenreiter, 1949.

——— "C. Ph. E. Bachs Variationenwerke." *Revue Belge de Musicologie* 6 (1952): 190–218.

——— "Eroica-Variationen op. 35 und Eroica-Finale." *Schweizerische Musikzeitung* 89 (1949), 282–286.

——— "Mozarts Klaviervariationen." In *Hans Albrecht in Memoriam,* edited by Wilfried Brennecke and Hans Hasse, pp. 168–173. Kassel and New York: Bärenreiter, 1962.

——— *The Variation.* Anthology of Music, vol. 11. Cologne: Arno Volk, 1966.

——— "Zur Theorie der Variation im 18. und beginnenden 19. Jahrhundert." *Festschrift Joseph Schmidt-Görg zum 60. Geburtstag,* edited by Dagmar Weise, pp. 117–130. Bonn: Beethovenhaus, 1957.

Fischer, Wilhelm. "Instrumentalmusik von 1750–1828." In *Handbuch der Musikgeschichte,* edited by Guido Adler. 3 vols. 2nd ed. Berlin, 1930; rpt. Tutzing: Hans Schneider, 1961; Munich: Deutscher Taschenbuch, 1977. Vol. III, pp. 795–833.

——— "Stilkritische Anhang." In Adolf Schnerich, *Joseph Haydn und seine Sendung,* pp. 225–262. Zürich-Leipzig-Vienna: Amalthea-Verlag, 1926.

Fisher, Stephen C. "Haydn's Overtures and Their Adaptations as Concert Orchestral Works." Ph.D. dissertation. University of Pennsylvania, 1985.

———— "Sonata Procedures in Haydn's Symphonic Rondo Finales of the 1770s." In *Haydn Studies,* edited by Jens Peter Larsen et al., pp. 481–487. New York: W. W. Norton, 1981.

Floros, Constantin. *Beethovens Eroica und Prometheus-Musik. Sujet-Studien.* Veröffentlichungen zur Musikforschung, 3. Wilhelmshaven: Heinrichshofen, 1978.

Flothuis, Marius. "Bühne und Konzert." *MJb 1986,* 45–58.

Flotzinger, Rudolf. "Die Barocke Doppelgerüst-Technik im Variationsschaffen Beethovens." In *Beethoven-Studien. Festgabe der Österreichische Akademie der Wissenschaften zum 200. Geburtstag von Ludwig van Beethoven,* pp. 159–194. Veröffentlichung der Kommission für Musikforschung, II. Vienna: Hermann Böhlaus Nachfolger, 1970.

Forkel, Johann Nikolaus. *Allgemeine Geschichte der Musik.* 2 vols. Leipzig, 1788–1801.

Forschner, Hermann. *Instrumentalmusik Joseph Haydns aus der Sicht Heinrich Christoph Kochs.* Beiträge zur Musikforschung, 13. Munich-Salzburg: Emil Katzbichler, 1984.

Framery, Nicolas-Étienne, Pierre-Louis Ginguené, and Jérôme-Joseph de Momigny. *Encyclopédie méthodique: Musique.* 2 vols. Paris, 1791–1818. Rpt. New York: Da Capo, 1971.

Freeman, Robert N. "Zwei Melker Musikkataloge aus der zweiten Hälfte des 18. Jahrhunderts." *Mf 23* (1970), 176–184.

Fuhrmann, Roderick. "Mannheimer Klavier-Kammermusik." Ph. D. dissertation. Marburg, 1963.

Fussell, Paul. *Poetic Meter and Poetic Form.* Rev. ed. New York: Random House, 1979.

Geiringer, Karl. *Joseph Haydn: A Creative Life in Music.* 3rd ed. Berkeley and Los Angeles: University of California Press, 1982.

Geminiani, Francesco. *The Art of Accompaniment.* London, 1755.

Genette, Gérard. *Figures of Literary Discourse.* Translated by Alan Sheridan. Introduction by Marie-Rose Logan. New York: Columbia University Press, 1982.

Gerber, Ernst Ludwig. *Neues historisch-biographisches Lexicon der Tonkünstler.* 4 vols. Leipzig, 1812–1813.

Gericke, Hannelore. *Der Wiener Musikalienhandel von 1700 bis 1778.* Graz: Hermann Böhlaus Nachfolger, 1960.

Gerlach, Sonja. "Die chronologische Ordnung von Haydns Sinfonien zwischen 1774 und 1782." *HSt 2* (1969–70), 34–66.

Gerstenberg, Walter. "Generalbasslehre und Kompositionslehre in Niedtens *Musicalische Handleitung.*" In *Bericht über den internationale musikwissenschaftlichen Kongress Bamberg 1953,* pp. 152–155. Kassel and Basel: Bärenreiter, 1954.

Gibbons, Thomas. *Rhetoric; or, a View of its Principal Tropes and Figures, in the Origin and Powers: with a variety of Rules to escape Errors and Blemishes, and attain Propriety and Elegance in Composition.* London, 1767.

Girdlestone, Cuthbert. *Mozart and His Piano Concertos.* New York: Dover, 1964.

Gombrich, E. H. *The Sense of Order: A Study in the Psychology of Decorative Art.* Ithaca, N.Y.: Cornell University Press, 1979.

Goodman, Nelson, and Catherine Z. Elgin. *Reconceptions in Philosophy and Other Arts and Sciences.* Indianapolis and Cambridge: Hackett, 1988.

Gottsched, Johann Christoph. *Ausführliche Redekunst.* Leipzig, 1736; 5th ed., 1759. Modern edition by Rosemary Scholl, *Johann Christoph Gottsched Ausgewählte Werke,* vol. 7. Berlin and New York: De Gruyter, 1975.

Gotwals, Vernon, trans. and ed. *Haydn: Two Contemporary Portraits.* Madison: University of Wisconsin Press, 1968.

Grant, Kerry S. *Dr. Burney as Critic and Historian of Music*. Ann Arbor: UMI Research Press, 1983.

Grassineau, James. *A Musical Dictionary*. London, 1740. Facsimile. New York: Broude Brothers, 1966.

Grave, Floyd K. "'Rhythmic Harmony' in Mozart." *MR* 41 (1980), 87–102.

Grave, Floyd K., and Margaret G. Grave. *In Praise of Harmony: The Teachings of Abbé Georg Joseph Vogler*. Lincoln: University of Nebraska Press, 1987.

Griesinger, Georg August. *Biographische Notizen über Joseph Haydn*. Leipzig, 1810. Facsimile. Leipzig: VEB Deutscher Verlag für Musik, 1979.

Gruber, Gernot. "Musikalische Rhetorik und barock Bildlichkeit in Kompositionen des jungen Haydn." In *Der junge Haydn,* edited by Vera Schwarz, pp. 192–201. Graz: Akademische Druck- und Verlagsanstalt, 1972.

Gurlitt, Willibald. "Musik und Rhetorik." *Helicon* 5 (1943), 67–86.

Guyer, Paul. *Kant and the Claims of Taste*. Cambridge, Mass.: Harvard University Press, 1979.

Harrison, Daniel. "Rhetoric and Fugue: An Analytical Application." *Music Theory Spectrum* 12 (1990), 1–42.

Haydn, Joseph. *Gesammelte Briefe und Aufzeichnungen,* edited by Dénes Bartha. Kassel: Bärenreiter, 1965.

Heartz, Daniel. "Thomas Attwood's Lessons in Composition with Mozart." *PRMA* 100 (1974), 175–183.

Heinichen, Johann David. *Der General-Bass in der Composition*. Dresden, 1728. Facsimile. Hildesheim: G. Olms, 1969.

Henderson, Judith Rice. "Erasmus on the Art of Letter-Writing." In *Renaissance Eloquence: Studies in the Theory and Practice of Renaissance Rhetoric,* edited by James J. Murphy, pp. 331–355. Berkeley, Los Angeles, and London: University of California Press, 1983.

Henneberg, Gudrun. "Heinrich Christoph Koch's Analysen von Instrumentalwerken Joseph Haydns." *HSt* 4 (1978), 105–112.

Herbst, Andreas. *Musica poetica*. Nürnberg, 1643.

Hess, Reimund. "Serenade, Cassation, Notturno und Divertimento bei Michael Haydn." Ph.D. dissertation. Mainz, 1963.

Hess, Willy. "Von Dressler bis Diabelli (Die Entwicklung der Variationentechnik Beethovens)." In *Beethoven-Studien,* pp. 72–79. Bonn: Beethovenhaus, 1972.

Heuschneider, Karin. *The Piano Sonata of the Eighteenth Century in Germany*. Cape Town: A. A. Balkema, 1970.

Hildesheimer, Wolfgang. *Mozart*. Translated by Marion Faber. New York: Vintage, 1983.

Hill, George R. "The Concert Symphonies of Florian Leopold Gassman." Ph.D. dissertation. New York University, 1975.

Hiller, Johann Adam. *Wöchentliche Nachrichten, die Musik betreffend*. Leipzig, 1767.

Hoffmann-Erbrecht, Lothar. *Deutsche und italienische Klaviermusik zur Bachzeit. Studien zur Thematik und Themenverarbeitung in der Zeit von 1720–1760*. Jenaer Beiträge zur Musikforschung 1. Leipzig: Breitkopf & Härtel, 1954.

Horsley, Imogene. "Improvised Embellishment in the Performance of Renaissance Polyphonic Music." *JAMS* 4 (1951), 3–19.

Hörwarthner, Maria. "Joseph Haydns Bibliothek—Versuch einer literarhistorischen Rekonstruktion." In *Joseph Haydn und die Literatur seiner Zeit,* edited by Herbert Zeman (*JbÖK* 6 [1976]), pp. 157–207.

Hosler, Bellamy. *Changing Aesthetic Views of Instrumental Music in Eighteenth-Century Germany*. Ann Arbor: UMI Research Press, 1981.

Huber, Eva. "Zur Sozialstruktur der Wiener Logen im Josephinischen Jahrzehnt." In *Aufklärung und Geheimgesellschaften: Zur politischen Function und Sozialstruktur der Freimaurerlogen im 18. Jahrhundert,* edited by Helmut Reinalter, pp. 173–187. Munich, 1989.

Huizinga, Jan. *Homo Ludens: A Study of the Play-Element in Culture*. Boston: Beacon Press, 1955; first pub. c. 1950.

Hurwitz, Joachim. "Joseph Haydn and Freemasonry." *HYb* 16 (1985), 5–98.

Huschke, Konrad. "Beethovens pianistische Wettkämpfe." *Allgemeine Musikzeitung* 60 (1933), 518–520.

Hutchings, Arthur. *A Companion to Mozart's Piano Concertos*. Oxford: Oxford University Press, 1948.

Jäger, Georg. "Zur literarischen Gymnasialbildung in Österreich von der Aufklärung bis zum Vormärz." In *Die österreichische Literatur: ihr Profil an der Wende vom 18. zum 19. Jahrhundert (1750–1830),* edited by Herbert Zeman *(JbÖK* 7–9 [1977–79]), pp. 85–118.

Jameson, Fredric. *The Prison-House of Language: A Critical Account of Structuralism and Russian Formalism*. Princeton: Princeton University Press, 1972.

Jander, Owen. "Romantic Form and Content in the Slow Movement of Beethoven's Violin Concerto." *MQ* 69 (1983), 159–179.

Jenner, Gustav. *Johannes Brahms als Mensch, Lehrer, und Künstler*. Marburg: Elwert, 1905.

Johnson, Douglas. "Beethoven's Early Sketches in the 'Fischhof Miscellany.'" Ph.D. dissertation. University of California, Berkeley, 1978.

———— "1794–1795: Decisive Years in Beethoven's Early Development." In *Beethoven Studies* 3, edited by Alan Tyson, pp. 1–28. Cambridge: Cambridge University Press, 1982.

Kahl, Willi. *Selbstbiographien Deutscher Musiker des 18. Jahrhunderts*. Facsimiles of Early Biographies 5. Amsterdam: Staufen-Verlag, 1972.

Kant, Immanuel. *Observations on the Feeling of the Beautiful and Sublime*. Translated by John T. Goldthwait. Berkeley, Los Angeles, Oxford: University of California Press, 1960; 1991.

———— *Critique of Judgment*. Translated by J. H. Bernard. 2nd ed. London: Macmillan, 1914.

Karbaum, Michael. "Das theoretische Werk Johann Friedrich Daubes: ein Beitrag zur Kompositionslehre des 18. Jahrhunderts." Ph.D. dissertation. University of Vienna, 1968.

Keller, Fritz. "Rhetorik in der Ordensschule. 'Palatium Rhetoricae' von Michael Denis: Ein didaktische Epos—seine literarische Tradition, künstlerische Gestaltung und sein Verhältnis zum zeitgenössischen Rhetorikunterricht bei den Jesuiten." In *Die österreichische Literatur,* ed. Herbert Zeman *(JbÖK* 7–9 [1977–79]), pp. 55–83.

Keller, Hermann. "Vieni Amore . . ." *Neue Zeitschrift für Musik* 122 (1961), 230–232.

Kellner, David. *Treulicher Unterricht im General-Bass*. 2nd enl. ed. Preface by Georg Philipp Telemann. Hamburg, 1737.

Kemmler, Erwin. *Johann Gottfried Müthel (1728–1788) und das Nordostdeutsche Musikleben seiner Zeit*. Wissenschaftliche Beiträge zur Geschichte und Landeskunde Ost-Mitteleuropas, vol. 88. Marburg: Lahn, 1970.

Kennedy, George A. *Classical Rhetoric and Its Christian and Secular Tradition from Ancient to Modern Times*. Chapel Hill: University of North Carolina Press, 1980.

Kerman, Joseph. *The Beethoven Quartets.* New York: W. W. Norton, 1966.

Kerman, Joseph, and Alan Tyson. *The New Grove Beethoven.* New York: W. W. Norton, 1983.

Kimbell, David R. B. "Variation Form in the Piano Concertos of Mozart." *MR* 44 (1984), 95–103.

Kinderman, William. *Beethoven's Diabelli Variations.* Oxford: Clarendon Press, 1987.

——— "Tonality and Form in the Variation Movements of Beethoven's Late Quartets." In *Beiträge zu Beethovens Kammermusik. Symposion Bonn 1984,* edited by Sieghard Brandenburg and Helmut Loos, pp. 135–151. Munich: G. Henle, 1987.

Kirkendale, Ursula. "The Source for Bach's *Musical Offering:* The *Instituto oratoria* of Quintilian." *JAMS* 33 (1980), 88–141.

Kirkendale, Warren. "Ciceronians versus Aristotelians on the Ricercar as Exordium, from Bembo to Bach." *JAMS* 32 (1979), 1–44.

——— *Fugue and Fugato in Rococo and Classical Chamber Music.* 2nd rev. ed., translated by Margaret Bent and the author. Durham: Duke University Press, 1979.

Kirnberger, Johann Philipp. *Die Kunst des reinen Satzes in der Musik,* 2 vols. Berlin and Königsberg, 1771–79. Translated by David Beach and Jürgen Thym, *The Art of Strict Musical Composition.* New Haven and London: Yale University Press, 1982.

Klein, Rudolf. "Wo kann die Analysen von Haydns Symphonik ansetzen?" *ÖMz* 37 (1982), 234–241.

Klingenbeck, Josef. "Ignaz Pleyel. Sein Streichquartett im Rahmen der Wiener Klassik." *Studien zur Musikwissenschaft* 25 (1967), 276–297.

Koch, Heinrich Christoph. *Musikalisches Lexikon.* Frankfurt am Main, 1802. Rpt. Hildesheim: G. Olms, 1964.

——— *Versuch einer Anleitung zur Composition.* 3 vols. Rudolstadt and Leipzig, 1782–1793. Rpt. Hildesheim: G. Olms, 1969. Translated by Nancy K. Baker as *Introductory Essay on Composition.* New Haven and London: Yale University Press, 1983.

Köhler, Karl-Heinz. "Zur Bewertung der Korrekturen und Provenienznachweise im Autograph zum Klavierkonzert KV 450: Ein Beitrag zu Mozarts Kompositionsweise 1784." *MJb 1984/85,* 52–61.

Kollmann, Augustus Frederick Christopher. *An Essay on Musical Composition.* London, 1799. Facsimile, with an introduction by Imogene Horsley. New York: Da Capo, 1973.

——— *An Essay on Musical Harmony.* London, 1796; Utica, N.Y., 1817.

Kolneder, Walter. "Evolutionismus und Schaffenschronologie: Zu Beethovens Righini-Variationen." In *Studien zur Musikgeschichte des Rheinlandes II. Karl Gustav Fellerer zum 60. Geburtstag,* edited by Herbert Drux et al., pp. 119–132. Beiträge zur Rheinischer Musikgeschichte 52. Cologne: Arno Volk, 1962.

Komlós, Katalin. "'Ich praeludirte und spielte Variazionen': Mozart the fortepianist." In *Perspectives on Mozart Performance,* edited by R. Larry Todd and Peter Williams, pp. 27–54. Cambridge: Cambridge University Press, 1991.

——— "Mozart and Clementi: A Piano Competition and Its Interpretation." *Historical Performance* 3 (1989), 3–9.

——— "The Viennese Keyboard Trio in the 1780s: Sociological Background and Contemporary Reception." *ML* 68 (1987), 222–234.

Konold, Wulf. "Normerfüllung und Normverweigerung beim späten Haydn—am Beispiel des Streichquartetts op. 76 Nr. 6." In *Joseph Haydn: Tradition und Rezeption.*

Bericht über die Jahrestagung der Gesellschaft für Musikforschung Köln 1982, edited by Georg Feder, Heinrich Hüschen, and Ulrich Tank, pp. 54–73. Regensburg: Gustave Bosse, 1985.

Korcak, Friedrich. "Luigi Tomasini (1741–1808). Konzertmeister der fürstlich Ester-hazyschen Kapelle in Eisenstadt unter Joseph Haydn." Ph.D. dissertation. University of Vienna, 1952.

Kramer, Lawrence. *Music and Poetry: The Nineteenth Century and After.* Berkeley and Los Angeles: University of California Press, 1984.

Kramer, Richard A. "Beethoven and Carl Heinrich Graun." In *Beethoven Studies,* edited by Alan Tyson, pp. 18–44. New York: W. W. Norton, 1973.

Krones, Hartmut. "Rhetorik und rhetorische Symbolik in der Musik um 1800. Vom Weiterleben eines Prinzip." *Musiktheorie* 3 (1988), 117–140.

Kunze, Stefan. "Anton Reichas 'Entwurf einer phrasirten Fuge.' Zum Kompositions-begriff im frühen 19. Jahrhundert." *AfMw* 25 (1968), 289–307.

———— "Die 'wirklich gantz neue Manier' in Beethovens Eroica-Variationen op. 35." *AfMw* 29 (1972), 124–149.

Küthen, Hans-Werner. "Beethoven's 'wirklich ganz neue Manier'—Eine Persiflage." In *Beiträge zu Beethovens Kammermusik. Symposion Bonn 1984,* edited by Sieghard Bran-denburg and Helmut Loos, pp. 216–224. Munich: G. Henle, 1987.

LaCapra, Dominick. *History and Criticism.* Ithaca, N.Y.: Cornell University Press, 1985.

La Laurencie, Lionel de. *L'École Française de violon de Lully à Viotti. Études d'histoire et d'esthetique.* 3 vols. Paris: Librairie Delagrave, 1922–1924.

Landon, H. C. Robbins, trans. and ed. *The Complete Correspondence and London Note-books of Joseph Haydn.* London: Barrie & Rockliff, 1959.

———— *Haydn: Chronicle and Works.* 5 vols. Bloomington and London: University of Indiana Press, 1976–1980.

———— ed. *The Mozart Compendium: A Guide to Mozart's Life and Music.* New York: Schirmer, 1990.

———— *Mozart and the Masons: New Light on the Lodge "Crowned Hope."* London: Thames and Hudson, 1989.

———— *The Symphonies of Joseph Haydn.* London: Barrie & Rockliff, 1955.

Lanham, Richard. *A Handlist of Rhetorical Terms.* 2nd ed. Berkeley and Los Angeles: University of California Press, 1991.

———— *The Motives of Eloquence: Literary Rhetoric in the Renaissance.* Berkeley and Los Angeles: University of California Press, 1974.

Larsen, Jens Peter. *Essays on Handel, Haydn, and the Viennese Classical Style,* translated by Ulrich Krämer. Ann Arbor: UMI Research Press, 1988.

———— *The New Grove Haydn.* Work-list by Georg Feder. New York: W. W. Norton, 1983.

———— *Three Haydn Catalogues.* New York: Pendragon Press, 1979.

Larsen, Jens Peter, Howard Serwer, and James Webster, eds. *Haydn Studies: Proceedings of the International Haydn Conference, Washington, D.C. 1975.* New York: Norton, 1981.

Layer, Adolf. *Eine Jugend in Augsburg—Leopold Mozart 1719–1737.* Augsburg: Die Brigg [1975].

Lee, Douglas. "Some Embellished Versions of Sonatas by Franz Benda." *MQ* 62 (1976), 58–71.

Le Huray, Peter, and James Day, eds. *Music and Aesthetics in the Eighteenth and Early-Nineteenth Centuries.* Cambridge: Cambridge University Press, 1981.

Leux, Irmgard. *Christian Gottlob Neefe (1748–1798).* Leipzig: Fr. Kistner & C. F. W. Siegel, 1925.

Levy, Janet. "Covert and Casual Values in Recent Writings about Music." *JM* 5 (1987), 3–27.

Lippman, Edward A. "The Problem of Musical Hermeneutics: A Protest and Analysis." In *Art and Philosophy: Proceedings of the Seventh Annual New York University Institute of Philosophy 1964,* edited by Sidney Hook, pp. 307–353. New York: New York University Press, 1966.

Lockwood, Lewis. *Beethoven: Studies in the Creative Process.* Cambridge, Mass.: Harvard University Press, 1992.

Loesser, Arthur. *Men, Women, and Pianos: A Social History.* New York: Simon & Schuster, 1954.

Löhlein, Georg Simon. *Clavier-Schule; oder kurze und gründliche Anweisung zur Melodie und Harmonie.* 3rd ed. Leipzig, 1779.

London, Justin. "Riepel and *Absatz*: Poetic and Prosaic Aspects of Phrase Structure in 18th-Century Theory." *JM* 8 (1990), 505–519.

Longinus. *On the Sublime,* translated by T. S. Dorsch. Middlesex: Penguin, 1965.

Longyear, Rey M. *Schiller and Music.* University of North Carolina Studies in the Germanic Languages and Literatures, no. 54. Chapel Hill: University of North Carolina Press, 1966.

Macdonald, Hugh. "Fantasy and Order in Beethoven's Phantasie Op. 77." In *Modern Musical Scholarship,* edited by Edward Olleson, pp. 141–150. Stocksfield, Northumberland: Oriel Press, 1980.

Maniates, Maria Rika. "Music and Rhetoric: Faces of Cultural History in the Renaissance and Baroque." *Israel Studies in Musicology* 2 (1982), 44–69.

Manley, Lawrence. *Convention: 1500–1750.* Cambridge, Mass.: Harvard University Press, 1980.

Marpurg, Friedrich Wilhelm. *Anfangsgründe der theoretischen Musik.* Leipzig, 1757. Facsimile. New York: Broude, 1966.

——— *Anleitung zum Clavierspielen.* 2nd ed. Berlin, 1765. Facsimile. Hildesheim: G. Olms, 1970.

Marston, Nicholas. "Analysing Variations: The Finale of Beethoven's String Quartet op. 74." *MusA* 8 (1989), 303–324.

Marx, Adolf Bernhard. *Die Lehre von der musikalischen Composition.* 4 vols. Leipzig, 1837–1847.

Marx, Hans Joachim. "Some Unknown Embellishments of Corelli's Violin Sonatas." *MQ* 61 (1975), 65–76.

Masurowicz, Ulrich. *Das Streichduett in Wien von 1760 bis zum Tode Joseph Haydns.* Tutzing: Hans Schneider, 1982.

Matthäus, Wolfgang. *Johann André. Musikverlag zu Offenbach am Main. Verlagsgeschichte und Bibliographie 1772–1800.* Tutzing: Hans Schneider, 1973.

Mattheson, Johann. *Der vollkommene Capellmeister.* Hamburg, 1739. Facsimile. Edited by Margarete Reimann. Kassel: Bärenreiter, 1969. Translated by Ernest C. Harriss as *Johann Mattheson's Der vollkommene Capellmeister.* Ann Arbor: UMI Research Press, 1981.

——— *Große General-Baß-Schule.* Hamburg, 1731.

——— *Kern melodischer Wissenschaft.* Hamburg, 1737.

McKeon, Zahava Karl. *Novels and Arguments: Inventing Rhetorical Criticism.* Chicago: University of Chicago Press, 1982.

Meier, Adolf. *Konzertante Musik für Kontrabass in der Wiener Klassik, mit Beiträgen zur Geschichte des Kontrabassbaues in Österreich.* Giebing über Prien am Chiemsee: Emil Katzbichler, 1969.

Melkus, Eduard. "Auszierung einer da capo Arie von Mozart." *Mozart-Jahrbuch 1968–70,* 159–185.

Méreaux, Amédée, ed. *Les Clavecinistes de 1637 à 1790.* Paris, 1867.

Meyer, Eve Rose. "Florian Gassmann and the Viennese Divertimento." Ph.D. dissertation. University of Pennsylvania, 1963.

——— "The Viennese Divertimento." *MR* 24 (1968), 165–171.

Meyer, Herman. "Schillers philosophische Rhetorik." In *Zarte Empirie,* pp. 337–389. Stuttgart: J. B. Metzler, 1963.

Meyer, Leonard B. *Explaining Music: Essays and Explorations.* Chicago and London: University of Chicago Press, 1973.

Michaelis, C. F. "Ueber die musikalische Wiederholung und Veränderung." *AMZ* 13 (1803), cols. 197–200.

Mies, Paul. "Ludwig van Beethoven's Werke über seinen Kontretanz in Es-Dur." *Beethoven-Jahrbuch* 1 (1954), 80–102.

——— "W. A. Mozarts Variationenwerke und ihre Formungen." *Archiv für Musikforschung* 2 (1937), 466–495.

Miller, J. Hillis. *Fiction and Repetition: Seven English Novels.* Cambridge, Mass.: Harvard University Press, 1982.

Misch, Ludwig. "Fugue and Fugato in Beethoven's Variation Form." *MQ* 42 (1956), 14–27.

Momigny, Jérôme-Joseph de. *Cours complet d'harmonie et de composition.* Paris, 1803.

Monk, Dennis. "Style Change in the Slow Movement of the Viennese Symphony." Ph.D. dissertation. University of California, Los Angeles, 1970.

Morrow, Mary Sue. *Concert Life in Haydn's Vienna: 1760–1810.* New York: Pendragon Press, 1988.

Mozart, Leopold. *Versuch einer gründlichen Violinschule.* Augsburg, 1756. Translated by Editha Knocker as *A Treatise on the Fundamental Principles of Violin Playing.* Oxford: Oxford University Press, 1945; 1988.

Mozart, Wolfgang Amadeus. *Briefe und Aufzeichnungen.* Edited by Wilhelm Bauer, Otto Erich Deutsch, and Joseph Eibl. 8 vols. Kassel: Bärenreiter, 1962–1975.

——— *The Letters of Mozart and his Family.* Translated and edited by Emily Anderson. 3rd ed. New York and London: W. W. Norton, 1985.

Mraz-Koller, Gerda. "Bildungsanspruch und Bildungsmöglichkeiten im aufgeklärten Österreich." In *Joseph Haydn und seine Zeit (JbÖK* 2 [1972]), pp. 105–120.

Müller-Blattau, Joseph. "Beethoven und die Variation." *Neue Beethoven-Jahrbuch* 5 (1933), 101–136.

——— *Gestaltung-Umgestaltung. Studien zur Geschichte der musikalischen Variation.* Stuttgart: J. B. Metzler, 1950.

Murphy, James J. *Rhetoric in the Middle Ages.* Berkeley and Los Angeles: University of California Press, 1974.

——— ed. *Three Medieval Rhetorical Arts.* Berkeley, Los Angeles, and London: University of California Press, 1971.

Neefe, Christian Gottlob. "Ueber die musikalische Wiederholung." *Deutsches Museum* 1 (August 1776), 745–751.

Nelson, Robert U. *The Technique of Variation*. Berkeley and Los Angeles: University of California Press, 1948.

Neubacher, Jürgen. *Finis coronat opus: Untersuchungen zur Technik der Schlussgestaltung in der Instrumentalmusik Joseph Haydns*. Tutzing: Hans Schneider, 1986.

—— "'Idee' und 'Ausführung.' Zum Kompositionsprozeβ bei Joseph Haydn." *AfMw* 41 (1984), 187–207.

Neubauer, John. *The Emancipation of Music from Language: Departures from Mimesis in Eighteenth-Century Aesthetics*. New Haven and London: Yale University Press, 1986.

Newman, William S. "Emanuel Bach's Autobiography." *MQ* 51 (1965), 363–372.

—— *The Sonata in the Baroque Era*. 3rd ed. New York: W. W. Norton, 1972.

—— *The Sonata in the Classic Era*. 3rd ed. New York: W. W. Norton, 1983.

Niedt, Friedrich Erhard. *Handleitung zur Variation*. Hamburg, 1706. 2nd ed., rev., enl., and with commentary and appendix by Johann Mattheson. Hamburg, 1721. Translated by Pamela L. Poulin and Irmgard C. Taylor as *The Musical Guide*. Oxford: Oxford University Press, 1989.

Nottebohm, Gustav. *Beethoveniana*. Leipzig: J. Rieter-Biedermann, 1872.

—— *Zweite Beethoveniana*. Leipzig: J. Rieter-Biedermann, 1887.

O'Malley, John W. "Content and Rhetorical Forms in Sixteenth-Century Treatises on Preaching." In *Renaissance Eloquence: Studies in the Theory and Practice of Renaissance Rhetoric*, edited by James J. Murphy, pp. 238–252. Berkeley and Los Angeles: University of California Press, 1983.

Ong, Walter J. *Ramus: Method, and the Decay of Dialogue*. Cambridge, Mass.: Harvard University Press, 1958.

Oppen, Jürgen von. "Beethovens Klavierfantasie op. 77 in neuer Sicht." In *Bericht über den internationalen musikwissenschaftlichen Kongress Bonn 1970*, edited by Carl Dahlhaus et al., pp. 528–531. Kassel: Bärenreiter, 1971.

Palisca, Claude V. "*Ut oratoria musica:* The Rhetorical Basis of Musical Mannerism." In *The Meaning of Mannerism*, edited by Franklin W. Robinson and Stephen G. Nichols, Jr., pp. 37–65. Hanover, N. H.: University Press of New England, 1972.

Paulson, Ronald. *Emblem and Expression: Meaning in English Art of the Eighteenth Century*. Cambridge, Mass.: Harvard University Press, 1975.

Peacham, Henry. *The Garden of Eloquence*. 2nd ed. 1593. Facs. ed. with an introduction by William G. Crane. Gainesville, Fla.: Scholars' Facsimiles and Reprints, 1954.

Pecman, Rudolf, ed. *Colloquium Musica Bohemica et Europaea. Brno 1970*. Brno: n. p., 1972.

Plantinga, Leon, and Glenn Pierr Johnson. "Haydn's *Andante con variazioni:* Compositional Process, Text, and Genre." In *The Creative Process,* Studies in the History of Music, 3. New York and Williamstown: Broude, in press.

Plett, Heinrich F. "The Place and Function of Style in Renaissance Poetics." In *Renaissance Eloquence: Studies in the Theory and Practice of Renaissance Rhetoric*, edited by James J. Murphy, pp. 356–375. Berkeley and Los Angeles: University of California Press, 1983.

Pohl, Carl Ferdinand. *Joseph Haydn*. 2 vols. Leipzig: Breitkopf & Härtel, 1878–1882. Vol. 3 completed by Hugo Botstiber. Leipzig: Breitkopf & Härtel, 1927.

Pollock, Carla. "Viennese Solo Keyboard Music, 1740–1770: A Study in the Evolution of the Classical Style." Ph.D. dissertation. Brandeis University, 1984.

Poštolka, Milan. *Leopold Koželuh: život a dílo*. Prague: Státni Hudební Vydavatelství, 1964.

Powers, Harold S. "Language Models and Music Analysis." *Ethnomusicology* 24 (1980), 1–60.

Primmer, Brian. "Unity and Ensemble." *19CM* 6 (1982), 97–140.

Proier, Gerlinde. "Abbé Joseph Gelinek als Variationenkomponist." Ph.D. dissertation. Vienna, 1962.

Pseudo-Cicero. [*Rhetorica*] *Ad Herrenium*. Translated and edited by Harry Caplan. Loeb Classical Library, vol. 403 [Cicero I]. Cambridge, Mass.: Harvard University Press, 1954.

Puchelt, Gerhard. *Variationen für Klavier im 19. Jahrhundert*. Hildesheim: G. Olms, 1973.

Puttenham, George. *The Arte of English Poesie,* edited by Gladys Doidge Willcock and Alice Walker. Cambridge: Cambridge University Press, 1936.

Quantz, Johann Joachim. *Versuch einer Anweisung die Flöte traversière zu spielen.* Berlin, 1752; 3rd ed. Breslau, 1789. Facsimile. Edited by Hans-Peter Schmitz. Kassel: Bärenreiter, 1953. Translated by Edward Reilly as *On Playing the Flute.* New York, 1966; New York: Schirmer Books, 1975.

Quinn, Arthur. *Figures of Speech.* Salt Lake City: Gibbs M. Smith, 1982.

Quintilian. *Institutio oratoria.* Translated by H. E. Butler. Loeb Classical Library 126. Cambridge, Mass.: Harvard University Press, 1921.

Ratner, Leonard. "*Ars combinatoria:* Chance and Choice in Eighteenth-Century Music." *Studies in Eighteenth-Century Music. A Tribute to Karl Geiringer on his Seventieth Birthday,* edited by H. C. Robbins Landon with Roger Chapman, pp. 343–363. New York: Oxford University Press, 1970.

——— *Classic Music: Expression, Form, and Style.* New York: Schirmer Books, 1980.

——— "Eighteenth-Century Theories of Musical Period Structure." *MQ* 42 (1956), 439–454.

——— "Harmonic Aspects of Classic Form." *JAMS* 2 (1949), 159–168.

Reicha, Anton. *Traité de haute composition musicale.* 2 vols. Paris, 1824–1826.

——— *Traité de Melodie.* Paris, 1814.

Reichardt, Johann Friedrich. "J. A. P. Schulz." *AMZ* 3 (1800), cols. 153–57, 169–176, 597–606.

Reichert, Ernst. "Die Variation-Arbeit bei Haydn." Ph.D. dissertation. Vienna, 1926.

Reimann, Margarete. "Zur Entwicklungsgeschichte des *Double.*" *Mf* 5 (1952), 317–332; 6 (1953), 97–111.

Reimer, Erich. "Idee der Öffentlichkeit und kompositorische Praxis im späten 18. und frühen 19. Jahrhundert." *Mf* 29 (1976), 130–137.

——— "Die Polemik gegen das Virtuosenkonzert im 18. Jahrhundert." *AfMw* 30 (1973), 235–244.

Reynolds, Christopher. "Beethoven's Sketches for the Variations in Eb, Op. 35." In *Beethoven Studies 3,* edited by Alan Tyson, pp. 47–84. Cambridge: Cambridge University Press, 1982.

——— "Ends and Means in the Second Finale to Beethoven's Op. 30, no. 1." In *Beethoven Essays,* edited by Lewis Lockwood and Phyllis Benjamin, pp. 127–145. Cambridge, Mass.: Harvard University Press, 1984.

Richards, I. A. *The Philosophy of Rhetoric.* Oxford: Oxford University Press, 1936.

Riedel, Friedrich W. "Der Einfluss der italienischer Klaviermusik des 17. Jahrhunderts auf die Entwicklung der Musik für Tasteninstrumente in Deutschland während der ersten Hälfte des 18. Jahrhunderts." *Analecta Musicologica* 5 (1968), 18–33.

Riedt, Friedrich Wilhelm. "Betrachtungen über die willkührlichen Veränderungen der musicalischen Gedanken bey Ausführung einer Melodie. Zur Beantwortung der Frage: Woran ein guter Veränderer von einem schlechten eigentlich zu unterscheiden sey?" In *Historisch-kritische Beyträge zur Aufnahme der Musik,* II, edited by F. W. Marpurg, pp. 95–118. Berlin, 1755. Facsimile. Hildesheim: G. Olms, 1970.

Riepel, Joseph. *Anfangsgründe zur musicalischen Setzkunst.* Vol. 1: *De Rhythmopoeïa oder von der Tactordnung.* Augsburg, 1752; Regensburg, 1754. Vol. 2: *Grundregeln zur Tonordnung insgemein.* Leipzig, 1755. Vol. 4: *Erläuterung der betrüglichen Tonordnung.* Regensburg, 1765.

Rigler, Gertrude. "Die Kammermusik Dittersdorfs." *Studien zur Musikwissenschaft* 14 (1927), 179–212.

Ritzel, Fred. *Die Entwicklung der "Sonatenform" im musiktheoretischen Schrifttum der 18. and 19. Jahrhunderts.* Wiesbaden: Breitkopf & Härtel, 1968.

Rosen, Charles. *The Classical Style: Haydn, Mozart, Beethoven.* New York: Viking, 1971; New York: Norton, 1972.

Rothstein, William. *Phrase Rhythm in Tonal Music.* New York: Schirmer, 1989.

Rousseau, Jean-Jacques. *Dictionnaire de Musique.* Paris, 1768. Facsimile. Hildesheim: G. Olms, 1968. Translated by William Waring as *A Complete Dictionary of Music.* 2nd ed. London, 1779. Rpt. New York: A. M. S. Press, 1975.

Ruhnke, Martin. *Joachim Burmeister: Ein Beitrag zur Musiklehre um 1600.* Kassel: Bärenreiter, 1955.

Ruile-Dronke, Jutta. *Ritornell und Solo in Mozarts Klavierkonzerte.* Tutzing: Hans Schneider, 1978.

Rywosch, Bernhard. *Beiträge zur Entwicklung in Joseph Haydns Symphonik.* Turbenthal: Furrer, 1934.

Sadie, Stanley. *The New Grove Mozart.* New York: W. W. Norton, 1983.

Said, Edward. *The World, the Text, and the Critic.* Cambridge, Mass.: Harvard University Press, 1983.

Salzer, Felix. "Haydn's Fantasia from the String Quartet, Opus 76, No. 6." *Music Forum* 4 (1976), 161–194.

——— "The Variation Movement of Mozart's Divertimento K. 563." *Music Forum* 5 (1980), 257–315.

Sandberger, Adolf. "Zur Geschichte des Haydnschen Streichquartetts." In *Ausgewählte Aufsätze zur Musikgeschichte,* vol. 1, pp. 224–265. Munich: Drei Masken, 1924.

Scaglione, Aldo. *The Classical Theory of Composition from its Origins to the Present: A Historical Survey.* Chapel Hill: University of North Carolina Press, 1972.

Schachter, Carl. "Idiosyncratic Features of Three Mozart Slow Movements: K. 449, K. 453, and K. 467." In *Mozart's Piano Concertos: Text, Context, Interpretation,* edited by Neal Zaslaw. Ann Arbor: University of Michigan Press, in press.

Schaeffer, John D. *Sensus Communis: Vico, Rhetoric, and the Limits of Relativism.* Durham and London: Duke University Press, 1990.

Schafhäutl, Karl Emil von. *Abt Georg Joseph Vogler: Sein Leben, Charakter und Musikalische System, seine Werke, seine Schule, Bildnisse etc.* Augsburg, 1888.

Scheibe, Johann Adolph. *Compendium Musices Theoretico-practicum, das ist Kurzer Begriff derer nöthigsten Compositions-Regeln.* Edited by Peter Benary as the appendix to *Die deutsche Kompositionslehre des 18. Jahrhundert.* Leipzig, 1960.

——— *Critischer Musicus.* New enl. ed. Leipzig, 1745. Facsimile. Hildesheim: G. Olms, 1970.

Schenker, Heinrich. "Beethovens Dritte Sinfonie zum erstenmal in ihrem wahren Inhalt dargestellt." In *Das Meisterwerk in der Musik. Ein Jahrbuch,* III (1930), 74–84.

———— *Beethovens neunte Sinfonie.* Vienna: Universal, 1912; rpt. Universal, 1969.

Schering, Arnold. "Die Lehre von der musikalischen Figuren." *Kirchen-Musikalisches Jahrbuch* 21 (1908), 106–114.

Schiller, Friedrich. *Naive and Sentimental Poetry* and *On the Sublime.* Translated by Julius A. Elias. New York: Frederick Ungar, 1966.

Schleuning, Peter. "Beethoven in alter Deutung: Der 'neue Weg' mit der 'Sinfonia eroica.'" *AfMw* 44 (1987), 165–194.

Schmid, Ernst Fritz. *C. P. E. Bach und seine Kammermusik.* Kassel: Bärenreiter, 1931.

Schmitz, Hans-Peter. *Die Kunst der Verzierung im 18. Jahrhundert: Instrumentale und Vokale Musizierpraxis in Beispielen.* Kassel: Bärenreiter, 1955.

Schoenberg, Arnold. *Fundamentals of Musical Composition,* edited by Gerald Strang. New York: St. Martin's Press, 1967.

———— *Style and Idea,* edited by Leon Stein. Berkeley and Los Angeles: University of California Press, 1975; 1984.

Scholz, Gottfried. "Der dialektische Prozess in Haydns Doppelvariationen." *Musicologica Austriaca* 2 (1979), 97–107.

Scholz-Michelitsch, Helga. "Georg Christoph Wagenseil als Klavierkomponist. Eine Studie zu seiner zyklischen Soloklavierwerken." 2 vols. Ph.D. dissertation. Vienna, 1966.

Schönfeld, Johann Ferdinand von. *Jahrbuch der Tonkunst von Wien und Prag.* Vienna, 1796. Facsimile, with afterword and index by Otto Biba. Munich and Salzburg: Emil Katzbichler, 1976.

Schor, Naomi. *Reading in Detail: Aesthetics and the Feminine.* New York and London: Methuen, 1987.

Schroeder, David C. *Haydn and the Enlightenment: The Late Symphonies and Their Audience.* Oxford: Clarendon, 1990.

Schubart, Christian Friedrich Daniel. *Leben und Gesinnungen: von ihm selbst, im Kerker aufgesetzt.* Edited by Ludwig Schubart. With an afterword by Claus Trager. Stuttgart, 1791–1793; rpt. Leipzig: VEB Deutscher Verlag für Musik, 1980.

Schulenberg, David. "Composition as Variation: Inquiries into the Bach Circle of Composers." *CM* 23 (1982), 57–87.

———— *The Instrumental Music of Carl Philipp Emanuel Bach.* Ann Arbor: UMI Research Press, 1984.

Schumann, Robert. *Gesammelte Schriften.* 3rd ed. Leipzig: Breitkopf & Härtel, 1875.

Schwindt-Gross, Nicole. *Drama und Diskurs: Zur Beziehung zwischen Satztechnik und motivischem Prozess in die Streichquartetten Haydns und Mozarts.* Laaber: Laaber-Verlag, 1989.

Scruton, Roger. "Public Text and Common Reader." *Comparative Criticism* 4 (1982), 85–105.

Šetková, Dana. *Klavírní Dílo Josefa Antonína Štěpána.* Prague: Státni Hudebni Vydavatelství, 1965.

Shklovsky, Victor. "Art as Technique." Translated by Lee T. Lemon and Marion J. Reis in *Russian Formalist Criticism: Four Essays,* pp. 3–24. Lincoln: University of Nebraska Press, 1965.

Sidney, Sir Philip. *An Apology for Poetry or The Defence of Poetry.* Edited by Geoffrey Shepherd. London: Thomas Nelson and Sons, 1965.

Sieber, Tilman. *Das klassische Streichquintett, Quellenkundliche und gattungsgeschichtliche Studien*. Neue Heidelberger Studien zur Musik, 10. Bern: Francke, 1983.

Simpson, Christopher. *The Division-Viol, or the Art of Playing Ex Tempore to a Ground*. 2nd ed. London, 1667. Facsimile. London: J. Curwen & Sons, 1955.

Sisman, Elaine R. "Brahms and the Variation Canon." *19CM* 14 (1990), 132–153.

———— "Haydn's Baryton Pieces and His Serious Genres." In *Internationaler Joseph Haydn Kongress Wien 1982,* edited by Eva Badura-Skoda, pp. 426–435. Munich: G. Henle, 1986.

———— "Haydn's Hybrid Variations." In *Haydn Studies,* ed. Jens Peter Larsen et al., pp. 509–515. New York: W. W. Norton, 1981.

———— "Haydn's Theater Symphonies." *JAMS* 42 (1990), 292–352.

———— "Haydn's Variations." Ph.D. dissertation, Princeton University, 1978.

———— "Small and Expanded Forms: Koch's Model and Haydn's Music." *MQ* 62 (1982), 444–478.

———— "Tradition and Transformation in the Alternating Variations of Haydn and Beethoven." *AM* 62 (1990), 152–182.

Smeed, J. W. *The Theophrastan 'Character': The History of a Literary Genre*. Oxford and New York: Clarendon, 1985.

Smiles, Joan E. "Directions for Improvised Ornamentation in Italian Method Books of the Late Eighteenth Century." *JAMS* 31 (1978), 495–509.

———— "Improvised Ornamentation in Late Eighteenth-Century Music." Ph.D. dissertation. Stanford University, 1976.

Smith, Barbara Herrnstein. *Poetic Closure: A Study of How Poems End*. Chicago: University of Chicago Press, 1968.

Smith, John H. *The Spirit and Its Letter: Traces of Rhetoric in Hegel's Philosophy of Bildung*. Ithaca, N.Y., and London: Cornell University Press, 1988.

Snook, Susan. "Daube's 'Der Musikalische Dilettant': Translation and Commentary." Ph.D. dissertation. Stanford University, 1978.

Solie, Ruth. "The Living Work: Organicism and Musical Analysis." *19CM* 4 (1980), 147–156.

Solomon, Maynard. *Beethoven*. New York: Schirmer Books, 1977.

———— *Beethoven Essays*. Cambridge, Mass.: Harvard University Press, 1988.

Somfai, László. "Albrechtsberger-Eigenschriften in der Nationalbibliothek Széchény, Budapest." *SM* 2 (1961), 175–202; 4 (1963), 179–190; 9 (1967), 191–220.

———— "'Learned Style' in Two Late String Quartet Movements of Haydn." *SM* 28 (1986), 325–349.

———— "Opus-Planung und Neuerung bei Joseph Haydn." *SM* 22 (1980), 87–110.

———— "Stilfragen der Klaviersonaten von Haydn." *ÖMz* 37 (1982), 147–153.

———— "The London Revision of Haydn's Style." *PRMA* 100 (1974), 159–174.

Spitzer, John. "Musical Attribution and Critical Judgment: The Rise and Fall of the Sinfonia Concertante for Winds, K. 297b." *JM* 5 (1987), 319–356.

Spitzer, John, and Neal Zaslaw. "Improvised Ornamentation in Eighteenth-Century Orchestras." *JAMS* 39 (1986), 524–577.

Sponheuer, Bernd. "Zum Problem des doppelten Finales in Mozarts 'erstem' Klavierkonzert KV 175: Zwei Versuche der Synthetisierung von 'Gelehrtem' und 'Galantem.'" *AfMw* 42 (1985), 102–120.

Steiner, George. *Real Presences*. Chicago: University of Chicago Press, 1989.

Stilz, Ernst. "Die Berliner Klaviersonate zur Zeit Friedrichs des Grossen." Ph.D. dissertation. Berlin, 1930.

Stötzer, Ursula. *Deutsche Redekunst im 17. und 18. Jahrhundert.* Halle: Max Neimeyer Verlag, 1962.

Street, Alan. "The Rhetorico-Musical Structure of the 'Goldberg' Variations: Bach's *Clavier-Übung* IV and the *Institutio oratoria* of Quintilian." *MusA* 6 (1987), 89–131.

Strohm, Reinhard. "Merkmale italienischer Versvertonung in Mozarts Klavierkonzerten." *Analecta musicologica* 18 (1974), 219–236.

Strunk, Oliver. "Haydn's Divertimenti for Baryton, Viola, and Bass." *MQ* 18 (1932), 216–251.

Sulzer, Johann Georg. *Allgemeine Theorie der schönen Künste,* 4 vols. Leipzig, 1771–1774. 2nd ed. 1792–1794. Rpt. Hildesheim: G. Olms, 1969.

Sumner, Floyd. "Haydn and Kirnberger: A Documentary Report." *JAMS* 27 (1975), 530–539.

Tank, Ulrich. "Die Dokumente der Esterházy-Archive zur fürstlichen Hofkapelle in der Zeit von 1761 bis 1770." *HSt* 4 (1980), 129–346.

Tischler, Hans. *A Structural Analysis of Mozart's Piano Concertos.* Brooklyn: Institute of Medieval Music, 1966.

Tobel, Rudolf von. *Die Formenwelt der klassischen Instrumentalmusik.* Bern and Leipzig: Paul Haupt, 1935.

Todorov, Tzvetan. *Theories of the Symbol.* Translated by Catherine Porter. Ithaca, N.Y.: Cornell University Press, 1982.

Tovey, Donald Francis. *Beethoven.* London: Oxford University Press, 1944; paperback ed. rpt. 1971.

——— *Essays in Musical Analysis: Symphonies and Other Orchestral Works.* New edition. London: Oxford University Press, 1981.

——— *Essays in Musical Analysis,* vol. 3: *Concertos.* London: Oxford University Press, 1936.

——— "Haydn's Chamber Music." In *The Main Stream of Music and Other Essays.* Cleveland and New York: Meridian Books, 1959.

Treitler, Leo. *Music and the Historical Imagination.* Cambridge, Mass.: Harvard University Press, 1989.

Trimpert, Dieter Lutz. *Die Quatuors Concertants von Giuseppe Cambini.* Tutzing: Hans Schneider, 1967.

Türk, Daniel Gottlob. *Klavierschule, oder Anweisung zum Klavierspielen für Lehrer und Lernende.* Leipzig and Halle, 1789. Facsimile. Edited by Erwin R. Jacobi. Kassel: Bärenreiter, 1962; 2nd ed. 1967.

Tyson, Alan. *Mozart: Studies of the Autograph Scores.* Cambridge, Mass.: Harvard University Press, 1987.

Uehding, Gerd, and Bernd Steinbrink. *Grundriβ der Rhetorik: Geschichte, Technik, Methode.* Stuttgart: J. B. Metzler, 1986.

Uhde, Jürgen. *Beethovens Klaviermusik.* 2 vols. Stuttgart: Reclam, 1968.

Unger, Hans-Heinrich. *Die Beziehungen zwischen Musik und Rhetorik im 16.–18. Jahrhundert.* Würzburg: K. Triltsch, 1941; rpt. Hildesheim: G. Olms, 1979.

Unverricht, Hubert. *Das Streichtrio.* Tutzing: Hans Schneider, 1969.

——— "Zur Chronologie der Barytontrios von Joseph Haydn." In *Symbolae Historiae Musicae. Hellmut Federhofer zum 60. Geburtstag,* edited by Friedrich Riedel and Hubert Unverricht, pp. 180–190. Mainz: B. Schott's Söhne, 1971.

van Reijen, Paul Willem. *Vergleichende Studien zur Klaviervariationstechnik von Mozart und seinen Zeitgenossen.* Buren: Frits Knuf, 1988.

Vickers, Brian. "Figures of Rhetoric/Figures of Music?" *Rhetorica* 2 (1984), 1–44.

———— *In Defence of Rhetoric.* Oxford: Oxford University Press, 1988.

———— "Rhetorical and Anti-Rhetorical Tropes: On Writing the History of *Elocutio.*" *Comparative Criticism* 3 (1981), 105–132.

Viecenz, Herbert. "Über die allgemeinen Grundlagen der Variationskunst, mit besonderer Berücksichtigung Mozarts." *MJb* 2 (1924), 185–232.

Vogg, Herbert. "Franz Tuma (1704–1774) als Instrumentalkomponist nebst Beiträgen zur Wiener Musikgeschichte des 18. Jahrhunderts (Die Hofkapelle der Kaiserin-Witwe Elisabeth Christine.)" Ph.D. dissertation. University of Vienna, 1951.

Vogler, Georg Joseph. *Verbesserungen der Forkel'schen Veränderungen über "God Save the King."* Frankfurt am Main, 1793.

Walther, Johann Gottfried. *Musicalisches Lexicon.* Leipzig, 1732; Facsimile. Edited by Richard Schaal. Kassel: Bärenreiter, 1953; 3rd ed. 1967.

Webster, James. *Haydn's "Farewell" Symphony and the Idea of Classical Style: Through-Composition and Cyclic Integration in His Instrumental Music.* Cambridge: Cambridge University Press, 1991.

———— "The Chronology of Haydn's String Quartets." *MQ* 61 (1975), 17–46.

———— "The Falling-out between Haydn and Beethoven: The Evidence of the Sources." In *Beethoven Essays: Studies in Honor of Elliot Forbes,* edited by Lewis Lockwood and Phyllis Benjamin, pp. 3–45. Cambridge, Mass.: Harvard University Press, 1984.

———— "The Form of the Finale of Beethoven's Ninth Symphony." *Beethoven Forum* I (1992), 25–62.

———— "The Scoring of Mozart's Chamber Music for Strings." In *Music in the Classical Period. Essays in Honor of Barry Brook,* edited by Allan W. Atlas, pp. 259–296. New York: Pendragon Press, 1985.

———— "Traditional Elements in Beethoven's Middle-Period String Quartets." In *Beethoven, Performers, and Critics: The International Beethoven Congress, Detroit, 1977,* edited by Robert Winter and Bruce Carr, pp. 94–133. Detroit: Wayne State University Press, 1980.

———— "When Did Haydn Begin to Write 'Beautiful' Melodies?" In *Haydn Studies,* ed. Jens Peter Larsen et al., pp. 385–388.

Weinmann, Alexander. *Beiträge zur Geschichte des Alt-Wiener Musikverlages.* Vienna: Universal, 1962–1973.

———— *Der Alt-Wiener Musikverlag im Spiegel der "Wiener Zeitung."* Tutzing: Hans Schneider, 1976.

———— "Verzeichnis der Musikalien des Verlages Johann Traeg in Wien, 1794–1818." *Studien zur Musikwissenschaft* 23 (1956), 135–183.

———— *Vollständiges Verlagsverzeichnis Artaria & Comp.* 2nd. ed. Vienna: Ludwig Krenn, 1978.

West, Meredith J., and Andrew P. King. "Mozart's Starling." *American Scientist* 78 (1990), 106–114.

Wheelock, Gretchen. "Marriage à la Mode: Haydn's Instrumental Works 'Englished' for Voice and Piano." *JM* 8 (1990), 357–397.

Williams, Peter. "The Snares and Delusions of Musical Rhetoric: Some Examples from Recent Writings on J. S. Bach." In *Alte Musik: Praxis und Reflexion,* edited by Peter Reidemeister and Veronika Gutmann, pp. 230–240. Winterthur: Amadeus, 1983.

Winkler, Klaus. "Alter und neuer Musikstil im Streit zwischen den Berlinern und Wienern zur Zeit der Frühklassik." *Mf* 33 (1980), 37–45.

Wolf, Georg Friedrich. *Kurzgefasstes Musikalisches Lexikon.* 3rd rev. ed. Halle, 1806.

Wolf, Eugene K. "The Recapitulations in Haydn's London Symphonies," *MQ* 52 (1966), 71–89.

———— "The Rediscovered Autograph of Mozart's Fantasy and Sonata in C Minor, K. 475/457." *JM* 10 (1992), 3–47.

———— *The Symphonies of Johann Stamitz: A Study in the Formation of the Classic Style.* Utrecht: Bohn, Scheltema, & Holkema, 1981.

Wolff, Christoph. "Mozart 1784: Biographische und stilgeschichtliche Überlegungen." *MJb 1986*, 1–10.

Wollenberg, Susan. "Haydn's Baryton Trios and the *Gradus*." *ML* 54 (1973), 170–178.

Wyzewa, Théodore de, and Georges de Saint-Foix. *W.-A. Mozart: Sa vie musicale et son oeuvre.* Rpt. New York: Dover, 1980.

Yudkin, Jeremy. "Beethoven's 'Mozart' Quartet." *JAMS* 45 (1992), 30–74.

Zaslaw, Neal. *Mozart's Symphonies: Context, Performance Practice, Reception.* Oxford: Oxford University Press, 1989.

Zenck, Martin. "Rezeption von Geschichte in Beethovens 'Diabelli-Variationen.'" *AfMw* 37 (198), 61–75.

Ziegler, Christian Gottlieb. *Anleitung zur musikalischen Composition.* Quedlinburg, ms. dated 1739. US:NYp Drexel 3290.

Zsako, Julius. "The String Quartets of Ignace J. Pleyel." Ph.D. dissertation. Columbia University, 1975.

Index

Aesop, 23

Albrechtsberger, Johann Georg, 50n, 113, 117, 235; String Quartet in D, Hob. III:D3, 114–116

Alternating variation, 41, 75, 107, 121, 150–162, 170, 174, 185, 190, 193–194, 197, 220, 246–248, 254–261; alternating rondo-variation, 121, 153, 159, 162, 174; alternating strophic-variation, 153, 159, 185, 193

Alternation, 72, 150, 152, 207, 226, 233, 243, 246; of mode, 151–152, 154, 156, 190

Amplification, 9, 29–39, 91n, 100, 105, 145, 243, 261. *See also* Rhetorical figures

Anderson, Emily, 219

André (publisher), 77

Aristotle, 12, 29, 30, 39

Arrangement, 159. *See also* Dispositio

Ars combinatoria, 52, 61, 69, 74, 83

Ars dictaminis, 24–25

Ars praedicandi, 26–27, 35–36; rhetorical model of exegesis from, 142

Artaria (publisher), 40, 77, 120

Aspelmayr, Franz, 117; String Quartet in Eb, 117

Attwood, Thomas, 80, 82n

Bach, Carl Philipp Emanuel, 3, 20, 32, 34, 53, 58–60, 69, 81n, 83n, 85, 133, 151, 158n, 163, 278–279; Six Sonatas with Varied Reprises, 51n, 58, 68, 72n, 133; No. 6 of that set, 153–154; variations on the "Folies d'Espagne," 253

Bach, Johann Christian, 106

Bach, Johann Sebastian, 1, 2, 49n, 50n, 67, 68, 74, 81n, 146; Goldberg Variations, 1, 2, 5–6, 68, 253; English Suites, 51n; "Art of Fugue," 68; Variations on "Vom Himmel hoch," 68

Bach, Wilhelm Friedemann, Symphony in F (F. 67), 227

Bass line, 6, 45, 52–55, 60, 61, 68–69, 110, 112, 113, 119, 130, 135, 137–138, 139, 160, 161, 216, 226, 255, 257–259, 260; varied bass, 69, 110, 126n, 132; walking bass, 92, 111, 132. *See also* Constant-bass variation

Basso continuo. *See* Thoroughbass

Beauty, the Beautiful, 12, 13–14, 236

Beer, Johannes, 23

Beethoven, Ludwig van, 1, 2, 3, 10; "new manner," 2, 235, 249–254; knowledge of Sulzer's encyclopedia, 68, 257; three creative periods of, 148; and alternating variation, 158, 246–249, 254–260; and *minore* variation, 163; and decorum, 238–242, 246, 247; letter to Eleanor von Breuning, 251

    WORKS

    Creatures of Prometheus, Op. 42, 254, 255, 259n

    Fantasy in G major, Op. 77, 165, 246n

    Quartets, strings: Op. 18 No. 5 (A major), 238–242, 246, 249; Op. 74 (Eb major, "Harp") 242–246, 249; Op. 132 in A minor, 254n

    Quintet, strings: Op. 29, 252

    Sonatas, piano: Op. 57 (F minor, "Appassionata"), 10, 108; Op. 109 (E major), 108n, 243

    Sonata, violin and piano, Op. 30 No. 1 (A major), 252

    Symphonies: No. 1 (Op. 21), 183n; No. 3 (Op. 55, *Eroica*), 1, 2, 3, 68, 107, 181, 250, 255–261; No. 5 (Op. 67), 152, 254n; No. 7

Beethoven, Ludwig van (*continued*)
(Op. 92), 108n, 243, 254n; No. 9 (Op. 125), 152–153, 243, 254n
  Trios, piano: Op. 1 No. 3 (C minor), 238; Op. 70 No. 2, 246–249
  Trio, strings: Op. 8, 238n
  Variations, piano: Op. 34 (original theme, F), 64, 250, 251, 252–253; Op. 35 (original theme, Eb, "Eroica," "Prometheus"), 64, 68, 71, 181, 239, 250–252, 253–254, 256, 257; Op. 120 (waltz by Diabelli), 75; WoO 63 (march by Dressler, C minor), 250; WoO 65 ("Venni amore" by Righini, D), 241n, 250; WoO 67 (theme by Count Waldstein, four-hands, C), 183; WoO 72 ("Un fièvre brûlante," by Grétry, C), 251; WoO 73 ("La stessa, la stessissima" by Salieri, Bb), 239; WoO 76 ("Tändeln und Scherzen" by Süssmayr, F), 251; WoO 80 (original theme, C minor), 64
  Variations for piano and cello, on "Ein Mädchen oder Weibchen," Op. 66, 251
  Variations for 2 oboes, English horn, on "Là ci darem la mano," WoO 28, 142n
Benda, Franz, 32; violin sonatas, 51n
Bernhard, Christoph, 21, 49
Binary (two-reprise) form, 75, 82, 83, 102, 105, 106, 133, 168, 169, 171, 198, 237
Birck, Wenzel Raimund, 117; *Trattenimenti*, 117
Blackall, Eric, 9
Blair, Hugh, 8
Brahms, Johannes, 1, 29; Sextet No. 1 in Bb major, Op. 18, 240n; Variations on a Theme of Handel, Op. 24, 252n
Brandes, Heinz, 21
Breitkopf (publishers), 191, 251–252, 253, 257
Brossard, Sebastien de, 41n 52n
Brown, A. Peter, 113, 149, 191
Bryan, Paul Robey, 149
Bücken, Ernst, 147
Buelow, George J., 21
Bukofzer, Manfred, 21
Burke, Edmund, 13
Burmeister, Joachim, 21, 33
Burney, Charles, 49, 109, 128

Cadenza, 39, 40, 49n, 59, 65, 99, 130, 131, 139, 150, 165, 172, 194, 195, 200, 210, 212, 221, 250
Cantus firmus, 5–6, 63, 127, 142, 150, 161, 162, 164, 175, 176–181, 183, 195, 203, 214, 217, 241, 246, 253, 254, 257–258, 259

Capriccio, 15, 164, 183, 253. *See also* Fantasia
Cavett-Dunsby, Esther, 197
Chaconne (*ciacona*), 5, 54, 69
Character, 3, 12, 17, 26, 37, 53, 56, 58, 65, 66–67, 70, 71, 73, 91, 106, 121, 142, 145, 158–159, 178, 192, 198, 223, 231, 233, 250–251
Character piece, 67, 160, 192, 250
"Character variation," 67
Characteristic variation, 1, 2, 6, 41, 67, 72, 165, 250–251, 253, 258
Chria, 37, 91–92
Christmann, Johann Friedrich, 69
Cicero, 29, 30, 36, 145, 237, 256
Clementi, Muzio, 64
Closure, 10, 39–40, 62, 95, 183, 195, 212, 220, 228
Coda, 15, 39–40, 41, 72, 75, 95, 99, 103, 107, 113, 137–138, 139–142, 150, 159, 161, 164, 165, 168, 169, 171, 194, 206, 210, 212, 216, 218, 219–220, 221, 228, 229, 230, 233, 241, 243–245, 246, 248, 253, 256, 259, 260
Coleridge, William, 15
Compositional process, 18n, 120, 261n
Concertante variation, 111, 113, 117, 130, 132, 135, 150, 153, 196, 207, 216, 220, 221, 229, 233, 256
Concerts, 48, 51, 64–65, 77, 196, 199, 203, 219, 228
Cone, Edward T., 36n, 261–262
Constant-bass variation, 68–69, 112, 117, 118, 127, 130, 135
Constant-harmony variation, 66, 68–69, 112, 118, 145, 153, 216, 250, 254, 258, 259
Constant-melody variation, 164, 176. *See also* Cantus firmus
Contrapuntal variation, 2, 6, 43, 45, 46, 68, 69, 112, 137, 150, 161, 186, 211, 212, 214, 218, 233, 234, 239–240, 253, 257. *See also* Counterpoint; Cantus firmus; Fugue
Contrast, 2, 4, 27, 37, 43, 63, 100, 107, 114, 121, 125, 130, 135, 137, 150, 160, 191, 237, 240, 247, 250, 257
Copiousness (*copia*), 27–29, 35, 37, 100, 142, 145, 191, 234, 260
Corelli, Arcangelo, 74, 240; violin sonatas, Op. 5, 51n
Corrette, Michel, 110n
Counterpoint, 1, 2, 34, 47, 49, 71, 109, 127, 132, 135, 137, 142, 150, 152, 161, 164, 171, 172, 175, 178, 181, 183, 184, 185, 186, 189, 191, 212, 214–215, 216, 217, 218, 219, 223, 239, 240, 241, 256. *See also* Contrapuntal variation; Cantus firmus; Fugue

Couperin, François, 68
Czerny, Carl, 64, 247

Da capo: form, 4, 158; in variations, da capo of theme, 6, 39, 92, 128, 130, 131, 220. See also Theme reprise
Dahlhaus, Carl, 255
Dance types. See Binary (two-reprise) form; Characteristic variation; Gavotte; March; Minuet; Siciliana; Suite
D'Anglebert, 50n, 68
Daube, Johann Friedrich, 12, 28, 32, 52, 61, 66, 67, 69, 87n
Decoration, 1, 2, 3, 4, 5, 7, 11–14, 38, 121, 159, 175, 195, 253. See also Diminutions; Embellishment; Ornament
Decorum, 3, 29, 236, 237, 238, 240, 241–242, 246, 247, 253, 254, 261
Defamiliarization, 241–242, 246, 253
Deleuze, Gilles, 5
Derrida, Jacques, 5
Descant, 36, 43, 54
Developing variation, 99
Development, 2, 52, 64, 75, 95, 103, 106, 107, 147, 163, 172, 175, 185, 241, 256, 260
Diminutions, 51, 53–54, 56, 60, 178. See also Embellishment; Ornament
Dispositio (arrangement, Ausführung), 16–18, 21, 108, 120, 159, 197, 198, 210. See also Arrangement; Realization; Rhetoric, five parts of classical
Dittersdorf, Karl Ditters von, 69, 117
Divisions, 21, 26–27, 54, 63
Double, 27, 53, 63, 68, 71, 243
"Double variation," 150–151, 255

Elaborated form, 261–262
Elaboratio (elocutio, Ausdruck), 12, 18, 21–22, 30, 197. See also Rhetoric, five parts of classical; Rhetorical figures
Eliade, Mircea, 5
Ellison, Julie, 6–7
Embellishment, 11, 18, 20, 32, 37, 49, 58, 101, 110, 121, 133, 219; necessity for adding, 20, 31; caution against overdoing, 20–21, 31. See also Decoration; Diminutions; Ornament
Erasmus, Desiderius, 27–28, 35
Esterházy, Nikolaus, 128
Exordium, 21, 39, 226, 256; as principium and insinuatio, 256
Expansion techniques, 82–100, 133, 145, 172, 224; varied repetition as, 61–62, 95, 100–101; repetitions, 83, 95; insertion, 83, 87; of

cadences, 83, 85, 93, 100, 103. See also Principal periods
Expression. See Elaboratio; Rhetorical figures

Fasch, Karl Friedrich, 74, 250
Fantasia (fantasy), 15, 65, 77, 83n, 164, 181–183, 185, 191–192, 253. See also Capriccio
Favart, Charles, 160
Feder, Georg, 110, 118–119, 122
Figured bass. See Thoroughbass
Fischer, Kurt von, 2–3, 53n, 255
Fischer, Wilhelm, 147
Fisher, Stephen, 160
Floros, Constantin, 255
Forkel, Johann Nikolaus, 23, 33, 34, 35, 39, 74, 217, 224; Variations on "God Save the King," 67, 69–71, 165, 251
Freemasonry, 25
Freud, Sigmund, 5
Froberger, Johann Jacob, 68
Fugue, fugato, 2, 15, 50n, 64, 67, 68, 71, 107, 113, 119, 142, 181, 184, 185, 220, 240, 251, 253, 256, 257, 259, 260. See also Contrapuntal variation; Counterpoint
Fürnberg, Baron von, 118
Fussell, Paul, 10

Galant style, 47, 133, 161, 184, 189, 194, 214
Gasparini, Francesco, L'armonico pratico al cimbalo (1708), 52
Gassmann, Florian Leopold, 111, 117; Symphony No. 65 in Ab, 113, 114
Gavotte, 224
Geiringer, Karl, 147
Gelinek, Abbé Joseph, 77, 158, 165; Variations on "Les Allemandes Saxones," Op. 67, 158n
Geminiani, Francesco, 53
Genette, Gérard, 3
Genre: choice of, 113, 196–197; weight of, 118–119, 186, 196, 238; characteristic elements of, 226, 228–229, 231, 233, 237
Gerlach, Sonja, 149
Gibbons, Thomas, 31
Gluck, Christoph Willibald, 65, 199; "Unser dummer Pöbel meint," 202; "Che farò senza Euridice," 212
Gombrich, E. H., 11
Gottsched, Johann Christoph, 33n
Grassineau, James, 52
Graun, Carl Heinrich and Johann Gottlieb, 32
Griesinger, Georg August, 23, 120
Ground, 5, 6, 52, 54, 61, 62, 63, 241, 262
Guignon, Jean-Pierre, 77n

Gurlitt, Willibald, 21
Guyer, Paul, 14
Gyrowetz, Adalbert, 164

Handel, Georg Frideric, 74, 146; Chaconne
with 62 variations, 253
Haydn, Joseph: acquaintance with rhetoric,
23–25; autobiographical sketch, 24; expansion of small forms, 80, 92–98; theme-
types, 111–112; method of composition,
120–121, 191; sonatas composed for Auenbrugger sisters, 120, 217; and *Regulatio chori
Kissmartoniensis*, 128–129; study of Bach and
Handel, 146; importance of 1772, 145–146;
creative periods, 146–150; *con espressione*
marking, 189; sonata composed for Breitkopf, 191; sonata composed for Marianne
von Genzinger, 191

  Works
  Baryton Octets, 150
  Baryton Trios (Hob. XI), 110, 111, 118,
  122, 128–132, 133, 152, 197; No. 2, 111n;
  No. 6, 111n, 130; No. 8, 112; No. 29, 112,
  127–128, 129; No. 38, 119, 121, 122; No.
  41, 111, 130; No. 45, 130; No. 50, 130; No.
  60, 130–131; No. 69, 130; No. 73, 132, 152,
  153; No. 81, 132; No. 95, 111n, 132; No.
  97, 152; No. 105, 132; No. 106, 111n, 132;
  No. 116, 111n, 132
  Capriccio in G major ("Acht sauschnei-
  der"), Hob. XVII:1, 183
  Divertimenti (Hob. II): No. 1, 111; No.
  11 ("Der Geburtstag"), 80, 92–94, 111; No.
  23, 133
  Duos for violin and viola (Hob. VI), 117;
  No. 2, 119; Nos. 3 and 6, 117
  Mixed chamber music: Horn Trio, Hob.
  IV:5, 117; Flute trio, Hob. IV:10, 189n;
  Flute trio, Hob. IV:2, 220
  Quartets, strings, 109, 151, 163; early,
  118, 119; Op. 2/6 in Bb major, 119, 121–
  125, 132, 133; Op. 9, 99, 110, 118, 119, 132,
  133; Op. 9/2 in Eb major, 110, 133–134;
  Op. 9/5 in Bb major, 112, 132–133; Op. 17,
  99, 110, 118, 132–133, 152; Op. 17/3, 132–
  133; Op. 20, 99, 132, 146, 152, 251; Op. 20/
  2 in C major, 183; Op. 20/4 in D major,
  109, 133, 135, 138–142, 174, 186, 238; Op.
  20/5 in F minor, 99; Op. 20/6 in A major,
  174; Op. 33, 147, 149, 172–175, 197, 219;
  Op. 33/1 in B minor, 99; Op. 33/2 in Eb
  major, 102, 103–105, 174; Op. 33/4 in Bb
  major, 60, 102, 174; Op. 33/5 in G major,
  102, 174, 207, 209, 220, 242n; Op. 33/6 in

D major, 102, 174, 175, 176; Op. 50, 149;
Op. 50/2 in C major, 99; Op. 50/4 in F#
minor, 175, 176; Op. 54/2 in C major, 99;
Op. 55/1 in A major, 175n; Op. 55/2 in F
minor, 149, 153, 193n; Op. 64/1 in C major,
176; Op. 64/2 in B minor, 175, 177; Op. 71/
3 in Eb major, 156, 242n, 247n; Op. 76,
175, 241, 246; Op. 76/1 in G major, 151;
Op. 76/2 in D minor, 151; Op. 76/3 in C
major, 151, 177, 240; Op. 76/5 in D major,
220, 241, 256; Op. 76/6 in Eb major, 112,
130, 142, 149, 176–185, 195, 220, 238, 242,
246, 257; Op. 77, 175, 246; Op. 77/2 in F
major, 101, 177, 195, 238

  Sonatas, keyboard (Hob. XVI), 132; No.
  19 in D major, 121, 150, 153; No. 22 in E
  major, 121, 151, 152, 153; No. 26 in A major, 152; Sonatas of 1776 (Hob. XVI:27–32),
  43, 111, 163; No. 27 in G major, 111, 153,
  163; No. 28 in Eb major, 111, 153, 163; No.
  29 in F major, 111, 153, 163; No. 30 in A
  major, 43–47, 111, 119; No. 31 in E major,
  111, 153, 163, 242n; No. 32 in B minor,
  121; No. 33 in D major, 153; No. 34 in E
  minor, 186, 247n; No. 36 in C# minor, 119,
  120–121, 217; No. 37 in D major, 151; No.
  39 in G major, 119, 120–121, 217; No. 40 in
  G major, 171, 186–189; No. 42 in D major,
  171, 189–190, 191; No. 43 in Ab major, 150;
  No. 44 in G minor, 151, 152, 153; No. 46 in
  Ab major, 99; No. 47 in E minor, 186; No.
  48 in C major, 149, 156, 189, 190–192,
  247n; No. 49 in Eb major, 191–192, 193;
  No. 50 in C major, 101; No. 52 in Eb
  major, 101; Hob. XVII:D1 in D major,
  111, 118

  Symphonies, 70, 72, 109, 204; No. 14 in
  A, 80, 92–94; No. 31 in D major ("Horn-
  signal"), 111, 220, 256; No. 42 in D major,
  61, 85–86, 99, 100, 153; No. 44 in E minor
  ("Mourning"), 99; No. 45 in F# minor
  ("Farewell"), 146; No. 46 in B major, 146;
  No. 47 in G major, 109, 112, 132, 135–138,
  139, 142, 152, 161, 186n, 203, 204, 207–208;
  No. 51 in Bb major, 153; No. 53 in D major
  ("Imperial"), 159–160; No. 55 in Eb major
  ("Schoolmaster"), 106, 153; No. 57 in D
  major, 142–145; No. 61 in D major, 150;
  No. 62 in D major, 203; No. 63 in C major
  ("Roxelane"), 151, 160–161, 174, 203, 207,
  208, 247n; No. 66, 150; No. 68 in Bb major,
  150; No. 69 in C major ("Laudon"), 150;
  No. 70 in D major, 142, 150, 160, 161–162,
  174, 186; No. 71 in Bb major, 150, 163; No.

72 in D major, 111, 112, 220, 256; No. 74 in
Eb major, 102, 106, 168; No. 75 in D major,
145, 150, 163, 168, 203, 204–209, 238; Nos.
76–78, 203; No. 77 in Bb major, 207; No.
82 in C major ("The Bear"), 161; No. 83 in
G minor ("The Hen"), 168; No. 84 in Eb
major, 150, 168; No. 85 in Bb major ("La
Reine"), 100, 168, 254; No. 87 in A major,
99–100; No. 88 in G major, 101, 168–170,
175n, 246; No. 89 in F major, 170; No. 90
in C major, 254; No. 92 in G major ("Oxford"), 169, 170; No. 93 in D major, 170;
No. 94 in G major ("Surprise"), 39, 150,
168, 238n, 254; No. 95 in C minor, 168,
169n, 238; No. 96 in D major ("Miracle"),
170; No. 97 in C major, 168; No. 98, 168,
169n, 170; No. 99 in Eb major, 168, 170;
No. 100 in G major, 169n, 170; No. 101 in
D major, 256; No. 102 in Bb major, 119n;
No. 103 in Eb major ("Drumroll"), 170–
171, 186n, 247n; No. 104 in D major ("London"), 170, 171–174, 256
    Trios, keyboard (Hob. XV), 185; No. 2
in F major, 118; No. 5 in G major, 185; No.
6, 151, 171; No. 13, 149, 153, 193n; No. 19
in G minor, 80, 93–98, 130, 149, 153, 186n,
220; No. 20 in Bb major, 185; No. 23 in D
minor, 149, 186–187, 247; No. 26 in F# minor, 119n; No. C1 in C major, 110n, 111,
118
    Trios, strings (Hob. V), 118, 119; No. 7
in A major, 119; No. 8 in Bb major, 111,
119, 122–127; No. 11 in Eb major, 111; No.
D3 in D major, 111
    Variations, keyboard (Hob. XVII): No. 2
in A major, 110; No. 3 in Eb major, 110;
No. 6 in F minor, 142, 192–194, 247, 252;
No. 7* (authenticity uncertain) in D major,
110; Hob. XVIIa:1 in F major for keyboard
four-hands ("Il maestro e lo scolare"), 119,
121, 122–123, 223
    Vocal music: *La canterina*, 112, 127; *Phile-
mon und Baucis*, 189n; *Missa Sancti Nicolai*,
146; Songs, 189n
Haydn, Michael, 203; Divertimento No. 105
in F, 133n
Hegel, Georg Friedrich, 5, 19, 24, 28–29
Heinichen, Johann David, 49, 52–53
Herbst, Andreas, 21, 23
Herder, Johann Gottfried, 9
Herz, Henri, 77
Hildesheimer, Wolfgang, 25
Hoffmann, E. T. A., 247
Hoffmeister, Franz Anton, 164

Hofmann, Leopold, 58, 69; "Andante varia-
tio" in keyboard concerto, 56–58
Hofstetter, Romanus, String Quartet attrib.
Haydn, Op. 3/2, 115, 117
Hogarth, William, 13
Hummel, Johann Nepomuk, 64
Hünten, Franz, 77
Hybrid forms, 3, 101, 109, 146, 150–163, 172,
183, 218, 219, 256
Hymn theme, 108, 145, 165, 168–169, 176,
198–199, 202, 204, 206, 240, 259. *See also*
Theme
Hypotaxis, 7–9, 101, 107. *See also* Parataxis;
Periodic style; Sequential form

Idea, 16–17, 112, 120–121. *See also Elaboratio;
Inventio*; Invention
Imitation of nature, 12, 34, 52
Inventio, 16–18, 21, 26, 108, 121, 197, 198,
203. *See also* Compositional process; Idea;
Invention; Rhetoric, five parts of classical
Invention, 1, 16–18, 59, 61, 189, 191. *See also*
Compositional process

Johnson, Douglas, 238
Joyce, James, 5

Kalkbrenner, Frédéric, 64, 77
Kant, Immanuel, 13–14
Kennedy, George, 30
Kerman, Joseph, 238, 240, 242
Kierkegaard, Søren, 5
Kirkendale, Warren, 255
Kirnberger, Johann Philipp, 81n, 87n, 90n
Klein, Rudolf, 101
Koch, Heinrich Christoph, 15–16, 21, 23, 61–
62, 67, 71–73, 79, 80, 82, 85–91, 92, 93, 94,
95–98, 100, 105, 110, 112, 217, 229, 237,
254, 279–280
Köhler, Karl-Heinz, 203
Kollmann, Augustus Frederick Christopher,
60, 64, 74
Kozeluch, Leopold, 158, 164, 165, 250; Piano
Trio in A major, 158n; Sonata in F major,
"La Chasse," 165–166
Kramer, Lawrence, 108
Kundera, Milan, 261

Lacan, Jacques, 5
Lamy, Bernard, 11
Landon, H. C. Robbins, 118, 148, 149, 160
Lanham, Richard, 29
Larsen, Jens Peter, 148

Learned style, 161, 184, 185, 216, 217, 219, 220, 226, 228
Lockwood, Lewis, 255–256, 261n
Löhlein, Georg Simon, 51n
Longinus, 38, 175

March, 67, 71, 231, 233, 250, 257, 258, 259
Marpurg, Friedrich Wilhelm, 23, 32, 34, 50, 51, 54, 63, 189, 193
Marston, Nicholas, 242
Martini, Padre Giovanni Battista, 154–155, 158n
Marx, Adolf Bernhard, 67, 75
Marx, Karl, 5
Mattheson, 12, 17, 22, 23, 28, 31, 33, 34, 50, 52, 53, 63, 68, 278
Melodic-outline variation, 66, 67, 68–69, 75, 110, 112, 118, 125, 131, 132, 133, 135, 137, 145, 151, 153, 159, 216, 248, 250, 254, 259
Melodic reprise. See Theme reprise
Meyer, Leonard, 10
Michaelis, Christian Friedrich, 17, 236–238, 241, 261, 280
Mies, Paul, 197, 255
Miller, J. Hillis, 5
Minuet, 68–69, 79–80, 110, 117, 118, 121, 135, 151, 235; Tempo di Menuet, 111, 121
Momigny, Jérôme-Joseph de, 2, 32, 64, 164, 165
Moral characters, 23, 91–92, 121
Moscheles, Ignaz, 64
Mozart, Leopold, 20, 24, 58, 60, 154, 156, 228
Mozart, Wolfgang Amadeus; rhetorical writing by, 8, 25; letters to Michael Puchberg, 25; performance of K. 382, 40; improvising variations, 65; and *minore*, 163; choice of genres, 196–197; models in other composers, 197, 202–209; placement of opposite-mode variation, 210, 219, 232
    WORKS
    Concertos, piano, 193, 206, 254; K. 175 in D major, 40; K. 382 ("Rondo" in D major), 40–43, 217, 218, 219, 223, 226, 231; K. 413 in F major, 217; K. 415 in C major, 217; K. 449 in Eb major, 60, 107, 218–219; K. 450 in Bb major, 198, 202–209, 215, 218, 219, 223, 226, 238; K. 451 in D major, 218; K. 453 in G major, 219, 220–223, 256; K. 456 in Bb major, 207, 223, 224–228, 230, 231; K. 459 in F major, 214, 219; K. 467 in C major, 219; K. 482 in Eb major, 207, 210, 219, 223, 228–231, 232; K. 488 in A major, 206n; K. 491 in C minor, 207, 210, 219, 231–234, 256, 258; K. 503 in C major, 219
    Divertimentos and serenades, 197; K. 334

in D minor, 231; K. 361 in Bb major, 197, 207, 208; K. 388 in C minor, 196n, 197, 199, 210, 232; arr. for string quintet, K. 406, 196n, 199
    Don Giovanni, 145, 207
    Duo in Bb major, violin and viola, K. 424, 210
    Quartets, strings: K. 170 in C major, 216; K. 387 in G major, 60, 214; K. 421 in D minor, 174, 198, 207, 209, 220, 231; K. 464, 198, 210–214, 219, 234, 238, 241
    Quintet in A major, clarinet and strings, K. 581, 197
    Quintet in Eb major, piano and winds, K. 452, 206n
    Sonatas, piano: K. 332 in F major, 51n; Sonata and Fantasy in C minor, K. 457/475, 60
    Sonata in F major, violin and piano, K. 377, 206n, 207, 209, 231
    Symphonies, 197; No. 36 in C major ("Linz"), K. 425, 169n; No. 39 in Eb major, K. 543, 106; No. 40 in G minor, K. 550, 106, 169; No. 41 in C major, K. 551 ("Jupiter"), 214
    Trio, piano, K. 564 in G major, 198–199
    Trio, strings, K. 563, 197, 206n, 214–217, 219, 239
    Variations for piano: K. 354/299a, on "Je suis Lindor," 64; K. 398, on "Salve tu, Regina" by Paisiello, 65; K. 455, on "Unser dummer Pöbel meint" by Gluck, 65, 199–201, 209n; K. 573, on minuet by Duport, 198; K. 613, on "Ein Weib ist das herrlichste Ding" by B. Schack or F. Gerl, 217
Müthel, Johann Georg, 250

Neefe, Christian Gottlob, 15–18, 21, 28, 236, 250, 276–277
Niedt, Friedrich Erhard, 49, 52, 53–55

Ordonez, Carlo d', 111, 113; String Quartet Op. 2/6, 113, 115; Symphony D6, 113, 115
Organicism, 1, 3, 12, 15, 107, 242
Ornament, 1, 3, 6, 11, 12, 18, 19, 21, 30–32, 33, 34, 38, 49, 51, 54, 56, 58, 60, 64
Ostinato, 2
Overture, 67, 142, 178, 181, 190

Parataxis, paratactic form, 7–11, 45, 99, 101, 107, 108, 145, 168, 172, 185, 195, 221, 223, 233, 260; as distinct from sequential, 7, 10, 260; as *oratio perpetua*, 8. See also Hypotaxis; Periodic style; Sequential form
Passacaglia, 99

Paulson, Ronald, 9
Peacham, Henry, 38
Performance (delivery), 12–13, 23, 36, 43, 186, 191, 226
Performance practice, 48–49, 51–60
Periodic style (*oratio periodica*), 8–9, 233. *See also* Hypotaxis; Parataxis; Sequential form
Peroration, 21, 25, 29, 39, 47, 142, 150, 220, 223, 234
Peucer, Daniel, 80, 91–92
Pichl, Wenzel, 164
Pleyel, Ignaz, 70, 164, 165
Porpora, Nicola, 133
Principal periods, 82, 87–92, 99, 100, 103, 106, 107. *See also* Expansion techniques
Puchberg, Michael, 25
Puttenham, George, 34–35, 37, 38, 39, 100–101

Quantz, Johann Joachim, 32, 51, 52, 56, 58, 60
Quintilian (M. Fabian Quintilianus), 13, 20, 27, 30, 33, 90, 192, 243

Rameau, Jean-Philippe, 50n
Ratner, Leonard, 2–3, 22, 255
Raupach, Christoph, 63
Rauscher, 32, 67, 87, 95. *See also* Setzmanieren
Realization, 16–18, 79, 120; of figured bass, 52. *See also* Dispositio
Recitative, 46, 133
Recurrence, 2, 4, 6, 7, 21, 109, 150, 151
Reicha, Anton, 73–76, 257
Reichardt, Johann Friedrich, 146
Repetition, 1–18, 19, 21, 28, 33, 36, 52, 53, 61–62, 72, 78, 83, 85, 87, 92, 95, 99, 106, 108, 153, 164, 183, 184, 185, 194, 195, 216, 230, 233, 236, 237, 238, 246, 255, 260, 261; in literature and poetry, 4–7, 9; Platonic and Nietzschean, 5; repetition without decoration, 164, 185, 233, 246. *See also* Rhetorical figures
Reynolds, Christopher, 252
Rhetoric, 4, 12, 18, 19–47, 50, 60, 70, 71, 78, 80, 91, 100, 109, 112, 118, 120, 135, 159, 164, 168, 172, 175, 178, 185, 190, 192, 194, 195, 197, 198, 223, 255, 260; five parts of classical (invention, arrangement, style, memory, delivery), 18, 21, 60; structure of oration (introduction, statement of facts, division, arguments and proofs, destruction of enemies' arguments, conclusion), 21, 22, 24–25, 39, 92; models for variation form in, 26–30, 35–40; epideictic (demonstrative), 29–30, 145; primary and secondary, 30; po-litical (deliberative), 30; forensic (judicial), 30; oration as series of proofs, 39, 46–47; and elaboration, 112, 120–121. *See also* Amplification; *Ars dictaminis; Ars praedicandi;* Copiousness; Idea; Invention; *Inventio; Dispositio; Elaboratio;* Performance; Rhetorical figures
Rhetorical figures, 3, 11, 18, 19, 20, 21–22, 25, 30–40, 49, 87, 137, 223, 224, 228; as word-figures, 33, 38, 194; as "sentence-figures," 33, 224; as "figures for the understanding/intellect," 34–35, 189, 217; as "figures for the imagination," 34–35, 189, 217, 224; as "auricular figures," 35; as "sensable figures," 35, 101; as "sententious figures," 35, 100

FIGURES
abridgement, 189
abruptio, 46, 191
anadiplosis, 224
anaphora, 168
antithesis, 29, 95, 159, 189, 194, 223, 228, 254, 261
apostrophe, 139–140
argument, 21, 43, 47, 108, 168, 186
arousal (*exsuscitatio*), 36, 43, 139–140
comparison (*similitudo, parabole*), 30, 37, 39, 43, 100, 108, 122, 168, 178, 223
congeries (accumulation, heaping up words), 30, 122, 184
contrarium (reasoning by contraries), 159
dialogue (*sermocinatio*), 36, 43
digression (*digressio*), 27, 37, 45, 139, 169, 194
dinumeratio (heaping up sentences), 37, 43, 45
dissembling, 38–39, 178, 253
dubitation (*Zweifel*), 33
dwelling on the point (*commoratio*), 37, 43, 168, 178, 260, 261
ellipsis, 33, 34
emphasis (*significatio*), 190
epanalepsis (repetition of beginning idea at the end), 142, 224
epistrophe (*Wiederkehr*), 33, 144, 168, 224
epizeuxis, 194
exclamatio, 228
figures of repetition, 7, 12–13, 18, 21, 33, 35, 36, 37, 194
forcefulness, 186, 192
gradatio (*climax, Steigerung*), 33, 45, 101, 108, 135, 137, 223, 228, 230, 242, 243, 246, 248, 257, 259
hyperbole (*superlatio*), 7, 20, 189–190, 243
imitatio, 209

Rhetorical figures (*continued*)
   incrementum (augmentation), 30, 243
   irony, 112, 135, 137, 178
   metaphor, 3, 6, 20
   paronomasia (*Verstärkung*), 33
   passus duriusculus, 224
   pathopoeia, 34, 142, 223, 224, 226, 233
   periphrasis (*circumlocutio*), 38–39, 43, 45, 144, 175, 226, 253
   pleonasm, 38, 43, 45, 110, 122, 125, 131, 139, 144, 161, 181, 189, 226, 253
   polyptoton, 228
   refining (*expolitio*), 36–37, 39, 43, 92, 95, 142, 186, 216–217, 260, 261
   saltus duriusculus, 34, 223, 224
   suspension (*Aufhalten*), 33
   synecdoche, 125, 137
   synonymy, 6, 37, 39, 128
   variatio, 49
[*Rhetorica*] *Ad Herrenium*, 4, 36–37, 43, 92
Rice, John A., 73n
Riedt, Friedrich Wilhelm, 54–56, 278
Riepel, Joseph, 26–27, 32, 49–50, 52, 61, 67, 79, 82–85, 87, 90, 128
Ries, Ferdinand, 64
Ritornello, 41, 43, 72, 150, 217, 218n, 230, 231, 255
Robbins, Jerome, 6
Rondo, 4, 9, 16, 40, 41, 60, 67, 72, 75, 82, 91, 95, 102, 103, 105, 113, 129, 149, 150, 151, 168, 169, 174, 200, 206, 217, 219, 232, 256
Rondo-variation, 41, 72, 106, 111, 121, 150, 153, 158, 164, 168, 170, 174, 195, 197, 228, 229, 243, 246, 254, 255
Rosen, Charles, 2–3, 10, 103, 106, 108, 175, 207
Rousseau, Jean-Jacques, 50n, 66
Ruile-Dronke, Jutta, 203
Rywosch, Bernhard, 149

Said, Edward, 5–6
Salon variations, 15, 77
Sandberger, Adolf, 147
Scheibe, Johann Adolph, 22, 33, 49n, 50, 68–69, 83, 110
Schenk, Johann Baptist, 158
Schenker, Heinrich, 255
Schering, Arnold, 21
Schiller, Friedrich, 14, 19
Schlegel, August Wilhelm von, 15
Schleuning, Peter, 255
Schoenberg, Arnold, 67, 70n, 99, 197
Schulz, Johann Abraham Peter, 50n, 66–69, 110, 112, 146, 193, 250, 257, 279
Schumann, Robert, 15, 75

Schwärmer, 32, 67, 189, 233. *See also Setzmanieren*
Schwindt-Gross, Nicole, 91
Sequential form, 7, 9–10, 99, 260. *See also* Hypotaxis; Parataxis; Periodic Style
Setzmanieren (figures of composition), 32, 38, 43, 51–52, 63, 193, 224, 226, 228, 231. *See also Schwärmer; Rauscher*
Siciliana, 67, 71, 117, 174, 198, 207, 220
Simpson, Christopher, 54–55, 63
Small form, 82, 85, 95, 99, 100, 101, 102, 103, 106, 107, 108, 261
Smith, Barbara Herrnstein, 5, 7, 9–10
Somfai, László, 113, 149
Sonata form, 3, 4, 9, 10, 15, 39, 67, 78, 79, 80, 82, 90, 91, 92, 95, 101, 102, 103, 106–108, 146, 149, 159, 168, 169, 170, 172, 183, 185, 195, 229, 255, 261
Sonata-rondo, 81, 105, 217, 218, 219
Sonata with varied reprises. *See* Varied-reprise sonata
Spielmanieren (figures of performance), 32, 51–52
Steffan, Johann Anton, 118, 250; Sonata Op. 2/6, 118, 154, 155, 156; 25 Variations for piano, 158; Capriccios, 183
Steibelt, Daniel, 64, 165
Steiner, George, 36n
Stone, Peter Eliot, 257n
Strophic variation, 7, 10, 43, 71, 101, 107, 109, 110, 118, 128, 133, 135, 142, 149, 163, 164, 168, 170, 174, 175, 194, 210, 259, 262
Strunk, Oliver, 118
Sturm und Drang, 9, 147
Sublime, the, 12, 13–14, 38, 175, 236
Suite, 53, 68, 111, 151, 255
Sulzer, Johann Georg, 12–13, 18, 66, 68, 257
"Symphony style," 175n, 220, 226, 254–255

Teiber (Teyber), Anton, 158, 164; Notturno for two pianos, 158n
Telemann, Georg Philipp, *Sonates méthodiques*, 51n
Ternary (ABA) form, 4, 41, 107, 135, 149, 150, 164, 169, 170, 255
Ternary (ABA) variation, 4, 75, 158, 163, 164, 168, 170, 171, 172, 185, 191, 197, 220, 241, 256, 259
Theme, 2, 3, 5, 15, 69, 71, 112; borrowed, 1, 2, 70, 165, 198, 205; original, 70, 198, 251–252; theme types, 111–112; "walking" melody, 111–112, 174
Theme reprise, 39, 106, 108, 122, 125, 130, 132, 133, 137, 144, 150, 159, 162, 163, 165,

190, 193–194, 212, 219, 232, 233, 247, 253;
melodic reprise, 39, 43, 45, 92, 108, 133,
145, 151, 161, 162, 171, 186, 207, 237, 247,
248, 254, 258, 259. *See also* Da capo
Thoroughbass, 49, 52–54, 69
Tomasini, Luigi, 117, 129
Tovey, Donald Francis, 133
Treitler, Leo, 102–103
Türk, Daniel Gottlob, 51, 60
Tyson, Alan, 219

Vanhal, Johann, 69, 117, 118, 158, 164, 250;
Capriccios, 158; Theme avec VII Variations
caractéristiques, 165, 167
Variations:
Adagio-Allegro pair of, 4, 200, 210, 220
as form, 1, 4, 5, 8, 14, 15, 16, 19, 21, 25,
26, 27, 38, 39, 47, 48, 53, 63–75, 80, 82
as technique, 1, 3, 5, 12, 21, 28, 47, 48,
51–62, 64, 65, 99, 100, 106, 170
changes of meter and tempo in, 41, 43,
64, 95, 210, 218, 220, 250n, 252–253
changes of theme's structure in, 2, 145,
150, 161, 163, 189, 195, 200, 212, 230, 247,
251, 260
disparaging critical assessments of, 1–5,
10–11, 14–15, 40, 47, 75, 77, 109, 164–165,
250n, 251, 253n
free motivic treatment in, 118, 121, 125,
127, 128, 133
improvised, 21, 48, 51–60, 63–65, 66,
217, 250, 251; improvisatory elements in, 3,
164, 189, 190, 191, 199–200, 250
maggiore, 152, 164, 186, 189, 190, 191,
210, 227, 229, 232–233
"middle section" in, 185, 231, 233, 256,
260
minore, 4, 39, 41, 43, 75, 100, 132, 152,
153, 154, 156, 157, 162–163, 164, 168, 170,
172, 186, 189, 190, 191, 193, 200, 207, 210,
212, 215, 216, 217, 220, 221, 223, 228, 233,
234, 240, 247, 254, 259
movement position of, 72, 110–111, 121,

128, 133, 135, 149, 164, 168, 174, 185, 186,
192, 197, 204, 256
ordering of, 63, 239–240
progressive diminution in, 41, 45, 101,
133, 135, 137, 186, 223, 242, 247, 257
propriety in, 237
transitions between, 2, 107, 165, 183, 195,
221, 247, 251, 254, 256, 259, 260
varied repeats (reprises) in, 39, 45, 46, 99,
101, 109, 117, 122, 125, 151, 152, 163, 168,
169, 171–172, 191, 195, 206–207, 212, 214,
215–216, 217, 227, 257, 259
weight of, 109, 149, 186, 238
See also Alternating variation; Cantus firmus; "Character variation"; Characteristic
variation; *Concertante* variation; Constant-
bass variation; Constant-harmony variation;
Constant-melody variation; Contrapuntal
variation; "Double variation"; Hybrid
forms; Melodic-outline variation; Rhetoric,
models for variation form in; Rondo-
variation; Salon variations; Strophic variation; Ternary (ABA) variation; Theme;
Theme reprise; "Variation rondo"
"Variation rondo," 72, 150
Varied-reprise sonata, 58–60, 85, 99, 117, 133,
151, 154, 164, 170, 174
Vickers, Brian, 22, 30–31
Vico, Giambattista, 5–6
Vogler, Georg Joseph, 25–26, 67, 69–71, 135,
234, 251, 277, 279

Wagenseil, Georg Christoph, 118, 155
Wahr, Karl, 146, 160
Walther, Johann Gottfried, 53, 71
Webster, James, 47, 146–147, 149
Williams, Peter, 22
Winckelmann, Johann Joachim, 12
Wyzewa, Théodore de, 147

Ziegler, Christian Gottlieb, 61, 62–63
Zimmermann, Anton, 113–114; String Quartet in F major, 116